LEADING LADIES
OF MAKEUP EFFECTS

Showcasing the Award-Winning Women of
Makeup Effects for Film and Television

Patricia L. Terry   Gary Christensen

Foreword by Michael Westmore

Edited by Erica Preus

A Publication of

One Off Publishing LLC
Laguna Woods, California

A Publication of One Off Publishing LLC,
Laguna Woods, California

ISBN: 978-0-9993432-0-3 (Hardcover)
ISBN: 978-0-9993432-1-0 (Softcover)
ISBN: 978-0-9993432-2-7 (E-Book)

Library of Congress Catalog # 2017913154

Compiled, Edited, Designed and Art Directed by Gary Christensen and Patricia L. Terry
Book Cover designed by Gary Christensen

LEADING LADIES
OF MAKEUP EFFECTS

LEADING LADIES OF MAKEUP EFFECTS

$\mathcal{C}$ONTENTS

PATRICIA L. TERRY

POV: The Genesis

The name of the class was "Life Reimagined" aimed toward people of a 'certain age' who are ready for the next adventure, the next challenge, the next phase of life. They asked the hard questions: What do you think is your responsibility to others? What do you stand for? What gives you energy? If you pay attention to surprisingly recurrent signs or suggestions, in what direction are they pointing?

Eeeeeek, we thought this might be simply an interesting seminar connecting interesting people to interesting things. Instead, they expected us not only to think, but to take a hard look at where we are, where we wanted to go, and how we might get there. The homework after the second meeting was to take a risk each day by talking to someone new, visit a new place, or try something new and inspiring.

Coincidentally, Son of Monsterpalooza was that weekend in September of 2015. Gary is the makeup artist in the family, so, armed with his new insights and an idea that had been percolating for years, Gary waylaid Lois Burwell and Eryn Krueger Mekash in the aisles of the convention and floated an idea: Isn't it time women makeup artists were represented as vigorously as men are? What do you think about a book that focuses exclusively on women makeup artists, their stories, their work??? Ever-gracious, both Ladies enthusiastically embraced the idea and offered to help when the time came.

And the idea began to stand on its wobbly legs. Several intense months of culling through websites, exploring awards, creating a viable list, contacting our Ladies, and setting up interviews followed. December 28, 2015, we had our first interview with Eryn in a Doubletree Hotel room. Desperately nervous, we set up the Go-Pro Camera and the audio tape and rearranged the furniture. Eryn's was the first of 26.

There were little bumps along the way: Tami was on a remote island in New Zealand without internet access, Vivian was on location in Atlanta, Frances, Julie, Christine, Jenny, and Jane live in the UK, Montse lives in Barcelona, Lesley in Australia, Tina had a 300th episode to shoot. But we managed to interview them all, with a little trip to London and another to Barcelona on the side.

The division of labor took on a life of its own: Gary, the makeup artist, follows make-up artists on Facebook, meets and maintains relationships with other artists, reads everything about makeup voraciously, teaches theatrical makeup at several Southern California colleges. He brings his understanding of the art and his expertise to the table. I am a theatre director and acting and literature teacher, I see big pictures and am fanatical about the written word. I bring my organizational skills, critical eye, and overall vision to the table. We are both artists, which makes for some pretty fiery exchanges, but there is a healthy respect for each other's talents which has served us well in this complicated, two-year process.

Then the hard work began. The writing. Our goals were clear: Honor, Encourage, and Inspire. Respect our Ladies and their work, draw a unique, individual, defining portrait of each Lady, and maintain our authorial/artistic integrity. Every time we sent a draft to one of our Ladies for fact-checking, we held our breaths until we received it back. We breathed easier for a day, then girded our loins, for the next step was to send it to Erica Preus, our dependable and talented editor. We stopped breathing until her edits came back. They were obvious improvements, tweaks that clarified, substantive commentaries. Phew, deep breaths. Uncounted internal edits, another round of fact-checking, and a final edit by Erica left us oxygen deprived. We did this 26 times, breathlessly facing the unexpected curves and speedy descents of living on a roller coaster!

Of course, we owe a great debt to our Leading Ladies, for without them there would be no book. To a woman, the interview process was delightful, insightful, honest. They were generous with their stories and patient with our endless emails and requests. *Leading Ladies of Makeup Effects* is a paean to the makeup industry, the artistry that drives it, and mostly to the women who are in the trenches day in and day out, bringing their talent and dedication to film and television.

I dedicate this work to my most excellent partner, my partner on these pages, off these pages, in my life - my Gary. Our life together careens from one adventure to another, complete only because you're there to share it. Your ideas and your creative eye enrich, spur, buoy us onward to ever-greater adventures and excellence. Your dedication to the Ladies has brought this book to life. None of this could happen without you. Together we are whole.

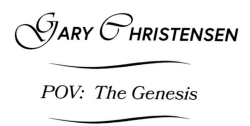

Gary Christensen

POV: The Genesis

The idea started simply enough.

In 2015, our friend, Beverly Norcross, contacted me because while updating Richard Corson's **Stage Makeup** to the 11th Edition, her new publisher asked whether she had any other book ideas. Beverly forwarded me the question and an idea began to form.

Originally, I thought an update to **Making a Monster** by Al Taylor and Sue Roy would be interesting. The book was published in 1981 and followed monster film makeup from its inception with Jack Pierce, who created iconic characters such as Frankenstein's monster, Dracula, and the Mummy, and continued through the years to a young up-and-comer, Rick Baker, with a mention of his work on **Star Wars.** I thought an updated version of the book could pick up with Baker and continue to 2015. But, when I started truly considering such an endeavor, it was overwhelming. Who to choose? How to choose? Hadn't **Make-Up Artist Magazine** been covering these gentlemen for almost 20 years? Hey ... wait a minute ... gentlemen? I went to my library and pulled my makeup books off the shelves. Yep, just as I remembered.

Flashback to 2013. I was invited to join Neill Gorton's *FX 911* Facebook group and I was smitten. I was sucked into the FB world and became completely immersed; every day, I had a full serving of special effects makeup. The makeup posts were from all the corners of the makeup world, individual artists, labs, special effects groups, and makeup schools such as Cinema Makeup School, Neill Gorton's Makeup Studios, Vancouver Film School. I loved seeing what the student artists were creating, but I also began to note something curious. In these class photos, the number of women far outnumbered the men, out of a class of 20 faces, 18 were women. What? I started checking the school photos, all the schools were showing similar trends. I'd also noticed this pattern at the International Makeup Artist Tradeshows (IMATS) in Los Angeles and London, as well as on the pages of **Make-Up Artist Magazine.**

Returning to 2015, two facts stood out: all the books about famous makeup artists on my shelves were about men, and the makeup effects world was filling up with women. The "Ah-ha!" moment struck like a thunderbolt--there needed to be the first book ever about the WOMEN working in makeup effects. A niche book within a niche market. This is a great idea!

Then the tsunami struck! Looking at the vast sea of women working in makeup effects, we couldn't possibly cover them all. We wanted to write a book, not create a telephone directory. We needed to set a specific course through the ocean of possibilities which included students, shops, non-union and union makeup artists, makeup designers, department heads, and award winners. Suddenly, a calm in the storm. Award winners! Those ladies already had received recognition by their peers in the industry. Our course was clear and now we had stars by which to navigate.

And so…this book, *Leading Ladies of Makeup Effects*, was conceived. A book to *honor* the best-of-the-best women in makeup effects! A book to *encourage* the women already working in what was deemed a man's domain! A book to *inspire* young women to learn and train in the makeup effects industry with *female role models*!

But an idea is just an idea. Until you begin to work on it, you don't know if it can live. If you've read Pat's *Genesis*, you know how it grew from there. We had interviews to set-up and conduct. Would these Award-winning ladies give us the time of day to sit and talk with us? Yes! The interviews with these Leading Lady makeup artists whose work we've watched and admired for years were glorious! Equally glorious were our interviews with our Emerging Artists, young women reaching their way into the industry with enthusiasm, excitement, and true grit. All these dynamic women shared generously of themselves, their stories, and careers. Whether for 90 minutes or four hours, in person or on the phone, each interview flew by too fast, but each was magical.

We owe a huge debt of gratitude to our Leading Ladies.

I owe an unpayable debt of gratitude to my wife, my Leading Lady, for partnering with me on this Odyssey. We never would be here now without her. At the beginning of every interview, I told our Leading Lady, "Pat will be conducting the interview. She's a questioner. I'm a talker. We want to hear from you." Pat has a natural ability to make people feel comfortable. The reason? When she talks to someone, she is truly more interested in them than herself. A rare quality. People trust her for that quality. It allows them to feel heard and, therefore, they speak from a place of truth. We knew these interviews came from that kind of truth, so we treated it with great respect and love. I'm also grateful to Pat because she is an actual writer, someone who cares about words and ideas as literature. Me, I tend toward casual, useful writing. How I ever thought I could write a book, only the universe knows. But Pat knew. She's the one ultimately responsible for this book, its structure, it attention to detail, its art …. and there is art to be found herein. This book would not be in your hands, right now, if Pat hadn't pushed, argued, cajoled, and persevered to bring you the best reading experience we could deliver. So, let me finish by saying, "Thank you, Pat! You've made a dream come true!"

So, with your kind indulgence, I'll finish by quoting Dr. Frankenstein, "It's ALIVE!!!!" I said I was a talker? I'll shut up now and let you start reading the *Leading Ladies of Makeup Effects!*

Michael Westmore

Foreword

*When I was supervising **Star Trek**,*
I would hire at least 100 artists per season and at least half of them
or more were women.

In Hollywood, there is always history behind every story in the Motion Picture Business and the Leading Ladies of Makeup Effects are part of that history. When I was serving my three-year makeup apprenticeship at Universal Studios, there weren't any female effects makeup artists; in fact, there weren't any professional female makeup artists at all except for those women that were schooled in the application of body makeup. Their responsibility was to apply cosmetics on female performers from the neck down. Also in the early days, makeup/lab men created and applied all the special makeups in the studio makeup department and most of the time behind closed doors. The knowledge of mixing chemicals, molding, prosthetic manufacturing, and latex application was a well-kept secret amongst a very few.

In the 1960s private makeup effects labs started to blossom outside the studio gates due to the quality work of the independent artists and lower costs. At one point, it was said there were over 50 independent outside labs of all sizes, including mine. This is where women would eventually be accepted for their talent. During the mid-1970s the movie business changed due to new regulations. The studios opened their doors and the individual crafts were allowed to hire whomever they desired. The new rules of eligibility made sense as women were already practicing as professional makeup artists in areas outside the studio system as demonstrators, sellers, painters, and teachers. Who knew more about the general makeup industry, application of color, and cosmetics than women? Then along came a few artistic women with a burning desire and a curious interest in getting their hands into wet plaster, molding clay, and mixing latex. Their special EFX interest wasn't fulfilled until they could enjoy designing, creating, and applying images of horror, aging, monsters, aliens, fantasy, characters, tattoos, burns, scars, cuts, and bruises. Shortly after their entrance, women became integral members of the labs. I bet each one of the Leading Ladies remember the first day they were given the opportunity to apply their makeup artistry on a real studio set.

Today the early women pioneers and the newly recognized EFX artists are Superstars. Over my time in the film industry I found these Leading Ladies to be extremely talented, dedicated, and passionate about their craft. They were and still are eager to learn more and more to improve their skills. Because of their desire to know more, I have always been willing and anxious to teach them all that I had learned from the masters. I expected them to surpass my teachings with all their imaginative creativity.

I never gave it a second thought that I had to give a woman a chance to prove her makeup ability. Introductions always started with a recommendation or a direct phone call. Next, we would meet and they would show me pictures and drawings of their contributions to previous assignments or projects. It was always their personality, reputation, and background that drove me to say, "I want you on my team because I can always teach you more." To be truthful, I don't think I ever interviewed any female EFX artist that I didn't hire if I had an opening. I discovered the women artists were excellent team players, kind, considerate, sympathetic, friendly, and dependable--I could count on them 110%. They could and do tolerate the rigors and demands of their craft and they bring specific touches to their art in their own inherent way. Certain character traits are very important and need to be respected as they assist their actors to survive the turbulence and competitiveness of the movie business

Time has shown Leading Lady makeup artists march into history. They didn't need to be embraced, their talent allowed them to be acknowledged and accepted by the film industry, it just needed a little time. From the beginning of their entrance into the film business, 40+ years ago, the women's membership in the union has grown to over 50%. I am so proud of all the Leading Ladies of Makeup Effects. Especially those I had the opportunity to see develop their talent and reputations and become Award Nominees, Oscar Winners, Emmy Winners, and Makeup Artist Guild Winners. I hope I had a little part in passing on, to all, my makeup knowledge that has been a legacy from the Master Artists that took me under their wings, including the men and women of the Westmore Family. This year, 2017, the family is celebrating its 100th year in Hollywood makeup history and was honored by the City of Los Angeles for the family's contribution as "Leaders in Studio Makeup." I am also celebrating the accomplishments of the Leading Ladies of Makeup Effects.

Michael Westmore

LEADING LADIES
OF MAKEUP EFFECTS

ESTABLISHING SHOT:
WHAT ARE MAKEUP EFFECTS?

As relates to this book, we define *makeup effects* as makeup used to create specific characterizations, something beyond a beautiful, cosmetic effect. These characterizations include minor and major aging (with or without prosthetics), historical characters and periods, illnesses and disease, quick-change disguise, and creatures, aliens, and monsters. All the Ladies in this book have created makeups which fit these parameters.

CLOSE-UPS:
THE PORTRAITS

On the following pages, you will meet and discover the lives and careers of our Leading Ladies. These are portraits, our impressions of these women. We have drawn lines along their paths of influence, revealed shapes within their early training and work choices, deepened the contours of their experiences, featured their projects which vibrantly color their professional careers, and illuminated their philosophies that have textured and nuanced their art and lives. While each is an individual, they possess similarities: strength, determination, passion, kindness, and deep, deep caring. It is these qualities that make them all Leading Ladies.

OVER-THE-SHOULDER SHOT:
THE SCRIPT

We interviewed all our Ladies from December 2015 through November 2016. We audio recorded all the interviews and many were videotaped as well. So we wouldn't miss a word of what each Lady said, the recordings were professionally transcribed becoming the raw materials for our book. Each of our Leading Ladies was given the opportunity to read the text, verify the facts and information, supply photographs, and finally, approve the content of her chapter.

WIDE SHOT:
COLLABORATORS

As will become obvious as you read the portraits, film and television makeup requires a team of collaborating artists to fulfill the job. From designers to department heads, key to crowd room makeup artists, prosthetics to effects specialists, hair and wig stylists, and a multitude of makeup shop personnel--life-casters, sculptors, mold-makers, prosthetic runners, fabricators, pre-painters, hair-punchers, facial hair and wig makers--each of these artists play a role in creating a successful makeup. But it is beyond the scope of this book to acknowledge everyone. Our Ladies have risen to the level of responsibility of overseeing the final makeup looks that appear on screen, whether they had an actual hand or brush on it. In other words, "the buck stopped" with them. These women are the first to acknowledge they can't do their jobs alone. We congratulate all the collaborators who work to bring makeups to screen; please forgive omissions. On these pages, our Ladies take the Sharp Focus.

Now, sit comfortably in your makeup chair and allow us to work....

HOW FILMS ARE NOMINATED FOR THE ACADEMY AWARD FOR

BEST ACHIEVEMENT IN MAKEUP AND HAIRSTYLING

Throughout the year, the members of The Makeup Artists and Hairstylists Branch of the Academy of Motion Picture Arts and Sciences (AMPAS) discuss films that include makeup and hair work of merit. There is discussion between and among members of the Branch via open forums and online about the work in the above-mentioned films.

In December, all the Branch members vote for up to seven films from the roster compiled by the Branch members. Selections are based on the work without regard for prior awards, union affiliations, or Academy membership. PricewaterhouseCoopers Accountants tally the votes and the top seven vote-getters are announced before the holidays. These seven films comprise the Short List.

In January, representatives of each of the films on the Short List attend the "Bake-Off" where they

* show a 10-minute clip of the film
* discuss the work
* explicate the design process.

The presentations are live-streamed to the Branch members to inform their voting.

The Branch members then vote for three of the films from the Short List, the votes are tallied, and the top three vote-getters are the chosen nominees.

Special Thanks to Tom Oyer,
Membership and Awards Manager,
Academy of Motion Picture Arts and Sciences,
for providing insight and information

Oscar Winners

Oscar Winners

The first Academy Awards for Makeup were presented as Special Honorary Awards. The first award was given to William J. Tuttle for **7 Faces of Dr. Lao** in 1964, and the second was given to John Chambers for **Planet of the Apes** in 1968. Both these films made extensive use of foam latex prosthetics to create their characters and tell their stories. Tuttle utilized his makeups to turn one actor, Tony Randall, into seven diverse characters, and Chambers astounded audiences with his ape makeups in the original **Planet of the Apes**. With these films and their awards, the makeup world was never the same again!

Not until 14 years later, when the Academy of Motion Picture Arts and Sciences (AMPAS) established the *Academy Award for Best Makeup*, was makeup elevated to annual award status. That first annual Oscar went to Rick Baker for **An American Werewolf in London** (1982) for his dazzling makeup transformations of a man into a wolf.

The following year, 1983, two women, Michèle Burke and Sarah Monzani, won the *Academy Award for Best Makeup* for their work on **Quest for Fire (Le Guerre De Feu)**. The makeups detail Neanderthals and other primitive men encountered on a search to reacquire fire.

In 1993, the award was expanded to include hair stylists and the award was renamed *Academy Award for Best Makeup and Hairstyling* to acknowledge the contribution of hairstylists to the appearance and effect

of the characters.

Since 1982, 139 men and women have been nominated for an *Academy Award for Best Makeup and Hairstyling*; 38 men and 22 women have won. Of the 22 women winners, 17 women have won Oscars specifically for their achievements in Makeup.

We focused our Oscar chapters on the women who have won the award for Makeup. 12 of these Leading Ladies appear on these pages: Michèle Burke, Lynn Barber, Lois Burwell, Jenny Shircore, Christine Blundell, Valli O'Reilly, Tami Lane, Montse Ribè, Julie Dartnell, Robin Mathews, Frances Hannon, and Lesley Vanderwalt.

We were unable to interview the unrepresented five because we were unable to contact them, we were unable to schedule an interview (either in person or by telephone), there was a conflict of interest, or they wished to be recognized for their work rather than their words. We are sorry we couldn't include all these Leading Ladies and congratulate them on their Oscar achievements: Sarah Monzani, Ve Neill, Lisa Wescott, Mindy Hall, and Elka Wardega.

Our Oscar winning Leading Ladies appear chronologically based on the year of their awards, beginning in 1983 with Michèle Burke, and ending in 2016 with Lesley Vanderwalt.

And now...the envelopes please....

1983
ACADEMY AWARD
BEST MAKEUP

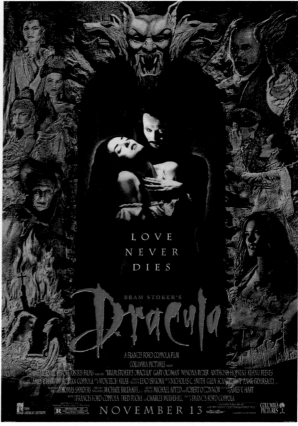

1993
ACADEMY AWARD
BEST MAKEUP

QUEST FOR FIRE (1982), (aka LA GUERRE DU FEU),
US poster art, 1981,
TM and Copyright ©20th Century Fox Film Corp. All rights
Licensed from Everett Collection, Inc. / Alamy Stock Photo

BRAM STOKER'S DRACULA, (1992)
US poster art, WINONA RYDER, GARY OLDMAN
©Columbia Pictures/courtesy Everett
Licensed from Everett Collection, Inc. / Alamy Stock Photo

Michèle Burke

My mother was an amazing woman. She came from that era, a Victorian-type era,
where she was going to marry and have children and be a housewife.
I think, truly, she yearned to be something else. She didn't ever want me to get
trapped in that Irish, be-the-mother-get-married-because-you've-nothing-else-to-do.
She wanted me to be independent, to get out there and explore the world.
She made it very clear to me that if I wanted to do something,
I had to just get on with it and do it. I guess that's why, in a way,
when you're a makeup artist you are a bit of a loner.
You have to forge and blaze the trails yourself.

"The Three Stooges. A picture of one of them pressing the other's face on a hotplate, his face screwed up in pain. The hotplate burner was glowing and smoke was coming off it. I kept looking at that and saying to my dad, 'How could he do that and not get burnt?'"

Michèle Burke laughs at her story about that picture in **Life Magazine**. With a twinkle in her eye and a lovely lilt to her voice, she is a consummate storyteller in the tradition of her homeland, Ireland. Surrounded by her paintings in a warm, comfortable home she shares with her husband, Michael Winter, Michèle is energetic, lithe, and whip-like with an expressive face and eyes that reflect a shifting sea of intensity.

"My father said to me, 'Oh, it's not real. It's Hollywood trickery.' But it looked so real to me I couldn't fathom it. It really sparked my mind, the idea that it looked one way, but it really wasn't that at all."

An Irish Girl Masters Trickery

In 1983, the second year an annual Oscar for *Best Makeup* was awarded, Michèle Burke became one of the first female makeup artists to win an Academy Award for the film *Quest for Fire,* an honor she shares with co-recipient Sarah Monzani. Then, in 1993, she became the first woman to be awarded two Oscars when she won *Best Makeup* for *Bram Stoker's Dracula*. Altogether, she has been nominated six times for Oscars, twice for the previously mentioned films and for four others: *Clan of the Cave Bear* (1986), *Cyrano de Bergerac* (1990), *Austin Powers: The Spy Who Shagged Me* (1999), and *The Cell* (2000). Additionally, Michèle won an Emmy Award in 1990 for *Alien Nation*, and was nominated for *Dr. Quinn, Medicine Woman* (1993). Her British Academy of Film and Television (BAFTA) Awards include wins for *Quest for Fire* and *Cyrano de Bergerac*, and nominations for *Bram Stoker's Dracula* and *Interview with the Vampire* (1994).

Michèle hails from Kildare, Ireland, where she was the second oldest in a family of 10 children. She grew up surrounded by six brothers and later, three sisters. "I spent a lot of my childhood with my brothers and their pals. It seemed there were no suitable girls in Kildare where I grew up because it's just a small town." Her mother was a traditional Irish housewife and her father was "a bit of a rogue" who was the managing director and owner of Tote Investors (Ireland), a racehorse gambling business, and a Ford dealership. "In my early days, my father was an amazing character, full of life, endlessly optimistic, and really very influential on me…we'd visit art galleries, discuss paintings, and look at *Life Magazine's* pictures of movies stars. His enormous love for the cinema made a lasting impression on me."

Their family home was a large Georgian style house in the middle of town, right next door to the town cinema where every Sunday they'd present a double feature of horror films which Michèle and her brothers were forbidden to see. "My mother felt we shouldn't be in there, she didn't think it was good for us." But the kids knew the projectionist would be testing his reels in the afternoon and running the film before the theater opened, so "we'd clamber over the wall from our house and sneak into the theater to watch. We got bits and pieces of horror films; my early memories of monsters were *Nosferatu* and *The Mummy*."

Since they were not allowed to watch the film's screening, the kids found the next best thing. "There were emergency exit doors at the side of the building, so we'd sit up on the wall next to the theater and wait, watching those doors. Within about 20 minutes of the film's start, those doors would burst open, BOOM, and out would dash all of these people running down the lane out into the town screaming, 'Ahhhhh,' the girls calling, 'Mammy, mammy'…we would know what film would get what reaction. That made a big impression upon me, but it didn't play into my world until I began to do a lot of horror films myself. I realized you can get a lot of bang for your buck just by scaring people the right way."

School Challenges

As a young girl in boarding school, Michèle was talented at art and sports, but had trouble with her academics. At the time, neither she, nor anyone else, knew or understood dyslexia. Michèle had problems inverting numbers, but the problem didn't extend to letters or reading. "My mother had a harebrained idea. 'Okay. If she's not going to be thriving academically, why doesn't she learn a language?' So they packed me off at 15 to a boarding school in France to learn French."

The transition wasn't easy for Michèle because no one spoke English. "It was gruesome. I was so lonely and I was so out of place." She learned French quickly because she "wanted to make friends and get along." In spite of the problems she'd had academically in Ireland, at the end of her studies, now fluent in French, she had a revelation. "I realized, I'm not as stupid as the head mother thought I was." Armed with a new feeling of empowerment, she returned to Ireland to attend a different school and finished her exams with honors in art and French. Finally finding some success at school "gave me the power to feel, 'I'm not a dud.'"

Now, faced with the prospect of attending university, Michèle decided to pursue languages rather than art. "My father said to me, 'Don't be an artist because that's not going to pay the rent.' He said, 'Keep that as the hobby. The art is your hobby. Use your languages.' I thought, 'Okay, I want to be a UN interpreter.'" Her first step towards fulfilling that ambition was to move away from home once again. "It was the early '70s. My family was having a difficult time financially, and the IRA was bombing London. I thought, 'I'll go to Madrid, I'll learn Spanish, and see what happens.'"

So, once again, Michèle packed herself off to a foreign environment, now not a wholly unfamiliar experience. In Madrid, she started taking art and art history courses that were available to foreign students at the university. To support herself, she taught English to children after school. She continued in that fashion for three years and became fluent in Spanish. One day, a friend told her of a school that taught interpreting, and Michèle decided now was the time to test her ambition as an UN interpreter. "They put me in this little booth with headphones on. Suddenly, I'm hearing Spanish and I'm meant to be quickly translating it into English. After an hour of that, I thought, 'Oh my goodness. This is not me.' My brain doesn't work like that. I realized I couldn't do it. I was devastated because my whole goal at that point was to be an interpreter. I thought, 'Well, okay, I'll have to switch gears and think of something else to do with myself.'"

Throwing the Dice

Returning to Ireland without a plan, Michèle found things were not going well at home; her father was drinking and gambling and the large family was floundering. Her mother once again had a novel idea: Michèle and her older brother would immigrate somewhere with better opportunities and the rest of the family would follow. Michèle thought, "Perfect. I have a new mission. I'll save the family." She and her brother made applications to Canada and Australia. "Being from a gambling family, we decided whichever one accepts us first, we'll go there."

The first reply was from Canada, so Michèle and her brother packed themselves off to Montreal figuring Michèle's French would help her find a job. "It was 1973 and I was in my early 20s, and I thought, 'This is a really great place to be.' I tried the BBC, but my heart dropped when they pointed me at a typewriter and a desk. I just thought, 'I can't do this.'" So Michèle got a job as a cocktail waitress at the Rainbow Bar and Grill where she began to meet people. A girlfriend at the bar suggested, "'Why don't you model? My family is in the fur business.' I thought this sounded like great fun. I modeled a bit, but I realized I was camera-shy and in all the pictures of me I looked geeky, stiff, and unhappy." Modeling wasn't in the cards, but through the fashion shows, Michèle found another interest.

Michèle and her friend put on a fashion show of vintage clothing. To do it right, her friend said they'd have to hire a makeup artist. "I didn't even know what a makeup artist was. She was much more savvy than I. The day of the show, in walked two makeup artists. One of them said, 'Do you want to see my portfolio?' I said knowingly, 'Oh, of course.' As he turned the pages, this light bulb went off and I thought, 'How come I didn't know you could do this?' At this point, I'm thinking, 'I could do this as a hobby, as a form of art.' The very next day, I couldn't wait to call him aside and ask him where I could learn how to do what he did."

He told Michèle about a course she could take where she'd learn beauty makeup. "I borrowed $200, my first ever in the world, and got my first credit card to afford to take this course three nights a week. I was thinking, 'This will be great fun.'" At the time, she didn't consider it a way to make money. "For me, it was an art form and I really wanted to be an artist. I wanted to be able to paint. Making these changes on faces was dramatic!"

Fashion Makeup wasn't Enough

When the course ended, Michèle heard that Revlon was hiring artists for their store promotions. She applied for the job and became their international makeup artist, doing demonstrations in department stores. "What was great about that job was women lined up and I did face after face after face." She found this an excellent training ground that led to other jobs. While working for Revlon, she heard about a couple, Electa and Corrado, the top fashion makeup team working in Montreal. They had their own line of makeup products and a boutique that offered makeovers. "At that time, they were the 'it' group and I got a job with them. They did all the top fashion shows and fashion spreads. In between those jobs, I would be in the store selling makeup and doing makeovers by appointment for clients. I became really good and became known as a fashion makeup artist."

As Michèle honed her craft as a fashion makeup artist and started putting together her portfolio, she stumbled upon Richard Corson's *Stage Makeup* book. "As I turned the pages, I thought, 'I'm not a true makeup artist.' I wanted to know how to do character work. I wanted to know how to do fake noses, witches, and aging. I wanted to know all that prosthetic special effects stuff." She started asking around and heard about a makeup artist, Mickey Hamilton, who was known for doing these specialty makeups. "I literally knocked on her door and said, 'Could I apprentice with you?' She was a bit of a tough nut, but she was really great. 'Yes, you can. I don't pay, but I'll put you to work.'"

TERROR TRAIN (1980) JAMIE LEE CURTIS
Licensed from Moviestore collection Ltd / Alamy Stock Photo

Horror and SFX

Because of Canadian tax breaks in the 1980s, Montreal and Quebec were becoming the centers for shooting horror and low-budget films. Montreal didn't have an abundance of available makeup artists, however, to get work, previous film experience was necessary. Michèle found a way to leap over the obstacles. "Mickey got me in the door. I worked three films with her and worked really hard. I mean long, long hours. I slept on the floor of her living room and I got fed on-set. The best part was I learned how to work on a film set; I was besotted by film, and became enamored with the power of makeup."

She also discovered Montreal had no effects shops. "If you wanted blood, you made blood. If you wanted scar material, you'd have to figure out how to make it. We had to do everything ourselves." She teamed up with Stephen Dupuis and they shared a lab. "It was great fun, a really great time. We used to experiment with sloppy mixtures all day. Basically, we learned from each other. We'd go to chemical companies and get the products and make whatever we needed. It was really an amazing learning experience. Everything we had and used we made ourselves. Everything I did, I had never done before."

Michèle's big break came when she worked on *Terror Train* (1980) as the head makeup artist with Roger Spottiswoode directing and John Alcott as director of photography. "Can you imagine, the famous John Alcott? Jamie Lee Curtis was 19 or something. It was really a challenging experience. Some of the stuff I did on that film, I'd read how to do a few days before. I remember this body lying with a slit throat and thinking, 'I don't know how to do this sort of stuff.' I quickly went to the Richard Corson book, read about how to stipple latex, then roll it up to create the cut, paint it, and apply blood. I used jam. I used a lot of raspberry jam on that show for blood gel."

"I knew my wounds were good because…I grew up Catholic watching the crucifixion, looking at the gash. I remember thinking, 'I could make a better gash.' The crown of thorns, I'd put much more blood on the crown of thorns and the nails. There was a lot of blood and gore stuff that I did. In fact, I was known as the Queen of Horror at one point. I like splashing blood around and I thought there was huge restraint used on the blood on the crucifixion images."

From **Terror Train**, Michèle learned an important lesson. "It taught me to never think there was only one way to do something. Every time I had a job, I approached it differently. On each job, I had more knowledge and was aware of more products. With that approach, I was unconventional. I think people began to notice what I was doing because I wasn't doing anything like anybody else. Why would I be? Here I am up in Montreal on my own. I'd never been to Hollywood. I barely knew anything about anything in the film world except for my little corner of it."

The World of Neanderthals

One day, she got a call to do **Quest for Fire** (1981). "I had no idea what this film was. All I knew was I was getting a call. They wanted me to leave in three days to do a film about Neanderthals, which I literally had to look up, 'What's a Neanderthal?' When I saw the pictures, I thought, 'Oh, my God, a Neanderthal! Hmmm…well, I guess I can do that.'"

The first part of the film was shot in Africa; Sarah Monzani was head of department and Michèle worked with her on the leads. After the African segments wrapped, the production broke for a period and the producers decided they wanted to shoot the rest of the film in Canada. The change of location took advantage of Canadian tax breaks and simplified the logistics of the production. It was all about money; they could use Canadian crews. The producers approached Michèle to run the rest of the shoot in Canada and head up the department.

QUEST FOR FIRE (CAN/FR/US 1981) Picture from the Ronald Grant
Licensed from Ronald Grant Archive / Alamy Stock Photo

"It was a very challenging film because, truthfully, it was way over my head, but I took it on. I was heading this huge department, having to run the logistics of the call sheet with all these crew people coming in to work on the two different tribes. It was complex. It was a very tough shoot, dealing with a lot of people, a lot of personalities. It really helped me understand how to be a head of department and having to delegate." She found she had to train her Canadian makeup artists to maintain continuity. "We did a makeup test and everyone did a Neanderthal. One had a dark brown face, one had a pink face, and one had a yellow face. I realized I had a problem. I had to take charge. So I gave them all one foundation and everyone used the same color because the tribe had to look like a tribe; I created a system." She also had to do new face casts, sculptures, molds, and run foam latex appliances. She discovered shortcuts, creating facial prosthetics in three sizes - small, medium and large - which then could be mixed and matched to create different prehistoric faces. It was a huge job. "Some days, we were driving to set holding warm appliances on our laps fresh from the oven."

Not only did she have to maintain continuity of the makeup, but she had to mediate the relationships of her crewmembers as well. "I had multiple personalities to deal with: this one fighting with that one, that one fighting with someone else. I fell back on my childhood skills. Being second in command to my mother, I had learned how to settle disputes, wipe tears, soothe, advise, improvise, teach, and manage time and chores. I was doing a lot of that on the film. Running a large crew, the personalities become key. It is important to have a compatible crew, a team that is creative and can work together. Those early skills I'd learned at home were important."

Quest for Fire was nominated for an Academy Award for *Best Makeup*. "Out of the blue, months after we finished the film, the production manager called me and said, 'Michèle, you've been nominated for an Oscar!' I had to ask him, 'What does that mean?' He laughed. I said, 'No, really, what does that mean?' Well, he explained, and then said, 'We're up against *Gandhi*.' I said, 'Oh, well *Gandhi* is a really popular film. We're not going to win.' So I took this film called *Iceman* (1984) working with Michael Westmore up in Canada. They said to me, 'We know you're nominated, but you can't go to Hollywood for the Oscars because we're going be shooting up in remote locations; you won't be able to get away.' I said, 'Oh, no, no. We're not going to win. *Gandhi* is.' I really wanted to do *Iceman*."

So, Michèle went off to work on *Iceman*, a Hollywood film about a Neanderthal man discovered frozen and re-animated in modern times. Michèle was department head working with Westmore as makeup designer.

In 1983, Michèle won the Academy Award for *Best Makeup* for her work on *Quest for Fire,* which she shares with Sarah Monzani. "It was very exciting. A few months later, I got a notice to come to the post office to claim a package. I was in Toronto at that time, so I went down to the post office and the postman said, 'Customs says I've got to open up this package.' It was the height of the drug era and this rectangular, coffin-like box weighed a ton, which caused suspicion. Of course, I knew what it was. I said, 'Open it' and he opened up the package. He looked up and gasped, 'It's an Oscar.' My sister, Adrienne, who was living with me at the time, said to him, 'Oh, why don't you present it to her?' He became solemn and very formal, reached into the box, and with a flourish, I was presented my first Oscar by the postman. The other post office patrons applauded and crowded around to congratulate me!"

Moving Again

Winning the Oscar pushed Michèle to make a decision about the next step in her career. "I thought, everyone is saying, 'Who is this person, Michèle Burke? Is this a fluke?' I decided, 'Okay, that's it.' I'm tenacious. I need to get down there, face the beast, and see if can I make it in Hollywood. I'm a big fish in a little pond in Montreal. Now I want to go to Hollywood and see how I can do." Once in Hollywood, Michèle found it was a bit like starting all over again, reminiscent of going to boarding school or immigrating to Canada. "I'm in a new country. I had to establish myself. I had to get into the union. So, I had to start over working non-union films." She also decided to open up a small lab, but Hollywood was different than Canada. "I noticed there was an attitude, 'The guys, we do this, the girls don't do this work.' But there was no disputing me, because I had been doing this work for years and intended to continue to do so."

Again, Michèle dug into the experiences from her youth growing up with six brothers. "Always, they were doing stuff to me like, 'No girls are allowed' or 'Girls don't do this.' I used to have to fight my corner from very early on. I remember one particular incident where I spent weeks building a beautiful fort of sticks and twigs with my brothers. At the finish of it, my older brother got this board and he painted, 'No girls allowed.' Well, I went berserk. My mother came out and she fought my corner saying, 'Under no circumstances is Michèle not allowed.' Of course, as soon as she turned her back, my brother says, 'Well, you can be the squaw, or maybe the nurse, or something.' When I saw how my mother stood up to them and

how they all took it, I thought, 'Okay, she's teaching me something. I'm not going to put up with this anymore.' From then on, I didn't. I decided, I'm going to be one of them and they'll have to accept me as I am, and that's it."

Michèle knuckled down and started doing non-union films building a new reputation in Tinsel Town. "I just got on with it, did the jobs and the work, and just kept plodding along." She got into the union as makeup designer for *LBJ: The Early Years* (1987), a three-hour miniseries for NBC. She created the prosthetics for 10 likeness makeups for Randy Quaid as LBJ covering a 30-year period. "That was the big thing for me because once I got into the union, I was able to do the bigger films and I began to get a lot of work."

CYRANO DE BERGERAC(1990) GÉRARD DEPARDIEU
Licensed from United Archives GmbH / Alamy Stock Photo

In 1986, Michèle was head of department for *Clan of the Cave Bear*, again with Michael Westmore designing the cave-people, but it wasn't the experience she had hoped it would be. She'd read Jean Auel's book, and the description of her Neanderthal with the sloping skull and other physical attributes inspired Michèle's creativity, but "…they didn't want that. It was nearly like *One Million Years B.C.*,

even though they kept saying to me, 'We don't want Raquel Welch.' Every time I tried to put more dirt on them or tried to make them look more like Neanderthals, they'd say, 'No, no, no clean them up.'" The film went on to be nominated for an Oscar. "In the end, what did we end up with? We ended up with a version different from the book. We did our best work, no one could fault what we did; it wasn't the book and it wasn't what I had envisioned. However, our responsibility is to the director's vision."

Avoiding the Stereotype

When she completed *Clan*, Michèle made a conscious choice to find projects that didn't include Neanderthals. She worked as makeup designer or as special effects makeup artist on several projects, including the 1989 television series, *Alien Nation*, the 1990 film, *Cyrano De Bergerac* (her third nomination for an Oscar), and in 1992, *Bram Stoker's Dracula* directed by Francis Ford Coppola.

Michèle's interest was piqued by the prospect of doing the film with Coppola. "They said that they wanted me to do a Dracula without the typical

BRAM STOKER'S DRACULA (1992) GARY OLDMAN
Licensed from AF archive / Alamy Stock Photo

fangs, widow's peak, and cloak; they wanted a Dracula that had never been seen before. Now I was excited; that's what I like. I want to do characters that haven't been seen before." **Dracula** was also Michèle's first collaboration with Costume Designer Eiko Ishioka who profoundly influenced Michèle's makeup and artistic designs.

Michèle was hired as makeup and hair designer and department head to coordinate the looks and hairstyles of all the characters, including the now-famous old-age Dracula, east-meets-west hairstyle. Greg Cannom and Matthew Mungle applied the old age, wolf, and large bat-creature makeups. **Bram Stoker's Dracula** presented Coppola's unique vision of the fabled vampire story and earned Michèle her fourth nomination and second Academy Award for *Best Makeup*, which she shares with Greg Cannom and Matthew W. Mungle, making her the first female makeup artist to win two Oscars.

As Ireland's only two-time Oscar winner, Michèle was invited back to her homeland to appear as a guest at the Galway Film Festival. She brought her Oscars with her which were displayed in an elaborate exhibition hall on a church-style pedestal at the front. "There was a long line of people waiting to meet me and view my Oscars up close. One woman got up the nerve to ask me if she could hold an Oscar. I said, 'Sure…but if you hold it, you have to make a wish.' She assumed a solemn stance and moved into serious wishing mode. Everyone behind her was watching closely. The line grew longer, snaked out the door and onto the street, and everyone that followed made a wish. I have continued that tradition and many-a-wish has been made on my Oscars." Authors' Note: When we interviewed Michèle, we, too, wished upon her Oscars.

In 1994, Michèle heard a film was being planned based on the Ann Rice novel, **Interview with the Vampire: The Vampire Chronicles**. "If I've read the book and I hear about a project, and I think, 'Oh, my God,

INTERVIEW WITH THE VAMPIRE; THE VAMPIRE CHRONICLES, (1994)
TOM CRUISE
Licensed from United Archives GmbH / Alamy Stock Photo

I want to do that. I seek out that job.' I see it as an artwork, not another job. **Interview with the Vampire**, I sought out. I contacted Neil Jordan (director) in Ireland, and again when I saw him at the Oscars." She was hired as makeup supervisor in collaboration with Stan Winston Studios to create the makeups for the film's all-star cast: Tom Cruise, Brad Pitt, Antonio Banderas, and Kirstin Dunst. On this film, she enjoyed creating vampires that differed greatly from those she had created for **Dracula.** "My mandate was the vampires had to look like they had translucent skin and like they were from earth, but not earth. During the day or in twilight, when they walk in the streets, they can't look like vampires, but at night, then yeah, vampires."

After working on **Interview**, Michèle had to again fight being typecast as a niche makeup artist. "At every phase of my career, I wanted something else. At one point I was in the fashion world. Then I was the Queen of Horror. Then I thought, 'I don't want to be the Queen of Horror.' Then I became the Queen of Neanderthals and I thought, 'That's a niche I don't want to be in.' All I got called for were Neanderthals. I did **Clan of the Cave Bear**, that's fine. Then I thought, 'That's it, no more Neanderthals.' Then, I started to do the vampire films, **Dracula** and **Interview with the Vampire**. Suddenly, 'Oh she just does vampires.' I'd say, 'No, I don't just do vampires.' I was always wriggling out of being typecast. I tried to make sure that I directed my career and where it was going, not taking all the calls that came in, because otherwise you become the 'Burn Girl' or 'The Male Lead Girl.' People often niche you."

"If you are a makeup artist in the film business, as much work will come to you due to your good straight makeup as your specialty stuff. I think being able to do a leading lady is a major achievement on many levels, because you have to make them look gorgeous and different every time they work. I see myself as a makeup artist who is capable of spanning the complete spectrum of what is needed: beauty, character work, the unreal, aging, prosthetic work. I have that ability and I can do most things that are required."

"I always tried to be versatile; if I did one film with effects then I wanted to do another one with beauty. I always tried to mix it up, but artistically, I always try to keep challenging myself. I like challenges. I always choose my projects for the artistic value and the fun I'll have working on them."

Variety is the Spice

The search for variety has led Michèle to work on an interesting mix of films with Tom Cruise: *Jerry Maguire* (1996), *Vanilla Sky* (2001), *Minority Report* (2002), *Mission: Impossible III* (2006), *Tropic Thunder* (2008), *Mission: Impossible – Ghost Protocol* (2011), *Rock of Ages* (2012), and *Oblivion* (2013). "Running a show like the *Mission: Impossible* films incorporates a variety of makeup effects. They have disguises, special effects, dirt, beauty, everything. I love that because that's a challenge. There's continuity and you've got to keep the team together and you're traveling. It's a real ride. I love that." Along with the action-packed thrill rides of those films, Michèle also found variety doing the comedies *Austin Powers: The Spy Who Shagged Me* (1999) for which she received her fifth Oscar nomination, and *Austin Powers in Goldmember* (2002).

One of Michèle's most artistic films was *The Cell* (2000) with Director Tarsem Singh, starring Jennifer Lopez, Vince Vaughn, and Vincent D'Onofrio. Michèle collaborated for the second time with Costume Designer Eiko Ishioka and KNB EFX Group did the prosthetic fabrication of her designs. The film is a stylized thriller about a social worker entering the mind of a comatose serial killer in order to help the FBI learn where he has hidden his latest kidnapping victim. The scenes inside the mind-space shared between Lopez and D'Onofrio are stylistically beautiful and horrific, a perfect blend of Michèle's talents for beauty and effects makeup. "Sometimes on a film, you're told to

THE CELL (2000) JENNIFER LOPEZ AND VINCENT D'ONOFRIO, AVERY PIX
Licensed from Entertainment Pictures / Alamy Stock Photo

back off and water it down, as happened on *Clan of the Cave Bear*. Other times, you're pushed further, which is what Tarsem Singh did with me on *The Cell*. I would give him my version and he'd say, 'More, more, no that's not enough.' Then I realized a film like that is fantastic to work on because you're pushed to your artistic limits." Her work on *The Cell* earned Michèle her sixth Oscar nomination, making her only the second woman in Oscar history to do so.

"You have to be in charge of your own life. You can't allow yourself be the ship on the rough seas being blown around and saying, 'I wonder which port I'll end up in?' At this point, I can pretty much pick and choose my projects, which is a lovely place to be. What would I like for my next project? To design a character that's never been seen before."

"I think artistic ability is what makes one makeup artist stand out over another." Her paintings lining the walls of her home are vivid with bright colors and moody contours; every piece is an evocative portrait with a face seen through her own a special lens. For Michèle, painting is a fine art, whether oil on canvas or makeup on skin. "If someone's artistic, you'll see the art."

OUTTAKES:

On Independence and Being a Loner:

"You may have a mentor and you may work with other artists, but I never thought like that. I always thought, 'You better just get out there, get your own work,' which I did. That's why really I was a 'one of one' basically when I worked. I didn't think of relying on anybody else. If I wanted a film, I'd go after it. I'd call them up, go for an interview, ask them could I work on it, and get the job. That's how I operated. I always tell makeup people, 'you know, you are a loner. You've got to know that this is a solo job and you've got to be able to rely on yourself more than anything. Then, of course, you work and rely on your team to follow your lead. It reminds me of a quote from Jazz musician, Miles Davis, in which he said [in relation to his fellow musicians], 'I don't want them to follow me. I want them to follow themselves, but to be with me.' Exactly!"

On Collaboration & Communication:

"I value collaboration and communication because I have worked with some that don't; they just expect you to work as the makeup girl down there doing the thing, but if suddenly something's wrong, it's 'Make-up!' I like when there's collaboration because we are a team; on a film you never work alone, you're never isolated. The work of a makeup artist must harmonize with whatever the costume designer designs. I must work with them. Our work must invisibly blend together. I don't work on an island. Everything comes together hand-in-hand. It's a painting or a tableau that we're all creating, so I like when there's a lot of communication and collaboration."

"I want to hire people that I know can listen to my direction artistically, help me execute that, or bring new skills and new ideas to the project. I feel each person on my team exponentially raises the level of art, so to speak, and I see it as an art form. I want my team to help me create. I never give the credit to myself alone; it's a team that executes the job."

On Meeting Challenges:

"Pretty much every film I work on has, not a problem, but a challenge I have to resolve. For example, in *Tropic Thunder* I designed Tom Cruise's Les Grossman. Ben Stiller, the director, called me up and said, 'Look, Tom has to have big, fat sausage fingers and hair on his hands and a huge hairy chest and he's got to look overweight and he's got to be balding.' Then Tom says, 'Yeah, but I don't want to be in the make-up chair any longer than an hour.' Now, that's a problem because that type of a makeup takes longer. I thought, 'Okay.' At the time we were doing multi-pieces, I cut down on the number of pieces we used. Also we pre-punched all the hair, which everyone does now, and pre-painted everything. When the pieces went on, they were pre-punched, painted, and mostly we just needed to do the blending."

On Trust & Confidence:

"I did a film with Roland Joffé called *There Be Dragons* (2011) and it had a major aging and, of course, they had no money. They were shooting in Buenos Aires, so I did it up here, prepping, working out of Spectral Motion, and Roland Blancaflor at RBFX ran the silicone for me. I needed the right people with the right skills. I called Tom Floutz to come work with me. Once I had designed the look, we went over to Spectral Motion. I wanted a one-piece silicone that had the neck, the chin, the face, the forehead, ending behind the hairline and then a wig went on it. We got it done and I pre-painted it. We had the hair punched in, which took ages. We did five of them.

"Then Tom and I flew down to Buenos Aires and, when I got there, I got whisked off the plane and told, 'The producers want to have a meeting with you right away.' I thought, 'Uh oh, what's going on?' They were all worried, they'd never seen the makeup, we'd never done a test. We were shooting the next day with it and one of the producers was saying, 'I'm worried about this,' because it was a really low budget film. 'Can we just gray out his hair and put glasses on him, that could age him?' I thought, 'Oh, no we can't do that.' They said, 'Well, why don't we do a makeup test tomorrow?' I explained we only had five sets of this makeup, enough for the five days shooting. I said, 'With a test, we'll lose a day's shooting with the makeup." Then I said, 'Look, I know this is going to look good.' Roland Joffé said, 'Stop the meeting. Michèle, look me in the eye and tell me that you feel confident that you can do this makeup.' I looked him straight in the eye and I said, "Roland, I am 100% confident that this makeup will be a success.' He looked around the room and he said, 'The meeting's over, we're shooting as per Michèle tomorrow.' I thought, 'Wow, phew.' At that point, I felt confident and everything went great. You've got to be confident in what you do because if you're not confident, you're not going to instill it in the people around you. Now, that confidence only came from having done millions of makeups before. You don't gain that confidence just out of nowhere."

"I always had to fight my corner to make sure that it was understood that no one was coming in to do the special effects makeup work. That was me. I also do that. It was more often to production managers and people like that who would say, 'Who should we bring in to do that particular makeup?' I'd say, 'Nobody. I'm doing it.' They would look surprised, 'Shouldn't we bring somebody in?' I'd say, 'No.'"

"I remember one day on *Vanilla Sky*, Tom Cruise's makeup design was a horrible disfigured face, the result of a car accident. I based the look on a Francis Bacon painting; it was a really strange makeup. The producers weren't sure if this was a good idea at all because they felt, well, Tom's iconic face…Tom and Director Cameron Crowe wanted it. I remember I completed the makeup and Tom looked at himself in the mirror and he said, 'Michèle, I look terrible.' I said, 'I know, Tom, you do.' He said, 'Are you sure I'm okay?' I said, 'You're okay.' He wouldn't have gone out had I not said, 'You're okay.' You have to be assured of what you do."

On Different Times:

"Back when I was doing a lot of work in Canada, every effect was a practical. I did *Trouble with Trolls* where an elf character had ears that moved when he spoke. I did that practically with a mono-filament. I'd be off camera always and as he spoke for his close-up, I'd move his ears up and down."

"I remember doing a film where this guy gets a bullet hit and part of his ear falls off. Well, I'm there with a fishing rod, and every time they'd say, 'Action,' the blood hits, the ear spurts, and I have to chuck the ear off with a mono-filament and a fishing line."

On Career Options:

"After you get out of school it's a strange quagmire. Do you do commercials? Do you go to fashion? Do you do the news? What do you do? Sitcoms? Feature films? There is such a big world out there, and how do you get in the door?"

On Dirty Work and Health:

"It's dirty work doing molds. Your hands get wrecked. Don't talk about your nails, they're ruined. You're breathing in all of this junk. It's not pleasant. At a given point, even I realized that I'm breathing in too much plaster dust and it was affecting my lungs. Now we are more aware of the hazards of breathing and touching chemicals and powder substances. And all of the solvents…it's not fun. If someone is working with fiberglass, do you really want to be around that?"

"You have to have good health because the hours are daunting. You're going to work split shifts. You're going to eat at odd hours. A lot of travel. You've got to have a lot of stamina and health."

"You've got to have the passion. Being a makeup artist is a lifestyle…It's very difficult if you work in film. It's a lot of sacrifices. Most of the people that I know, they live it, it's their life. Maybe if you do commercials, or TV, it can be different. In film, it's never, 'I go out and I'm a mechanic for eight hours of the day, then I come home to the husband and kids.' This, no, it's a way of life."

On Makeup Artistry:

"Two people can apply a foundation differently, and when you see the same product on the same face done by two different people it becomes apparent who is the artist. With one, the actress' skin looks amazing, luminescent. Whatever they've done, however they've blended it…and then the other person does it and you wonder, what has happened? That's the artistic ability."

"It's 'being in service to.' When I watch *Downtown Abbey* and you see the ladies' maid or butler. They basically were like makeup people. They were a dresser, did their hair, and got them ready. They stand back. In the same way, it's not about us, it's about your actress or actor. It's your bedside manner, everything has to be conducive so that they feel their best when they walk out, and they are that character you've created. That's the whole thing."

"I try to bring my makeup artistry to the forefront. I'm just someone who applies great makeup. That's how I work, sticking to the job. I try to bring that to the table by the way I dress and by the way I approach and deal with the work that is at hand. We're there to execute the job we got hired for and we should give them the best of what we can give them. That's professionalism."

Catching Up!

We interviewed Michèle on January 14, 2016. Since then, she has worked on

The Super
Makeup Designer for Val Kilmer

Marshall
Makeup Designer for Kate Hudson

Honorary Professor: Shanghai Vancouver Film School
Presentation and Workshop in Shanghai, China, 2016

Continued Development and Design of Makeup applicators and blenders
with Geka Worldwide

Custom Makeup Courses and Workshops

For more of Michèle's Work and Credits, visit:

www.micheleburke.com
Instagram: micheleburke_mua
www.imdb.com

1990
ACADEMY AWARD
BEST MAKEUP

DRIVING MISS DAISY, (1990)
MORGAN FREEMAN, JESSICA TANDY, ©Warner Brothers/courtesy Everett Collection
Licensed from Everett Collection, Inc. / Alamy Stock Photo

I love working. If you're always the department head you forget what it's like to come and be a day player. As a department head, I don't need a day player to come in and try to be department head, I need a worker bee.
So, when I'm a day player I come in and I'm the worker bee.

Like many other eight-year-old girls, Lynn Barber had Barbie dolls. But unlike other eight-year-old girls, she used to erase their painted-on faces and redo them using nail polish. "I think I always knew I wanted to do makeup. For a minute, I thought I might want to be a flight attendant, but at 5'2" it might have been a problem. Then I saw a magazine cover with Susan Dey from **The Partridge Family** on it and I told my mom, 'I want to do her makeup.' My mother said, 'Honey, it's not a real job.' 'Well somebody did her makeup. Somebody made her look like that.' And that was that. When I was at West Seneca West Senior High School and my friends were vying for the lead in the school play, they asked me what I wanted to do. I said, 'I don't want to be on stage. I want to do the makeup.' And I did. I'm very comfortable behind the camera making other people look good."

Her Family

Hailing from Buffalo, New York, Lynn's entire family has an artistic bent. Her father was a musician, her mother a portrait painter, her younger brother, James Nowak, can build anything and is a construction foreman, her older brother, Bruce Nowak, is a Grammy-nominated musician, and her daughter, Micah Laine, is also a makeup artist. "I was fascinated watching my mother make a flat piece of paper come to life with a beautiful face of a woman. I wanted to do that. And my dad impressed upon me my life's philosophy: 'If you're like water everything will be okay. Sometimes water is like an iceberg, it sunk the Titanic, and sometimes water is a baby's tear. Water can change everything depending upon the situation.' He was a poet."

Lynn's confidence in her makeup skills (and her mother's trust in those skills) came into play even when she was a little girl. One day in the 1960s, wearing a blue chiffon dress with matching blue eye shadow, Lynn's mother was preparing to leave for a wedding. But Lynn, at age nine, said, "'You can't leave; I have to fix your makeup.' She had just the blue shadow on, which they did back then. I sat her down, softened it up and she said she got complements all day." Lynn's talent and her discerning eye were evident even from a very early age.

While in high school, Lynn went to Potter Road Technical School (now renamed Potters Road Vocational School) and studied cosmetology. She knew she was interested in makeup, and this training provided her with a foundation that has stayed with her to this day. "Vocational school was a great thing to have because it was like an apprenticeship program. There's nothing like hands-on training. I hope this country goes back to more occupational schools. Pretty soon, the young ones won't know what a hammer and nail are."

Marching to Her Own Drum

When she was 17, Lynn graduated from high school, did some traveling, then worked in an office "which was a disaster." Feeling restricted, she moved to New York City where she felt less confined and could ply her creativity in a hair salon where she did both makeup and hair. "I loved New York and all the clothes, but I couldn't afford them, so I got a sewing machine and started making my own. Everything I had was something I made. I'd go to the fabric store to buy the material for my wardrobe. Then, of course, the hair, the makeup, the wigs, I did all of that. It fit my bohemian frame of mind."

It's said it isn't *what* you know, but *who* you know, and that, coupled with being in NYC, opened a door to Lynn's future. Lynn had a friend, Franky, whose mother ran the Holiday Inn where Director James Caan and the cast of *Hide in Plain Sight* (1980) happened to be staying. Production needed someone to cut and style hair for the 1960s-period film, so they asked Franky's mom if she knew anyone. She sent the cast to see Lynn at the salon and she was "bitten by the movie bug. We weren't allowed on-set because it was a union film, but we got to visit it. That was it. I wanted to work in film and do makeup."

Atlanta and Daisy

In the early '80s, Lynn moved to Atlanta from NYC. Atlanta was, and still is, a booming film town. At that time it was a hub for commercials, which provided Lynn with lots of work opportunities between getting married and giving birth to her daughter. Georgia is a right-to-work state, so Lynn could work in film and television there without belonging to the union. Eventually, she joined NABET (National Association of Broadcast Employees and Technicians) which folded into IATSE (International Alliance of Theatrical Stage Employees) Local 798 in 1990. Among the film opportunities she had in Atlanta, Lynn worked on *A Killing Affair* (1986), *Pals* (1987), *Alone in the Neon Jungle* (1988), and *Caroline?* (1990), a Hallmark Hall of Fame TV movie.

While working on *Caroline?*, Lynn was told there was a film coming up that needed a makeup artist for aging that would span decades. She was asked to audition in order to show the director what she could do. Lynn was on-set for 16 hours a day and just didn't have time to do the test, so she asked, "Can the director come to me? Come to my set?" Everybody agreed. Lynn got a friend to be the model, and between takes, on her lunch hour and breaks, Lynn went into the makeup trailer to age her friend. The agreed-upon hour arrived and the director, assistant director, and unit production manager descended upon the makeup trailer. "The director said, 'I don't know the woman you've aged, how do I know what she looks like without makeup?' 'I aged only half her face.' To make the point, I covered half the model's face to show her without makeup and then uncovered the half with the age makeup. Right then and there I got the job. The director was Bruce Beresford, the movie was *Driving Miss Daisy*, which led to an Academy Award nomination, which led to a win."

Potter Road Technical School may have trained Lynn on the basics like street beauty, hair, and general aesthetics, but she needed more sophisticated skills to succeed in film work. *Driving Miss Daisy* required

Lynn to age Morgan Freeman, Dan Akyroyd, and Jessica Tandy incrementally over a 25-year period. The year was 1989 and silicone prosthetics that are now the industry standard weren't even invented yet. Atlanta didn't have a makeup supply house; everything had to be shipped in from LA or New York. **Driving Miss Daisy** begins in 1948; the characters age slowly and subtly, which presented a challenge for the makeup crew. Miss Daisy Werthan (Jessica Tandy) is 72 at the start of the film and 97 at the end; Hoke Colburn (Morgan Freeman) is 60 at the start, 85 at the end; and Boolie Werthan (Dan Akyroyd) ages from 40 to 65.

"I instinctively learned how to age an actor. Just playing around, figuring things out. We didn't have tutorials. We couldn't go on the internet. We had to read books. Watching my mom do those portraits, manipulating highlight and shadow to create a three-dimensional illusion fed my imagination. Then I started figuring things out. I learned how to make a wrinkle by using the actor's own aging, using the existing lines, not imposing something that wasn't there naturally. That's what I did for **Driving Miss Daisy**."

Manlio Rocchetti was department head on the film. Together, he and Lynn tested looks and found the products that would create subtle, realistic aging for each stage of the process, and determined how each subsequent year would be reflected in the makeup. Even the thinnest foam latex would have been too thick. It was therefore decided that old school stretch-and-stipple would be the technique of choice. Stretch-and-stipple

DRIVING MISS DAISY (1990) DAN ACKROYD, JESSICA TANDY, AND MORGAN FREEMAN
Licensed from Moviestore collection Ltd / Alamy Stock Photo

was used around the eyes, mouths, and jaw lines on all the characters to create gentle aging. "Morgan was 50 years old at the time. We tried pieces, we tried everything, but the stretch and stipple worked best for him. I put age spots on him then greyed his hair. The challenge was getting him to look old, he had and still has, great skin." Lynn tried using contact lenses to simulate cataracts for Morgan Freeman's eyes, "but they were huge and thick and he couldn't handle it. That's when we went with the glasses he has in those last scenes." Additionally, bald caps created receding hairlines on Dan Akyroyd and Morgan Freeman, showing the slow progression of time. Rocchetti was responsible for Akyroyd's makeup and Lynn was responsible for the rest. She received the Academy Award for *Best Makeup*, which she shares with Rocchetti as makeup supervisor, and Kevin Haney as makeup consultant.

DRIVING MISS DAISY (1989) MORGAN FREEMAN & JESSICA TANDY
Licensed from AF archive / Alamy Stock Photo

Mama Bear

"I had to work for everything. I didn't know anybody in the entertainment industry. I didn't have a brother or an uncle or a sister to introduce me to someone. I just plugged along. I had to work for it and I'm glad I did because it reinforced my belief that I'm a survivor and independent, always have been."

This sense of independence and survival is one Lynn has instilled in her daughter, Micah Laine. Micah trained as a makeup artist in Atlanta, earned her esthetician license, then eventually worked her way into the makeup union. Once in the union, Micah asked her mom if she would hire her to work on *Army Wives (2007-2011)*, which Lynn department-headed for four seasons. Lynn's response: "'I need to see your resume. You need to go out and work with other people and see how that works out because we're too close.' I was hard on her, harder than I would have been on most people. She thanked me later. Now people call me up and tell me what great ethics she has, what beautiful work she does, and what talent she displays."

Of course, Lynn was like a mother bear if her child was bullied. The night before the 1990 Oscars, Lynn received a call from a crying six-year-old Micah. "I asked, 'Why are you crying?' 'One of the kids at school said you don't love me anymore because you haven't picked me up in a week. I told him you're going to win an Oscar. And he said, 'You're a liar.'" The night of the Oscars, on stage, under the lights, in front of millions of viewers, Lynn held up her Oscar and said, "'Micah, you can take this to show-and-tell on Friday.' We flew home and Micah took the statue to school on Friday and guess who didn't come to school that day? The kid who made her cry."

Traveling the World, then Home

Atlanta was a haven for Lynn, her time there gave her steady work, established her reputation, and brought her success. Part of that success was working with well-known actors who requested her. Kate Jackson, of *Charlie's Angels* fame, asked Lynn to come to Toronto to be her personal makeup artist for two films, *The Silence of Adultery* (1995) and *The Cold Heart of a Killer* (1996). "I like being a personal. I get to take care of my actors. It's different than running a department because you work with just that one person."

Young Hercules (1998) took Lynn to New Zealand, a right-to-work country, where she lived and worked for three years. New Zealand presented challenges for Lynn. "I miss the food. I miss the people. I don't miss the weather. It's hard weather. It could be beautiful, hot, and sunny, and then all of a sudden, a big storm comes in…it was hard work. Also, they didn't have proper makeup trailers. Of course, this was 16 years ago, so I'm sure it's a lot better now." One of her fondest memories is working with a youthful Ryan Gosling as Young Hercules.

In 2000, Lynn received a call that her father was ill, so she moved back to the States, landing in Los Angeles. Luckily, her father regained his health, leaving Lynn free to pursue work in LA, but she hit some roadblocks because she didn't belong to the Southern California branch of the makeup union. She received a call to do a film in Charleston, South Carolina, and because she belonged to Local 798, the East Coast local, she could take the job. On that set, Lynn met a young actress named Jena Malone who asked her to come back to LA for her next film. Lynn took that job, which happened to be as department head on

Donnie Darko (2001), and officially qualified for union membership in Local 706.

Obtaining union membership on both sides of the country involved two very different processes. Local 798 (East Coast union) required a two-day test that included a 12-hour written portion and a 12-hour practical where a mastery of bald caps, aging, beauty makeup, and male grooming was necessary. Lynn took that test in 1990 and passed. Whereas by 2000, Local 706 (West Coast union) had done away with the test. In its place, freshly sworn in trainees were required to take eight eight-hour classes, each one focusing on a different skill, such as: aging, prosthetics, proper maintenance of the makeup kit, and facial hair. At the completion of the eighth class, the trainee is elevated to journeyman status. Lynn finished her courses and qualified as a journeyman, but she still continues her education whenever she can.

DONNIE DARKO (2001) JAKE GYLLENHAAL
licensed from Moviestore collection Ltd / Alamy Stock Photo

"I think it's important to keep up. There are videos and classes available on aging, beauty, contouring, highlighting, how to pour molds, everything. I take as many courses as I can fit into my busy schedule."

Lynn remains in Los Angeles in a spacious, modern condo that is central to many LA locations. "We call our home base camp. It's quiet. There's many times on a show, we call it Fraterday, where we go in mid-day on Friday, work into Saturday morning at 6 AM, and have to be back at 5:30 Monday morning. I've got to get everything done within a limited number of hours: see my husband, do the laundry, shop at the market, go to the DMV, get my teeth cleaned, have my hair colored, all that stuff. It's busy, always busy. But I prefer to be too busy."

Smiley Face and the Twinkle

"My mom taught me if you draw a smiley face, the circle and two dots for eyes don't ever change. But you can make him sad or angry or perplexed with the eyebrows. Like the emoticons on our phones. Then the mouth changes. People always say it's the eyes, the eyes, the eyes, but it's the brows and the lips. Those are my go-to things."

Lynn's creative process always begins with the script and concept meetings with the director, whether she's working on film or television or runway. "I know exactly what the character should look like. It pops into my head." The actor is usually the last partner brought into the discussion, but he or she usually has strong ideas about the character. Lynn fulfills the director's vision, satisfies her vision, and pleases the actor. "My job is to bring them ideas. Usually a woman will say, 'Oh, I want to look….' Everyone doesn't like something about their face, so I work to minimize that. Or, sometimes they really like something about their face they want focused, the lips, the eyes. I bring out the best and make them feel like they own it. Make them feel comfortable.

"I don't leave my actors. I'm right there with them on-set. I'm watching the camera, I'm watching video village to make sure if I need to do something I'm there. I don't go back and sit on my phone while they're acting. A lot of times I have to come in with a tear stick, or a blower if they can't get the tears going. If they have to look drunk and crazy, I've got to come in with a pencil and put it in. Sometimes we'll add the blood or sweat during the hold or freeze; I'll drop it in or spray it on. I run in, do it, run out. And they continue. An actor once told me, 'When you're my makeup artist, I don't feel like I'm up there alone.' That made me feel good, because they're not."

Lynn works on the right side of the actors she makes up and when she is finished, the actors stand up, look at themselves in the mirror, then "they give me that nod of approval. They don't say anything, but I can see it in their eyes. Oh, I get goosebumps. Ann Margaret did it when I worked on her in *Ray Donovan* (2013-2014), she had that little twinkle. I got it from Larry Hagman, I got it from Linda Gray in *Dallas* (2012), that little twinkle they get in their eye when they stand up and they feel...Larry felt like JR. Linda felt like Sue Ellen. They feel like their characters. It's the greatest compliment I can get."

Water Revisited

Holding her father's advice close, Lynn has found strength and inspiration when she follows his mandate: "If you're like water, everything will be okay." Lynn assesses situations and decides the best way to handle them, flowing river, or solid block of ice. For example, "On the show I'm currently working on, the producers don't want last looks. They don't want the actors to look polished, or too together. Okay. I can't be that rigid person, 'my way or the highway.' I need, in this instance, to flow with the current." On the other hand, Lynn tells of a time in the '80s when she called the union in New York, about a problem for which she received no help and often, no return calls. "I remember somebody I spoke with, a man with a heavy New York accent, who said, 'Good Luck, kid' and hung up. I thought, this time I can't be a drop of water. I've got to be an ice cube."

RAY DONOVAN (2013) JON VOIGHT & LIEV SCHREIBER
Licensed from AF archive / Alamy Stock Photo

Lynn has worked as department head on *Donnie Darko* (2001), *Like Mike* (2002), *Marilyn Hotchkiss' Ballroom Dancing & Charm School* (2005), *Bottle Shock* (2008), *Beverly Hills Chihuahua* (2008), *Army Wives* (2007-2011, 72 episodes), *Ray Donovan* (2013-2014, 24 episodes), and has happily acted as makeup artist, key makeup artist, and personal on a number of other films and television shows. "If you are a day player, be a day player. If you are a department head, be a department head. If you're key, be a key. If you're a personal, be a personal. If you're coming in as cleanup crew, just be the cleanup crew. Don't overstep your position."

With a CV that encompasses film, television, and runway, Lynn clearly enjoys it all, but prefers television over film because "it's faster, quicker, you always have to be on your toes. If you're doing episodic TV and you're doing 12 episodes, things change every single day. You've got 12 scripts instead of one. As you're shooting one, you're probably re-shooting another, and prepping for the next one. I like it because my brain has to have that stimulation. They used to call me the Energizer Bunny."

"Many is the time I look around and think, 'Aw, I get to do this and get paid.' I'm so thankful that I've been able to do what I do and love what I do and make people happy. Whether it's making them look hot and sweaty, or drunk, or bruised, or beautiful, I love every bit of it. Every bit of it."

OUTTAKES:

On Longevity:

"This business is a little big world. Once you get a bad reputation, you're lost. If I'm about to do a job in Vegas, I'll call on the people I know who work in Vegas. You only want to work with people who are there to work."

On Future Projects:

"I would really love to do something like *Dancing with the Stars* which is almost like doing theatre. Not stressful, but in the moment. You've got to change those dancers out and get them out, boom, boom. It would be fun and creative."

On Location:

"When you're on the road, you're in a strange kitchen, a strange bed, strange bathroom. It's somebody else's and they furnished not to your taste. And you're in a strange city. When you're on location all that has to be factored in. You're travelling, you have to have mud boots, rain boots, rain gear, clothes for the heat, for cold, sun hats."

On Last Looks:

"Some projects demand last looks more than others. *Shameless* (2011-current) a gritty, domestic dramedy, should look windblown and unkempt, which doesn't need last looks. However, a more style-driven, society piece does. I got to do the reboot of *Dallas*, Season one, with Larry Hagman, Linda Gray, and Patrick Duffy. We got everybody ready, then it was time for last looks. We powder, refresh, make sure no hair is sticking out, and the actors walk on-set to begin the shoot. The DP [Director of Photography] on Season one wouldn't do last looks! Sue Ellen had to walk from the trailer through the Dallas wind in a beautiful Chanel outfit; it was important to take a few minutes to be sure she looked just right. We asked for last looks, but the unit production manager said, 'No.' The ladies were not happy, but after the first day, we had last looks."

On the Industry:

"We in the entertainment business can influence people; let's do it for good. You can find enough sadness and darkness in the news. I'd rather go for the light. Influence people in a positive way."

Catching Up!

We interviewed Lynn on March 6, 2016. Since then, she has worked on

Kevin Hart: What Now?
(Documentary)
Makeup department head: Casino segment

Mother's Day
Key makeup artist: second unit, Los Angeles

For more of Lynn's Credits visit: www. imdb.com

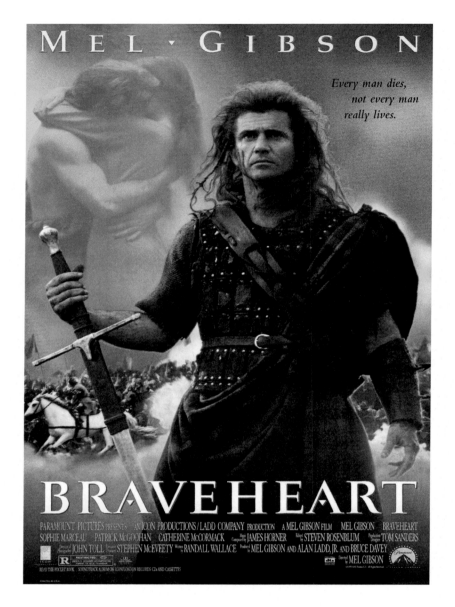

**1996
ACADEMY AWARD
BEST MAKEUP**

BRAVEHEART (1995) POSTER, MEL GIBSON
Licensed from AF archive / Alamy Stock Photo

Lois Burwell

All creative activity requires a certain bravery because we expose ourselves to the
very core. It's a risk that could bring failure as well as success.
All the great filmmakers I have worked alongside have that ability to go out on a limb,
have embraced and supported others to be courageous.

From the Beginning...

"My love of film and makeup comes from what people today might consider inappropriate parenting," laughed Lois Burwell as she described the beginning of her love affair with film. As a young girl whose parents loved going to the cinema, Lois recalls seeing Vincent Price in **The Raven**, Kubrick's **Paths of Glory**, and anything with Peter Cushing, including **Dracula, The Curse of Frankenstein**, and **The Mummy**, all by the age of five.

"My early influences in makeup were as something that altered someone's appearance rather than giving them a flattering look. When I saw something that alarmed me, like **Bambi,** where I screamed the place down, my parents reassured me, 'That's not real, that's makeup. Someone's done that to someone to make them look that way. They're just actors.' I was five, I needed the reassurance."

With piercing green eyes, her trademark cropped hairstyle, a calm demeanor, dry wit, and generous spirit, Lois Burwell reflects the values and roots of her London upbringing. Her father was an electrician by trade, her mother a telephonist who, in her youth, worked for a court dressmaker. Both parents enjoyed working with their hands, and the household was a hands-on, make-at-home, D-I-Y collaborative. As the only child of older parents with a grandmother at home, Lois spent much of her youth with adults, having adult conversations undaunted by and embracing big ideas and a large vocabulary. "Being precocious or show-offy was never encouraged in my household, and that may have influenced what I do because makeup is behind-the-scenes. You're encouraged to express yourself and yet you're not encouraged to be in the limelight. It's the work that speaks, not necessarily you."

At some level, Lois has known since childhood that she wanted to work in the film industry. Distant memories of her first moments of inspiration came bubbling back when Michael Key interviewed her for an article about the film *War Horse* (2011) for *Make-Up Artist Magazine*: "[Key and I] were in a back room of the Alexandra Palace in North London where IMATS [Inetrnational Makeup Artists Trade Show]used to hold its conference, and I recognized the room as one I visited when I was fourteen. The BBC [had been] filming a program and the prop chap asked me and my friends, 'Are you interested in seeing the set, girls?' I said, 'Absolutely, wonderful, we'd love to see behind-the-scenes rather than just watch the filming.' He took us into a dark room lit only with light bulbs around the mirrors. It was the makeup room. I stood there, looked around and said, 'I'm going to do this.' The prop man said, 'You know, I believe you will.' I'd forgotten that memory until the moment Michael Key asked me, 'How did you begin?'

"Film has always been here for me. I like the permanence, good, bad, indifferent, there it is. I love that. It's the difference between a book and an app. I like the physicality of it. I love the fact you sit with a group of strangers in the dark and life stops. It's not the same as watching it on the television where the phone goes, you go for a pee, you have a cup of tea…the film's reduced even if you've got the biggest television screen in the world. In the cinema it doesn't, except if you're sitting next to some numpty with an iPhone checking her latest tweets."

Listening to Her Heart

After school and on weekends, a young Lois attended dance school. She was an accomplished enough dancer that when there was a show, she'd dance with the older girls, and she quickly evolved into the makeup "go-to gal" for the older dancers in her troupe. When she was nine, she was making up the 13-year-old dancers as dolls, soldiers, or rainbows. "Then I just put it on the back burner…any idea of a career in makeup didn't make sense to me because it wasn't a real career. But I still loved doing makeup."

Undeterred, Lois kept coming back to makeup. She was attracted to makeup, she had an obvious talent in the field, so she took steps to learn about the career options available. There were no makeup training schools as there are today, and the makeup union was a closed shop (one had to have a card to work, and one had to be employed to get a card), or one had to be lucky enough to be taken on as a trainee. Consequently, Lois found herself limited when it came to furthering her experience and education in the UK.

The BBC (British Broadcasting Corporation) did offer training to women in both hairdressing and makeup (historically, women were limited to the roles of hairdressers or body painters, not makeup artists for films), but that wasn't the direction Lois wanted to go. "I know I would have had training, but it would have been in television. I didn't want to work in television. I wanted to do what made my heart sing. Film."

The Puzzle

While at Polytechnic of Central London, Lois met and began collaborating with film students from the National Film and Television School. By working for free on student films with third year directing students at the NFTS, Lois began to hone her makeup skills. The directors would bring her on, like her work, then seek her out for paying gigs later as their careers advanced. "They worked on rock videos…and I might get paid expenses. It was a good early experience, finding out what worked on film and what didn't. But I wasn't getting what I wanted."

Lois's goal was to gain formal entrance into the film business via a union card, and she knew she had to evaluate the steps that would take her there. "You look at what you want, how you want it to be…and you dial it back to its component parts. It is a bit like having a jigsaw puzzle without the picture on the lid."

In 1981, Lois was part of the crew for a student film shot in the Scottish Highlands where everyone did everything. "I was twiddling the knobs on the Nagra [sound recorder] because that's how you did sound then, or holding the boom, or making the sandwiches, and making the frocks. We stayed in holiday caravans in October and had no heat or hot water. When the shoot wrapped, we headed to Glasgow and stopped at the Halt Pub, [the] hangout for everyone in the Scottish film industry." There were drinks and chats, and connections were made. "A year later, the phone rang and a young woman said, 'Bill Forsythe wants you, if you're interested, to work on *Gregory's Girl*.' 'I don't know Bill.' 'Yes, you do, you met him at the Halt Pub, he was the quiet one in the corner.'" As a result of that phone call, Lois became the makeup department head for *Gregory's Girl* (1980), heading a crew of one, herself, with special dispensation from the union since no one else would take such a low budget film at the time. *Click*: the first critical piece of that jigsaw puzzle fell neatly into place.

A Restoration Dream

Following *Gregory's Girl*, Lois was hired to work on Peter Greenaway's *The Draughstman's Contract* (1982) for BFI (British Film Institute), a charitable organization founded in 1933 which promotes and preserves filmmaking and television in the United Kingdom. To ensure its longevity, the BFI received a special dispensation from the union stating that non-union talent could be hired for their projects and all members of a production team received equal pay. Because the wages weren't high, working for the BFI appealed to young filmmakers seeking status and experience, as well as established artists seeking interesting, challenging projects. For Lois, it remains one of her all-time favorite projects to this day. "My God, I loved doing that film," she recalls fondly. "At that time, I really thought that every film would be like that. It isn't, and they're not.

THE DRAUGHTSMAN'S CONTRACT (1982)
Licensed from Photo 12 / Alamy Stock Photo

It was a wonderful, wonderful time. Beautiful place, fabulous cast, a real peach of Restoration makeup, highly stylized, but realistic, too."

While working on *The Draughtsman's Contract*, Lois met union makeup artists and hairstylists who influenced and educated her, including the women who would sign her application into the union, Christine Allsopp and her mother, Connie Reeve. "When Connie came into the trailer I was working with an actor who started to be tricky. Whatever it was, whether it was our work, his response, he was having a conversation with me, and I don't know which, but that meeting decided Connie. She had seen my work on the film [but] it was actually how I handled the actor's concerns that tipped the favor in my direction. Both Christine and Connie signed my application, which led to an interview, which led to my sitting for the test, which I passed. I got my union card, but then I didn't work for a year."

Click. Click. Two more puzzle pieces snaps into place...but one was upside down. Now she needed to find union work.

Fate Steps In

The union only allowed members to work on union films, meaning all those connections Lois made doing non-union work became useless once she received her card. They couldn't hire her, she couldn't work for them, and no one in the union knew her well enough to call her for jobs yet. "Saying no to people who had employed me before...it was a very tricky time." To make a living, she taught ballet and modern dance lessons, worked early mornings in a bakery, and made archival quality paper envelopes for a legal firm on Knightrider Street.

Then came the train strike.

THE LORDS OF DISCIPLINE (1983) DAVID KEITH & MARK BRELAND
Licensed from AF archive / Alamy Stock Photo

The Lords of Discipline (1983), a union film with Pauline Heys at the helm of the make-up department, was being shot at The Royal Military Academy Sandhurst outside of London. They needed 22 makeup artists and 22 hairdressers for two days of shooting. With the train strike, the drive was long, traffic was terrible, and many makeup artists didn't want to make the trek. Lois arranged to borrow a car, turned up on-set with 21 other makeup artists and received a position. "I had maroon hair and was wearing - I thought I looked very nice - a sort of black, not punk, but new wave kind of outfit. Smart, not greasy, clean, and maroon hair."

Veteran makeup artists such as Alan Boyle, George Frost, Eric Allwright, and Roy Ashton flanked Lois in the crowd room. "They gave me the benefit of the doubt to a certain degree. We'd do the day's work, get the call out, I'd go on-set, I'd stand by. By the end of the first day the conversation started, 'What brought you to this? Why do you want to do it?' And on the second day, during slow times, Eric said, 'Do you know how to cover a black eye? Because it's one of things you're going to have to do.' Roy Ashton shared his blood recipes and wax nose technique with me. I said to Eric, 'That's really good of you to help me like that.' He said, 'You know what? Sharing information is exactly what everyone should do because...I can tell you and show you anything, but can you actually make it work? There's no fear involved.' That's how it began." Click. Click. Click.

The Evolution of a Department Head

Eric Allwright understood both the nature of the work and the inherent good in sharing information without fear, and Lois credits her strong relationships with other artists in part to Allwright's generosity. "I never understood why people view another person as competition. There is no competition. If you've got two makeup artists who are going for the same job with similar resumes, similar films, similar age and you walk into that room, where there's the line producer, the director, whoever's the grownup in the room who will be deciding whether you're going to be employed or not. Now, one man's meat is another man's poison, they're either going to want you, or me, or neither of us. So, there's no such thing as being in competition. The person I'm in competition with is myself, because that drives me and I won't let go of that drive. The day I do, the day I'm doing it just for the money, just to get a wage check, that's the day I have to stop, because the work's too hard and it's too special to be treated that way. That's how I feel, that's how I truly feel now."

Several years and several films followed *The Lords of Discipline*, and Lois worked in various makeup departments as a day player, coming in for a day as needed without any long-term commitment **from the** production. Then one day she received a call from Tom Smith, department head for *Indiana Jones and the Temple of Doom* (1984), to come in as a day player. "The call came in because the makeup artists were talking to each other and they remembered my work…it came from my work." Click.

Tom Smith became a mentor to Lois during those weeks she worked on *Temple of Doom*. He believed in fully immersing and testing his trainees, hands-on, on-set, with the actors. He invited Lois to watch him hand-lay a beard then, without warning, the next day ask her to lay a beard as he had done the day before. There was no room for error.

"You're sweating bullets but somehow it gave you more than just confidence…you had to step up to the plate. You had to sink or swim. I think that was quite good immersion." Based on that positive experience, Lois always has a trainee on a film, if she can, to provide real life experience of working as a makeup artist on-set. "It's not like being in a classroom…there's no red carpet, there's no glamour, absolutely none. Zero. It's about doing the work under sometimes inhospitable, unfriendly, and difficult circumstances. Sometimes it's delightful, of course, but that's what it's like. A trainee learns quickly whether this is a profession he or she wants to pursue."

And for Lois, *Temple of Doom* only solidified her desire. "I'll never forget my first day on-set. My heart was pounding; I got there early and there was no one around. It was completely empty and dark, pitch black. I went to H Stage, walked in and I walked through the Temple of Doom. I could have just cried. This is a film I could only dream about working on, and here I am, I'm working on it. That's the thing about youth and dreams, and I remember that feeling. If you had asked me at the time if I thought I'd ever work with Steven [Spielberg], I'd have said, 'Never in my wildest dreams.' There's something extraordinary about that." And she clearly made an impression as well; since 1984 and *Temple of Doom*, Lois has worked with Spielberg on seven more films, including: *The BFG* (2016), *Bridge of Spies* (2015), *Lincoln* (2012), *War Horse* (2011), *War of the Worlds* (2005), *Catch Me if You Can* (2002), and *Saving Private Ryan* (1998) as makeup designer and department head.

During her time working under Tom Smith, Lois learned not only makeup techniques, but also the intricacies of department heading. She vividly recalls an incident when an assistant director demolished a young makeup artist for a mistake. Smith approached the AD: "'You don't speak to one of my department like that. You have a problem, you come and speak to me, because this is where the buck stops. Not there. Here.'" Then Tom asked the makeup artist to step into the trailer. "He ripped him a new bottom. He just tore into him and said, 'That AD was absolutely correct in everything he said apart from one thing, he said it to you and not to me. Don't you ever do it again.' I thought, 'That's really good.' United. There was a united feel. Not us against them, but a feeling we are the makeup department. It's not all about me. It's not about being in competition with each other, but it's about the 'we' that comprises the department's work as a whole. That has never left me. You talk about things that never leave you, and that never has."

The Responsibility to the Film

"I fulfill the obligation and responsibility of being head of department, which sometimes means you're not liked or not pleasing. Sometimes you have to have the hard conversations, particularly when it involves staffing and money, but you don't have to be abrasive. I am there in service of the film. I say to all my team, it's not a democracy. You have an idea? Bring it to the table. I might say, 'no,' because I know what's underneath the water of that iceberg and you don't. It isn't your place to know. That's why my head's on the block and not yours. I'm your safety net. I'm also the person that you should be wary of at the same time. My first obligation is to the film.

"You're only as good as the team. Getting everyone together as an orchestra. Some of you are string section, some of you are wind instrument, others percussion, and at different times all of you are important, but you're all there in service of the same thing, which is to play that piece of music. Obviously, in film terms, you are there to make the film and tell the story. The stronger the other players are, the better everyone becomes."

Ever-inspired by that passion for both strong camaraderie and equally strong work she learned from Smith, Lois now instills that same drive in the members of the departments she now runs. She tells the story of one remarkable night during the filming of **War Horse** when the call was cancelled and everyone was excused to go home for the night with full pay. One crew member asked a specific question about the blind prosthetic on Jeremy Irvine, who played Albert, and Lois and the main team offered to demonstrate the technique. "The daily makeup artists could have gone home, but they stayed until after midnight, as did the hair stylists. We were all working on each other, trying this new technique, making up each other. There was something about that that was really magical. I think it was one of my favorite nights at work ever, because it was the work bringing us together. They stayed for the work."

LINCOLN (2012) DANIEL DAY-LEWIS
Licensed from AF archive / Alamy Stock Photo

Lincoln presented a different kind of challenge to Lois. She had to figure out how to make up Daniel Day Lewis as Lincoln in less than two hours. "The makeup was a process called stretch and stipple for aging, which is a mix of attagel and green marble concentrate...every day you paint it on, stretch the skin, when it dries, it snaps back into the shape you want the crumple and wrinkle to be. It was a three-hour makeup that we needed to cut down to an hour and 15 minutes." Lois credits her key makeup artist, Kenny Myers, and his ability to work in concert with her throughout the process as one of the major reasons for the successful transformation. "You know when you fold a blanket with someone who doesn't know how to do it? Somehow the blanket doesn't work. It won't fit into the heirloom cupboard any more. If you're folding a blanket with someone like your mom or your sister, a thousand times, you have that movement. Double-teaming is exactly the same thing. Not everyone can double team, not everyone's fast, so you have to be both of those things and careful with the work. Kenny Myers is fast, careful, and able to double team. I would have been lost without him."

Constructing the Story

Long before her team is in place, Lois begins her research and design process. Everything begins with the first reading of the script, understanding the story and characters. She then creates a makeup script with looks, followed by a mood board for visual reference. "It's [made of] things that remind me of something. I literally take colors, or a painting, or a photograph of something similar, or a still from another film, or something of the actor or real character, and I glue it on a board and have them for individual characters or scenes or an environment. My mood boards are old-fashioned and chimpy, but they seem to work."

Lois then takes her concepts to the director or to "whoever is the grownup with the most power. He who pays the piper calls the tune. If you're fortunate enough to be on a film set with someone of the caliber of Steven Spielberg, there's only one captain of that ship." The costume designer is also a vital contributor to the look of a character; Lois confers and works with the costumer to find the whole character. "I'm not there as fluff and fold to pander to an actor's vanity. Nor am I there to put three dots here when told to by the costume designer, I'm too old for that." Once a director has approved the designs, Lois works collaboratively with the actors because "if the actors don't wear their makeup, which helps them become the character, the production isn't going to fire an actor, they will fire you...but that is where your work is, it's on a human being. A human being who's making themselves very vulnerable by being in front of a camera...I understand people's peccadilloes as long as they're not rude, hostile, or offensive. There's never an excuse for that. Oh, I hope I don't come over as a really bossy boots saying that!"

Achievements On and Off-Set

Lois Burwell's career has now spanned over three decades, and during that time she has worked on many iconic, high-profile, blockbuster films such as: *The Princess Bride* (1987), *Shirley Valentine* (1989), *Hamlet* (1990—Mel Gibson), *The Muppet Christmas Carol* (1992), *Braveheart* (1995), *Saving Private Ryan* (1998), *The Green Mile* (1999), *The Last Samurai* (2003), *War Horse* (2011), *Lincoln* (2012), and *The BFG* (2016). Lois has three nominations for BAFTA Awards (The British Academy of Film and Television Arts) for *Braveheart, Saving Private Ryan*, and *Lincoln*, two Oscar nominations for *Braveheart* and *Saving Private Ryan*, and one Oscar for *Braveheart.*

Braveheart was of both professional and personal significance to Lois. Personally, she met her future husband, cinematographer John Toll, during the production. Professionally, the film won five Oscars, including: *Best Sound Editing, Best Cinematography, Best Director, Best Picture*, and Lois received the Academy Award for *Best Makeup* which she shares with Paul Pattison and Peter Frampton. "It was the best it could ever be. It was an extraordinary time. None of us would have thought it standing on that film set, not in a month of Sundays."

As Mel Gibson's personal makeup artist, Lois worked with Gibson to create the iconic war paint the Scots donned on the battlefield. Originally, Gibson wanted a St. Andrews cross on his face, but the war paint design evolved through collaboration with Lois into the award-winning final product. The blue dye worn in battle by the ancient Britons (who later became the Scots) historically came from the leaves of a flax plant called woad. Lois was able to come up with a facsimile of this plant's dye for the film, working to recreate the exact color of blue of the woad plant.

BRAVEHEART (1990) MEL GIBSON
Licensed from Moviestore collection Ltd / Alamy Stock Photo

Creating Battle Plans

"I love doing battle films. I actually really do enjoy them. There's something exhilarating about the number of people, the drive to do it, and the fact that you're following a battle plan. Actually, filmmaking is a bit like that anyway, it follows a strategic plan of action."

SAVING PRIVATE RYAN (1998) MEDIC SCENE ON BATTLEFIELD
Licensed fromAF archive / Alamy Stock Photo

To prepare, Lois researches each film extensively: the period, the politics, the social mores, the characters, and relationships. For **Saving Private Ryan** (1998), she visited the British Imperial War Museum and found a book containing photographic references of the injuries received on D-Day at Omaha Beach on the coast of Normandy, France. "Every single wound in the first 20 minutes of **Saving Private Ryan** actually happened on that day, on that beach. The one that stands out is the radioman who lost his face in an explosion. The dummy that Conor O'Sullivan made had a concave face, as you'd expect. But the actuality was the man's face was split straight down the middle, the hair intact, but peeled back, and there was so little blood. I never mind re-creating it if it's in service of a story that needs to be told. If you're showing a life being taken, or a life that's been sacrificed, then there's a certain obligation that you have, that you do it to the best of your ability, and you're always mindful of the real loss of life."

For Lois, who has experienced the harsh conditions of literally shooting in the trenches, there are times when the production of a battle film feels like being in battle. "On **War Horse**, when we were in those trenches, it was hard. It was so hard. I cannot tell you how awful it was; grown men were struggling in this storm, freezing cold, rain lashing. We were pulling each other out of the mud. We were up to our hips in mud. It was like being in the trenches in WWI, the Great War, but without ammunition. We got a sense, a taste, a small taste of what those lads went through."

The Importance of Humility

When working on **The Last Samurai** (2003), one of the biggest challenges Lois and her team faced was making up 500 soldiers. The film was shot in New Zealand, and the burn time for sunburn is approximately eight minutes because of a hole in the ozone layer. The Samurai's heads were freshly shaven, so the makeup crew had to spray them all with sunblock that wouldn't run or burn their eyes, and would dry before any makeup was applied. Lois remembers asking one of the members of her crew to spray the soldiers, to which the crewmember said, 'I'm a makeup artist. I don't stand and spray sunblock on. I'm here to do makeup.'" Lois stepped into the tent and sprayed sunblock on soldiers. "No one ever questioned a request on that film again. We learned two lessons: one, no one is bigger than the project she's working on and, two, no one's more important than another." The battle here was both on-set and backstage.

"Having a piece of paper saying you're a makeup artist actually means that you're competent at certain techniques, not all. You might not have learned set etiquette, you might not have learned how to handle actors, you might not have learned, just a wild possibility, how to behave on a film set until you've been on one. Or understand the politics, which are always present…the iceberg is this big above the water and there's all of this to learn underneath the water line."

When Lois is asked what she does for a living, her answer is eloquent and inspiring. "I still say, well, I do makeup. I find it really hard to be a makeup "artist" because to me that's the thing I hope to achieve before the end of my career, the "artist" part. You're always ongoing. Learning, wanting to improve. It's the passion that drives, it's the passion that makes you want to do it. It's the passion of standing there and getting it right. Walking onto a set and just standing back from it and going, 'Oh, we nearly did it, you can't see the artifice.' Or watching a film that you did nearly 20 years ago and saying, 'You know, it's not too bad.' It's the passion, it's the drive, it's working as a team, working as a group. The group coming together, whether it's makeup, hair, costumes, cinematography, sound…it's sort of circles within a circle, that's how I see it."

Of course, after decades of an inspiring career, Lois is much more than a woman who "does makeup." Lois Burwell is a makeup artist. She is also a gardener, a lover of horses, a woman both respected and respectful, a woman filled with passion for her work and her life, a woman with great humility and pride. Her jigsaw puzzle is still a work-in-progress, but the picture is beautifully clear.

OUTTAKES:

On Alternatives:

"I had a young mortuary assistant contact me about doing a makeup course…he was appalled at some of the end results, people's loved ones looking badly. He was shocked and wanted to improve that ability. Obviously, on someone who's deceased, you can go slightly more extreme. You don't have to worry about the comfort factor. What you do have to do is create, maybe recreate, the face that has been damaged, or changed color, or whatever. Now, I found that fascinating, although it's obviously not everyone's cup of tea."

"Physical Deformities…rather than have a National-Health-Groucho-Marx nose that's attached to glasses or ears…why not use film techniques to help these people to actually be able, in their own microwave, every day, make a new nose and add droppers of color to it that will blend to their skin? Imagine the courage to continue with life if people are looking at you. You either become completely inured to it or stay in your room. Or if they're going out on a date that evening or going out to dinner, make a fresh ear or a fresh nose. The film industry, to a certain degree, is at the sharp, pointy end of innovation in those ways. We need to be able to recreate things without a huge amount of trouble. We need it to be durable, we need it to work in all temperatures, and it needs to be actor-friendly. There you have it. There are lots of exciting possibilities for people, from one extreme to the other."

On Life Lessons:

"I've never regretted a single moment I said 'no' to a film…[and there isn't] a single moment that I regret a film I've said 'yes' to, even if it was a miserable experience, and some of them are. You learn something in every process. Actually, it doesn't matter what you do in life, whether it's makeup, whether you're a director, an actor, a bus driver…you always have something that you can use at some point. Something good, even if it's 'I won't be doing that again.' I think you learn that as you go along."

On Being a Woman in the Industry:

"There are certain haltering moments that happen to a woman and not necessarily to a man. For a woman, the thing that comes up, sooner or later, is do I have a child? Not, do I get married or have a partner these days, but do I have a child? I think that's something you need to think about quite carefully because some women will want to have it all. It's what we'd all like, a career and a family. The reality is very few manage to do so without sacrifice on one level or another. If someone goes out of the circuit for a while in order to have children, then enters back in, sometimes they get two steps down the ladder because other people have come in. Those people they've worked with have found a new crew. Juggling the private life with this working life is hard and one the biggest challenges."

"The people who made some of the most 'boys-ee' stories I've worked on, whether it's **Saving Private Ryan, Warhorse,** or **Lincoln** aren't sexist in any shape or form. Steven Spielberg would no more consider women to be less than their male counterparts than fly to the moon. He put me in charge of war films. He never thought for a moment that I couldn't do it because I'm a woman."

"I think too much can be diminished by focusing on gender when you talk about a career in the film industry. It's about opportunity, whether you're a man or a woman, it's opportunity."

"I think, 'Can I do a good job? Do they want me? Do I match you? Do you match me? Can we work together?' That's what I'm thinking, not, 'Am I a woman? Am I a man?' What I'm thinking is, 'Can I do the work?'"

On Being the Boss:

"You know you have to be able to say you're wrong. You have to say to everyone, 'You know what? I muffed up. What a muff up. I'm so sorry. How do we get out of this pickle? Come on, everyone, what do you think?'"

On Logistics:

"What do I need in order to pull this together as a whole? You take the actor, you take the character, and you find the place where they meet. Then you have to take into consideration the rest of it which is how long do you have, how much money do you have, what are your resources? What do I need to achieve in service to the story? These are the practical things that you must work out, you must be mindful. Now, being mindful might mean on certain scenes you fly by the seat of your pants, use 18 people when you could use 25, then you can ramp up on the scenes where the actors are going to be hot and sweaty with 60% facial hair. You have to do all those calculations all the time. You have to mind the budget. You don't spend your budget on glitter eye shadow when you actually need spirit gum."

On Ageism:

"You've only got so many films inside you. Now, I really want those films to be fantastic, if I'm still wanted. I could be past my 'sell by' date, you never know in this business. It's something that everyone needs to think about. It's an ageist business. It doesn't mean I can't do work. I can still climb a mountain, I can even climb the mountain and probably be in a trench the same as a 30-year-old, but that might not always be the case. I'd like to be the one who knows when to stop, not be the one that's waiting for the call that never comes. "

On Doing Demos:

"Doing a demonstration makeup is about the technical craft; you're in the cul-de-sac known as the makeup world. It's not going somewhere else, it's the technical enjoyment of putting a makeup together. I actually don't like doing demonstrations, I have to be honest, I don't. Although I'm obviously not short on words and can chat, what I can't do is talk and do makeup. I actually can't do it. And I get the horrors at the very thought of being watched doing the work. I lose all sense of myself while applying a makeup and that's how I like it. Actually, Daniel Day was the perfect actor for me because he wanted silence. He didn't want any conversation at all, so it was heaven."

On Last Minute Deadlines:

"I think, 'How can I do this in 10 minutes? What the hell am I going to do and with what?' I say, 'Can you leave it with me?' You can't say, 'I can't do this,' or 'You're having a laugh, aren't you?' Because it's actually what you want to say, but you can't. So you say, 'Can you leave it with me?' Because it buys you some time to actually put your head on and think and come up with something that works."

On Becoming a US Citizen:

"How I became a citizen, which I'm pleased to be, is that I met my future husband. I knew if we were going to date, we had to be on the same continent, basically. We couldn't be a gazillion miles away from each other just for it to stand a chance of working. I didn't even know if it would because when we first met on *Braveheart*, it looked like it was going to be a dalliance; he lived on one side of the world, I lived on the other. I applied for a green card in my own name and without putting pressure on our relationship, I could work and be on the same continent as John. That way we could see where it would go, or not."

"I ran into a difficult situation trying to get back into the country after a four-month shoot in Greece. John and I were married by this point, and I never wanted to go through the agony of the immigration line again. That and knowing where I was going to live made citizenship my choice. When I finally gained my US Citizenship, the officer said, 'Come on in and welcome!' He had, you know, one of those university rings, one of those big, huge, knuckle dusters. At home, we called it a knuckle duster. 'Welcome to the United States of America,' he boomed. I'm not given to that at all, but I was so pleased and relieved, I had the desire to kneel and kiss his ring."

"You can contribute. You can actually vote and do things that affect your life and the life of others. So that's why I did it."

Catching Up!

We interviewed Lois on February 4, 2016. Since then, she has worked on

Ready Player One
Makeup designer and head of department

Hotel Artemis
Personal makeup artist for Jodie Foster

Book Club
Personal makeup artist for Diane Keaton

Lois also serves as a Governor on the
Makeup Artists and Hairstylists Branch of
Academy of Motion Picture Arts and Sciences

For more of Lois' Credits, visit: www.imdb.com

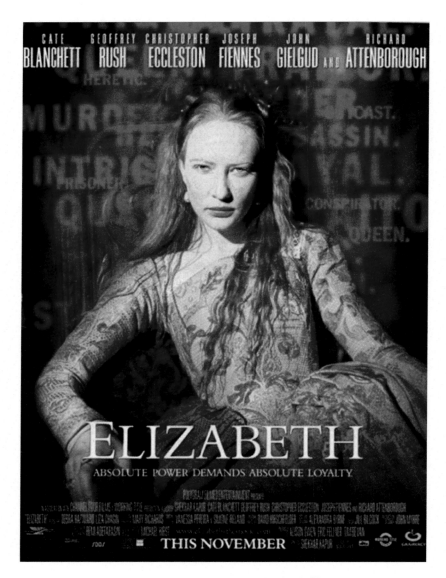

1999
ACADEMY AWARD
BEST MAKEUP

ELIZABETH (1990) UK Film Poster
Licensed from The Advertising Archives / Alamy Stock Photo

Now, as I've grown older, I've learned to broaden the way I think and become more sophisticated in my thinking patterns. Who is this person? Where is he? What is he? I consider all aspects of society. I bring all sorts of elements into it so that that person starts to take shape, and from there, I can go deeper and further into what would have been his history, his geography, his influences. In the end, his whole look is formed because of all these layers being drawn into him.

If Jenny Shircore could spend her time doing anything she wanted, she'd be in her library researching. Anything. Everything. "I would research in my spare time. I could just give myself a project and research it." For example, she is fascinated by the barber surgeons of Medieval Europe. The barbers were also the medical practitioners because the physicians considered surgery beneath them, so the barbers used their razors to cut hair, pull teeth, amputate legs, and blood-let. "It also would be fantastic to research and recreate something in the 11th or 12th century. I'd have your eyebrows off in a shot! There were some beautiful, beautiful faces and hair back then. You know there are interesting subjects everywhere."

Jenny combines her love of research with her love of makeup and design. Interestingly, in her full and varied career, Jenny has designed only four contemporary films: **Notting Hill** (1999), **Gangster No. 1** *(2000)*, **Starter for 10** (2006), and **Burton & Taylor** (2013). As a result, she has been able to devote herself to in-depth exploration of the periods represented in her films, everything from Restoration England (**'Tis a Pity She's a Whore**, 1980), to 17th Century Holland (**Girl with a Pearl Earring**, 2003), to 1936 New York in **W.E.** (2011), to World War II France in **Suite Française** (2014).

For **Macbeth**, the 2015 film directed by Australian Justin Kurzel and starring Michael Fassbender and Marion Cotillard, Jenny researched the history and mythology of the 1050s, and applied her findings to the three witches. "Justin wanted the witches to be three wandering women with facial markings-self-inflicted, ritualistic marks." Jenny's research led her to an ancient Celtic alphabet called Ogham whose patterns consist of short parallel lines crossed by a short diagonal slanting line. "I thought these patterns would work wonderfully as tattoos on the body. I practiced and perfected the lettering, even trying to form words from it. My assistant and I created a tattoo for the whole back of one of the women. I thought it looked perfect! Sadly, that scene was cut out of the film! Ah well, that's show business!"

MACBETH (2015) MARION COTILLARD
Licensed from AF archive / Alamy Stock Photo

"Again, in *Macbeth*, I designed a makeup for Marion Cotillard for the scene where she moves from being Lady Macbeth to becoming the Queen. I used a pale blue color, which in those days would have been extracted from the woad plant. I diluted this color to achieve the merest hint of blue tone and then used it right across her eyes. It was symbolic of her change in status. It's regal, it's tribal, it's war paint. It encompassed all three meanings."

"If I can back up anything unusual that I want to do with hair and makeup with solid reasoning…then I'll go ahead and do it. I have to have total conviction for why I'm doing something and I can only have that conviction with shed-loads of research under my belt."

Exotic India to Emigration

Jenny's journey to the UK is as complex as her family's background. Her mother was French Burmese and her father was Armenian French. Her father's family immigrated to India from Armenia after World War I, and her mother's family went to India for business opportunities during the period of the British Raj. Both her parents were born in India where they met, married, and had their six children: three girls and three boys.

Their life was one of privilege. Jenny's father worked in international shipping. The girls went to boarding school, the boys to a private day school. Living in India had a profound impact on Jenny, one that resonates in her approach to life and work. "I saw so much poverty there that ever since it has made my flesh creep to see unnecessary waste or excessive indulgence. My parents instilled in us a great sense of right and wrong, respect for the people working for us, a morality that holds me back sometimes. I could never consider any film offer without having an overall sense of balance. For example, I would never take on a film that I thought was rubbish or offensive, even if they offered me lots of money. I love the small independent British films."

The school system in India "is fantastic." Each of the private schools has a sister university and the students take their exams as if applying to that university. "If you do eventually want to go to one of those universities, for example Oxford or Cambridge, there is extensive follow-up." In addition to vigorous academics, the arts were also a driving force in school. Jenny and her sister took dance classes, everything from ballet and Indian dance, from the ages of three. "Very theatrical, which involved us in shows and performances." Additionally, they were shown films every Sunday night and a Shakespearian touring group brought Shakespeare plays to the school regularly. "There's a huge history of live storytelling in India. They gather the children around in villages and schools and somebody tells a story and, for the evening, they sit around and listen. There's no television. The stories fire the imagination and the kids are inspired. I think that probably triggered my sister's love for teaching and directing in the theater and my love for storytelling. I love dreaming up plotlines!"

When India gained its independence in 1947, the school system changed some of its requirements. The change with the biggest impact was students were now expected to read, speak, and write Hindi to pass their classes. "English was our first language. We could speak Hindi, yeah, very badly, but we would never be able to read or write it well enough to pass the language requirement. My father realized this was an impossible situation for us and made the biggest decision of his life. He'd always loved the UK, so for the good of our education he decided to move the family. We had a beautiful, comfortable life in India. My parents made a big sacrifice. The transition wasn't smooth and my father suffered a bit in the process."

"In India, we had maids and cooks and, as a result, I never had to do anything. My mother had never cooked a hot meal or made a bed in her life because she hadn't had to. We had good fun at her expense while she was learning. Sometimes we wouldn't like dinner because it was burnt." Her father took them on the bus to school until they told him they could manage without him. Other cultural adjustments were more difficult. "Color. Whatever we went through in the way of insults…I don't think we ever told our parents because it would be too hurtful and we just lived with it. Things changed, times changed, we changed, and it was okay." Jenny's parents placed education as the top priority for the family, so they uprooted their life so their children would have excellent schooling and enrichment opportunities.

Makeup, Hair, and Boats

After high school, because she always wanted to do makeup and hair, Jenny went to the London College of Fashion to train as a beautician and an instructor. Her goal was simple: "Get my training and travel the world on a luxury cruiser."

"I'd been on those boats with my father and I loved it. But then I met a girl who had done that job and she said, 'What you've experienced as a passenger on those liners, you won't experience as a member of the staff.' So, I thought again."

At about the same time, the staff at London College of Fashion suggested Jenny apply to the BBC for their film and television training program. "I think I would have been quite happy in a hairdressing salon down the road from my parents. I could have lived out my life perfectly content." But the people at the London College of Fashion insisted she apply at the BBC, and "that was the start of my TV and film work."

There were thousands of applicants for 20 positions. Jenny interviewed, did a puzzle which tested her visual perceptions, got the position for the two-year training program, and stayed with the BBC for 16 years. "The BBC training encompassed the full spectrum of makeup: straight, glamour, effects, aging. When I started, TV was still in black and white. That taught me about light and shade and tones in color. Blue, green, and red can appear the same on a black and white screen if they are all of the same depth. It was a learning experience that still comes in handy today. Just as I was leaving the BBC, prosthetics were born. So yes, you could say we had learnt it all! The BBC training was across the board."

Pennies, Shakespeare, Dr. Who

During her tenure at the BBC, one of Jenny's favorite projects was **Pennies from Heaven** (1978) written by Dennis Potter (of **The Singing Detective** fame) and starring Bob Hoskins. The BBC production was a six-episode series that follows a sheet music salesman through his dreary life which he punctuates with flights of fantasy based on the songs he sells. This was innovative television. "Dennis Potter was one of our greatest writers. I watched it again last year and it stands the test of time, I think, in what it is. Makeup is more sophisticated now, we've developed our skills, our eyes are attuned, we've got better wigs, but I think we still nailed it then. That was a lovely project to do, it was really enjoyable." The script was later sold to MGM for an American production starring Steve Martin. "The American production didn't have the soul of our piece."

"In those days, there was a TV program called **Armchair Theatre** which aired a big drama or theatrical piece every night. Shakespeare at least twice a week. It was a lot and we were learning all the time. Today, TV doesn't have the programs we had years ago."

Doctor Who, a British institution since 1963 (with a sixteen-year break in production 1989-2005) "was a simple little program with dust bins moving around when I started it. Now, the effects are amazing. To this day, I get **Doctor Who** fans sending me photographs from all the episodes I did, asking me to sign them. They collect all the memorabilia."

Movin' on Out

In 1985, Jenny was at a crossroads in her life. She had lost her father and was ready for a change, but didn't know where or how that would exert itself. Then, she was asked to do **Dreamchild**, a film written by Dennis Potter, produced by Kenith Trodd and directed by Gavin Millar, all part of the team on **Pennies from Heaven.** "I just couldn't bear walking down the same BBC corridors anymore. I just had had enough, really. Since I was asked and since I'd be working with people I'd worked with before, I thought, 'Yes, let's make the move. Time to make the move.'"

DREAMCHILD (1985)
Licensed from United Archives GmbH / Alamy Stock Photo

Dreamchild revolves around the childhood relationship between Alice Liddell and Lewis Carroll. As an octogenarian, Alice Liddell attends a reception in honor of Lewis Carroll and realizes, as the model for Alice in his books, the relationship was odd and unusual. "It was a beautiful film. Really lovely. It was the first time I did aging on Coral Browne using the industry standard of the day: stretch the skin, stipple on latex, dry, powder, and release. It was also the first time I went to rushes where I could see my makeup on the big screen. I think she looked great. It was a lovely experience. That was my first film." Jenny was nominated for a BAFTA (British Academy of Film and Television Arts) for *Best Makeup Artist* for her work on this film.

Jenny's second film was **Personal Services** (1987), a film about a woman, Cynthia Payne, who lived outside of London and offered personal, sexual services, out of her home. She specialized in fetish/kink roleplay with older men and received quite a bit of notoriety in the tabloids. Terry Jones, from Monty Python, directed the film, David Leland wrote it, and Julie Walters played Cynthia Payne. "I am very lucky to be able to move from one lovely project to another."

"I've worked very hard. I put everything into whatever I do. I am lucky, though. It's come my way."

"Let it Live"

"I had a supervisor at the BBC, Eileen Mair, who, one day while I was doing a makeup, said, 'Now Stop. Let it Live.' That's stayed with me forever. When you've created something, you then breathe life into it or it's just a lump of whatever. That 'Let it Live' thing, you have to give it life. You can see that in front of you when you're working. When it's just a solid block or a lump, you have to know how to bring it to life."

"A lot of my friends with whom I've grown up have helped me develop, helped me think, helped me look and see and broaden. They all think their problems through. They'll think about the human race and life, with depth of thought. I think that is so important to think below the surface; it's too easy to think superficially. That's often where my makeup takes me, think it deeper and deeper, sideways, clockwise."

When Jenny creates a makeup design, she always starts with the script and visualizes the actor in her mind's eye. The makeup content is a major consideration, then the director's vision and the costumer's vision come into play through discussion and collaboration. Jenny develops the broad picture, an understanding of the whole, and knows what every character looks like and where each character fits. "I have the balance of the look. The actor has his individual character in mind. It's my job to make each character work with the next. I discuss that with the actors. Of course, gradually, you draw each one of them into the whole picture. You can influence them as well. I worked with Ralph Fiennes when we did *The Invisible Woman* (2013), it was fantastic. Of course, you don't argue with Ralph. You wouldn't want to, because he's perfection.

"As a designer, you have to listen. You have to listen and understand what the director wants. You've got to put the director's vision at the fore, or help him create one. You have to listen and understand what the actors are saying to you about their characters. The rest of it is understanding your actors, just being with them. Sometimes you have to whack them on the head, you don't have to mollycoddle them. Give yourself to them and receive as much as you can. It's observing every single thing so you bring to the project the greatest amount you can give it.

"It's about the truth. It's what you're finding for the look, for the makeup. It's when you're comfortable with that and you're comfortable in what you've put out there and it answers all the questions, is it right, is it true, is it just? Does it live?"

A Rich Career and Favorite Effects

Jenny Shircore's career covers decades, and in that time she has designed the makeup for large, block-buster films and television series, as well as small, independent films. The script, subject matter, makeup challenges, director, costumer, and actors all figure into her decision whether to take the job. These days she has the luxury to pick and choose her projects. She has worked on such varied projects as *A Month in the Country* (1987), *The Secret Garden* (1993), *The Phantom of the Opera* (2004), *Mrs. Henderson Presents* (2005), and *Clash of the Titans* (2010).

At the time of this interview, Jenny had just completed the pilot for *Will* (2017), a TV miniseries about William Shakespeare's youth written by Craig Pearce and directed by Shekhar Kapur. It has everything Jenny likes in a project: it has a definitive period, the 1570s; it deals with the issues of the day, the conflict between the Catholics and Protestants; it involves the writers of the day, Shakespeare and Marlowe; and it contains specific makeup challenges, creating a novel look for a prostitute. "We had a prostitute to do and it's not just Elizabethan, it's Elizabethan punk. Both periods flatter each other and work together really well. We used a bald cap to create a high forehead and then placed a bleached blonde wig with dark roots over the bald cap. We cut the front two inches of the wig down to stubble to show the dark roots. This shows the prostitutes would bleach their hair and shave their hairline to achieve the fashionable high hairline of the day. We then plastered over the stubble and the face with thick white makeup. Lots of scarring. Fun!"

In 2011, Jenny was faced with a different type of challenge, making up Michelle Williams to look like Marilyn Monroe for *My Week with Marilyn*, directed by Simon Curtis. "From the outset, it was a totally collaborative process between Michelle and me. We know it's not Marilyn Monroe. Who are we going to kid? The difficulties were technical, her mouth is bigger than Marilyn Monroe's, her eyes and face and cheekbones are different shapes than Monroe's. The wig helped create the image, and, as her figure is neat and tidy, the costume designer, Jill Taylor, made her look voluptuous and sexy. We didn't use

MY WEEK WITH MARILYN (2011) WEINSTEIN COMPANY FILM
MICHELLE WILLIAMS AS MARILYN MONROE
Licensed from Pictorial Press Ltd / Alamy Stock Photo

VANITY FAIR (2004) JAMES PUREFOY & REESE WITHERSPOON
Licensed from AF archive / Alamy Stock Photo

THE YOUNG VICTORIA (2009) GK FILMS PRODUCTION WITH
EMILY BLUNT AS THE QUEEN AND RUPERT FRIEND AS PRINCE ALBERT
Licensed from Pictorial Press Ltd / Alamy Stock Photo

prosthetic bits and pieces, we made up Michelle every day to get the 'essence' of Marilyn. To give the actress what she felt she needed to go on stage. The lingering close-ups of Michelle Williams show a supernaturally beautiful, talented, and complicated female icon." Jenny was nominated for a BAFTA for *Best Makeup and Hair* for her work on this film.

Vanity Fair (2004), adapted from a 19th Century novel by William Makepeace Thackeray, was directed by Mira Nair, and stars Reese Witherspoon and Gabriel Byrne. The demands of the huge cast and the complicated Regency period made this design a complex undertaking. Covering two decades from 1802-1822 and all the social classes, Jenny designed the makeup and intricate hairstyles for both men and women, incorporating tiny curls and sweeps and ringlets while maintaining authenticity. "I was so busy I never ever left the makeup trailer because we had so many actors with so many different looks. I think it's probably one of the busiest films I've ever worked on, and from that point of view, probably one of the most enjoyable. We were exhausted at the end of it."

Recognition

"I know for me it's quite sad when there are awards, because everybody works hard. Everybody puts as much into their films and their projects. Then it becomes a competition and then somebody has to be chosen as best. I'm always surprised because you never go into a job thinking there's an award at the end of this. You go into the job in order to work."

The Young Victoria (2009) explored the days of Queen Victoria's youth and early years of her reign. Jenny's challenge, as always, was to authentically reproduce the period looks. She worked closely with Director Jean-Marc Vallèe and Sandy Powell, the costume designer, to create a youthful look for the young Victoria (Emily Blunt) that was colorful and truthful. Emily Blunt had misgivings about wearing her hair like Queen Victoria wore hers for the coronation. That hairstyle is "historical fact, there are paintings galore. There's no way I could let her hair be anything else but that. She's beautiful, but I had to reassure her she was beautiful in that look. I can tweak a curl or lower the hairline, but it's basically there."

Once she ascended the throne, Queen Victoria wore a hairstyle she was comfortable with most of her life, and that is what Jenny designed. Jenny was nominated for an Academy Award for her design in **The Young Victoria** and won a BAFTA for *Best Makeup and Hair.*

Elizabeth (1998), directed by Shekhar Kapur, presented both different and similar challenges to Jenny. She had to create authentic looks while showing, through makeup and hairstyles, the evolution of the character Elizabeth, played by Cate Blanchett. The hair began long and loose, as was appropriate for a young girl, and metamorphosized into a high, tight, coiffed, off-the-neck hairdo. To aid this transition, there were 16 pre-styled wigs that slowly moved further back on Cate's forehead indicating age, maturity, and seriousness. Blanchett, wanting to help create as much realism as possible, shaved her hairline

and bleached her eyebrows and eyelashes. The other challenge was creating the white makeup, a sign of wealth and beauty during the 16th Century. Elizabeth's white makeup became more prominent through the course of the film, again symbolizing the maturity with which Elizabeth accepted her role as queen.

Jenny received the Academy Award for *Best Makeup* and the BAFTA for *Best Makeup/Hair* for her designs on *Elizabeth.*

In 2016 Jenny won the BAFTA for *Best Makeup and Hair Design* for **The Dresser**, a TV film directed by Richard Eyre about an ageing Shakespearean actor (Anthony Hopkins) and his dresser (Ian McKellen) who has taken care of him for years. "I was waiting to start doing **Beauty and the Beast** and I thought I didn't want to do anything beforehand, but then I thought, how many times do you get an offer with Ian McKellen and Anthony Hopkins playing the lead roles? I had Sir Ian McKellen in this chair, Sir Anthony Hopkins in that chair, and Richard Eyre giving me notes - what could be more perfect? Every morning these guys were going down memory lane, telling their stories about Peter O'Toole and about this one, that one, and that theater director going back 40-50 years. There was such a hush in the makeup room because we were all listening. How many times has that ever happened? That was my prize on that film."

ELIZABETH (1998) CATE BLANCHETT
Licensed from AF archive / Alamy Stock Photo

Jenny Shircore is delightful. With her mane of beautiful grey hair and sly sense of humor combined with honesty, candor, and fierce intelligence, she is a force. Of art. Of creativity. Of social conscience. When asked what her secret weapon is, she quipped, "charm and bullshit."

<u>OUTTAKES:</u>

On Influences:

"I was so lucky because I was surrounded by people who were thinking, creative people. I learned from them how to develop those things."

"I've collected an enormous number of books and have a large library at home, so I can do all my research there. My partner is an architect and he also has a lot of books and a wealth of knowledge about periods, manners, all sorts of societies. Society and houses go together. Makeup, clothes, and how people look are all interrelated."

On Lessons Taught:

"I had a trainee in my last film, *Beauty and the Beast*, and I asked her what her boyfriend did for a living. She said, 'He's a so-and-so.' I asked what company he works for and she said she didn't know. I told her, 'The next time you come in I want you to know that.' Just make them not flow easily over everything. Just get their brains working, get them to think, get them to see. Get them to observe and to be aware of what they're doing. In that way, you can look at the leaf and not just walk past that whole hedge, without even taking it in. Seeing one tiny leaf, and the beauty of it. It's stop, look, and observe."

On Lessons Learned:

"I think, for most of my work, I have to fulfill the comfort factors in myself, mentally, spiritually, all those things. I think that's what guides me. If suddenly something in me is saying, 'no, that's wrong.' then I wouldn't do it, I would steer away and go somewhere else."

"If somebody's forcing me one way and it doesn't sit comfortably, then my truth guides me. I guess that's why some directors and producers ask me to come and do a film. Because they know what I'm going to put out there, they know and they trust that truth."

On the Makeup World:

"I think there's greater camaraderie in the makeup world these days. There's no great divisions and splits. I mean, we realize we all need each other. The makeup world is not that big. We're friends together."

"I just wonder what's going to happen to all these young people who want to be in the film world and do makeup. Every day I get CVs and letters and phone calls, all asking if they can come and train. I don't see how the film world can accommodate them. Certainly not in England."

"However, with the way TV is booming with companies such as Amazon and Netflix making their own films and long series, and with less in-house employees, I'm hoping there will be new opportunities for young freelancers starting out in the industry."

On the Work:

"The makeup/hair designer designs 'the look' for all the characters in the film, working closely with the director, the production designer, the actors & especially the costume designer. That's my job!"

"I always choose the makeup and hair artists who work with me, and have usually worked with them over many films. We have a close working relationship and an understanding of each other's ways! The makeup artist's job is to apply the makeup, bringing all of their skills to the fore, thereby giving life to the character."

On Men and Women:

"I know a male makeup artist who is always away. Always. Always. Always. With children at home he says, 'it's to put them through school.' For him, as long as the indoors is happy, the children are going to a good school, his wife's got the washing machine, got this, got that, then that's fine for him. It's exactly what I did it for, but the male justification is different. I don't think there's any sense of guilt, which we, as women, feel."

"Family comes first, every time. It has to. Whether it's somebody's ill, or whether somebody psychologically needs you, or whether you just have to be there. That's where you have to be."

Catching Up!

We interviewed Jenny June 1, 2016. Since then she has worked on

The Nutcracker and the Four Realms
Walt Disney feature, directed by Lasse Hallström
Hair and Makeup Designer
starring Keira Knightley, Morgan Freeman, and Helen Mirren

Leading Ladies Speak Out

PROFESSIONALISM

MICHÈLE

"I try to bring my makeup artistry to the forefront. I'm just someone who applies great make-up. That's how I work, sticking to the job. I try to bring that to the table by the way I dress and by the way I approach and deal with the work that is at hand. We're there to execute the job we got hired for and we should give them the best of what we can give them. That's professionalism."

"First thing in the morning, it's comforting for the actors to have you there because you create an atmosphere they can come into and be vulnerable. We get them in their most vulnerable moments, when they come in feeling tired, or angry, or frustrated, and you're there to make them look the best they can. We have to stand back and be that person. That's being professional."

LOIS

"Professionalism is multicolored and multifaceted. I think one of the most important things is you put the work before yourself. I am there in service of the film. It doesn't mean I'm a servant. I'm there to do the work. I'm not about to put myself before the job at hand."

JENNY

"100% commitment and focus. I'm there on the job, attentive to it. It has to become your being, I think. You go to a meeting, you have to be armed with anything, everything. You have to be focused. You have to know what you're going in with and you have to be committed."

LESLEY

"I remember professionalism being described to me as one of the few relationships in the world that is one-on-one, like a doctor-patient relationship. I think you have to have really good boundaries and really good skills, people skills."

"Understanding the hierarchy of the leadership and working with people to support them is important. I think you need to be professional, firstly, to the people who hire you. You should be loyal, stand by them always. It's not like you get there and suddenly you are top dog. Someone hires you."

FRANCES

"Being true to yourself is one way of staying professional across the board. If you try and adjust your personality and everything about you to everybody who come along, you won't have a name. Don't aim for success, just work hard. Do it as perfectly as you can."

ERYN

"I keep trying to reassure these young women. You need to be supportive. You need to be supportive of your fellow artist. You need to not be involved in gossip and not to be involved in...It's hard not to because you're working together for 17 hours a day. It's exciting to talk about other things that are going on. There's a nice way and a kind way to approach something. I think a really important thing is to try to be supportive of one another and being professional at work."

"There's that funny saying, 'You do you.' You just do what you're doing. Don't look at all this other stuff that's going one. You do your best job. You shine as what you're doing. Don't get distracted by what other people are saying about you or saying to you. Come in, be professional and do your job. That gets noticed."

VIVIAN

"For emerging artists, I think handling yourself with dignity is something that will change the climate of women in the industry. We have to look professional in every way. How we dress, how we carry our stuff. We are equal in our ability to everything a man can do, we may have to show it a little more."

"Flexibility defines Professionalism."

JANE

"Be flexible. Keep your head. Have a broad skill base, as broad as you can get it, because even if you want to specialize in something, you'd be surprised by how much it all crosses over. I've seen other prosthetic people get frustrated when they've done a beautiful prosthetic and there's a bad wig put on it or bad facial hair. As broad a skill base as possible."

"Professionalism is a way of conducting yourself. Listen to what other people have to say. Don't be upset when they don't agree with you or don't like your ideas. Everybody's entitled to their opinion and you know we're all different. Just be able to set yourself aside and be objective."

2000
ACADEMY AWARD
BEST MAKEUP

TOPSY-TURVY, (1999) US poster art, from left: Jim Broadbent, Allan Corduner, (as Gilbert & Sullivan)
©October Films/courtesy Everett Collection
Licensed from Everett Collection, Inc. / Alamy Stock Photo

CHRISTINE BLUNDELL

I love being a hairdresser. I always have; it's in my bones. I am good at makeup and, yes, I'm very good at hair, but I'm better at knowing what I want to see and at knowing the skills that people with me are bringing to the table.

I know what I want and what my job is...what I do as a designer is bring in people who are able to pull off the look the director wants.

An adventurous, colorful, gypsy-like childhood often produces adults who either live life on those same terms or go to the opposite extreme of a staid, comfortable, predictable lifestyle. Or, as in the case of Christine Blundell, an amalgam, a life full of adventure, travel, and creativity peppered with a family, home, and a successful business.

It was a crisp spring day in London and the Borough of Camden bustled with life. The business suits walked smartly, the mothers leisurely pushed the babies in prams, and the cafes filled with lingering patrons enjoying a full English breakfast. Around the corner and down a nondescript street is an industrial building with big letters, CBMA, Christine Blundell Makeup Academy, on the window. The inside is a combination of funky and modern. With a vibe similar to the backstage in a theatre, the makeup rooms are filled with mirrors and lights and photos that punctuate the brick walls, exhibiting student work as well as iconic makeups designed and executed by Christine. "I've always referred to myself as a Camden person, born and bred. Although I wasn't born here, I moved here when I was a teenager. I love Camden. It's my home, and wherever I go in the world I can't wait to get back to Camden, which is why I've got a makeup school here."

Kitty, the French bulldog, and Yoda, the pug/schnauzer scampered ahead of Christine, sniffing around for water, a scratch, and beds on which to curl up. Christine, just back from a holiday in Greece, filled with energy and purpose, walked briskly into the school. Her speech is crisp and fast, her office full of books, scripts, photos, files, and a makeup mirror, and she is always within earshot of Petar Agbaba, her business partner, at the front desk.

The Adventure Begins

Christine was born in Watford, UK, 17 miles northwest of London, to non-traditional parents. Her father was a car dealer, her mother a dog breeder and horse dealer. Together they bought, renovated, and sold houses. "We had a very eclectic childhood. They'd park me and my older brothers in a caravan [trailer] outside and do up the house. Then we'd all move in for a couple of months, and then we'd move on." By the time Christine was 15, "we'd moved our home about 16 times. I went to 11 different schools."

Animals played a large part in her childhood and are a significant part of her adulthood. "We always had a lot of animals when I was growing up. My earliest memory was when my mom worked on a dairy farm and she let me ride on the back of a pig. We also had horses, so I was on horses. When my mom worked for a horse dealer, I rode the horses to find out if they were broken in for the horse sellers and buyers."

Christine left school at 15, "which you could do at the time. I didn't pass any exams." She now has two sons, Stan, 18, and Alfie, 16, who are ready to take their GCSE tests (General Certificate of Secondary Education). "There are times I really wish I had studied harder and done exams and stayed on to do A levels and GCSEs, especially because my kids are now doing them. I tell them, 'You've got to get your exams, you've got to study.' Stan tells me, 'You didn't.' My response, 'That doesn't matter. The School of Life doesn't exist anymore.'"

The Lure of Music and Hair

In the late '70s the punk movement had started, and at 16, "I was very much a punk. I used to play bass guitar in a band called Filthy Habitz." Christine spent most of her time touring around with punk and new wave bands. "[I was] very much on the road, very organic. I would load everything in the back of my Escort van, because I was the only driver, and drive up and down the motorways. It was what all the bands did at the time." The one constant in her itinerate life was hair dressing; she cut the band members' hair, but never held down a steady job. "It was the one thing I always had to fall back on."

"I messed about a lot in my teenage years until I got to my early twenties when I decided I needed to knuckle down a little bit more." Christine got an apprenticeship in a salon in Stevenage, 34 miles north of London, cutting hair. Wanting to live in London, she moved to a salon in Kensington Market, Vision, and then on to Tenor Salon. "It was really punk and buzzy and really good fun. It was always fun to be in London." A few years later, Christine moved back to Stevenage and opened her own salon called Scallywags. She wanted to run it "with a bit of a twist. People would pop in. It was a very friendly, very funky little hairdresser. On Saturdays, we used to cut hair until lunchtime, and then in the afternoon we had a policy where we only did friends, and they would have to pay with wine. Then we'd all go out. It was a really good time to be around. It was vibrant."

After four successful years, the bank approached Christine with an idea. Franchise. Because Scallywags was doing so well, the banker thought she should expand or sell to maximize her financial success. "I didn't want to become a hairdresser who just went on and on. Because of how I'd been brought up, I decided instead of keeping the salon, I would sever every safety net I had. I sold up and decided to move back to London and do a makeup course."

The Phantom's Lessons

Christine's makeup education was a freelance short course taught by what she remembers to be "amazing teachers." Now that she had some training under her belt, her friend, Trefor Proud, (with whom she would eventually share the Oscar for *Topsy Turvy* as her key assistant) put Christine in touch with the woman doing the makeup for the theatrical production of *Phantom of the Opera* who was looking for someone to pick up the swing shift position. "Trefor was working in theater, and at that time, you had to have a union card to be able to work in makeup for anything. The easiest way to get the union card was to do some theater work because they were always crying out to people to come and help. That was how I got my union card."

Unfortunately, Christine wasn't very good in the theater. "I'm a bit bad in the dark. There was one occasion, I think Dave Willetts was the Phantom at the time, where there is an explosion and the whole theater is thrown into darkness. At that point the Phantom is ready for his touchups. I was standing there, I had to have his glass of water here, and hold my fingers over the top of it so the straw didn't move the prosthetics around. As he was doing that, I had to use my thumb to lift his lip and pop more glue in there and push it down whilst he was drinking. The theater was thrown into darkness and all I could do or say was, 'Oooh.' He was really nice about it and when I was taking his makeup off at the end, he said, 'Maybe you're not cut out for the theater.' Because I've always been a bit funny with darkness, it didn't occur to me there would be a problem." Christine stayed with the production and got her union card, which opened up additional professional opportunities for her.

From **Phantom,** Christine got a freelance position with London Weekend Television. And that job led to another job that would impact Christine's film career for the rest of her life. One of the designers on LWT was working on a film that needed a hairdresser. "All of the actors needed something done to their hair and because she wasn't a hair dresser, she wanted me to do it. That was the first time I ever worked with Mike Leigh; the film was **Life is Sweet** (1990)."

The Film Family

Since **Life is Sweet,** Christine has been designer for all of Mike Leigh's films: **Naked** (1993), **Secrets and Lies** (1996), **Career Girls** (1997), **Topsy-Turvy** (1999), **All or Nothing** (2002), **Vera Drake** (2004), **Happy-Go-Lucky** (2008), **Another Year** (2010), **Running Jump** (2012), **Mr. Turner** (2014). Mike has a core group of people he relies on to be with him during his lengthy and complicated process: Dick Pope, cinematographer; Jacqueline Durran, costumer; Susie Davis, production designer; and, of course, Christine Blundell, makeup designer. "Mike Leigh and Dick Pope are my filming family. They really are. I did my first film with them, and fingers crossed, I'll do my last film with them. I've worked with Mike for 25, 30 years."

LIFE IS SWEET (1991)
JANE HORROCKS TIMOTHY SPALL & CLAIRE SKINNER
Licensed from AF archive / Alamy Stock Photo

"He's the master. We all love and adore him. We usually all kind of want to whack him at the end of the film, in the nicest possible way, but at the beginning of the film we're desperate to get back." Mike Leigh's films begin with an overarching idea. If the film is a period piece, there is extensive research into the period details such as politics, homes, society, clothes, careers, values. If the film is about real, historical people like in **Topsy-Turvy** or **Mr. Turner,** all the biographical information that can be gathered is assembled. "Mike is known for being a realist, so the researcher has begun work before we officially start. At the official start, this last film was at Christmas dinner, he tells us the outline of the story. He's got a skeleton of what he wants to happen or an idea. Then he'll develop it and we all get very involved in it."

When it's time to begin rehearsing with the actors, Leigh uses improvisation to develop the life of each character from birth to his/her shooting age at the beginning of the film. "If anything happens to the character during this period, like they might lose an eye, there'll be a point where he'll bring me in. We'll discuss that and they'll continue rehearsals with whatever damage has been done. That's a whole story in itself. In *Life is Sweet*, one of our characters had had a car crash when she was 18. I was called into rehearsals and we researched the crash, which had happened in the early seventies, how the wound would have been stitched up at that time, the convalescence, everything. Then, from that age onwards, [the character] would carry the scars. I mocked up a scar so when she went into improvisations with somebody she hadn't met before, they would see something had been done to her face."

Once the actors have worked through their characters' back-stories, Christine, Jacqueline Durran, and Susie Davis conduct interviews with the characters. "I host what we call surgeries. We talk to the actors. We all sit with pen and paper and take notes. We're not allowed to talk about any other actor or anything Mike might have told us. Mike will quite often give us little tidbits and things he wants us to find out. We ask them things like, 'Where did you go to school? What bands did you like?' When you're finding out about them, it's quite amazing. Say, for example, if it was me, I was a punk. I used to like The Cure and Siouxsie and the Banshees. I'd be writing all of that down and the set designer might think, 'Oh I'll get some posters of Siouxsie.' When the actor goes into their on-set house, they'll see little memorabilia bits, maybe a record collection from the punk days. For me, it's a common-sense approach to building character."

And then filming begins. Mike has the idea of the scene, the actors spend two to three days improvising it, and Mike writes down the improvised dialogue. "Then we come in. They'll show us everything they've rehearsed. Dick Pope will decide on the lighting, and Josh Robertson, 1st AD, will decide we'll need four to five days to shoot that scene. We'll all film the scene, then we all pull back, and Mike will begin rehearsing the next scene, and we do it all over again. That's how it goes."

The Rewards

Actors often ask Christine how they can work with Mike. Christine responds: "You've got to think of it as a workshop. There might be months and months of research for your character that ends up in one scene. That happens a lot. However, you've had an in-depth character workshop for a year."

It is understood by actors and the creative team on a Mike Leigh film that the entire process, from idea to finished film, usually spans a year. His actors and team happily commit that time to him. "I make no money whatsoever out of Mike, and I wouldn't want to. He really is my filming family. When he's doing a film, I want to be there. I literally want to be there. I understand his process. I love everyone that works on his films, and I understand his need for what I bring to his films. For that, it's invaluable. I will be free for the year for him to film. I will be around London should he need me to pop in. That's how we work."

"I hope I bring a little golden nugget when I talk to actors: I understand what they're trying to bring out in a character because I work with Mike. I totally believe we can help them bring it out."

"Every time Mike does a film, one of the things I find really interesting with him and Dick Pope as a working collaboration, is they always want to try something new in every film. They both want to try and experiment every time. They'll use a different film stock that's just come out or do a desaturation of color. I'm always learning something new on these films."

Collaborating, building a project from its inception, creating multi-layered looks for characters, understanding and participating in the creative process, committing to a project for the love of the experience bring Christine back, again and again, to her creative home.

Gilbert & Sullivan to Angelina Jolie

Christine's CV includes a wide range of projects, from large-budget block busters like *Wonder Woman* (2017), *Casino Royale* (2006), and *Legend* (2015), to smaller, independent films like *The Full Monty* (1997), *The Constant Gardener* (2005), and *One Chance* (2013) about opera singer and *Britain's Got*

Talent winner, Paul Potts. Among all her work, Christine has several favorite projects.

Topsy-Turvy

TOPSY-TURVY (1999)   ALLAN CORDUNER & JIM BROADBENT Licensed from AF archive / Alamy Stock Photo

Topsy-Turvy (1999), explores the tumultuous, creative relationship between Sir Arthur Sullivan (Allan Corduner) and W. S. Gilbert (Jim Broadbent) over a 15-month period from 1884-1885 when they wrote **The Mikado.** *Topsy-Turvy* was Mike Leigh's first period film, so the challenge for the designers was to create detailed and authentic Victorian looks, including the knick-knacks on the mantel pieces, brothel furniture, clothing, and the intricate hairstyles. In preparation for the film, Christine, costumer Lindy Hemming, and the rest of the creative team had a room at The Victoria and Albert Museum where they had access to the archives for research. Both men and women's hairstyles involved a variety of swirls and twists, complicated upsweeps, and varied parts. Facial hair also played a prominent role during that era, ranging from long, bushy beards, to clipped and curled mustaches. Christine had all the wigs and facial hair handmade as per the period. Because the script was improvised, she didn't know if the wigs would stay on the actors' heads or be bandied about, so they needed to be strong enough to withstand a tussle if necessary.

Gilbert and Sullivan produced their operettas at the Savoy Theater, which was built in 1881 and is still producing today. It was also the first theatre to use electricity, which is a minor plot point in the film. The theater was available to the creative team of *Topsy-Turvy* to aid in the production design.

Layered on top of the realism of the daily Victorian look was the theatrical makeup necessary for all **The Mikado** scenes onstage. Theatrical makeup at that time was heavier and broader than street makeup, with eyebrows whited out, bald caps ill-fitted on actors' heads, and heavy, broadly painted lines. Christine discovered in her research at the V&A that there were seven colors actors used for stage makeup in the 1800s. The complication of using those colors to duplicate the look led her to ask for a special week of rehearsal devoted to teaching the actors about putting on theatrical makeup, which she was granted.

The final look of *Topsy-Turvy* is complex, multi-faceted, authentic, and utterly charming. Christine won the British Academy of Film and Television Arts (BAFTA) award for *Best Makeup/Hair* and received an

MR. TURNER (2014) ©Sony Pictures Classics/Entertainment Pictures
TIMOTHY SPALL as J.M.W Turner.
Licensed from Entertainment Pictures / Alamy Stock Photo

THE CONSTANT GARDENER (2005) © Scion Films.
RACHEL WEISZ AND RALPH FIENNES
Licensed from Entertainment Pictures / Alamy Stock Photo

Academy Award for *Best Makeup* that she shares with her key assistant, Trefor Proud.

Christine has also been nominated for three additional BAFTA Awards for her work on **Finding Neverland** (2004), **Vera Drake** (2004), and **Mr. Turner** (2014).

The Constant Gardener

Another project that remains close to Christine's heart is **The Constant Gardener** (2005) which is based on a John le Carré novel of the same name starring Ralph Fiennes and Rachel Weisz. The film (and novel) revolve around an unscrupulous pharmaceutical company giving untested drugs to the Kenyan natives, the murder of Tessa (Rachel Weisz), and the search for the culprits.

Directed by Fernando Meirelles and produced by Simon Channing Williams, there was a symbiotic relationship between the Kenyans and the production team. The extras were not hired actors, but children from the town of Kibera. A bridge was built for the set that remains permanently in town. 2000 jobs were created, and Christine and Lesa Warrener, Christine's key assistant of 18 years, trained two local women to be makeup artists. Christine recalls Channing Williams, "[saying] to me, 'Chris, we're going to Nairobi, Kenya, and you can take one person with you and I want you to train people there to do the rest of the work. Every set piece we build will be left there to help create jobs. Don't go there expecting to get pampered, expecting to have someone to bring you afternoon sandwiches, because we will be in the middle of poverty, the most extreme you will ever come across.'" Christine and the rest of the team signed on. While there, because the region was unsafe, she constantly had two guards, Kenyan natives who wore tribal wear, one named Samuel, the other, Jackson. "Again, like most of these things, it wasn't the money…it was something that I can say I did and I'm very proud of that."

Hackers

Hackers (1995) revolved around a group of high school kids in New York who were proficient in hacking long before it became a daily occurrence. Directed by Iain Softley, the film starred Johnny Lee Miller and featured, for the first time, a young actress by the name of Angelina Jolie. "Angelina came over with her hair down to here and when I first met her I said, 'You know, I'd really like to do something like a manga, cartoony kind of hair on you. And she was like, 'Yeah, cut it off.' I literally cut this really jaggedy haircut and she was the coolest, coolest person, up for anything. And Johnny, **Trainspotting** (1996), let us bleach his hair. *Hackers* just had its 20th anniversary; it's become a bit of a cult classic."

Process and Guiding Philosophy

Christine's design process follows a predictable pattern: read the script, list the characters, identify makeup challenges, meet with the director, research, and meet with the actors. "I see my actors on a one-on-one with them first so they can talk to me, not me talk to them. I want them to tell me what they're seeing and what they want to achieve out of this. Then I'll have my notes and the director's notes and I will then incorporate what the actor says and adapt it and fluidly incorporate what they're saying so that it all comes together."

"I'm very proud of what we can do as makeup and hair designers and as prosthetics people. I'm very proud of any illusions we can create. However, unless specifically asked otherwise by the director, I will keep them as simple as possible."

HACKERS (1995) LAURENCE MASON, JONNY LEE MILLER, ANGELINA JOLIE & MATTHEW LILLARD. Courtesy Granamour Weems Collection Licensed from Granamour Weems Collection / Alamy Stock Photo

"I love the ability to play on people that come in for one or two days because we have the time and freedom to do a five hour makeup on them. We had David Beckham in *King Arthur: Legend of the Sword* (2017) in full prosthetics. Guy Ritchie, the director, said, 'We don't want people to know it was David Beckham. We don't want people to recognize him until 10 minutes after they've seen him.'" So, Christine brought in Krystian Mallett, prosthetics designer, and between them they were able to create a completely unrecognizable character; knowing they had David Beckham for only a few days the complex application process also lasted for only a few days.

The One That Got Away

The one project that never came to fruition and is a great disappointment to Christine is *Don Quixote* directed by Terry Gilliam. The pre-production meetings had a madcap quality fit for the screen. Terry called her to meet with him about the project, and having never met him, she asked how she would know him. "Meet me at Café Rouge at 10:00. Bring a copy of *Don Quixote."* At the end of the meeting, he said, "'I would love to have you do the film.' Who wouldn't want to do a Terry Gilliam film? 'I'd love to do the film, but I can only do it on the condition that you will sit with me over the next week and will talk me through the whole script from start to finish. Just me and you, and you will tell me what you're seeing in every single scene. I need to know from your words what you're seeing."

The next morning at 10:00, Christine met Terry in the attic of his home where he used "play mobile little dolly things" [action figures] to demonstrate the action. "We read the script aloud and he grabbed this action man and said, 'Then the giant comes from over here, like this. Don Quixote sees him and he's like, 'Woo, the giants are here.'"

Then "'we go into the palace into the huge banquet scene. All the servants come in, but they're not servants, they're kind of like men, and suddenly they become goats.' I was like, 'Okay, man becomes goat. How many men-become-goats do you want to see?' 'Ummm, 10.' 'Oh god, let me get a cost on that."

"One day Terry said to me, 'Chris, I want to take you out somewhere.' We got in the car and drove out to some stables in the country where he brought out four horses of various shades of gray. He said, 'These are the Rocinantes, can you make them look all the same?' 'So you want me to do the animals as well?' 'Yeah, great.' At this I thought, 'Oh...okay. Paint the horses.' He's so brilliant to work with, Terry. It's heartbreaking that it never actually came together that film."

CBMA - Christine Blundell Makeup Academy
Used with permission of Antonio PaganoAlamy

Giving Some Back...The Makeup Academy

For years, Christine carried a notebook around and made notes about the needs of the professional makeup world. "What do people need to know? What don't trainees know when they come to me? Things like how to dirty down people, how to read the scripts, what a first AD is, where to stand when you're on-set, all the things a trainee needs to know, not just knowing how to do big monster makeups, which is a whole different thing."

One day, on the set of **Casino Royale**, Christine was talking about the makeup trainees and the gaps in their training and that she "really needed to find a way of being at home a bit more. Maybe I should do a school." Linda Hemming said, "'Can you stop talking about it and just do it?' When she said that, I said, 'Oh, I suppose I better crack on and do that.'"

Enter Petar Agbaba, family friend: "Look, I don't know much about it, but would you consider me as your business partner?" They found the space in Camden, remodeled, Christine developed the curriculum, advertised for students, and Christine Blundell Makeup Academy opened 10 years ago. Part of the curriculum is to train with working professionals and to experience a real life working situation on one of Christine's films. "My graduates will come out for paid work experience on my films as trainees. My crowd room supervisor, Charmaine Fuller, is there, obviously, but she's always got at least four to eight of my ex-students or graduates working in it full time. When my students finish here, they come into the crowd room and the graduates that are there will look after them and show them what to do as a trainee. It's lovely to see people understanding they're going to do a trainee internship to become a junior and then, hopefully, move up."

"I've got a lot of students of mine, those who first started out with me, who are now designing their own films. I know all of them and what they're up to. I want people to succeed. Because I work in the industry, it's important they do well, otherwise I look a bit like a schmuck. One of my graduates, Stephanie Smith, won an IFTA (Irish BAFTA) last year."

"We've got a connection with the National Film and Television School and we do student films there. It is an opportunity for our students to work with film students on-set in a creative, low-budget situation. I love doing student films because you sometimes learn more on low budget when you don't have the access to thousands of pounds worth of product. Suddenly, you have to make up dirt from Vaseline and bits of color from the art shop and things."

Christine also works with North London Schools on a project called Films Cool, a creative way to challenge the students' imaginations and involve them in film-making. The students make 10 minute trailers for gore films on a budget. "We have this thing called a 10-pound budget [about $15] and I'll go to Sainsbury's and get 10 pounds worth of gelatin and syrup and food coloring and show the kids at the local school up the road how to make their blood and gore and everything else on that budget."

"Whenever I film abroad, it's always fun for me to go and see the local supermarket and what they sell. To make sure I can get gelatin or camp coffee's always a good one. All those things you kind of forget you can use. I've been in Thailand where I actually cut hair off a goat and laid it on someone. We've all done it. It is the sort of thing where you're suddenly in the middle of nowhere and your director will say, 'Can you do a burn down one side of his face?' And you're, 'Yeah, of course I can.'"

Kiss of Death

"Working on films can be the kiss of death to relationships. I'm single, I'm very happy single, and I've always been a single parent, always. From the moment my kids were born, I think my partner was with me for the first couple of years, but he wasn't really with me. He was off doing stuff that was much more fun, he said."

Christine has been very fortunate with childcare because she has had only two nannies during her boys' growing up. One of the nannies, Kathy, is still with them and even joins them for vacations. Christine also has a large cadre of friends who have been in her life for years, and "as long as I've got my mates around me, male and female, I'm the happiest bumming around. When I go off in films, I might go to ground, and when I resurface I'll have a quick holiday, and then it's 'Okay guys let's just start going out, having a drink and catching up.'"

"I never really felt the need to be living with somebody other than my kids. Again, it goes back to my childhood. We were brought up to be very independent; I've always enjoyed time on my own, with my animals. I've always been at peace with who I am and I think that if I ever was to meet somebody, probably the only way it would work nowadays is if we had different houses. I'm a bit of a stickler in my own sort of ways."

Christine Blundell brings unique vision and experience to the film industry. Fiercely independent and loyal, inviting forthright and open exchanges, Christine has no affectations. Her eclectic upbringing forged a woman clear about her priorities, her work, her family, her art.

OUTTAKES:

On Influences:

"I watch people all the time. I'm a compulsive, addictive people-watcher and they will eventually turn up in characters. It's all in here. There's certain traits I snatch from people. I enjoy faces."

"I'm very much like a bit of a magpie, just a bit of there or there, my whole life to this point has been, 'Oh, I do this and I'm not having fun anymore.' It was how I was brought up. We'd dump a house and move every six months. The longest we were in a house was two years, shortest was six months, and that's kind of been a pattern throughout my life."

"My life is my boys. I had my first son, Stan, when I was living just around the corner. Then I moved up the road when I had Alfie and I've been there for 15 years. Funnily enough, I did all the moving around as a kid and now, with my own family, I'm in one place."

On Secret Desires:

"I'd like to do a western. It's my whole thing, cowboys and Indians. I grew up on horseback; I really would love to do a western."

"All-night shoots in arctic conditions I pass on to somebody who's younger and more energetic."

"I'm a lover of teams. I use my same four core people, Lesa, Charmaine, Chloe, and Scarlett who I like to have on my main makeup bus. Then I bring in specialists for prosthetics, for example."

"I don't like egos. I'm really rubbish with egos and I don't like arrogance. I'm very obsessed with the fact we're technicians and we're there to do a job."

On The Vanities:

"People don't use that term with me because they know I don't tolerate it. It's usually nipped in the bud very quickly. I don't give out anything that really allows that to be tolerated."

"I'd like to think that's behind us. So much has been going on about women in film now and ethnic minorities. All the sludge has been brought up to the top, if you'd like. I'm kind of hoping that now everybody is beyond it."

On Staying Healthy:

"Doing a film is like running a marathon. When I'm doing a film, I literally live, eat, and breathe that film. I very rarely go out. I go to bed at like 9:00 because I need eight hours sleep and I need to be alert in the morning. I need to be on a very even keel all the time so I very much take care of myself."

Catching Up!

We interviewed Christine on June 6, 2016. Since then, she has designed Hair and Makeup for

King Arthur: Legend of the Sword
Director Guy Ritchie

Wonder Woman
starring Gal Gadot and Chris Pine

Life
starring Jake Gyllenhall, Ryan Reynolds, and Rebecaa Ferguson

Paddington 2
starring Hugh Bonneville, Sally Hawkins, Julie Walters, and Hugh Grant

Peterloo
Director Mike Leigh

Aladdin
Director Guy Ritchie

For more of Christine's Credits, visit: www.imdb.com
For further info about CBMA go to the website: www.cbmacademy.com

LEADING LADIES OF MAKEUP EFFECTS

2005
ACADEMY AWARD
BEST ACHIEVEMENT IN MAKEUP

LEMONY SNICKET'S A SERIES OF UNFORTUNATE EVENTS (2004)
JIM CARREY HOFFMAN EMILY BROWNING & LIAM AIKEN
Licensed from AF archive / Alamy Stock Photo

Some people think doing straight makeup is easy. You get somebody who has dark circles under their eyes, or has bad skin, or discoloration...it's a challenge to cover the imperfections without the makeup showing. Someone may want their eyebrows to be lifted ever-so-slightly, but they want to look natural. Maybe someone wants to lay some little hairs in and look like they have absolutely no makeup on at all, that's a special effect. Just because it's not rubber doesn't make it less; it's corrective makeup under HD conditions. It's a challenge to make up, cover things on people.

Valli O'Reilly is like a jazz musician who is ever-riffing on a motif. She is outspoken, vivacious, passionate, and grounded. She loves her job, enjoys the creativity, stimulus, and comradery of a project, thrives on working with top-notch directors and actors, but she insists on having a life outside of the industry. "I found I needed not to work all the time because I have a lot of interests I like to do outside makeup and the film business. Maybe because I didn't grow up in the US, I make sure I take a holiday every year no matter what. My family took long vacations every year. Even when I did back-to-back jobs, I made sure I went away for the weekend."

Valli was born in Alberta, Canada, and raised in Montreal and Toronto. She loved the movies and **The Munsters**, **The Addams Family**, and **The Twilight Zone**. "When you live in Canada, you don't think you're going to be living in California and working in the film business or going to the Academy Awards. None of my family members are in the film industry; my father is a pharmacist and my mother used to own a modeling agency and is a writer. My parents were always excited about anything we were interested in. They were always very supportive."

Sculpture has been a passion for Valli since she was young; she began taking adult classes when she was 14 and studied under May Marx, who was head of the Sculptors Society of Canada. Her love of art continued through college as she earned her degree in fine arts from York University in Toronto, and her passion for art drove her to advanced studies in sculpture at the Ontario College of Art and Design. "I was an artist and I was a sculptor and I just fell into makeup. I actually never went to makeup school."

In the early '80s, Valli spent a summer in New York studying sculpture, making up models for fashion shoots, and taking film classes because "it was something to do." And this, more than anything else, opens a window onto what makes Valli tick. She has always had a restless curiosity that needs feeding; she is constantly searching for a new way to express herself, to challenge her talent. From those early days in New York through to today, Valli explores artistic outlets to satisfy her drive: photography, ceramics, classes, drawing, painting, fashion, travel.

Learning While On-Set

Valli began to work on student films doing makeup. "I bought Richard Corson's book [*Stage Makeup*], the original one, and looked up what they wanted. If they wanted blood and stuff, I went to a makeup supply house and bought whatever little budget thing they had. I used things like popcorn with blood on it to be brains. I was creative. I taught myself."

Having been initiated into the film business, Valli travelled between New York and Toronto, working on films and sharpening her makeup skills. She met her future husband, an actor, in Miami, and they settled in New York - two artists looking for work. He was from California, so they eventually decided to move to the heart of the film industry, Los Angeles, where rent was cheaper and opportunities greater. In LA, Valli met people in the industry, established herself, built a reputation, and did makeup on many non-union films and music videos. "I did tons of MTV music videos. I worked with Jennifer Warens, Leonard Cohen, Talking Heads, Traveling Wilburys, INXS, so many different musicians. Bryan Adams. Now I work with him as a photographer."

"As time went on, I worked with people who had trained at makeup school. I was a good monkey-see-monkey-do kind of person. Greg Cannom [three-time Oscar winner] is a friend of mine, I met him in the '80s and he showed me how to do a lot of stuff. When I started doing non-union films in LA, he would make and apply all the difficult effects for me. He did a great head of Super Dave Osborne."

With her MTV and non-union film experiences under her belt, Valli was asked to be Antonio Banderas' personal makeup artist on *Mambo Kings* (1992) which made her eligible to get into the union. "Also, I was told I needed an esthetician's license to get into the union, so I took some classes and passed the State Board Exam." She also passed the union test (a prerequisite at the time) and professional doors opened for Valli in both film and television.

It's the People

Valli has worked on major motion pictures, applied makeup on top talent, and collaborated with award-winning directors and designers. "Sometimes the movies were amazing because of the people in them. I've done a bunch of movies with Emma Thompson, who is a fun person, Dustin Hoffman, Annette Bening, Jennifer Aniston, Sharon Stone, and Warren Beatty who I've worked with for 25 years. *How to Make an American Quilt* (1995) had Ellen Burstyn, Anne Bancroft, Winona Ryder, Maya Angelou, and Alfre Woodard. I also made up Whitney Houston in *The Body Guard* (1992)." The star-studded client list continued in 2016 when Valli did a movie for HBO, *Mosiac*, directed by Steven Soderbergh with Sharon Stone, Paul Reubens, Beau Bridges, and Garrett Hedlund.

And this is the uniqueness of Valli. She creates working relationships with actors that transcend years based on established trust and mutual respect. "I've gotten along fabulously with the actors I've worked with. I want them to like my work enough to want to use me again, and to feel the experience in the makeup trailer has been fantastic."

Valli has been Dustin Hoffman's personal makeup artist on ten projects: **Lemony Snicket's A Series of Unfortunate Events** (2004), **Meet the Fockers** (2004), **Stranger than Fiction** (2006), **Perfume: The Story of a Murderer** (2006), **Mr. Magorium's Wonder Emporium** (2007), **Last Chance Harvey** (2008), **Little Fockers** (2010), **Luck** (HBO series, 2011-2012), **Chef** (2014), and **Barney's Version** (2010) for which

she received the Genie Award, given by the Academy of Canadian Cinema and Television, for *Best Achievement in Makeup*, which she shares with Adrien Morot, Rejean Goderre, and Micheline Trepanier.

Barney's Version is the story of Barney's life (Paul Giamatti) told in flashbacks and colored by dementia. Hoffman plays Barney's father, providing advice and ballast to his life, as he himself ages. This is a stylized, period piece where "Dustin had to have mutton-chop side-burns at the beginning of the film and brown hair. I had to age him for the end of the film; I think I gave him a chipped tooth."

Warren Beatty is another actor with whom Valli has had a long-term working relation-ship. Beatty is frequently the writer, produc-er, director, and actor in his films; as such, he hires Valli either as his personal makeup artist or head of department for the whole film. In 1994, Valli was head of department for **Love Affair**, and again for **Bulworth** in 1998. She was also Mr. Beatty's personal makeup artist for **Town and Country** (2001), and depart-ment head for **Rules Don't Apply** (2016).

BARNEY'S VERSION (2010) *PAUL GIAMATTI, DUSTIN HOFFMAN*
MOVIESTORE COLLECTION LTD
Licensed from Moviestore collection Ltd / Alamy Stock Photo

Rules Don't Apply focuses on a relationship between Howard Hughes' chauffeur, Alden Eh-renreich, and a new starlet, Lily Collins. "We chose to create a realistic, every-day look. Some women had bushy eyebrows and every-body had red lips and eyeliner on. The hair and clothes were, naturally, of the period."

Actors are not the only long-term professional relationships Valli has acquired over the years of her career; she credits many of her job op-portunities to costume designer, Colleen At-wood. They worked together for the first time on **Mars Attacks!** (1996), again in 2004 on **Lemony Snicket's A Series of Unfortunate Events**, and in 2010 on Tim Burton's **Alice in**

LOVE AFFAIR (1994) ANNETTE BENING & WARREN BEATTY
Licensed from AF archive / Alamy Stock Photo

Wonderland. "Colleen was responsible for me working with Tim Burton and on **Lemony Snicket's**." An-other long-term relationship Valli has is with Milena Canonero, costume designer, who introduced Valli to Warren Beatty, Annette Bening, and Francis Ford Coppola which has resulted in years of collaboration and work.

Choices

"In the beginning of 2000, my career changed. I decided I wouldn't go on location to places I didn't want to go. I don't mind going to London, or Germany, or New York, but a small town in Texas or Baton Rouge? No, thank you. And I don't like the cold. I grew up in the cold, so I'm not a big fan. It's different being in the cold when you're in the film business…you stand in it, at night, outside, for 12 hours…I love my friends and my family and sleeping in my own bed."

Valli is an artist who has controlled her career, not allowed her career to control her. She is in the enviable position of being able to pick and choose her projects, which she credits to some savvy business decisions when she was younger. "I was smart in the beginning of my career; I was conservative. I saved my money, bought real estate in Venice [California], which is really thriving now. I didn't rush out and get a Hermes this or a Louis Vuitton that…I didn't spend my money that way. If I didn't want to take a job because I knew it would be something I wouldn't enjoy, I didn't have to.

"What makes me happy are jobs that are artistic and challenging. I need to be around culture. I wouldn't be happy, no matter who was in the movie or what the makeup was, if I was someplace that didn't allow me to enjoy myself in my down time. I build in time for my own life.

"I've tried to mix up my career; I've been diverse. I do editorial stuff, I do commercials, movies. In order to be happy, I have to have a lot of friends that aren't even in the business…you can get pulled onto the roller coaster of, 'What's your next job?' 'What are you doing next?' I used to…say, 'My next project is The Valli O'Reilly Show, The Story of My Life.'"

Using the Lessons

Working on non-union and low-budget films laid a foundation for Valli to acquire on-the-spot creative problem-solving skills. "When you have no money, you have to get creative. I remember once we took some bristles off a broom and made whiskers for a lion. Even now, suddenly the director will want something fast. I have to look in my kit and think, 'What's going to make that shine? Put some red there, have the actor hold his hand in a certain way, put KY jelly on it.' A lot of the time, if you're working with a really good hairdresser, you can really problem solve together. I like the challenge and the collaboration."

THE JOY LUCK CLUB (1993) CAST PHOTO
Licensed from Entertainment Pictures / Alamy Stock Photo

Valli's favorite project of all time is ***The Joy Luck Club*** (1993), a film adapted from the 1989 novel written by Amy Tan that focuses on four Chinese-American immigrant families in San Francisco who start a club which revolves around the game of mahjong, The Joy Luck Club. As the ladies are playing the game, mother-daughter relationships become the heart of the film while Chinese history from 1900-1992 is the backdrop. Working on the film demanded that Valli think on her feet, research the period, and work with a small budget, all with little or no prep time. "I didn't get any sleep the first two weeks. I spent my weekends in the library, researching. We had advisors there from the Chinese Historical Society of America in San Francisco, so everything had to be historically correct. We had no wigs, we had no special effects. I had to make everything out of the kit."

One of the actors in the film had to look younger for the flashbacks. "Even though he was in his early thirties, he had a receding hairline. The hairdresser, Terry Baliel, and I cut up hair that I had for beards and used spirit gum to glue on hairs, one-by-one, to fill in his hairline. We used to say, 'Next they are going to ask us to do the catering.' But in the end, everything just fell together perfectly."

Fantasy Work

Valli has evolved her own distinctive style which comes from her art training, her experiences in fashion, on-set work in film and television, print work, in-depth research, and talking with and learning from other special effects makeup artists. "My friends say to me, 'I can always tell when it's your work in a movie because you have your own little quirky sense of style.' I'm good with fantasy. If producers look at my work, they would know what to hire me for. It has more of a fashion look. I shine in period makeup and in fashion and in fantasy makeup with a small amount of effects. Basically, I follow my own rules, as if I was painting."

A fine example of a fantasy/fashionable film is *Alice in Wonderland* (2010). "For something like *Alice in Wonderland* there were lots of concept meetings with the costume designer, Colleen Atwood, who does pretty much all of Tim Burton's movies, and a really short meeting with Tim who told me to look at Bette Davis from *The Private Lives of Elizabeth and Essex* (1939) as an inspiration for the Red Queen (Helena Bonham Carter) and Kirk Douglas in *The Vikings* (1958) who had a huge scar down the side of his face as inspiration for the Knave of Hearts (Crispin Glover)." Valli, as makeup designer for the film, created a mood board that included all kinds of inspiration: colors, furniture, shapes, smudges of lipstick, a beach. "It helps me tap into my creative juices." When they tested the makeup in the trailer, Valli had the still photographer take a lot of pictures of the different looks she tried. "I'd number the pictures and Tim went through the stills and see what he liked. He'd say, 'I like that on that picture, this on that one.' Then we put them all together and came up with something he liked."

"I was a fan of this artist named Margaret Keane who did those big-eyed kids in the '70s, so I based a lot of my looks for the film on her work. For the White Queen, I also took a little bit of Carolyn Jones from *The Addams Family* and mixed it in with Margaret Keane and the image of a beatnik doll I had as a kid and came up with the final look."

For the Red Queen, Valli had to adapt the design to Tim Burton's vision and Helena Bonham Carter's heart-shaped face and thick eyebrows. "Tim decided he didn't want eyebrows on her…so we made a decision to have a prosthetic made for her that came down past her eyebrows, one that was light and flexible enough to allow Helena to act through. When we started the process, I was drawing her eyebrows on her, but I thought, 'the more the movie goes, the more tired I'm going to get and these aren't going to match day-to-day.' So, I made myself a stencil and drew them on. And then I thought a stencil for the heart-shaped lips would work, too."

"Because the film was CGI, HD, and 3D, everything had to be perfect. I did Helena, Mia Wasikowska (Alice), and Anne Hathaway (The

ALICE IN WONDERLAND (2010) HELENA BONHAM CARTER
©face to face/Entertainment Pictures)
Licensed from Entertainment Pictures / Alamy Stock Photo

White Queen) pretty much every day." For the White Queen, "the skin couldn't look like Kabuki makeup, so I looked for a product that is very thin, but gives coverage." The White Queen's lips are a dark plum, brushed on with a fine brush; her nails are a black-plum. "Leslie Devlin was my key and made up Crispin Glover as well as other cast members."

"It's fun. It's fun putting up all the pictures because it inspires the actors, too. Color and everything. I'll talk to them about what they think which, of course, influences the final decisions." Valli O'Reilly received a BAFTA Award (British Academy of Film and Television Arts) for *Best Makeup and Hair* for **Alice in Wonderland**, which she shares with Paul Gooch.

LEMONY SNICKET'S A SERIES OF UNFORTUNATE EVENTS (2004)
EMILY BROWNING JIM CARREY LIAM AIKEN
Valli O'Reilly, Head of Depart., with Bill Corso as Personal MUA to Jim Carrey
Licensed from Moviestore collection Ltd / Alamy Stock Photo

Fortunate Events

Lemony Snicket's A Series of Unfortunate Events (2004), a neo-Victorian film that follows three orphans who are perpetually trying to escape their evil guardian, is a prime example of complicated, well-oiled, creative collaboration on a grand scale. Valli was head of department on the film and therefore responsible for ensuring the designs were realized and camera-ready. Bill Corso was personal makeup artist to Jim Carrey who had four different looks.

The characters for the large crowd scenes replicated Eastern Bloc films of the 1950s and '60s, and everything was exaggerated and whimsical. Mustaches were three inches longer than normal. The women all had the same painted face. Count Olaf's troupe had subtle, stylized makeups which included a hooked man covered in scars who can't stop scratching himself, the white-faced women who resembled a Victorian doll, a large, androgynous person, and a small man with blue hair and an eye tattooed on the back of his head.

The film has a unique look: it is dark and moody, ornate and foreboding, other-worldly and old-worldly. To attain such a successful look involves a lot of people working toward the same goal, guided by clear communication and achieved with open minds. Valli O'Reilly received an Online Film and Television Association (OFTA) Award for *Best Makeup and Hairstyling for **Lemony Snicket's***, as well as the Academy Award for *Best Achievement in Makeup* which she shares with Bill Corso.

The Full Life

Valli O'Reilly has a full work life. She works on films as head of department or as a personal, she does print work, commercials, documentaries, and red carpet, all the while balancing her work with a life full of friends and creative outlets.

OUTTAKES:

On Long Term Success:

"I think it's important to be well-versed in everything and know your limitations. I can lay on a beard. I know how to do some effects. I know how to do beauty. I can run a show. When there are areas that are bigger than what I'm capable of doing, I will hire somebody else whose specialty I don't have and need."

"Get some type of art training. Learn what highlighting and shadowing is all about. You don't put highlights on the same spot on everybody, you have to look for it and understand it; art school helps with that."

On Collaboration:

"I'm not one of those people who doesn't want anybody to input anything. I do like it if they tell me they've got a great idea. I like to have people working with me that I think are as good as me or better. I don't like to hire people that aren't very good. I like to recommend good people."

"Keep all your opinions about other people on the show, other makeup and hair people, to discuss at home, not in the trailer."

On Passion:

"While I was working to live, I wanted to make sure my work was something I had a passion for. Otherwise you're spending a lot of hours in the day with a lot of people doing something you don't like. I like to have fun. Actors like me because I like to have everybody laughing."

Catching Up!

We interviewed Valli on February 13, 2016. Since then, she has worked on

A Little Something For Your Birthday
with Sharon Stone, Tony Goldwyn, and Ellen Burstyn

Valli has been working primarily on press junkets and a lot of commercials in 2017.

For more photos of Valli's Print work, visit www.zenobia.com
For more of Valli's Credits, also visit: www.imdb.com

2006
ACADEMY AWARD
BEST ACHIEVEMENT IN MAKEUP

THE CHRONICLES OF NARNIA: THE LION THE WITCH AND THE WARDROBE (2005)
Licensed from AF archive / Alamy Stock Photo

There's no real roadmap. If you talk to anyone, every story's different. From Eryn Krueger Mekash to Lois Burwell to me, everybody got here in different ways. That's the beauty part of this. It's not like what you're promised: you go to college, you get a degree, and you get a job. That's not the way it works, not in the real world anymore. You have to be a little bit gutsy and naïve. I attribute my naïveté in the beginning as a positive thing because I was just so blown away by everything.

Also, you have to be willing to put yourself in the way of opportunity.

"You have to put yourself in the way of opportunity" may well sum up Tami Lane's journey from Illinois to Hollywood, to New Zealand, and back to Hollywood as one of the best prosthetics makeup effects artists in the business. Being gutsy with a dose of naïveté has served her well, but she also has had a cadre of teachers, friends, and mentors guiding and nudging her to put herself in the way of opportunities.

In February 2015, Tami went back to Bradley University in Peoria, Illinois, which she attended in the mid-nineties on a softball scholarship, as one of the honorees at the university's first annual celebration of female athletes. "I thought that was a good reason to go home." While Tami was home, she reconnected with her high school band director, Mary Jo Papich. "If anybody was my biggest inspiration, it was her."

A Strong Female Model

Tami remembers Papich not so much for her discipline or the way she taught, but for her interest in the arts. "She always dressed flamboyantly. She was sparkly." Tami was a trumpet player, as was Papich, which is unusual because trumpet is widely considered a man's instrument. Also, at the time, most band-leaders were men, so "she was a woman in this men's club. I didn't realize what that meant until later."

Often the most active students have conflicts balancing academics with extracurricular activities. Tami's conflicts were balancing all her many extracurricular activities, band and softball and basketball, with each other. "I had to go to parades or jazz music fests on the weekends. So sometimes I had to miss games or part of practice. During basketball season, I was always in Harper's Hellhole running laps because I'd miss half of ball practice to do jazz band rehearsals every Friday. [Papich] would go head-to-head with these male coaches to fight for her students' participation. She'd make contracts, 'you get her this weekend, I get her on another.' She stood up for herself and for what she did. She wasn't a flute player. She was a trumpet player."

During her week back home for the Bradley event, Tami caught up with Papich, who is now retired from teaching and focuses her energies on organizing jazz festivals. "She recently moved back to Peoria from Chicago where she did wonders with the city's music programs. However, because they've taken all the arts out of the schools in Peoria, she feels she can do more for Peoria by helping bring the arts back into the schools. She's still a fighter."

Other Early Influences, Film and Theater

"While I was growing up, my mother was obsessed with films and movies and theater. Every Friday night, my mom and dad took us to the movies or one of the two community theaters, Peoria Players or Corn Stalk. I always wondered, 'What would it be like to work backstage?'"

One year, the Peoria Players was presenting **Sweet Charity** and Papich was the music director. Tami asked if there was something she could do to help out. "[My mother] almost flipped. 'You're already in too much stuff.' I was in the band, I was in sports, I was in student council, and I had a 3.9 grade point average. I was an overachiever. But this was something to do separate from school. I said, 'I promise. If I get one B, if anything falls, I'll give up community theater.' Well, I just kind of ran with it."

While she was working at the theater, she met Harold Breitenbach, the construction foreman for the theater who also happened to build haunted houses and loved doing effects. Tami found herself working with him painting scenery, building effects, hanging lights, and running the light and sound boards. But soon, she discovered makeup.

"The last show of the season we always did a *Best Of...* featuring our favorite musical numbers. For this show, there were numbers from **West Side Story** and **Cats**. 12 dancers had to get into **Cats** makeup in eight minutes. I was working the light board with my headset on and the stage manager said, 'Tami, you paint. Get down here. One of our makeup artists didn't show up.' I said, 'I don't know how to do that.' 'Well just get down here.' The sound guy took over my cues and I ran down to the green room. They had all this Krylon grease paint and pictures of **Cats** from Broadway. They said, 'Whoever sits in your chair, just pick one and do it.' That was how it happened. It was the best eight minutes of my life. It was the adrenaline. We were laughing. It was so much fun painting these people. I'd never used a grease palette before in my life. I think I was 17 then. I really, really loved that. I started doing more makeup."

Course Correction ... Steppin' Up to the Plate

In her senior year of high school, Tami needed to make some decisions. She was offered a softball scholarship at Bradley, but that meant she had to choose a major. Music seemed a natural choice, but, according to Tami, "I'm a terrible audition. I get so nervous. I didn't feel confident enough to major in music." Strike one. Then she thought maybe she'd like to be a physical therapist. "The dean [at Bradley] said I had to give up playing ball to be in that program. I thought, 'Hell no, that's how I'm paying for this!' My parents are teachers. My Dad is a P.E. teacher and coach. My Mom was a school secretary. They're not rich people and this is an expensive school. I guess I can't major in that." Strike two. Next up, Tami was sitting in calculus class, drawing. The teacher, Ms. Canty, was discussing matrixes and Tami, not particularly interested, continued drawing. "My teacher came up behind me, picked my notebook up, took a look, and said, 'Did you ever consider going into art?' She put it back down and kept on lecturing. I kept drawing and she let me. I went home that day and I said, 'Mom, I think I'm going to major in art.'" A hit...safe on first base.

Following the Art Path...Sort Of

Tami entered Bradley as an art major on a softball scholarship. In her junior year, she met her graphic design instructor, Val Carlson, who introduced her to the world of computer graphics. Carlson had a significant influence on Tami who describes them as being "still friends" to this day. However, in her senior year, Tami had a revelation - she hated computers. She'd been working at a job doing clip art, day after day, and was bored silly. She no longer wanted to pursue graphic design. She was in a quandary. What could she do from here? She had spent four years in school and didn't want to waste her degree.

"It was a Wednesday night and I went to a bar, fittingly called Desperado's, with my friend Amy, and I asked her, 'What am I going to do?' Amy said, 'You're into community theater, right? And you love to do that makeup stuff, right? Well, at Bradley there's this class that goes out to Los Angeles for two weeks and they introduce you to the entertainment industry and you meet all these people. I think one of the things they do is tour a makeup effects shop.' 'What's that?' 'Well, it's a studio where they make all the makeup stuff.' 'Oh. That could be fun. I've never seen the ocean.'"

The problem with this new plan was the class was only open to Communication Department students and Tami was an art major. Seizing the incentive, "I went to see the professor, Dr. Bob Jacobs, and said, 'I know you go to LA with your class and I'm really interested in the makeup effects thing that you tour. I don't know anything about it, or anything else, but I'd like to go.'" There were slots for ten students, five guys, five girls, and there were 60 applicants. Dr. Jacobs put the students through an intensive interview process that included writing an essay. "I guess I wanted it pretty badly because I was lucky enough to be chosen to go on this class trip." Another hit...safe at second base.

Fate Moves in Mysterious Ways

The trip had a price tag of $2500 and Tami didn't have it. She went to her parents, and "My mom, just heartbroken, said, 'Oh Tam. We don't have that kind of money. I'm sorry, you can't go. We just can't afford it.' I was gutted and upset. 'What am I going to do? I don't want to do graphic design.' I was in the total panic mode of a senior. Typical." In a haze of disappointment, Tami drove to Chicago to visit a friend for the weekend.

When she arrived back at school on Monday morning, Tami discovered someone had broken into her house and stolen her jewelry. "I was devastated; my grandmother's ring was among the things taken. I called my mom up in tears. A half an hour later, Mom called back. 'Since you're still a student, you fall under our homeowner's insurance. You're insured for the loss, $2500. Let's go shopping!' 'Mom, do I have to buy jewelry with that money? Can I use the money for that class trip?' My mom said, 'It's your money. Do what you want with it.' I got the check from the insurance company and signed it over to Bradley University. That's how I went on the class trip." Another hit...safe on third.

A Trip of a Lifetime

On the trip to Los Angeles, Tami met a "Who's Who" lineup of Hollywood filmmakers: Howard W. Koch, head of Paramount Studios; Ray Bradbury, science fiction writer; Saul Bass, graphic designer for film titles, trailers, and posters; Henry Winkler, actor; John Hench, lead designer at Disney Imagineering. But the most significant event for Tami was visiting KNB EFX Group and meeting Robert Kurtzman, Greg Nicotero, and Howard Berger. "When I walked into that shop, my life changed. I was in awe. I said to Howard, 'How could I work here?' He told me, 'Go back to school. Graduate. Then move out to LA and call me.' And that's just what I did." Hit to deep to center...comes home for the run.

Road Trip: Movin' Out To LA

Two weeks after she graduated, Tami and three other Bradley grads headed to LA. When they arrived, the four of them shared a two-bedroom apartment in a grungy Hollywood neighborhood, a typical story. "We're all still here in LA, one is a leading CGI artist, another is a CPA, and the third has a traveling spa."

Tami called KNB EFX, per Howard Berger's directions, but she couldn't get to talk with him. "I told them to tell him I was the girl who gave him the paddleball." During Tami's senior year, one of her design projects was to create a special, self-promotional calling card that wasn't a business card.

"I was playing around with street signs, you know, 'Tami Lane.' Then I was in a toy store, and I saw a paddleball, one of those wooden paddles with the rubber ball. I thought, 'Ah ha!' I bought a dozen of them, took the elastic off and I sanded them down to the bare wood. Then I created a logo with my name, my phone number, and address. Well, when I met Howard, in order for him to remember who I was, I gave him one. Then he said, 'Well, I have three kids.' So, I gave him one more. It's a toy. Everybody at KNB is just a big kid."

The strategy seemed to work because the front desk took her calls. "I kept calling. They'd say 'He's in a meeting. He's on-set.' Whatever. I almost gave up because I didn't want to hound him." Foul ball.

To bring in some money, Tami got a job at UCLA Opera painting scenery. She'd moved to LA with her car, a television, and $1000 cash from graduation gifts which lasted about three months. With the job at the Opera, money issues relaxed. The day before her birthday, "I got a phone call from Howard Berger saying, 'Hey, I'm sorry I haven't called. We've just been really busy, are you still interested in work?' I said, 'Yeah, of course!' He said, 'Well, we just got this big movie called *Spawn* (1997) and need someone in to clean clay out of molds, sweep the floors, stock shelves, empty the trash, whatever. It's $7 an hour.' 'When do I start?!' I started the following Monday. That was the beginning of our relationship." Grand slam home run!

Getting to Work

With minimum experience in makeup and effects, Tami got on-the-job training at KNB. The first task she was assigned was cleaning out molds. "They were stone and fiberglass molds back then. My hands and knuckles were bleeding from digging the roma plastilina out of those molds."

One day while she was cleaning molds, "This guy, 'Big Al' Tuskas, one of the head mold makers, said, 'Tam, come here. You know how to make a mold? I'm going to teach you.'" He taught Tami how to make a two-part stone mold. He taught her about keys and flashing and undercuts. "I was actually kind of okay at it."

She also picked up some valuable advice from a co-worker. "'If you don't want to do something, mess it up, they'll never ask you again.' They threw me in the fiberglass spray booth. Yeah, I didn't like fiberglass. I kind of messed up and never was asked again to 'tap glass.' Truly, part of the reason was because fiberglass messes with women's reproductive organs and I was

Tami at KNB FX   Used with Permission of Tami Lane

22-years-old. I think even Howard and Greg agreed, 'Don't put her in that. Keep her away from that shit.'"

From there she learned about polyfoam and chemicals and casting. She started casting up molds and making parts; the logical next step was trimming the edges and seaming joints. Then Gino Acevedo asked her if she'd ever used an airbrush. "'You want to paint?' To me, he's one of the best airbrush artists in the business. He took me under his wing, showed me different tricks with the airbrush, how to use different paints." Airbrushing tapped into Tami's already-established talents; she'd studied painting as an art major, but she'd also been painting all her life.

"I love painting and I really love working in oils. I used to do big canvases in college, a lot of figurative stuff. I don't get to paint much anymore, but I do a lot of sketchbooks. I'm on planes a lot, so I use coffee and red wine for color. In my life, art has always been there. When my Mom sold our old dining room table she turned it over and saw all these drawings underneath. I used to sit under the table with markers or crayons and color."

Proficient at many tasks, Tami became very useful around the shop at KNB. Next, she learned techniques for hair transfer and punching hair, the process by which hair is inserted into silicone or foam so it appears the hair is growing out of the skin. "It's kind of my thing. I love punching hair." She started learning how to foam fabricate fake animals with Beth Hathaway, a creature puppet maker, one of the only other women working at KNB in the shop. "She taught me how to manipulate L200 along with all the other different types of foams to build all sorts of things."

Getting On-Set

After working in the shop for a year, in July of 1997, Tami got her chance to go on location in New Mexico with Greg Nicotero for the John Carpenter film, *Vampires.*

"At the beginning of my experience at KNB, I was working exclusively with Greg Nicotero. He actually gave me my first real break by taking me onto *Vampires*. Of course, I love John Carpenter, so [Nicotero] said, 'I just need somebody to come and help set up the trailer. It will probably just be for a week. You won't stay the whole time.' I said 'Yeah!' Well one week turned into two weeks and then he let me go to second unit alone to do the blood gags, shooting the close ups with John's wife, Sandy, who was directing that unit. Every day we were getting up really early to get to work because there were only three makeup artists doing seven hero vampires. They were all airbrushed makeups and this was back when there was no Skin Illustrator makeup. We were breaking down rubber mask grease paint with alcohol and putting it through the airbrushes, not easy, and labor intensive. Greg said to me, 'You want to do makeup, right?' 'I would love to do makeup.' 'I figure if you do two hero vampires, Scott does two, Doug does two, and Bruce does two, we don't have to come in at 5:30. We can shorten our pre-call and come in at 6:30.' Scott taught me how to do the makeups. I ended up staying on the show the entire time, doing lead makeups, blood gags, and background. When we came back after that show, that was it, Greg and I were friends."

With her first on-set experiences under her belt, Tami got another opportunity to work on-set, this time on *Talos the Mummy* (1998) with Howard Berger. "Howard was going to Luxembourg and he needed to bring somebody. Greg told him, 'You need to take Tami. She'll run. She'll do anything. Take Tami. She's great on-set. She'll be great.' Howard asked me to go and that was the show where Howard and I bonded. He looked out for me. We have the same twisted sense of humor. After that, Howard took me on everything."

Friends Move in Mysterious Ways, Too

"This is a crazy story. I was working a lot in the shop. I got into making dead animals, fake animals. I made Mr. Jingles for *The Green Mile* (1999), six puppet ones. I did a lot of dead animals for *Ravenous* (1999). I got called into Greg's office he said, 'After Friday we don't have anything for you. You might want to look for something else.' This was a Wednesday. 'What?' 'No, no, we'll keep you. When we get something, we'll call you.' I'd heard about being laid off for either two weeks or six weeks and never getting hired back again. I was thinking, 'What did I do?' Howard reiterated what Greg had told me, 'Yeah. Sorry man, we're just doing a bunch of lay-offs. After this, after you finish this stuff on Friday, we're just going to have to let you go for a while.' I had just moved into my very first apartment on my own in Silverlake. I'd been working steadily at KNB for nearly four years and I'd never been laid off. I'd seen people come and go but I didn't think…I don't know what I thought. I was just devastated.

"Thursday night about 10:30 my phone rang; it was Richard Taylor from Weta [a conceptual design and prosthetic makeup company in New Zealand]. I thought it was my friend Bill Hunt playing a joke, he was a sculptor at KNB and then got hired at Weta to sculpt for them for *Lord of the Rings* in 1998. He'd been gone almost a year, so this is now 1999. I said, 'Ha-ha-ha, very funny Bill,' and I hung up. The phone rang again. 'Tami, this is really Richard Taylor from Weta Workshop.' I said 'Oh, no, you're kidding. Oh, I'm so sorry Rich, I'm so sorry.' I'd met him before when I'd gone down to New Zealand to work on *Xena* and *Young Hercules* (1998) with Howard. He said, 'We need another on-set prosthetics makeup artist and you come recommended. Would you be interested in coming down to New Zealand for the next 15 months?' I said, 'Let me think about that…yes." He said, "Well, I was wondering about your availability.' 'Well lucky for you, I just came available.' 'When do you want me?' 'When can you get here?' 'Two weeks.' 'I was hoping sooner.' 'What are you thinking?' 'Four days.' 'How about seven?' 'Five.' 'Done.' I got a U-Haul truck, two guys from out in front who packed me up and put everything in a storage unit in Eagle Rock. Next thing I knew, I was on a plane for what I thought would be a 15-month stint in New Zealand to work on *Lord of the Rings* on-set doing orcs and feet and whatever. That changed my life.

"It turns out Richard Taylor and Howard are good friends. Richard Taylor had a stack of 5000 resumes from all over the world and it was just too daunting to pick one artist. He finally called Howard and said, 'I need an on-set prosthetics artist that can do monsters and whatever else we need.' Howard basically said, 'You need Tami Lane.'

"That phone call from Richard came in the prior Tuesday, and Howard and Greg had put a plan in place. Howard said to me, 'Tami I knew you wouldn't take the job. You would never leave KNB unless we got rid of you. But you have to promise me when you get back from *Lord of the Rings* you will come and work for me again.' That's a good friend, to fire you so you can do something else."

Lord of the Rings and Orcs

Tami left for New Zealand for 15 months, which turned into six years, working on the *Lord of the Rings (LotR)* trilogy, *The Fellowship of the Ring* (2001), *The Two Towers* (2002), and *The Return of the King* (2003). "I loved it there so much that I stayed and kept getting work."

Tami came onto *LotR* working as a prosthetics makeup artist on the "monster crew" making up the orcs. Most of the orcs were played by stuntmen, so maintaining continuity wasn't an issue. "You knew he was going to die that day. Basically, continuity schmontinuity. Do whatever you want. We had boxes of chins, boxes of noses, boxes of scars, and stuff like jewels and bones. Basically, nothing was pre-painted. So, it was a matter of pick, choose, and paint. New day, new orc." Until one day…

Tami had a stuntman, Lee, sitting in her chair, and even with boxes and boxes of bits and pieces she found she was starting to run out of ideas for things to do. Crunch! Tami had stepped on a piece of chainmail and it had cracked in half. She'd been doing scars and piercings already, so "I started breaking up the chainmail. I thought, 'Football players have those stickers on their helmets for good plays. Well, this chainmail could represent kills or whatever.' I started embedding the chainmail bits into the foam of the piece and painting them like they were embedded all the way down his face, down his nose, all over. I'm looking at it and thinking, 'That's kind of cool. Something different.'" It was so different that when the director, Peter Jackson, saw this particular orc, he pulled him out of the background and gave him lines. "Lee was just an orc that was supposed to get killed, head chopped off or something, and now he's in the movie in a scene with Christopher Lee. His line is something like, 'Oh, the roots grow deep, my Lord.' For me, as a makeup artist, that orc was supposed to be a one-off. Well, we shot that scene for five days so I was scrambling to recreate the look. 'What piece did I use? Lee, was it this chin?' I couldn't really remember. They all melded together. We didn't have digital cameras then, we used Polaroids, but we didn't take them of orcs because they were supposed to die! So, we had to guess and do the best we could to duplicate his look. Recently, Lee contacted me through Facebook. The first thing he said was, 'I'll never forget you because you gave me the opportunity to be in the movies.' That was nice. What your makeup artist can do for you."

A Special Mentor

"While I was Down Under working on **Lord of the Rings**, there was a woman that took me under her wing, a New Zealander named Dominie Till. What I didn't learn at KNB from Howard or Greg or Bob [Kurtzman], she taught me. Because she's a New Zealander, she doesn't have access to a lot of the things we have here in LA, so she really has to be resourceful. She taught me how to solve problems in a pinch. She taught me about wigs and hair punching, about straight makeup, and thinking fast on your feet. She does everything from wig knotting to straight makeup to glamour to monsters to application. She's a great friend and mentor to me to this day and I work with her on a lot of projects."

More Tales from Down Under

In 2004, Tami was still in New Zealand when she got a call

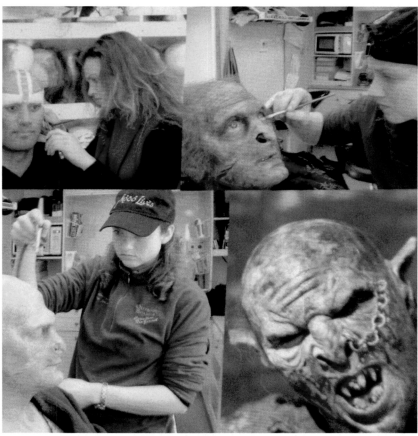

Tami making Orcs for **Lord of the Rings** (1999)   Used with Permission of Tami Lane

from her buddy, Howard Berger: "I got this movie and it's filming in New Zealand. I guess if you're not coming home, I'll have to come to you." "That's when he asked me to be the key and his second on **The Chronicles of Narnia: The Lion, the Witch and the Wardrobe**."

Tami's favorite makeup in **Narnia** was Mr. Tumnus, played by James McAvoy. Originally, McAvoy was only supposed to work for 12 days, but the director, Andrew Adamson, loved the character so much that McAvoy ended up working 56 days. "James McAvoy is such a beautiful man, and for him to allow us to glue hair to his body like that, day in and day out, shows his commitment and good humor. Tumnus was such a good character. Really fun." Working on McAvoy's makeup, Tami also discovered a secret weapon.

"Silicone wasn't a thing back then, it was just starting to evolve, so we used gelatin appliances to have translucency. It was hot in the sun, so with sweating and condensation we were having problems with corners lifting. To compound the problem, James had a cold. So, he had this prosthetic nose tip, snot and sweat eating away at the piece on the oiliest part of the skin. I had to think, 'Oh my God. What can I do?' I ran back to the trailer and I microwaved some gelatin in a CC cup. With a metal spatula, I went in and I lifted the corners of the nostrils and put in this goop. There's nothing stickier than liquidy gelatin. I just pressed it in and then took a powder puff with powder on it and kind of mushed it in until it set. The powder puff gave it some texture. That thing didn't move the rest of the day. I still use this trick for patching foam or even silicone; you just have to be sure you don't burn the actor."

Chronicles of Narnia: The Lion, the Witch, and the Wardrobe (2005)
Tami working on Mr. Tumnus   Used with Permission of Tami Lane

In 2006, Tami and Berger shared the honor of winning the Academy Award for *Best Achievement in Makeup & Hairstyling* for their work on **The Chronicles of Narnia: The Lion, the Witch and the Wardrobe**. Tami went on to work with Berger on the full **Narnia** trilogy, **The Chronicles of Narnia: Prince Caspian** (2008), and **The Chronicles of Narnia: The Voyage of the Dawn Treader** (2010).

Friends Step in Again

Having returned to Los Angeles in 2006, Tami spent the next five years working on various projects as a makeup artist, prosthetic makeup artist, key prosthetic makeup artist, and prosthetics supervisor for films such as: **The Hills Have Eyes II** (2007), **The Final Destination** (2009), **Surrogates** (2009), **Splice** (2009), **Edge of Darkness** (2010), **Don't Be Afraid of the Dark** (2010), **Water for Elephants** (2011), and **Fright Night** (2011).

In 2011, she was lined up to work with Berger on two films, **Oz the Great and Powerful** and **Hitchcock**, when she received a call on Thanksgiving, "How would you like to come home and be the prosthetics supervisor on **The Hobbit**?"

Tami, Howard Berger & Oscar   Used with Permission of Tami Lane

"They called me on Thanksgiving. I'm lined up to do these shows with Howard that I really wanted to do. I said, 'Can I have 24 hours to think about this?' Then I called Howard, 'This is a big decision.' He said, 'What do you mean it's a big decision, stupid? You're going to go do **The Hobbit**. That's the prosthetic supervising job on the biggest prosthetics show ever made to this date.' Then he said, 'No, you're fired. Consider yourself not on **Oz** or **Hitchcock**, you're fired. Go.' He finished with, 'Even if you stay, you're stupid and I don't hire stupid people.' He gave me no choice. I called **The Hobbit** people the next day and accepted the job. I was on a plane two weeks later."

The Hobbit, the New Trilogy

When Tami arrived in New Zealand, the Weta crew,

which included 30 concept artists and ten sculptors, had done all the concept work. Tami's contribution to the process was to talk with the sculptors and lend her technical and practical knowledge of application. "Things like recommending the blend would be better here, or adjusting the shape of noses, or suggesting what material would work best for the appliances, foam, gelatin, or silicone. The sculptors need to know these details because it makes a difference to the sculpts. With some materials, you need more of an edge, some less. Then my crew and I did all the test makeups."

Tami ran into a major hurdle when it came time to test the makeups because the production was using a new technology, the Red Camera. "We were shooting 48 frames with the Red Camera in 3D. It was basically seeing stuff that the human eye can't see. It was doing

Water For Elephants (2011)   Used with Permission of Tami Lane

weird things. Our first camera tests were with all our dwarfs, who looked great leaving the trailer. My photographs all looked great. When I went to rushes the next day, I thought I was going to get fired because the prosthetics were throwing yellow. All the reds were drained out. I'm thinking, 'Oh my God, we have to fix this somehow.' It wasn't just the prosthetics. It was screwing with the costume colors, the set colors, any color. But the faces especially, these guys looked jaundiced. It was horrible. So, I started experimenting. Katherine Brown, my key, and I started thinking, 'We're going to have to put the red back into it.' We had to over-redden the pieces. In some behind-the-scenes pictures they look really sunburned in their appliances."

To make matters worse, Tami found that there were various degrees of redness for which she had to compensate. Eventually, she started having all the appliances, foam and silicone, run pinker than usual. Once the makeup color was determined, she and her team painted masters that were glued to vacuform faces to use as references for how red the artists needed to go with the makeups.

In the end the problems were solved, and in 2013 Tami was nominated for an Oscar along with Peter King and Rick Findlater for their work on ***The Hobbit.*** She didn't win that year, and neither did her buddy Berger, who was also nominated for ***Hitchcock***. With a laugh she says, "When we're nominated individually, we don't win. So, we need to work together and be nominated together to have better chance at winning."

Tami went on to work on the other two ***Hobbit*** films, ***The Desolation of Smaug*** (2013), and ***The Battle of the Five Armies*** (2014), as well as ***Ted 2*** (2015), ***Concussion*** (2015), and ***The Shallows*** (2016).

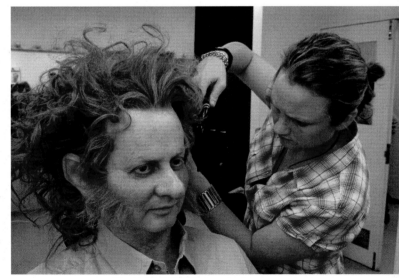

The Hobbit (2012)   Used with Permission of Tami Lane

Finding Her Niche

Tami's niche is her expertise in executing prosthetic makeups. Usually, "the ball is already rolling when I get pulled in for ideas on materials. Should this be a 3D transfer, or should this be a silicone piece, or should we use foam? Technical aspects like that. Sometimes they're working on computers so I can advise on what will happen when it's live on-set. Some of the greatest sculptors in the business are not makeup artists. I can't do what those guys do. But as far as putting it on, that's my expertise. I can ask a lot of the sculptors to make slight changes to help me on-set, but not create a different look. It's a teamwork effort. The biggest part of my job, the most gratifying part, is to take what a designer or a sculptor has done and put it on the screen. I want them to look at their work and be happy about it. That's my goal. I just want those guys that live with it much longer than I do, to look at it and say, 'Yep, that's exactly what I wanted it to look like.'"

Concussion (2015) Tami with Albert Brooks
Used with Permission of Tami Lane

What's Next?

Looking toward the future, Tami would like to do more character, likeness, and old-age makeups. She had particular success transforming Albert Brooks into his character for *Concussion* which involved putting him into a silicone bald cap that had been hand-punched with hair (Brooks has a full head of hair that he preferred not to shave for the role). Tami helped Brooks realize the character by convincingly applying and blending the appliances and by incorporating a special wig that blended into his hair and eyebrows. Brooks had been worried the makeup would look fake.

"He paid me the biggest compliment afterwards. We're standing at baggage claim in LAX and he basically said, 'You know what, Tami? I would love to do this again with you. You can do anything to my face, and I don't need to shave my head or whatever. You proved to me that with makeup you can do anything.' I'm waiting on that phone call, Albert. Let's go do something."

CODA: *Molto Vivace*

"I asked Howard a while ago, 'Why would you hire somebody like me that didn't know anything about what you do?' I didn't know who he was. I didn't even know who Dick Smith was at the time. Howard said, 'I hired you because you're enthusiastic. You know, anybody can learn anything as long as they have the right attitude. You were eager and enthusiastic, that's why I hired you.'"

With her honey-hued, leonine mane of hair, her quick smile and even quicker laugh, saying Tami is highly motivated is an understatement. From being a high achiever in high school sports and band, to a full-ride scholar in university, to a successful prosthetic makeup artist, she pursues every endeavor with gusto. In Tami's life, there have been many coaches on and off the playing field - family, friends, colleagues, and mentors - all who engender her trust and loyalty. As a team player, she knows when to listen to the coach, step up to the plate, and swing for the fence.

OUTTAKES:

On Directors:

"What do I like in a director? Decisiveness, consideration, and humor are the top three things."

"Decisive. Decisiveness. There's too many directors that are, 'Oh, um, I don't know. Just keep going, I'll know it when I see it.' It's also a complete waste of time if you can't...you have no direction."

"That he - or she - treats the crew with consideration. Not just, 'Me, me, me. I, I, I. I want this, I want this. I'm going to shoot for 15 hours without consideration for anything.'"

On the Boys' Club:

"I talk a lot about the boys' club. It exists. You just have to ignore it and do the work. The guy next to you might be better. You can't say, 'You're doing that makeup because you're a guy, and I'm doing this because I'm a girl.'"

"You know what? You have to be better or you just ignore the fact that they're men and they might be getting paid a little more than you. They might be, but you just keep working."

"What's my best advice? I say ignore the boys club...and learn practical jokes."

On Women in the Shop:

"When I started, it was me and another girl in the shop who weren't working the front office. The other girl, her name was Rachel, did all the sewing of the spandex suits and under things like gloves. She was a seamstress basically. Then we had Beth Hathaway, an amazing creature puppet-maker, and then there was Deborah Galvez. They had the first female sculptor in the shop, her name was Lori. We called her Lori Pie. I was like, 'A female sculptor?' At the time, you didn't see female sculptors, ever, in any shop. I also met Cristina Patterson, who does contact lenses. She's probably one of best lens painters in the business. Now she has her own company, Eye Ink FX."

On the Girls' Club:

"I do a lot of speaking. When I was on my latest show, ***The Shallows*** (2016), I was in the Gold Coast Down Under. IMATS was happening in Sydney and it happened to be my only two-day weekend. Michael Key calls me up and he goes, 'Hey, you're in Australia.' I said, 'Yeah, but I'm not in Sydney.' He went, 'All right, I'm emailing you. Here's your flight. Here's your hotel. You're coming down to Sydney for IMATS for the weekend.' I thought, 'That's nice of you, thanks.' He said, 'You're talking at 11:00 on Saturday.' I went, 'No, no, no. What?' He said, 'You didn't think I was going to bring you down here and you not do anything.' 'I thought you wanted just to have dinner. You have a successful magazine, come on.' He went, 'Oh no, you're going to work.' I said, 'I don't have a demo. I'm not prepared. I've been so busy.' I'd been on Lord Howe Island which is the most remote island in Australia. No WiFi, no cell phone, no nothing.

"But I went down there for the Saturday morning 11:00 slot. I figured maybe a dozen people might show up. I didn't sweat it. I'd just flown in that morning and went straight to the center near Fox Studios. I walk in and da-da-da, I'm behind the curtain and Michael Key gives me this incredible introduction. I come out onto the stage and it is, I shit you not, every seat filled. Standing room all on the sides, all in back. I don't even know, there were probably 200 people there, all girls, maybe a few men.

"I got a little choked up, I was just so blown away. Michael says, 'Don't worry, it's just an interview. We're just going to discuss what you've been doing lately. People want to hear about that.' I couldn't believe it when I saw a sea of women out there. They'd only just announced I'd be there two days before. It wasn't even in the program. And here are all these women, in ages ranging between 15 and 30, and some old friends that I worked with on *Narnia,* all just sitting out there.

"After the interview, a couple of girls came up and wanted to meet me and say thank you. That was nice. Then this one girl came up, she was super shy and her mother was with her. Her mother said, 'Well, go on,' to her daughter. I think her name was Jasmine, she was literally shaking. Her mother finally says, 'All right fine, I'll talk to her. My daughter follows your career and wants to do what you do. She's very shy, obviously. Well, when we saw you were talking and you were actually in Australia and we saw that you were doing this, we flew in from Melbourne.' Her daughter was 16. I just thought that was amazing for that mother to buy those plane tickets, get a hotel room at the last minute, and then come up just to see me. That was mind blowing. There's something happening right now."

On Sometimes It's All About a Nose...and a Helicopter:

"There was a situation on *Prince Caspian* where Trumpkin is tied up in a boat and they throw him overboard into the water. I was in charge of Peter Dinklage's makeup. His regular nose was gelatin, so for the scene in the boat, I said, 'Well, we can't use his gelatin nose [gelatin melts in water], we'll have to use a foam one.' I put a foam nose on him while he's beat up and whatever. He gets tossed in, like five or six times. Then, I said, and I had stated this up front when planning for the day's shooting, 'This is a foam nose, not a close-up nose. Don't shoot his close-up until after lunch.' But nobody listens to the makeup artist.

Chronicles of Narnia: Prince Caspian (2008)
Tami working on Trumpkin (Peter Dinklage)
Used with Permission of Tami Lane

"As soon as they got him to the shore, they wanted to pop in and shoot the close-up. I say, 'Andrew, he's wearing a foam nose. I need to switch that nose out and put his real nose on.' He says, 'How much time?' I said, 'Give me 20 minutes.' Basically, I called back to base camp, which for this location meant we had to be helicoptered in. In other words, our base camp is a ten-minute helicopter ride away. I call back to somebody in the trailer. I say, 'Can you pull a gelatin Trumpkin nose for me and give it to a pilot and get it over here as fast as possible?' We peeled off Trumpkin's nose and I cleaned it with alcohol, which is horrible around the nose area. Peter, he's a trooper. Yeah, within 20 minutes I had the nose flown in, the foam nose popped off, new gelatin nose on, painted it up, and the close-up got shot.

"We literally had a nose choppered in to set on a beach. That's one of my favorite stories."

One last story ...

"I did a short film for these two guys last year (2015). I had to take a woman who was about 45 years old and age her to 65, and then age her to 95. It was a short film and it was all their own money, so it was catch as catch can, when actors were available, the DOP, and all that stuff. It kind of sat in the background for a long time, for over a year. I worked on the sculptures for those two makeups and blocked them out.

"Then all of a sudden, they called me up, and they're like, 'Okay, everybody's available.' This is January

4th, 2015. 'All right, we have everybody ready. Actors, DOP. We have the locations. Everything. February 9th.' Jesus. I'm working on *Ted 2*. I'm like, 'I'm working full-time and I don't have time to finish the sculpts and do the lab work.' I had a little studio in the house I was living in.

"I called up my good buddy, Jason Collins. He runs Autonomous F/X, Inc. and it's just around the corner. I was living in Van Nuys. He was so good. I said, 'I have this amount of money. Give me an estimate.' He hired a sculptor to finish the sculpts. I went in and cut them where I wanted to cut them. They floated them. They did everything. They did all the lab. I went and got two wigs, John Blake wigs at Nigel's. I cut them and I styled them. It was something I did at night.

"Jason, I don't know how he did it, but he and his shop, Autonomous F/X, were able to do two age make-ups, five days for the 65, and three days for the 95. He gave me all my pieces so I could pre-paint, hair punch the eyebrows, two days before we started filming. It was just an incredible amount of work. I'm not saying it's the best age makeup in the world because it's not, but it was just...I had to pull in some help for application. Howard donated hands for me. We used the Rachel Weisz hands from *Oz Great and Powerful*.

"It was amazing and this actress just really sold the makeup. I pulled in favors...Dominie Till helped me on the 65-year-old makeup, and Vivian Baker assisted me on the 95-year-old, and it was just crazy. These directors, these up-and-coming guys, were totally blown away because the makeup is a huge part of the short film.

"Yeah, so I really got into that. Now, I want to do more of these age and character type makeups."

Catching Up!

We interviewed Tami on February 5, 2016. Since then, she has worked on

Patriots Day
Key make up artist working with Howard Berger, Directed by Peter Berg.

The Wall
Make up and Hair Designer, Directed by, Doug Liman
The film shot 14 days in the desert, she created tattoos, prosthetics, and blood gags.

The Exorcist
(TV Series for Fox)
Key Make up and SFX Artist working with Tracey Anderson.

The Orville
(TV Series for Fox created by Seth MacFarlane)
Key Make up Artist, Personal artist to Seth MacFarlane, working with Howard Berger.

For more of Tami's credits, visit: www.imdb.com

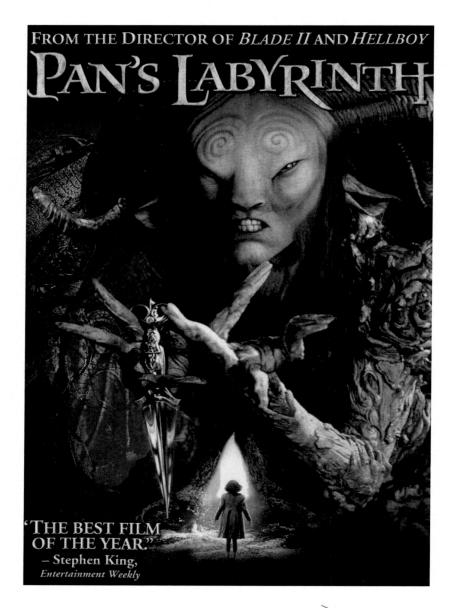

PAN'S LABYRINTH (EL LABERINTO DEL FAUNO) (2006)
Licensed from AF archive / Alamy Stock Photo

 Montse Ribé

When people see our work I expect it to be realistic and believable;

I don't want people to think, 'Oh. It's a makeup.'

I want them to see it as a real thing;

I want the prosthetic to disappear, no?

The last time we saw Montse was in London at the International Makeup Artists Trade Show (IMATS) in June 2016. She was sitting in a makeup chair undergoing a full makeup transformation complete with full face and cowl prosthetics. If we didn't know it was Montse, we wouldn't have recognized her. Montse is petite, Puck-like with a pixie haircut, laughing eyes, ever-gesticulating hands, and a charming, infectious laugh. With the prosthetics on, she was a balding man of 65 or so with a permanent grimace that spanned her jaw line. Why did Montse subject herself to this grueling process? Six hours of makeup, one hour to walk around showing it off, photos, then off it came. Why? "Because it's good to be on the other side."

This Barcelona native has built a career that spans several languages and continents. Although she is a native Spanish speaker, she communicates beautifully in English. She laughingly asked us to change the verb tenses and some word choices in her quotes for clearer understanding. "If not, they will say… 'What?'"

As a child, Montse was always drawing and sculpting in her father's studio at the top of the house. "I was living in a fantasy world, always imagining little creatures sitting there. I was not happy just to see the creatures on paper, I really wanted to see them in three-dimensions so I could talk with them. I wanted to see them alive."

Montse's father designed and made wood furniture, then switched to designing and making lamps which he sold out of his shop. Her mother still helps her father at home and at the shop, while Montse's sister

Montse in makeup by Nacho Diaz, IMATS London (2016)
Used with Courtesy of David Marti Mayor

is a history buff and insatiable world traveler. "My father, I think he has an artist's soul, but when you have to work, you have to leave a little aside."

They're Alive!

When Montse was a child, she watched Jim Henson and Frank Oz's *The Muppet Movie* (1979). When she saw *Star Wars: The Empire Strikes Back* (1980), she was enamored with Yoda. When she was ten (1982) she saw *E.T. The Extra-Terrestrial* and *The Dark Crystal*; when she was twelve, she saw *Gremlins;* and when she was fourteen, *Labyrinth*. All these films have a common thread: "[The creatures] have soul. I love the characters that have personalities; they're not just bad and die. They have a life. Yoda was perfect; he was a mystic, like the Dali Lama. I knew I would like to do something like this with creatures that have personalities. I see them and it's like I love them. I knew I wanted to do something like creating these creatures."

Montse's grandmother encouraged the family love for fantasy when one Christmas Montse received a copy of *Faeries,* written and illustrated by Brian Froud and Allen Lee, and her sister received *Gnomes* by Wil Huygen, illustrated by Rien Poortvliet. "When I saw the fairy book it was to me a bible of creatures because the creatures are brought into your reality. At the end of the book, there are pictures of little creatures in the forest, proof they are real."

Anime Kept Her Working

Montse knew she wanted to pursue an artistic life, and what she knew was drawing. So, daily after school, she went to drawing classes and continued to draw at home in her father's studio. Her parents encouraged her to take a degree in fine arts, thereby melding her drawing talents with art history in order to pave the way to a stable teaching position. "My parents are pretty traditional, and in Spain, at the time, there were not many places to learn special effects." One day she saw an ad for Mascaro School, a school that specialized in teaching cartooning and visual special effects. Montse was intrigued, so she went to night school to finish her high school degree and studied cartooning during the day. "It turns out we learned cartooning but not special effects." However, because of her training at Mascaro, Montse landed her first job at nineteen as a cartoonist with D'Ocon, which produced a television series in Spain. "I hardly drew anything. They gave us a storyboard and we had to look at the past chapters to find images that were similar. Okay, in chapter one there's this shot that could fit here. If you couldn't find anything, then okay, you'd have to draw it."

But Montse wasn't being creatively challenged. When a friend started a business making anime trading cards, Montse finally started drawing for a living. She kept her job at D'Ocon, and after work she drew trading cards for a series similar to *Mazinger Z*, a Japanese super robot manga series. "I was drawing hours and hours…I did twenty-four hours a day working at one place and then the other." The days were long, but at least she was drawing.

Screamin'

In a tapas bar one evening, Montse shared her frustrations with some friends: she was creatively stymied, reproducing others' designs and filling in storyboards with existing, unoriginal artwork. She felt she wasn't actually creating anything herself. When pressed, Montse told her friends she'd like to learn how to bring her two-dimensional drawings into three-dimensional characters, like in the movies. Coincidently, these friends knew David Martì who ran a school called Screamin' that taught special effects for film.

David Martì has been a film and special effects buff all his life: watching films, reading **Fangoria Magazine**, and studying famous pictures of special effects. But in the late 1980s and 1990s there were no training opportunities available in Spain. So David signed up for the *Dick Smith Basic 3-D Makeup Correspondence Course.* He completed the projects and mailed the photos to Dick Smith, who, in turn, would critique his work. David didn't speak English at the time, so it was a challenge for both David and Dick Smith to ensure they were communicating productively. Once the course was complete, David wanted to provide a similar opportunity for other Spanish artists to learn these techniques, so he opened a school, Screamin'. Montse remembers beautiful things about the school. "They were too good at teaching. They didn't care about money. For example, if you pay for a month to make a course and didn't finish, they kept you going until you did finish. Maybe you were there for one year."

Montse & David   Screamin' (2016)
Used with Permission of Gary Christensen

In addition to Screamin', David was one of three partners in DDT SFX, a special effects workshop that had a lively commercial base. While Montse was taking courses at Screamin' she also "started helping them [at the shop] and finally I didn't finish the course because I was working and learning more in the workshop." Eventually, there was so much work for DDT SFX that when one of the original partners quit, David and the remaining partner realized they were taking on too much, and closed the school.

The first six years Montse was with DDT, they worked exclusively on commercials. Eventually, the second original partner also moved on and Montse filled the spot. In 1998, Montse joined David as a 40% partner in the business. To further complicate matters, David and Montse had become romantically involved in what would become a twenty-one year relationship. "Some people say, 'How can you work twenty-four hours together?' For us it wasn't hard. Two years ago we decide…we love each other a lot, but not as a couple." As of this writing, Montse and David continue to be business partners. "It was hard, but now it's okay. Now we are very good."

No Shortcuts

"David is my teacher. He taught me everything about special effects. Mostly, I learned I must practice, practice, practice. We learned together that doing things at home and watching videos and studying pictures and trying to duplicate images through practice, practice, practice, made our work better."

It's not unusual for Montse and David to spend twelve to fifteen hours a day in the shop, even today, after more than twenty years in business. "At the beginning I was a little bit crazy. I was working night and day and it didn't matter. I enjoyed it. We have students come into the shop and who say, 'Oh, special effects are my life. I will do anything.' And they pull an all-nighter and it's not so easy. It's not that I don't want people to sleep, it's something that happens. You do it because you are enjoying it, you love it. But now, I'm older and I need more relax, *jeje.*"

"Students go to school and it seems they want somebody to teach them, but they don't do anything on their own. They are much too comfortable. They're not doing the work, not putting the time in. I think it's because society says you have to get everything quickly. Get famous quickly without going through the steps. No, you have to work to get things done. It's like the mother bird that brings food to the babies already chewed up. It makes me sad because if you don't have a passion and you don't want to work for it, you can't expect it to be handed to you."

Growing Pains

In 1994, DDT did the special effects for their first film, a short, **Aftermath**. A year later they did **Atolladero (Quagmire)**, then another short, **Dr. Curry** in 1997, then a second full-length film, **Los Sin Nombre**, in 1998. Up to this point, "we were doing mostly commercials, but we wanted to do film." Then a group of young directors and Brian Yuzna formed a Spanish production company called Filmax that produced fantasy and horror films using international directors like Stuart Gordon for **Dagon** (2001) and Jack Sholder for **Arachnid** (2001). Fantastic Factory (a label under the Filmax umbrella) provided DDT with lots of work and experience in the film industry. "When they started to call, we didn't say no. We were beginning and we had to demonstrate what we could do, so we said yes to everything. We worked every day for two or three years, Monday to Sunday. I came into the workshop and didn't know when I would be leaving. It was horrible. We were completely exhausted, but we were young and determined to do it. But you can't work like that forever."

In 2000, DDT did the special effects for seven films. Seven! **Arachnid, La Comunidad, El Espinazo del Diablo, Lucia y el Sexo, Torrente 2, Desaliñada,** and **Dagon.** What began as a small commercial shop had finally burst into the film industry with a passion.

Growing Up

As DDT grew and the work evolved, they moved into a new, larger space that covers the fourth floor of an industrial building in Barcelona. The ceilings are 25 feet high with a large central creature-making room, a sculpting room, a mold-making room, an office, a studio, a museum, and from the ceilings hang large effects: a giant's foot made from tree limbs, a whale skeleton, a monster head. But most obviously, there are the windows. "We chose a workshop with daylight because when you're working you go inside, then it's night, and you don't know what happened. The light is dead and I don't like that. We were very concerned about working in a place where we felt comfortable, where we can see the sun rise and set, whether it is day or night."

Santi cracked face makeup for **Devil's Backbone** (2001)
Used Courtesy of DDT/SFX

"Now we have a nice team. Everybody's happy, but it came year-by-year, trying to get better. During the hardest time people came and left, 'I can't do that; we can't work like this.' It was super hard. We knew we couldn't work that way forever." As of this writing, DDT is the premiere special effects shop in Spain.

The Bull

In 1995, director Nacho Cerdá entered his short film, **Aftermath**, in the International Fantastic Film Festival of Catalonia in Stigas, Spain. Also in attendance for his feature film, **Cronos**, was Guillermo del Toro. "When the **Aftermath** finished and the credits rolled, Guillermo stood up and screamed, 'Where is DDT? Where is DDT?' Cerdá and David looked at each other, wondering if they should hold up their hands or run out the door. They introduced themselves to Guillermo and he said, 'Wow, the corpses are incredible. I like your work a lot. The next time I come to Spain to shoot a movie, I will call you.'" Six years later he called.

Montse and David's first film for del Toro was **El Espinazo del Diablo (Devil's Backbone)** (2001), a story about a 12-year-old orphan boy who discovers the orphanage is haunted. They created a young boy ghost whose skin was like cracked porcelain. "I think it was a very elegant makeup." Following **Devil's Backbone,** DDT did effects for three more del Toro films: Oscar winner **El Laberinto del Fauno (Pan's Labyrinth)** (2005-2006), **Hellboy II: The Golden Army** (2007), and **Crimson Peak** (2015).

It was at del Toro's request that Montse made her first foray into costume acting. "Guillermo asked me to be behind the makeup for Young Hellboy in **Hellboy II: The Golden Army** because he needed someone small. I'm not an actress; I'm a super-bad actress in fact. When I came on-set, I was in makeup and John Hurt, who played the father, didn't recognize me (he knew me from **Hellboy**). We were waiting to start and I asked John, 'Do you know what we have to do?' But someone called, 'Action,' and we started our lines. I was very nervous, but finally it was fun and Guillermo was happy."

From the Inside

Probably the most significant byproduct of the Young Hellboy experience was Montse's immersion in the makeup and
its removal. "We always say to the actors, 'Don't pull it off.
We have to go very carefully.' Even if it doesn't hurt, the
skin, it could be damaged. I'm very patient, but one night
I couldn't stand it. 'We have only three hours to sleep. We
have to remove it!' So I pulled a little bit, and I gave myself
a little wound, so I validated my advice to actors. It's good
to be on the other side. I would do it again, but maybe I
say that because it was only one week of shooting."

A year later, director Joann Sfar needed an actor inside
the character *La Gueule, enfant* in the film **Gainsbourg: La
Vie Heroique (Gainsbourg: The Heroic Life)**. *La Gueule,
enfant* was a large potato-like character with tiny arms
dangling from a large, rotund body. To keep everything
in scale, Sfar needed an actor with shorter legs and small
feet: enter Montse. There were no lines and the shoot was
short, but Montse was willing to step into the character,
creating for herself a new perspective from the other side.

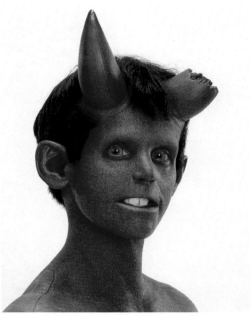

Montse as Young Hellboy *Hellboy II* (2007)
Used with Courtesy of Guillermo Del Toro

The Faun

"Pan's Labyrinth, it's good and bad. We learned a lot. We
love the characters we did…and we were very happy we had the chance to do something fantastic."

The Design

Del Toro approached DDT with the script and a clear idea of the characters he wanted them to create: Pan and Pale Man. But, of course, things evolved and changed. "The Pan, at the beginning, was a boy, a small boy. Now it's more like a human with goat legs. Then because he lives in the forest, it changed again." Then money became an issue. Half-way through pre-production, they were out of money; they'd spent their budget. Del Toro "is a very sweet guy, a friend to us, but he's passionate to have it all. For him it's like toys. He would love to have as many creatures as he can, no? So he pushes a lot to have as many things as possible with less money…we didn't know how to finish. We had to finish a movie and we didn't have any more money." The solution? Montse and David spent their salaries to make the effects for the film. They worked for three and a half months for free so the film could have the special effects it needed and del Toro wanted.

PAN'S LABYRINTH (2006) IVANA BAQUERO, DOUG JONES GUILLERMO DEL TORO (DIR)
MOVIESTORE COLLECTION LTD
Licensed from Moviestore collection Ltd / Alamy Stock Photo

Pan's Labyrinth (2005)
Licensed from Moviestore collection Ltd / Alamy Stock Photo

The Pale Man was another challenging metamorphosis. Originally, del Toro wanted a creature that transformed into a horse-like character with four legs that could run. "'No, no, no,' we said to Guillermo. 'There's no time. There's no money.' Then he came up with this idea of a more simple character. It's just the character and nothing else. I think sometimes when you don't have money, it's when better ideas come. I think he is a more iconic character because he's more simple."

The Reveal

"This was the nicest experience in showing a makeup we ever had." They were shooting on a hilltop with the makeup tent in the valley below. Montse and David walked out of the tent dwarfed by Doug Jones in the seven-foot-tall Pan suit, and slowly made their way up the hill to del Toro. "Usually when you do a makeup you show it to the director and the rest of the people and they react with 'Oh wow,' 'That's cool,' or whatever. But as we walked up the hill through the forest, there was silence. The entire crew was in two lines, we walked between them and Guillermo was at the end of the line, waiting…complete silence. David and I whispered to each other, 'They don't like it. What happened?' Guillermo stopped, looked, walked over to Pan, then he smiled, hugged Doug Jones, and said, 'I love it.' And the people started to clap. There're no words. It was fantastic. One of the few times I've seen Guillermo really touched. I think that was the most weird and nicest response to a makeup we ever had."

The Costume Actor

Montse is quick to point out that Doug Jones, who played both the Pan and the Pale Man, "is very intense and very talented." As a former contortionist, Jones is known for roles in fantasy and horror genres in which he wears heavy prosthetics, and for him "acting is a full body experience." (Topel, Fred. "*Fantastic Four 2*: Doug Jones: Doug Jones talks sequels, *Fantastic Four* and *Hellboy*." *Crave Online*, June 15, 2007)

There were particular challenges to playing Pan, such as balance (with the stilts, he was seven feet tall), vision (the eyes of the mask were wide-spaced so he could only see through the tear ducts), and hearing (the mask covered his ears, and the mechanics inside the headpiece that controlled the ears and eyebrows were constantly buzzing). And yet this actor succeeded in creating a realistic, believable character despite the challenges.

Jones has now done four films with DDT: *Hellboy II: The Golden Army*, *Gainsbourg: La Vie Heroique*, *Pan's Labyrinth*, and *Crimson Peak*. DDT requested him specifically for *Gainsbourg* because he had a history working with them and in their creations. "We choose a song for each movie, and at the end of the shoot we sing that song to mark the end of the shoot. It's a nice, and a funny good memory. Doug Jones is very theatrical."

Crimson Peak (2016)
Montse & David with Doug Jones as Lady Sharpe
Used with Courtesy of DDT/SFX

The Lessons

First and foremost, Montse and David were terribly unhappy that they had spent their budget so early in the process. The biggest lesson they took away from the experience was the importance of submitting a budget that is realistic and sticking to it as much as possible. "David and me suffered a lot." Secondarily, their team was evenly split between veteran and novice technicians, which unfortunately impacted the workload. "What we learned is you can have novices, but you must have a good balance between experienced technicians and novices. Actually, there should be more trained technicians who know how to do the work. Some technicians after the movie said, 'Okay. I quit. I don't want to do makeup effects anymore.' We were not happy. All the people we burned. We made them work more than they could, and we are not proud of that. But we learned a lot of how to organize things and not go down on the budget. Things we have used ever since. Of course, you learn more each time you work. It's like before and after, you know?"

Montse & David at the Oscars (2007)
Used with Courtesy of DDT/SFX

Pre-Oscar

Prior to the Academy Awards, *Pan's Labyrinth* won several prestigious awards in the makeup/special effects category: Online Film and Television Association Awards for *Best Makeup and Hairstyling* as well as *Best Visual Effects*; Ariel Awards, Mexico, for *Best Special Effects*; Goya Awards, Spain, for *Best Special Effects*. Then Academy Awards week arrived. "The production company and distributors treated us really well…we flew to LA first class, stayed in beautiful hotels, and David said, 'We are staying in the best hotels and surrounded by famous people and we have no money in the bank.' It was weird, super weird, and it was painful, but," she laughed, "we won the Oscar." They had a little trouble with TSA getting the statues on the airplane in their carry-ons, but logic prevailed and their statues now sit proudly in the DDT office in Barcelona.

Post-Oscar

"The Oscar changed the way producers talk to us; they respect us more." But immediately following the awards, their phone stopped ringing. Producers thought they'd moved to LA, or were more expensive, or had changed. Production companies didn't call with projects and after three missed opportunities, "David finally said, 'I'm going to call them' and things returned to normal. I think it's called the Oscar Curse because we heard this happens to a lot of people. After that, you have to keep working as always."

Montse Ribé does it all. She sculpts and makes molds and applies prosthetics and paints them. She is devoted to her work and her company and her business partner. She is candid, humble, and charming, bringing her European sensibilities to a Hollywood-driven field. When all is said and done, the young girl who drew in her father's study is finally able to bring her characters to life.

OUTTAKES:

On Meeting Mentors:

In 1997, Montse and David went to the US to attend the first International Makeup Artist Trade Show (IMATS) in Los Angeles. It was a whirlwind trip that included a visit to their mentor, Dick Smith. "We went to New York first to meet Dick Smith because he was living in Connecticut. We call him the Yoda of Special Effects. I make little sculptures, little figures, and I made one of Dick Smith to give to him, but it wasn't finished when we were in New York, so I gave it to him at IMATS. But he was so busy surrounded by lots of people, that he couldn't tell me anything. Some days later, we went to Rick Baker's workshop and Dick was there, by chance, and he first saw David, then asked for me. 'Where's Montse? Montse! I love so much your little sculpture. It's like the best little Dick Smith.' Awww, I was melting. He was really nice! And I remember him with lots of love."

"Rick Baker was really nice to us as well. I remember Rick Baker has a very nice sense of humor. He said, 'I'm waiting for my little Rick Baker.'"

"One movie that really influenced me was **Amadeus** with the makeup by Dick Smith. I was a child and didn't understand how a man could become older in one movie."

On Techniques and Skills:

"I'm very intuitive, I'm not very methodical. I'm a little bit of a disaster. Sometimes I try this, next time I try that. I really like it when I discover things, like when I'm sculpting with brushes, metal brushes. It's super quick and good for smoothing and for making textures, things you don't think about."

"There are some makeups that change when you put them on, they don't come alive until you put them on a face."

"I think you have to have a lot of illusion first. One thing is technique, which you can learn, you can practice, but I think a person has to have passion and illusion to do this job."

"It's important to be a perfectionist and to know you always have something to learn. Don't think 'Okay, I know everything.' You can still learn. You have to be happy with what you do, but you always have to think that you could do it better."

"I love sculpting, but I don't feel like I'm a sculptor because I didn't go to school for classical training. I just practice, practice, practice."

On Interesting Projects:

Montse : The Spanish director, Pedro Almodóvar, hired us to do the special effects for **Talk to Her**. This director is charming crazy. He asked us to do a big pussy.

Pat: Yeah? Like a cat? No?

M: No, no (pointing to her lap). Pussy, like a…

P: Oh. Okay. All right then. All right.

M: A big one.

P: A big one? Yay.

M: Yeah. It was six meters [18 feet] tall.

P: Oh my God!

M: By four meters [12 feet] wide.

P: Oh my God!

M: It was super. What I like about this job is that you get a range of things from a little makeup to a giant pussy. That's what I like. In the movie a guy had to walk into it, that's why it was so big

P: That's big.

M: We had to rent a workshop to build it in. I remember when we moved it we had a big truck come and pick it up. Because it was silicone, to protect it, we covered it only with see-through plastic. We were so concentrated on the work, we didn't think about what it looked like. People in cars stopped and looked twice. People on the street stopped working to look at the truck with the big pussy on it. It was very funny.

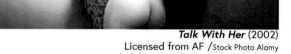

Talk With Her (2002)
Licensed from AF /Stock Photo Alamy

Catching Up!

We interviewed Montse on May 10, 2016. Since then she has been working on

El Faro De Las Orcas
Supervisor and technician for an animatronic orca

Museum Exhibition
'Guillermo del Toro: At Home with Monsters'
Supervisor and technician
Guillermo del Toro figures: Faun, Pale Man and Santi

Ella Es Tu Padre - Avelina
Supervisor and technician
Prosthetic make up transformation of a male actor into a female character

For more of Montse's Credit, visit: www.imdb.com

Leading Ladies Speak Out

MAKING A CAREER

LYNN

"This is a tough business and you're competing with a lot of people. You have to know how to talk to actors, people who have egos, people that scream and yell. You can't gasp. You have to have confidence."

'You have to be able to promote yourself. You have to be a photographer to take the continuity pictures and keep a continuity book. You have to do a little bit of everything. If you can't do that, if you just want to do makeup, maybe go into bridal makeup. There your focus is on making a bride and her party happy."

TAMI

"Richard Taylor gave me some of the best advice. He says, 'A good career is not only based on the jobs you do take, it's also based on the jobs you don't take.' I've always remembered that."

JULIE

"Go to the theater. Get your wig experience. Maybe do your haircutting. Do a private makeup course. The more you can do, the bigger chance you have of getting a step up the ladder."

ROBIN

"The most important thing to figure out is what type of makeup artist you want to be. Everybody is seduced by the glamour of film and Television but you have to remember the hours and the travel. Don't expect to have any other type of life."

"Networking is really, really important. It's not something that's my favorite thing to do, but it's important to constantly keep up your networking."

BARI

"Study drawing. Study the anatomy. Understand how the muscles work. Do self-portraits. You don't have to spend a lot of money, put a mirror in front of yourself, study its effects, train your eye to see, and see more every day."

MICHÈLE

"Emerging Artists have to be able to learn how to network and how to make cold calls and try to open doors that are closed. Call up photographers. Call up commercial houses. Find out what films are coming into town, low budget films, anything, and do whatever work they can do. It's not an easy journey, not in the beginning, that's for sure."

"Start collecting pictures of your work and start doing the work, because you've got to do the work, and start getting a portfolio together, a great portfolio, and really show your work. Then, start calling up people and saying, 'Can I come and show you my work?'"

JENNY

"I would say look at everything until you see it. Observe everything. Take in as much as you can. Of course, that comes with age, with time, with development."

LESLEY

"I always try to impress upon newcomers that it's not going to be two years of your life because that's what they expect. They expect to be doing what I'm doing in two years. I'm, 'No, no, no. It'll be 10-15 years minimum just to get to run a small budget film.' They'll say, 'What? Are you kidding me? I'm 20-something years old.' 'You're probably not going to head a department until you're 35-40. It's a long hill in front of you. Understand that.'"

"My best advice I can give is to also do a hair course. Have some hair skills because even if it's commercials, they're going to want you to do hair and makeup. It might be one guy and they're going to want you to do his hair and makeup. They won't hire two people. The person who has both skills in Australia will always get employed above the person that's single-skilled."

ERYN

"A brush is not a magic wand. You have to figure it out on your own, how to use it. Practice, take pictures, listen, and learn, just like with anything else you do in life."

CAMILLE

"Hair work has gotten me through so much, you know? And I did learn punching and ventilating in makeup school. Boy, that's just gotten me through everything, if I come to think of it."

"Dress as if you were androgynous, asexual. I've seen makeup artists wear bikini tops on shows. 'Okay not appropriate.' Always dress appropriately. It's a profession. You're not there to be the actress."

"Be prepared, completely prepared. Many times makeup departments are looked down on as the vanity crafts, you really have to have your self-esteem without being belligerent OR arrogant through being prepared. Bring your best to the table."

JENNIFER

"People want to hire people that want to be part of the team. That keeps people wanting to bring you back."

TINA

"Start working in a shop, start at Ground Zero. Take that job in the shop even if it's just cleaning up after the mold makers. Learn how to build, then get really good at applying."

VIVIAN

"I believe as an artist you should know your materials and tools. Having experience with them and some good practiced finesse allows you to create from your vision and not be hindered by your practiced skills."

2013
ACADEMY AWARD
BEST ACHIEVEMENT IN
MAKEUP AND HAIRSTYLING

LES MISERABLES (2012)
RUSSELL CROWE HUGH JACKMAN ANNE HATHAWAY EDDIE REDMAYNE & AMANDA SEYFRIED
Licensed from AF archive / Alamy Stock Photo

 JULIE DARTNELL

I know in some industries you have to really prove yourself as a woman, don't you?
But at the end of the day, it is a hard job and I think there's mutual respect
for what you do from everyone around you. You're all in it together.
I think you generally have to prove yourself across the board as a human being.

Julie Dartnell's mum, Anne, found out about her daughter's Oscar nomination for **Les Misèrables** (2012) when she saw Julie's name on the internet. "We knew over Christmas she had made the final seven, but we just found out she made the final three and received a nomination. Her phone doesn't work where she is at the moment, so we can't speak to her. We're not sure if she even knows!"

Born and raised in Stanford-le-Hope in Essex, east of London, Julie's childhood sounds idyllic. Her father is a retired welder with Procter & Gamble and her mother was a stay-at-home-mom and entrepreneur. "My mum wanted to be a hairdresser, but in those days, you went to secretarial college or you got married. Her dad would have none of it. Maybe because of that, my parents always said, 'If you want to try something, try it. You know, what's the worst that can happen? Give it a go.' Mum used to do all the neighborhood ladies' hair and makeup and loved it. Maybe that's where I got it from."

With a house full of four children, Anne Dartnell, along with three other women, (who also had children at home) started a dressmaking business designing and making children's clothes. "They went around to people's houses and had clothes parties and quite often I'd help." Anne's dressmaking talents were also a boon to Julie, her sister, and their friends, since she could make their clothes in all the latest fashions upon request. "She was just brilliant. Really clever, actually, the more I think about it and look back on it. She was really inventive." Julie's mother served as a model of industry, creativity, determination, and inspiration, all of which are reflected in Julie's journey into makeup.

Bert and Blue Peter

One day while she was in high school, where she studied dance and drama, a guest speaker, Bert Broe, came to give a makeup demonstration for the students. "I remember being quite fascinated by it all. I was blown away." Shortly thereafter, while watching the television show *Blue Peter*, a British children's series that highlights different careers, she saw an episode that spotlighted the BBC Makeup Department. "I was probably 15, I think, and I just thought, 'Oh, that's really interesting. I want to do that.' I sent off for information and got a leaflet back saying what I needed to apply for a trainee position in the BBC Makeup Department. My mum never said, 'Oh, don't be ridiculous,' she said, 'Well, let's look at this.'"

When Julie graduated from high school, she originally had planned to attend art school. But plans changed when Bert Broe contacted Julie's high school drama teacher with a job opportunity. He was looking for an apprentice. "Basically, he had two shops in the middle of theaterland, right in Covent Garden, called Theater Zoo. It was a costume hire and they sold theatrical makeup, wigs, anything to do with the theater, and animal costumes. He needed someone to work in the shop and be his apprentice out on jobs."

"I got the job and went to visit my sister in London. It was the early '80s, a lively time. We went to a party, met two girls looking for flatmates, and the next day I rung my mum and said, 'Mum, I'm moving to London!' She calmly said, 'Oh, okay. Where are you going to live? We'll just come up and meet the two girls.' We moved to London without really thinking too much about it. We were 17, that's why. And we had a lovely Irish landlady, Mrs. P."

"I found myself in situations where 'I just did it.' I suppose that stems from my parents telling me to always give something a try. I knew it's what I wanted to do. Well, try it, you know, and see how you get on. So yes, that's what I did."

The Zoo

Bert Broe was a third-generation theater makeup artist and wig maker who worked in a shop opened by his grandfather. All the major theatrical companies would come to him for wigs and masks and costumes, and he would go to the theaters and do the makeup on the actors. The back room was the mold room where Julie learned to mix latex, make masks, and paint them. "It probably wasn't very good for us, there wasn't any ventilation. Breathing all those fumes probably wasn't good, but nobody really thought about things like that then. Downstairs, there were makeup mirrors and lights and sometimes Bert would teach a class or do a demonstration down there."

"It was an amazing experience. I would go out with him and do all the Greek tragedies, Shakespeare, plays, musicals, and watch him work. I was there with him doing it, thrown into the deep end. He could lay hair on in a matter of minutes and the things he could do with a couple of grease sticks was just amazing. I just followed him really. Bert was an excellent, talented mentor. His wife worked in the shop, too, and they were really like another family. My mum actually came up and used to mend costumes when they got a little worn."

For three and a half years, Julie worked at Theater Zoo learning the business from the ground up. But her goal was clear: she wanted to get into the BBC Makeup Department. To qualify, Julie needed to get her A Levels in art (advanced classes) and be 20-years-old. She went to night school and completed her A Levels, took a course in TV makeup at Greasepaint Makeup School, and picked up makeup jobs to get as much experience in the industry as she could to round out her CV before she auditioned for the BBC

Only Two Colors

Admission to the BBC Makeup Department was highly competitive in the early '80s; there were 24 openings and 1400 applicants when Julie applied. There was a preliminary interview, which Julie passed, followed by a practical test that involved character aging, a hair-piece, and a beauty makeup. When Julie began her beauty makeup, everything was laid out for her. "I thought, 'This is odd, I've only got two colors of eye shadow and they were quite odd colors, an orangey-bronze color and a cream color. But I thought, 'I'll do my best.' When they came over to do the marking they asked why I chose those colors and I told them that was all I was given. 'Oh, did you not have this palette with 24 colors on it?' 'No.' 'Oh dear.' I think that probably ended up being in my favor."

Following the beauty test there was the hair challenge. Julie had to attach a hairpiece in a bun or pony tail which had to stand up to the pull test. "They pulled it and if it stayed on, you passed." Then there was the aging makeup, then another interview in front of the department head and senior designers, both of which Julie passed. She was one of 24 accepted into the school of 1985. There were four months of intensive training and 20 months as a trainee where she was learning on-the-job.

Nine Years of Everything

The reputation of the BBC Makeup Department is superb, mainly because the trainees learned every aspect of both makeup and hair while working on every conceivable type of project. "You could be doing the news one day and the next you'd be on *Pride and Prejudice* or a crime drama or a soap or *Top of the Pops*." *Top of the Pops* was a weekly television program that consisted of performances from some of that week's best-selling popular music artists with a rundown of that week's singles chart. "It was brilliant. All the top bands performed and you'd never know who you'd be making up that week."

Julie was 22, immersed in her training and "I wasn't sitting on the side lines. We were thrown in the deep end, especially if we were on a period drama or live entertainment with all those fast-moving shows, quick changes, and different characters. It was good because we had to do everything." Julie worked on the TV mini-series *The Chronicles of Narnia: The Lion, the Witch, & the Wardrobe* (1988-1990, 18 episodes) as well as *The Chronicles of Narnia: Prince Caspian* (1988-1989, six episodes) with Sylvia Thornton who was at the forefront of prosthetic use in television. Additionally, there was extensive in-house support. The wig department was well stocked, and if a piece needed to be constructed, it was, and then it was put into the system for future use. "It was a brilliant experience."

THE CHRONICLES OF NARNIA: THE LION, THE WITCH, AND THE WARDROBE at the BBC (1988) Licensed from Ronald Grant Archive / Alamy Stock Photo

A Family and Redundancy

In 1992 Julie had her first child, Holly, and three years later, her son, Tom. The birth of Holly coincided with rumors of redundancies at the BBC and as Julie wanted to spend more time with her baby, she decided to freelance. "There were no concessions if you had a child or children. They could send you to Yorkshire for four months to work on a drama and I wanted more control than that. I wanted to be at home as much as it was possible. I didn't want to be doing a big film, so I did lots of smaller projects."

Having a family forced Julie to redefine her priorities and life choices. "We've always been really open with our children, and said, 'Look, you know this isn't a normal household.' My husband works in the flower industry, so he gets up at 2:30-3 o'clock in the morning, and my job requires me to leave very early and be gone 12-14 or more hours a day, or to be on location for periods at a time. I think you just have to be honest with yourself about what you want. You know, your family's important. Your family will always be there and is the stability the film industry does not have."

And much like her parents before her, Julie and her husband, Dave, encourage their kids to "give it a try." Holly, after finishing her university degree, started travelling. "She wants to work, save, go somewhere else. Come back. Work. Save. Go somewhere else. She's going to do that for another year and then decide what she wants to do."

Tom decided at 15 he wanted to do a six-week charity trip to Uganda with the Scouts. "He said, 'Mom, I want to do this.' I said, 'Are you sure?' He said 'yes' and I said, 'okay.'" He raised the money, took the training, learned to cook the local food. In Uganda, he worked at two orphanages and helped build a chicken coop for 1000 chickens.

"I think you have to strike a balance somehow. If you don't work, you're not earning. All those elements come into it as well. For me, when I finish a job, it's always been important to have time off. I'd work, earn some money, go home, have a family holiday. I try to buy myself a bit of time to regroup and bring back that family environment."

The Goal

When Julie begins a project, she always starts with the script, meets with the director or head of department, and the actor. Sometimes there are concept drawings, sometimes not, depending upon the situation and the project. "We all work together. Most of the time it's been a process that has ended up with a happy end product."

Ultimately, "It is the character within the script, making him or her believable and actually bringing the character to life that I enjoy doing. That's what I aim to do."

SHAKESPEARE IN LOVE (1998) BEN AFFLECK & GWYNETH PALTROW
Licensed from AF archive / Alamy Stock Photo

Back to Work

For about six years after she went freelance, Julie stayed away from films. "I'd guest, come in and do days, do actors that are in and out. I chose to dip in, dip out. I did commercials, photo shoots, things like that. And then I got to the point where I thought okay, I really want to do a film."

In 1998, Julie worked on *Shakespeare in Love* with Lisa Westcott as her department head. Julie had worked with Lisa while they were both at the BBC, and this working relationship continues to this day. "It was my first big film back and it was great, I loved it. It was just brilliant. Wonderful director, John Madden, great team. I was looking after Ben Affleck. It's who I'm looking after now almost 20 years on, yeah."

"After that, I think people realized I was back doing films all the way through again." There followed a lot of television work with Lisa Westcott and Frances Hannon, both BBC connections. She was makeup and hair artist to Judi Dench on *The Last of the Blonde Bombshells* (2000), a made-for-TV movie; *Dinotopia* (2002), a fantasy mini-series which takes place on an island with talking dinosaurs; *French and Saunders* (2002-2003, 2 episodes), a BBC sketch comedy show; *The Lost Prince* (2003) which tells the story of

Prince John who was locked away because of epilepsy; *The Cambridge Spies* (2003) which explores the recruitment of Cambridge students as Soviet spies in the 1930s.

And Then There Was One

"I probably prefer looking after one of the main actors, being involved all the way through. I quite enjoy doing the journey with them, especially if their character evolves. You know, you kind of bring them to life. It's one of those situations where, especially with Lisa [Westcott], I've always been brought in to do the main character. We always have had a great working relationship."

Designers introduce Julie to the actor she will be making up early in the process. "A lot of the time these actors would have the designer make them up, but if the show is too busy for the designer to do the lead, they bring me

THE LAST OF THE BLONDE BOMBSHELLS (2000)
JUDI DENCH & IAN HOLM
Licensed from AF archive / Alamy Stock Photo

in early so I'm on a good footing to start with. You know you've got to fit in with the whole look, haven't you? You've got to be involved in what the designer is doing to get the overall picture and feel of everything."

Working with the lead actor, Julie is frequently involved in concept meetings with the director and department head, product and process discussions, and numerous camera tests. The balancing act is to make sure the actor has confidence in her while bringing to the film what the director and head of department need. "So, you're always keeping the balls in the air."

In 2004, Julie looked after Billy Crudup in *Stage Beauty*, adapted from the play *Compleat Female Stage Beauty* by Jeffrey Hatcher. Placed in the 17th Century, the film is based on the career of Edward Kynaston, an actor who exclusively played female roles. As it was illegal at the time for women to appear on stage, men made careers playing women's roles and, to do so believably, they were carefully and meticulously made up. Julie was charged with making up Crudup, balancing the correct period, wigs, and makeup to highlight his feminine bone structure and beauty, which then contrasted with his everyday look as a man. "It was all about theater. As you can imagine, it was right up my street."

In 2006, Julie looked after Javier Bardem in *Goya's Ghosts*, a 1792 Spanish Inquisition film. Then, in 2007, Lisa Westcott asked Julie to design Paul Giamatti's Santa in *Fred Claus*, which was her first time to work in the US. Later she looked after Chris Evans in the 2011

STAGE BEAUTY (2004) BILLY CRUDUP
Licensed from AF archive / Alamy Stock Photo

film *Captain America: The 1st Avenger*. Frances Hannon brought Julie on as key makeup artist and hair to look after Jesse Eisenberg in *Now You See Me 2*, and as key makeup artist for *The Grand Budapest Hotel* (2014), where she was hair and makeup artist to Adrien Brody, Tilda Swinton, Jeff Goldblum, and Owen Wilson. Julie won two Hollywood Makeup Artist and Hair Stylist Guild Awards for *Best Period and/or Character Makeup* as well as *Best Period and/or Character Hair Styling* for *The Grand Budapest Hotel*, both of which she shares with Frances Hannon.

Julie draws a distinction between "looking after" an actor and being an actor's personal makeup artist. In the previous films, Julie was hired by the makeup and hair designers to take care of the lead actor and to fulfill other duties as needed. When she works as a personal, she is requested by the lead actor and is responsible for the hair and makeup for that actor alone. She works closely with the actor and the director to ensure the character is true to their visions.

In 2015, after working with Julie on *Les Misérables*, Hugh Jackman asked her to be his personal for makeup and hair on *Pan*, a prequel to J. M. Barrie's *Peter Pan*. Jackman played Blackbeard and had several makeup effects that needed to be addressed in pre-production. "We sat down with Joe Wright, the director, and Hugh, because there were no guidelines to the period. We came up with some ideas. He needed to be grungy, quite nasty looking, and we wanted the audience to wonder if he was wearing makeup. I had to shave Hugh's head, as under all the hard-front wigs he was completely bald. One wig was quite elaborate, the other was kind of a variation on a samurai, kind of crossing over to a pompadour wig."

"There was a point in the film at the end, a battle scene, where his wig gets knocked off and underneath is scarring. We discussed the design and decided it would be great for Blackbeard to have scalping scars that never really healed up, but we wanted older scars on there, too. The whole thing evolved into a patchwork quilt with scars. There was no time so I had Bondo scars made and I applied them on top of one another. I ended up with about 14 different scars on top of his head. It became a production line of Bondos!"

Les Misérables

Lisa Westcott, the hair and makeup designer for *Les Misérables* (2012), asked Julie to look after Hugh

Jackman in this adaptation of Victor Hugo's novel, which she happily did. "*Les Miz*, as hard as it was, was really enjoyable. It did push every element of what you have ever learned or done. There was so much involved showing the passing of time with wig dressing and aging makeup. It was hard work, but we had a fantastic makeup team. Lisa was amazing as usual. I think, in terms of comradery and the cast, everything was extraordinary."

"The beginning of the film was actually our first day; you know when he's up on the mountains? Hugh came in and we, Lisa and I, had to breakdown his whole body. Feet, legs, everything was weathered and worn. We were told we were going to the top of the mountain. Lisa had her summer footwear on. We never thought we were going to be going there. There were no toilets. There was no food. We were hiding behind these rocks where they were filming so we wouldn't be in the shots. Everybody hid. We looked at each other and asked, 'How did this happen? We're on top of the mountain.'"

LES MISERABLES (2012)   HUGH JACKMAN
Licensed from AF archive / Alamy Stock Photo

"Luckily, if nothing else, we had our big jackets with us. When it got dark, we asked how we were going to get down the mountain. Someone said, 'Don't worry. Somebody is bringing up some head torches.'"

"We were staying in Nice, on the promenade, right by the sea. Other crewmembers told us how much they were enjoying the city and the food. I didn't even know that's where we were, I hadn't seen it in the daylight. There you go. The glamour of filming. The glamour of being in Nice."

Tom Hooper, the director, wanted Jackman's convict character to have an unkempt beard to show his position outside of society. Jackman's own beard wasn't long enough, so Julie had to figure out how to lengthen it and waterproof the extensions to protect them during the scenes in the water. She attached the extensions with eyelash extension glue, which worked perfectly.

The film was shot chronologically, hence Jackman had to be transformed from the convict, gaunt and bearded, to the successful, fleshed-out mayor without beard, literally overnight. "There was no time to even do makeup tests for the mayor: the mayor had no beard, the convict did. It would have been useless to put the bearded convict in front of the camera with the mayor's wig." Once the convict's scenes were finished, Julie shaved the beard, as close as she could to the skin and "it was done within minutes, gone."

"The next morning Hugh came in and I was, right, okay, I've got to turn him into somebody looking really healthy and prosperous. I used color, healthy tones. He had long side burns and I had dressed the wig to look lovely and true to the period. There was no trickery in post-production with visual effects for any of Hugh's looks."

As the film progresses and Jean Valjean ages, Julie used wigs to show Hugh's aging, as well as stippling around the eyes, and contact lenses. *Les Misérables* is an epic film, covering decades, following characters through their lives as they change social positions, economic situations, age, and die. The makeup and hair team was presented with many challenges: large crowd scenes, water scenes, a distinctive period that included all the social classes, and, of course time, and budget limitations. Julie and Lisa met these challenges and were awarded a BAFTA (British Academy of Film and Television Arts) Award for *Best Makeup/Hair* and the Academy Award for *Best Achievement in Makeup and Hair Styling*.

Life Imitates Art

Les Misérables explores injustice and morality. While the film soars to a rousing, satisfying conclusion, there was a fevered behind-the-scenes fight for better working conditions and pay. "When you go into a job, one you're excited about, one that's creatively challenging, you have to remember it's also a business. You can't be taken advantage of. It's conflicting. It creates a bit of angst."

The makeup crew comes in early every day to prepare for the actors and they stay late to take makeup off and clean up. "Almost every department has pre-calls. We don't. We give a certain number of hours for free... no other department does that apart from ADs and costume. This can be between 1 ½ to 2 hours a day."

"One night I stayed behind longer because I needed to wrap Hugh's convict look; we were filming him as the Mayor the next day. His beard had to come off, there was no going back. It was late when we finished, 1 AM, and I had to drive 130 miles to get to the next

LES MISERABLES (2012) HUGH JACKMAN
Licensed from AF archive / Alamy Stock Photo

location for the morning's shoot. It's dangerous when you're working those hours and driving as well. I mean we were literally following each other on the motorway to make sure we were going to get there."

Project Bushfire was born. The UK union for hair, makeup, and costume professionals, BECTU (Broadcasting, Entertainment, Communications, and Theater Union), stepped in to organize and protect its members while trying to negotiate better conditions, hours, and pay. One union organizer said, "The important thing about these negotiations is we are going to be paid for every hour we work. It will be the end of the old culture and we won't be giving any hours for free." The crew of **Les Misérables** was at the forefront of this conflict: filming regularly overran, sometimes into days off; crowd hair and makeup had huge makeup calls before shooting began; they were expected to put in "Goodwill Hours" that included prep and clean up time without pay; they had broken turnarounds for which they were not compensated. The hair and makeup team took to the barricades and demanded changes.

"I think it would be so much easier if there were proper guidelines as to what you bring to the table. 'These are the hours that you do and get paid for.' The main issue was to fight for a pre-call before unit call. It's been hard to make changes, even now, three years later. It's still ongoing." And like Valjean, the ladies and gentlemen of the makeup union continue to fight.

Julie Dartnell has grit. As a young girl, she knew what she wanted and pursued it. "It's a precarious industry, isn't it? You might turn down something and then something might not come along for a while. It is a hard industry to get into, but I believe if somebody has passion they will succeed."

Julie has lived her life "giving it a try," exploring options and following her heart in her work and for her family.

OUTTAKES:

On Health:

"You've got to have stamina. I think when people first come into the industry, they are shocked at the hours you do and how it can encroach into your personal life. Stamina is a big thing. You've got to be prepared that you will be working long hours. You've got to try and keep healthy."

"I think you've got to have a bit of a break between films. You need to regain your health, and so many people I know do it. We begin a healthy regime and join a gym! You try and get yourself back on track."

On Mentors:

"Bert Broe, Sylvia Fulton from the BBC, and Lisa Westcott."

On Freelancing:

"It's got peaks and troughs. One minute you're working and doing really well, and then suddenly it all goes quiet. Nature of the beast."

"I'm just working on a film and I've just had an availability check, something I quite like to have done. But I also want time at home. This can be conflicting as being a freelancer you never really want to turn work down. Hopefully, you will be asked again."

"You've got to have a good backup at home. There's only a couple of films I've done where I've been away for a long length of time. My parents came and helped with the kids. It worked, you know, but I wouldn't choose to do that a lot. I've turned down films that have been away when the children were young."

"We have been lucky considering both our working hours that we only ever had two people look after Tom and Holly. One was Natalie, but she wanted to travel and be part of the film industry, I kind of got her a step-in as a production runner. And when she left, her mom took over, so there has been some consistency in our crazy household."

On Hair, Makeup, and Prosthetics:

"A lot of us that came out of the BBC, where we were trained in all aspects of hair and makeup, did a lot of our own prosthetics. We just did it. We didn't think anything about it. My head doesn't work around the division of labor between hair, makeup, and prosthetics."

"There's a mixture of hair and makeup and prosthetics in the UK. Sometimes, especially when you go in for your checks and you've got three things going on, like with Hugh in *Les Miz*, who had beard extensions, character makeup, and prosthetic scars, I'd have to check all three things. I enjoy being part of it all, but I also enjoy just concentrating on the hair or the makeup."

On Tricks of the Trade:

"I always make the beards as natural as possible. Mixing the colors and having extra hair for laying on."

"I always have my favorite go-to palettes that have been part of my kit for years. Kryolan grease palettes and Dermacolor and now Reel Color and Skin Illustrator palettes."

"I think various Bondos [transfers] are always good to have. I've always got some of them at home because they're really quick. Somebody wants a scar or a wound and you know they're quick to put on."

"I don't believe anybody that says they don't get nervous still, no matter how many years they've been doing it. I think it's because you care. You have to control your nerves. You have to keep calm, don't you? I think that's quite important."

On Wishes:

"I think I'd like to do another musical. One that is really colorful and different from *Les Miz*. Something really vibrant with show girls. I'd like to do something like that. Going back to my theatre roots."

On Success Defined:

"Everybody brings something different to the table, don't they? Maybe you can't be brilliant at everything but you can try, and if you can look back and say you have always done your best, remained true to yourself, enjoyed it with a personal sense of achievement and been proud of your work, in my mind that's what success is all about."

Catching Up!

We interviewed Julie on June 5, 2016. Since then, she has worked on

Now You See Me 2
Key Make-up and Hair for Jessie Eisenberg, Cast 1, Daniel Atlas

Justice League
Hairdresser to Ben Affleck, and Diane Lane.
Hair and Make-Up for Connie Nielson.

Robin Hood
Personal Hair and Make-up for Taron Egerton , Cast 1, Robin Hood.

For more of Julie's Credits, visit: wwww.imdb.com

2014
ACADEMY AWARD
BEST ACHIEVEMENT IN
MAKEUP AND HAIRSYLING

DALLAS BUYERS CLUB (2013) MATTHEW MCCONAUGHEY
Licensed from Photo 12 / Alamy Stock Photo

ROBIN MATHEWS

It's not about the makeup, it's about the character.

It's about the actor on the screen.

The makeup is a tool; it's not about the makeup.

Combine a grandmother who performed in vaudeville, a grandfather who was a famous portrait photographer, a mother who sings professionally, a father who is a photographer, and holiday gatherings where she was expected to sing and perform monologues, and Robin Mathews' desire to be in the film and television industry was a *fait accompli*.

Vaudeville, Opera, and California

Robin's grandmother, Ruth Moore Mathews, was half of a vaudevillian team called The Moore Sisters who sang, danced, and told stories on the vaudeville circuit for years. Ruth eventually returned to her hometown, New Orleans, where she continued performing in theater and appeared in a film, **Panic in the Streets** (1950), directed by Elia Kazan. She was also active in the Daughters of the American Revolution, where she helped mount the yearly event celebrating the memory of the war. Robin, part of that entertainment, sang and danced dressed in an 18th century costume. "It was always very important to my grandmother for me to have a piece that I could recite in public and a song that I could sing at a party. I recited '*The House with Nobody in It*' by Joyce Kilmer, but the singing was a little complicated because my mother is an opera singer, the greatest singer that lives."

Vicki Fisk, Robin's mother, is a *coloratura* soprano who has performed all over the world. She moved to New York to concentrate on her career when Robin was eight while Robin stayed in New Orleans, lived with her grandmother, and got the acting bug. "Acting was my whole life as a kid; I was in a lot of musical theater and even performed with my mother in the opera **The Ballad of Baby Doe** at the age of five. I spent my whole life on the stage; I grew up there." The two strongest women in Robin's life influenced her career choices through example; she wanted to continue the legacy of her grandmother and mother by performing.

After she graduated from Mount Carmel Academy where she acted in plays and worked on makeup crews, Robin went to Louisiana State University as a theater major, but quickly became disenchanted with the lack of roles available to undergraduates. "I didn't want to go to New York. I didn't want to be a Broadway star. I wanted to work in film and television. I wanted to be in Hollywood, that was my goal. I researched conservatories and decided I wanted to attend the American Academy of Dramatic Arts in LA. It is the oldest acting conservatory in the country with a wonderful reputation and, ironically, it is located a few blocks from where I live now." Robin auditioned for the AADA, was accepted to the first year, and before attending, took a year off to save for the tuition. The American Academy of Dramatic Arts is very competitive. Students may attend the second year of training only if they are invited back; Robin was invited back. "The AADA is a wonderful acting conservatory. They are classically training actors. You're not allowed to work while you go there. It's eight hours a day, five days a week. It's very intense. I can't say enough about what it taught me, not only about the business, but about life in general."

Metamorphosis from Actor to Makeup Artist

School Influences

Part of the curriculum at the American Academy of Dramatic Arts is theatrical makeup, taught by Scott Ramp, which instructs actors how to do their own makeup for the stage. Scott has taught makeup at the AADA for over 20 years, bringing his experience from The Scream Team (the movie-quality foam latex appliance company he owns and runs), *Face Off* (Season Five contestant), and as the head makeup creator for Six Flags Magic Mountain Fright Fest. As the special effects makeup designer for Fright Fest, Scott offers his best students the opportunity to work during the Halloween season putting full facial prosthetics on the "scaractors" who work the haunt. Because Robin enjoyed the makeup class and showed obvious talent, it was an easy decision to expand her skill set. "I was working as an actor, auditioning, bartending, and I worked Fright Fest for Scott every Halloween for seven years. Scott taught me how to do prosthetics and effects. Eventually, I went to his lab and helped him make the pieces in his shop."

Many aspiring actors cobble work together to ensure availability to attend auditions and pay the bills. Bartending and waitressing, while seen as cliché, often provide actors the freedom they need to pursue acting. Straddling two worlds, Robin added makeup artist to her job list. "I taught myself beauty, read every book out there, and continued to bartend and go to auditions."

A Friend Steps In

A friend of Robin's, producer Brian Glazen, needed some special makeup effects done for his HBO-Sexy-Skinemax-type show and offered Robin the job. Robin agreed and was able to hone her special effects skills while on the job. A series of music videos and commercials followed including Super Bowl commercials for directors Michael Mann and Joe Pytka. "These were really a great training ground. There's no telling what you have to do in a commercial or music video, it could be high glamour, it could be period work, it could be handling hair. It was all fast, fast, fast."

In the meantime, Glazen had landed a job as head of production for Playboy Television. "Playboy Television was brand new at the time. They were doing all kinds of different things, from talk shows to scripted fake reality series, to competitions like American Idol but with playmates." Robin asked Brian if she could department head one of his shows, he agreed, and Robin's first department head position was for *7 Lives Xposed* (2001-2002). "For the next several years, I was corporate makeup artist for Playboy TV."

Although Robin was busy with Playboy TV, commercials, music videos, and her first department head position on a feature film, *The Rose Technique* (2002), she was still auditioning for acting roles and meeting with some success. However, "I still hadn't made the switch in my head over to the rest of my life, my career. I could have joined the makeup union a lot sooner, but part of my head was still on acting."

Back to New Orleans

In 2003, Robin went to New Orleans for the holidays and met a friend in the film industry who told her about all the work opportunities in Louisiana due to new tax incentives available to production companies shooting there. Coincidentally, this friend was working on **Home of Phobia** (aka **Freshman Orientation,** 2004), a film that needed a makeup artist. Initially, Robin wasn't interested in working outside of Hollywood, but the job was a department head position and as it filmed in Louisiana, a right-to-work-state, she was hired and became eligible to join Local 798, Makeup Artists and Hairstylists Union, New York. Once in the union, Robin began to work a lot more in both film and television, completing such projects as **Frankenstein** (TV movie, 2004) as makeup department head, **Torn Apart** (2004) as makeup department head and special effects makeup department head, and **Waiting** (2005) as makeup department head. Since she was working union films, she was supporting herself as a makeup artist. "Maybe in the back of my head I still thought I might act again, but I was so busy working I didn't really have much time to think about it."

The Sean Penn Connection

Robin's professional makeup life touched Sean Penn's acting and directing life several times between 2002 and 2007. "My friend John Scheide, who directed **The Rose Technique**, was Sean's first AD, and he introduced me to Sean. John told Sean, 'You've got to meet this girl, she does really badass makeup effects.' At that time, girls were not thought of as special effects makeup artists. Ve [Neil] broke that ceiling for us. It was a rarity when a girl like me was happy to be covered in blood and dirt. Sean met me and I did one little thing for him, then another, and he kept using me for the little things he was doing." The little things led to bigger things that impacted Robin's professional life.

FAMILY TORN APART, (2004) NEIL PATRICK HARRIS, JOHNNY GALECKI
Licensed fromUnited Archives GmbH / Alamy Stock Photo

In 2002, Sean asked Robin to be the head of department on the "USA" segment of the film **September 11**. The film used 11 different directors, each from a different country. Each segment asks the people of that country their reactions to the September 11th attacks. The film is an emotional, international montage of the day. Sean Penn was the writer and director for the USA segment.

All the King's Men (2006) is a film based on the Pulitzer Prize-winning novel of the same name by Robert Penn Warren. The story is about the life of Willie Stark (Sean Penn), a fictional character resembling corrupt Louisiana governor, Huey Long. Robin was a makeup artist on the film, Sean Penn was the lead actor. Additionally, Robin worked with Sean as key hairstylist on **The Assassination of Richard Nixon** (2004, Omaha, NB), and as special effects makeup department head on a music video he directed for Peter Gabriel entitled **The Barry Williams Show** (2002) that "culminated in an entire talk show studio audience randomly bleeding from different places of their bodies."

Nature Steps In

All the King's Men was shot in Louisiana, Robin's home state, and when the film wrapped in August 2005, she went back to New Orleans to visit family. While she was there, Hurricane Katrina struck. "There were breeches in the levee in two different spots, one was in Lakeview in Orleans Parish, which is where my entire family lives. We lost six houses in my family...there were 12 feet of standing water in that area,

ALL THE KING'S MEN YEAR (2006) SEAN PENN
Licensed from Photo 12 / Alamy Stock Photo

in the house. We lost every single picture, every single item, every single paper, including my entire makeup kit. I had lost everything in a fire before that, so since Katrina I don't hold on to personal things as much anymore. I don't collect anything. The things I really care about I tend to keep on my body or in my purse."

Two weeks after Katrina, Sean called Robin and said, "I have this project coming up. But I don't know, I've got to talk to you about it. It's going to be difficult. It's a true story of this guy who backpacked across the country all the way into Alaska and eventually dies of starvation. We're going to shoot in the desert in the summer, in Alaska in the winter. We're not going to fake any locations. We're going to take the actual journey he took, all the way from Atlanta across the country, down to Mexico, all the way up to Alaska. We're not

going to have makeup trailers. I don't even think we're going to have hotels in some locations. We might be sleeping outside in tents. This is going to take a very special makeup artist to be able to handle this." "I said, 'Sean, I just went through Hurricane Katrina. I promise you I can do this.' That job changed my whole life. That opportunity."

Into the Wild (2007) shot for nine months in seven different states, two countries, and 30 cities. "We slept on the Colorado River on pontoon boats with no sleeping bags, tents, nothing. No bathrooms, no electricity. He wanted the filmmakers to have the same experience as the character and bring that to the film, which I think it really did."

INTO THE WILD (2007) EMILE HIRSCH © Art Linson Productions.
Licensed from AF archive / Alamy Stock Photo

Then one evening, in a little bar in Alaska, Sean and producer Art Linson asked Robin to audition for a role in the film. "I finally get my first big role in a huge motion picture directed and written by Sean Penn. I'm also the makeup department head for my first huge motion picture written and directed by Sean Penn. I was like, what the hell? Then to complicate matters, Sean, after seeing dailies, said to me, 'You're meant to be an actor. Act and I will do whatever I can to help you.' I had so much to worry about makeup-wise I couldn't concentrate on this wonderfulness that had just happened acting-wise."

The film flipped and earned Robin entrance into the LA branch of the makeup union, but she finally had to make a decision: did she want to be an actor or a makeup artist? "To act, I would have to start all over from scratch. Getting an agent. Auditioning. Did I really want to give up everything I'd worked for during the last 10-12 years as a makeup artist? I finally had my big break as a makeup artist, to start over again as an actor…it was a hard decision, but I went with the makeup. I chose the makeup."

The Maturation of a Makeup Artist

Robin begins her design process with the script, a discussion with the director, followed by discussions with the actors. "I'm a much different makeup artist than a lot of others. I didn't know this until I worked with other makeup department heads. I break down the character as an actor would because that's the only way I know how to break down a character; I approach makeup design as an actor." Robin does a good deal of research and creates extensive back stories for all the characters, which, of course, inform the characters' looks. "Sometimes we use it all, and sometimes we don't, but even if the actor doesn't know that it's there or doesn't want to use it, in my head I know it's there and I've got a reason for doing the makeup I'm doing. I really do see a big difference between the way I create a character and the way other artists, who trained as makeup artists, create characters." Robin's two worlds neatly dovetailed, giving breadth and depth to her work.

Dallas Buyers Club

In **Dallas Buyers Club** (2013) Matthew McConaughey plays Ron Woodroof, an AIDS patient diagnosed in the mid-1980s when HIV/AIDS treatments were unavailable or cost prohibitive. Based on a true story, Woodroof smuggled unapproved pharmaceutical drugs into Texas for treating his symptoms and distributed them to fellow AIDS patients by establishing the "Dallas Buyers Club." The goal of everyone involved in the film was to depict the epidemic and its victims in a respectful, compassionate manner and tell the story truthfully, honestly, and without sentimentality. Woodroof, a homophobic Texas electrician, found a way to fight for AIDS victim rights and provide the medical treatment that the establishment eschewed; as a result of his determination, new treatments were discovered and AIDS victims were humanized.

Jean-Marc Vallée is a French-Canadian director who brought a unique approach to shooting **Dallas Buyers Club**. He shot it all with hand-held cameras using only ambient light; the cameras never stopped rolling, not for a location change or makeup touchup or lighting adjustment. This, of course, presented challenges for actors, costumers, camerapersons, and makeup artists. Robin said, "This is a very different way of shooting. Jean-Marc and Yves Bélanger, his DP, developed this style when they were doing commercials. I believe **Dallas Buyers Club** was the first feature he tried it on."

When Robin was hired for the job, Jean-Marc told her of the unconventional camera work he would be using and emphasized the short, 25-day shooting schedule. Additionally, **Dallas Buyers Club** was a very low-budget film. "He told me all the parameters, so I knew there was no way I could use any appliances on the actors and I had to use products that were movable, extremely movable. I had to figure out a different way to do the makeup than I would normally. Normally, I would use alcohol-based products because they don't move and they last as long as you want them to on the skin. I had to figure some other way. I didn't have the time or money to take prosthetics on and off. We had to use something that I could wipe off with my hands or with a baby wipe in a few seconds."

The evolution of an illness, out of sequence

Showing the progression of the illness, specifically the stages of the characters' degeneration and the devastation of AIDS, is integral to the impact of the film. As usual **Dallas Buyer's Club** was shot out of sequence, but it was unusual because they sometimes shot a healthy scene, a bed-ridden scene, and an outdoor mid-illness scene all in same day. The makeup had to change for every scene to reflect the stage of health/illness accurately. Therefore, there were often major makeup changes between takes. "The only time the camera was not up and rolling was during lunch or during a makeup change. Guess how much pressure that put on me?" There were days when Robin made five changes per character.

To achieve the realistic look of gravely ill people, both McConaughey and Leto each lost 40-plus pounds.

During the 25-day shoot, they were shown at their healthiest, their sickest, and at every stage in between. To make them look healthy at the beginning and middle of the film when the medications kicked in, Robin used upper and lower dental plumpers, which mold to the teeth like a retainer, to fill out their faces, and also "reverse highlight and contour to augment fullness and provide the illusion of health." When Matthew and Jared's characters were at their sickest, "I painted with highlight and shadow to contour every bone, tendon, and vein I could find on them to make them pop. Then I used pictures of skulls and skeletons to draw in the ones I couldn't see. This created the illusion of the various degrees of sickness emphasizing the gaunt, wane look."

Creating the makeup for Rayon, Jared Leto's transgender character with AIDS, tapped into Robin's actor training. When Jared Leto came on-set the day before shooting began, he was in character, he was Rayon. He never spoke as Jared or acted as Jared or dressed as Jared, he was always Rayon. He

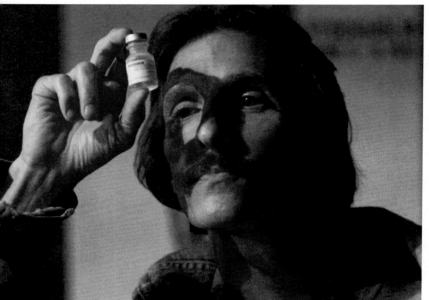

was always "she." While this may have caused some makeup artists a little trepidation, Robin embraced it. She understands the process actors use while developing a character and she could relate to it.

While Robin created the back story for her makeup design, she conferred with Rayon in making some final decisions. She decided Rayon's major influence was her mother, whose heyday would have been in the '60s. "I pulled pictures of all those '60s icons like Twiggy, Endora from *Bewitched*, Brigitte Bardot. I asked Rayon what she thought and she said, 'Yes, I quite like that.'" So her eye shadow, lipstick, and foundation were reflective of that period and those icons.

DALLAS BUYERS CLUB (2013) MATTHEW MCCONAUGHEY
Licensed from AF archive / Alamy Stock Photo

As depicted in the film, Rayon's lifestyle is a major influence on her skin, makeup, and health. She needed to take female hormones daily, but had little money and frequently spent what money she had on drinking and drugs. Hence, in the film, her look changes daily, dictated by how she spent the night before, whether she takes her hormones, or if she has time to shave. Jean-Marc wanted Rayon to be a "hot mess" in obvious disarray, or spectacularly unsuccessful in her attempt to always be beautiful. So, in the back-story, Robin created reasons for her different appearances. "Sometimes she's clean-shaven, sometimes she doesn't have time to wax her eyebrows. When she doesn't have money for her hormones, sometimes her beard will grow in a little bit and she just packs more makeup on."

Rayon also develops AIDS-related lesions during the film. Robin used Bondo transfers to create the lesions, then covered them with heavy Joe Blasco crème foundation because she [Rayon] would try to hide the wounds.

Seborrheic dermatitis, a red, flakey, itchy skin condition, is also a side effect of AIDS and was evident on both the main characters. The challenge: how to show the irritation realistically without using extensive appliances or pieces. Through experimentation, Robin hand-painted the rash, layered stretch and stipple using Green Marble Concentrate over it, and topped it by tweezing on grits and cornmeal one piece at a time. Though time-consuming, the simulation was disturbingly realistic.

A makeup artist's friend is lighting. Working only with ambient light complicated Robin's design and decision-making, forcing her to be flexible and quick-thinking. "I had no idea what lighting situations I was going to be shooting in, I didn't have any help with lighting. How many times do we shoot with prosthetics that have to be lit properly? There were a lot of times we'd be in the hospital in this crazy green and blue fluorescent light and then two seconds later we'd be shooting the continuation of the scene out-side in daylight. There was no chance to adjust the makeup beforehand, the makeup had to be adjusted on-set. When you don't stop in between, there's no breaks in between to relight. You just walk outside from the fluorescent light into the daylight and continue shooting."

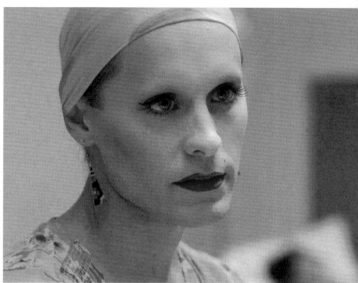

DALLA BUYER'S CLUB (2013)   JARED LETO
Licensed from Photo 12 / Alamy Stock Photo

Between the progression of the illness, the hand-held cameras that never stopped rolling, the use of only ambient light, a tiny budget, and a 25-day shoot, Robin's creativity was certainly challenged. The film is a paean to independence and the fighting spirit, humanizing those who are marginalized. The film received three Academy Awards: Matthew McConaughey for *Best Performance by an Actor in a Leading Role*, Jared Leto for *Best Performance by an Actor in a Supporting Role*, and *Best Achievement in Makeup and Hairstyling* which was awarded to Robin, which she shares with the film's hairstylist, Adruitha Lee.

Wild

Following *Dallas Buyers Club,* Robin worked on another Vallée film, *Wild* (2014), with the same set of challenges. "Jean-Marc shoots without any camera or lighting set ups, there's no grip or electric crew. All the camera work is handheld and all the lighting is ambient. So, whether we'd be running up a mountain or down into a gully, the camera is always shooting." Robin was makeup department head as well as personal makeup artist for Reese Witherspoon. *Wild* is the biographical story of Cheryl Strayed's 1100-mile solo hike up the Pacific Crest Trail. The film opens with a close-up of Cheryl's toe, bloody and torn, which is actually a silicone prosthetic overlaid on top of Reese's real toe, complete with a removable nail that she rips off on-camera as she overlooks magnificent scenery. "We really did shoot that on the side of a cliff. We had to take a ski lift up the precarious side of a mountain, then we had to hike another 45 minutes to get to the spot where we shot. We were tethered in on straps and a harness just to be able take care of Reese."

One of Robin's biggest challenges in the film was maintaining the continuity of Reese's cuts, scrapes, and bruises. "The hike takes place over a three-month period, and because they show title cards of what day it is in the hike on screen, the audience knows exactly what part of the journey we're on, which means I had to make sure those injuries healed properly. I couldn't take dramatic license, I had to do it in real time. I kept a gigantic file of continuity photos."

Jean-Marc wanted "gritty reality. No beauty makeup on Reese. Even though she has the no-makeup look, she had corrective makeup on occasionally, but it was so hidden you couldn't see it. I used some dental plumpers for her younger look, some highlighting materials around her eyes, giving her a little bit of a glow. Then when she becomes a heroin addict I added bags under her eyes and chapped lips and hand-painted blemishes."

As the hike continued, the character got dirtier and dirtier. "Dirt's really tricky to do properly because

WILD (2014)   REESE WITHERSPOON © Fox Searchlight Pictures
Licensed from Entertainment Pictures / Alamy Stock Photo

it needs to look like it's sunken into the pores, the crevices of the skin, wrinkles, under the nails. For this part of the hike we went without any cosmetic corrective beauty make-up. For the dirt, I used a spray dirt with different colors. I took dark brown spray dirt and sprayed it over her arms and worked it into the skin with my hands, really massaging it so it got in there. Then I took a baby wipe and wiped most of it off, gently, so parts remain stuck in the crevices and pores. I then repeated the process with differ colors of dirt. Then I did a light misting and started removing portions of it, random portions, and then sprayed a couple more times with different colors of dirt. Then I used stipple sponges to create little patterns on the skin and sometimes I used powered dirt on top of it all. As we got to the final part of the trail when she's really found herself, we added a little corrective makeup to make it look like she was settled into her spirit."

Although Robin relishes the challenges of working outdoors and overcoming nature's obstacles, "After ***Into the Wild*** and ***Wild***, I think any film with the word 'wild' in the title, I'm good. I've done enough of that."

An Ambassador

In 2010 when Robin was working on ***The Runaways***, a true story about the all-girls rock band, she used Make Up For Ever products because "they had the widest range of colors for this 1970s-era film where everyone, both men and women, were wearing a lot of makeup with glitter and bright pigments. Make Up For Ever was the only brand that offered those ranges." As a result of her work on that film, Robin was offered a contract with the international company. She has the luxury of going to Dubai several times a year to demonstrate new Make Up For Ever products, teach film and television master classes twice a year at the *Cite du Cinema*, Make Up For Ever TV and Film Academy Makeup School in Paris, and travel the world teaching master classes to publicize the Make Up For Ever TV and Film Academy Makeup School and products. "I've been so fortunate to be able to work with this fabulous company and their products. I'm so gratefull for all the opportunities they've given me."

Robin has had an adventure-filled journey. Her projects range from ***Heart, Baby*** (2017), to ***The Paperboy*** (2012), to ***Sons of Anarchy*** (2008 and 2012), to ***Twilight Saga: Eclipse*** (2010) where she was Kristin Stewart's personal, to speaking and teaching master classes while travelling the world. It is a life filled with variety and creativity and great satisfaction. "My whole life is my work. Literally, my dog, who was 20-years-old when he passed away, was my life. My dog and my work and that was it. I've chosen that. I'm happy with that. I've devoted everything I have to my career. Everything. I eat, breathe, and sleep film and television. That's my whole life. When you're that emotionally invested in something, it brings joy."

OUTTAKES:

On Women:

"We have more maternal instincts and we're able to take care of our actors in a different way than men do. A lot of being a good makeup artist is being a good therapist."

"The original makeup masters were all men, even if women were doing the work, the men were getting the credit. Ve [Neil] broke the glass ceiling for us, she got her name out there and got the public attention of being an effects artist and being a female. If it wasn't for her, I wonder if any of us would be here even now."

"I had to pay my dues by getting down and dirty and showing examples of my work before I got the opportunities."

"At the end of the day, it's still a boy's club. If I go into a meeting with a director and there's a ton of effects and gags, I tell the director, 'You don't have to hire a makeup effects company. I can handle anything that's in the script.'"

"People are much more critical of women, like they're expecting us to fail. I've spent time on-set when I was sick, but I didn't say anything, because it's seen as a weakness. You're already seen as weaker than a man, so anything else that might make you seem weaker, you've got to keep to yourself. That's my feeling on it."

"Hours are crazy long. God bless people who figure out a way to raise children and have a family while being in this business. I don't know how they do it. I really don't. God bless them."

On Staying Power:

"The best thing I can do for someone is to teach them the top five to ten things that they really need to do to be in film and television makeup. If you can do those top things perfectly, you're going to be okay, you'll always work."

"Ten necessary skills: learn how to cover a tattoo for high definition that is completely rub- and waterproof, know how to break down a script and do continuity, understand set and trailer etiquette, know how to do a real no-makeup makeup on men and women, good dirt, cuts and bruises, proper blood, hand laid hair and working with lace facial hair pieces, transfers, how to make, apply, and color small prosthetics."

On Options:

"Why not try music videos and commercials? Those are short. You can shoot on-set, turn down jobs, and get jobs. You don't have to be gone for six months at a time in another country."

"Maybe you want to do bridal makeup. People make a very good living doing red carpet and publicity makeup in bigger cities."

"If you want to be an effects makeup artist but you still want to have a life, one option would be to work in a shop. Although the hours are still long, you can have more of a life working in a shop than being on a set, because you can't leave the set. We're first in and last out. We're there a lot longer than everybody else."

"I've always wanted to do a *Gone-with-the-Wind-type* epic."

"I'm never going to turn down a script that I'm in love with because it's a really small budget. I take films because of the content, not because of the money."

"I wouldn't want to go back to acting again, but I really enjoy on-camera interviewing."

On the Critical Eye:

"I'm not completely able to get lost in films in anymore, not just because of makeup, but all departments. If you notice the makeup on the screen, then I haven't done my job properly because it's taken you out of the film."

"I see it so often where a makeup artist thinks it's all about the makeup and how great the makeup looks. Well, watching a movie, I shouldn't notice the makeup. If I notice the makeup, then it was a bad job, in my opinion."

On Mentors:

"My grandmother and mother would be my two major life influences, but in the industry, Scott Ramp, obviously, Sean Penn, and Matthew Mungle. I've learned so much from Matthew. He's giving with information and teaching and just the kindest, most wonderful, sweetest guy. I can't say enough. I owe him the world."

On Achieving Dreams:

"My entire life, since I began acting as a child, my biggest dream was to win an Academy Award. Since I've been working as a makeup artist my dream has been to have a major cosmetic contract. It's very odd to acheive the dreams you thought were unachievable. You just kind of sit completely stunned. Happily stunned. I spent most of 2014 in a completely happy daze. But what now? Honestly, it's a very strange feeling."

On Sharing:

"Being back in front of the camera, as a host and representative and teaching makeup, I'm getting to share the 20+ years of my career with new makeup artists just starting out. I want them to know I wasn't 'connected' in Hollywood; I just worked hard and devoted myself to my career. If I could do it, they absolutely can do it too."

On Man's Best Friend

"Who knows what else the future holds for me, but I'm positive it will include helping dogs. Although memories of my accomplishments will always fill me with humble, yet complete fulfillment, they, dogs, are what really make me smile now."

Catching Up!

We interviewed Robin on November 1, 2016. Since then, she has worked on

Teaching Master Classes at *Cite du Cinema* in Paris every six months.

Knuckle
A boxing movie with prosthetics and MUFX,
with Gary Oldman, Kelsey Grammar, and John Leguizamo.

Partnering with Lida Beauty, she's developing a line of revolutionary cosmetic products,
such as the Cleopatra Cat Eye Stamp, a pen eyeliner with a cat eyeliner stamp.
She will be the brand ambassador and spokeswoman for her products
on shopping networks, QVC and HSN

For more of Robin's Credits, visit:
www.robinmathews.com
www.imdb.com

LEADING LADIES
OF MAKEUP EFFECTS

2015
ACADEMY AWARD
BEST ACHIEVEMENT IN
MAKEUP AND HAIRSTYLING

THE GRAND BUDAPEST HOTEL (2014) WES ANDERSON (DIR) MOVIESTORE COLLECTION LTD
Licensed from Moviestore collection Ltd / Alamy Stock Photo

Frances Hannon

It's very important to be open-minded and inclusive in our industry in every way.

Open-minded. Everybody's input. Absorb it all.

Always, at the end of the day,

you will get what you think is right if you listen to everything.

Hoarding has its Purpose

"I invested hugely in my storage space because I'm a hoarder and I think everything has a use. If it hasn't got use on this film, it will on the next." Frances Hannon collects things: makeup products from the 1930s, hair accessories from the 18th and 19th centuries, eye shadows, used prosthetics. Everything is in boxes, and "there are some interesting labels there you know: dirt, filth, snow, sweat. Every box has got something useful."

"I've always loved antique fairs…and I used to go around and buy up old lipsticks and compacts, those little methane heaters, the little beard and mustache combs which have tiny little teeth. And oh, mustache pots of wax, you'd never use those, but replicas can be made from them."

Frances uses the old lipsticks to match color and texture for period pieces. "Not only can you get a good carmine, you can get the right texture match as well. When you are in close-ups you've not got shiny, glossy lips that would never have been in the '30s or '40s. The eye colors they used are so different from anything we produce now. These collectables are a valuable resource for period pieces, especially for something like **The King's Speech** or **The Grand Budapest Hotel**."

Once Frances has designed a prosthetic piece, she often uses it again and again for different films and different situations. She has actually used one piece in six separate films! "You know, one morning when I went in to work on **The Life Aquatic**, the call sheet said, 'Start: Bill injured.' Then I went through my stash. I found this piece and stuck the big, open gash on Bill Murray's head. There's always something useful if you keep it, so I built this enormous storage and everything is in there."

This English-Irish Rose

Frances is a statuesque woman, confident, open, with classical looks and bearing. Both her parents were born in Ireland, but each left to find work in London and met there over 70 years ago. "[They met] around the corner from this very place we are sitting [Shepherd's Bush]." Now both 87, they've been married 62 years, had six daughters, nine granddaughters, and are happily retired. Without any formal education, her father ran a successful business buying, renovating, and reselling public houses and restaurants. "Hard work, good brains, hard work. Really, my parents were my mentors. There was nothing artistically that I hooked into, but I saw lots of hard work."

THE LIFE AQUATIC WITH STEVE ZISSOU (2004) BILL MURRAY
Licensed from AF archive / Alamy Stock Photo

"As a child, I was addicted to Jacques Cousteau. I watched his television show religiously. As a result, I decided I wanted to study marine biology. My parents were doing very well financially and they said to all us girls, 'You don't have to choose now what you want to do. Feel free to keep studying.' I loved doing makeup on myself and my sisters...I could only have been 17 or 18, but I thought I did a good job, so I decided to go to the London College of Fashion for the three-year film and television makeup course and never looked back. Marine biology studies went out the window, but I did get a taste of marine life when I worked as Bill Murray's personal makeup artist on *The Life Aquatic with Steve Zissou* (2004), which is based on the life of Jacques Cousteau."

The arts are not an unusual or surprising occupation for members of Frances's family: her oldest sister, who died young, was a graphic artist, another is in arts education, a third sister was a producer, one daughter is a gifted artist and mathematician, another daughter works in the film industry for the camera department, and her youngest daughter works in film PR. "I haven't seen it in my parents, but I do believe there are great combinations like maths [sic] and art that are linked in the brain. My parents were extraordinarily successful in the maths and I feel if I researched it, I'd find a good grounding for the combo - art and maths."

Training, Sketch Comedy, and Churchill

After training at the London College of Fashion, Frances went into the highly competitive BBC Training Program that only accepted 12 trainees a year. There was a four-month training period, then an additional two years of designated trainee status. "You might not be doing a trainee's work by any means, but that was your title. After you finished your basic training, you were given a mentor: Pam Meager was mine. She was one of the senior designers...she was really opening doors in our industry."

At the BBC, a makeup artist was assigned work. "You didn't choose your work, you didn't have to apply for a position, and people didn't interview you, for you were already employed." During her 14-year tenure with the BBC, Frances was introduced to prosthetics when they were employed to create aging makeups for the first time in the series *I, Claudius* (1976) and *The Voyage of Charles Darwin* (1978). Using prosthetics for aging had never been done before: "It may be very crude now, but in those days it was something amazing and new." She continued her prosthetic work for the sketch comedy series *French and Saunders* (1987), and also mastered historical character makeups in *The Gathering Storm* (2002) for which she won a British Academy of Film and Television Arts (BAFTA) Award.

The French and Saunders Show presented unique challenges. It was a sketch comedy show featuring two comediennes, Dawn French and Jennifer Saunders, who played to a live audience and did quick changes over the course of the show. "The challenge was finding the essence of the look-a-like characters in a matter of minutes - to look at something, a nose, a chin, the eyebrows, and find the essentials in the face."

The Gathering Storm is an historical piece that follows Winston Churchill (Albert Finney) and his wife Clementine (Vanessa Redgrave) in the years prior to WWII. The challenges here were to create recognizable historical characters without completely disguising the actors. Frances shares her BAFTA for *Best Makeup and Hair Design* with Daniel Parker and Stephen Rose.

Psoriasis

In 1986 Frances was asked to design the makeup, hair, and prosthetics for *The Singing Detective*, which remains one of her favorite projects. The script, the director, the actors, and her team all came together to form a cohesive, successful, creative entity. *The Singing Detective* was comprised of six hour-long episodes that each contained four different time periods plus full-body, advanced stage psoriasis makeups. "It was hugely successful because it was so original; it was the BBC in the great days of really innovative TV." Directed by Jon Amiel, *The Singing Detective* was a professional milestone for Frances. She received her first BAFTA for her work on the show, and she began a professional relationship with Amiel that changed the course of her career.

The Singing Detective revolves around Philip E. Marlow, a writer of detective fiction who is hospitalized for psoriatic arthropathy, a chronic skin and joint disease. While he is hospitalized, we are

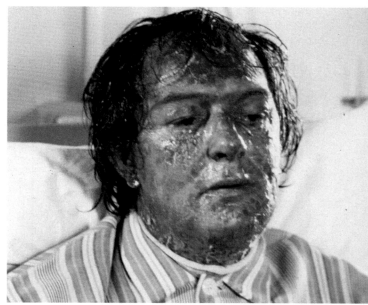

THE SINGING DETECTIVE (1986) MICHAEL GAMBON
Licensed from AF archive / Alamy Stock Photo

introduced to the various worlds in which he exists: the hospital reality, wartime England, the *noir* thriller he is writing in his head, and the fictional interactions of all of the above, usually in the form of a musical number. "All the makeups were complicated to achieve because we did the episodes out of order. [Lead actor] Michael Gambon's skin progression was dictated by the shooting schedule. One day we'd shoot Episode 5, then Episode 1, but within each episode were four layers of period so Michael would have three different looks. Patrick Malahide, who played the wife's lover, had three different looks. Within those there were two different periods and one contemporary. Joanne Whalley, the most beautiful nurse in the world, wasn't she? Different periods for her as well. Everybody was so complicated. Nobody was one thing."

Working out the psoriasis was a creative challenge. In some scenes, it covered Gambon's entire body and was often shot in close-ups. The skin appeared to be peeling off his face in irregular patterns showing discoloration at various depths. To achieve the look she wanted, Frances employed a technique she uses to this day: layering. "I really like makeup effects to be really fine and layered more than putting it on heavy to start with. I'd rather work towards the end effect than just paint it straight on, giving it a bit more texture."

"The psoriasis makeup only had a certain life on Michael Gambon's face. Sometimes, come late afternoon, half of the makeup would be gone. It wasn't super glued onto his face, you couldn't do that to him every day for 6 months."

Once the makeup was sorted, Frances went a step further; she asked Amiel if he could shoot his close-ups of Gambon at the beginning of the day. "The director always prefers, in my life of experience, particularly with TV, to start wide and move in to mids, then close-ups. I think it gives them time, one for the actor to get where they want to be, and secondly, the director is able to see what he wants to cut into. Jon was wonderful to adjust his shooting to the demands of the makeup."

Collaboration between the makeup designer and all other designers is crucial to the final outcome of any character's look. Lighting particularly impacts the makeup artist, defining and honing the colors and textures. Frances asked the DP (director of photography) to light the makeup room to match what the set lighting would be that day. "Because of Michael's complicated makeup, it couldn't be shot in the on-set light and then outside in the white light because it would look wrong. I made him up every day within the light he would be filmed. There are small things like that that make a huge difference that aren't always taken into account."

Frances won the BAFTA for *Best Make Up Design* in 1987 for her work in **The Singing Detective**, making her the youngest person to win this accolade. In the midst of her success, Frances suffered a personal loss; four weeks prior to the BAFTA awards, her son had died at birth. "It was an awful tragedy. It took many years, but I did get my girls."

Life, Work, Life

Frances and her husband have three daughters, one being her adopted niece. "Maybe I've been very lucky, but my husband and children have come to wherever I've gone away to work. You might be working very hard, and you won't end up putting money away at the end of the day, but you've done amazing work, hopefully, and your family has been with you." For eight months in 2000-2001, Frances was Bill Murray's personal makeup artist on three back-to-back films in America: **Charlie's Angels, Osmosis Jones,** and **Speaking of Sex.** Her girls were still young, so her husband home-schooled them on location. "There was a point when we couldn't do that, but at that point I thought about what jobs I would take, how long I'd be away, did I want to leave? I must've been very lucky, for when they were young I never left them for longer than four weeks."

"They're all grown up now. Now they jump on a plane and come and see me. **Jason Bourne** [2016], the film I just finished, shot in Las Vegas for five weeks and they all came to visit."

"I am fortunate to be able to pick and choose my time off. The hardest thing to do is say no to someone I like working with; I just said no to Ron Howard and it breaks my heart. But now I do need to be with my daughters for a while. They're all at home, all finished university recently. They're all starting new jobs, which is marvelous, and it's nice to have mum around to cook."

Leaving the Nest

In 1997, Jon Amiel asked Frances to do a film called **The Man Who Knew Too Little,** starring Bill Murray. For Frances to do the film, she would have to leave the BBC and begin to freelance, which she knew was "not an easy world to break into. I had my children by then, but I left the BBC, did that project, and never looked back. Then Bill asked me to be his personal on **Rushmore**, I met Wes Anderson, director, and life has gone from strength to strength, really."

To date, Frances has worked on four films with Director Wes Anderson: *Rushmore* (1998), *Life Aquatic with Steve Zissou* (2004), both as Bill Murray's personal, *The Darjeeling Limited* (2007) as hair stylist and makeup artist, and *The Grand Budapest Hotel* (2014) as makeup designer, hair designer, and prosthetics designer.

"Wes has a wonderful imagination; he pictures everything in his head. He is a true perfectionist. I mean every shade of every hair color, every brush on the skin, the size of the Mexico-shaped birthmark [on Saoirse Ronan's face] in *Grand Budapest* mattered to him. When someone wants that much perfection and that much detail, it's a great environment in which to work. It has to be as perfect as you can get it."

From Zombies to Kings

Frances' CV runs the gamut of genres: apocalyptic, dystopian zombies in *World War Z* (2013); fantasy in *X-Men: First Class* (2011); adventure in *The Da Vinci Code* (2006); historical England in *The King's Speech* (2010); fictional/fantasy in *The Grand Budapest Hotel* (2014). Guiding Frances' design decisions are two golden rules: be open-minded, and research, research, research. "After I have read a script, I do research for whatever it is, contemporary or period. The research is equal quantities whatever date it is set in, past or future. I think it's the most important part of my job. Share everything with your director. Listen. Be open to every input."

Preparing for *World War Z*, Frances watched every single zombie movie ever made. She was relentless, looking for treatments and designs that inspired her, and when she designed her own zombies she aimed to create something unique. "They were very vocal about wanting something different." Frances teamed with Mark Coulier, with whom she worked on *X-Men*, to create the zombies. "Mark doesn't do hair at all, so we split that."

Conceptually, the zombies incorporated dance and animal movements as they moved quickly across the screen. "Consequently, my work and Mark's needed to be strong because the zombies are never standing still. In the split second the audience sees them, the zombies need to stand out."

And then there are also the restrictions and realities imposed by the industry as a whole that every film artist confronts at some point. Most decisions are based on numbers: how can the maximum number of people see this film? What rating will engender greater viewability? "You can't show blood, you can't show something too vicious. The blood has to be black. There can't be too many wounds. You can't frighten the kids. You'd like to put a caption up saying, 'My zombie wouldn't have looked quite like this! This is a gentle version of where we would have taken it.'"

World War Z (2013)   Alamy Stock Photo

Frances had great fun working on the film despite the restrictions. "It was great, marvelous. Brad Pitt is a wonderful, wonderful artist, with a wonderful attitude. He's so clever; he's a pleasure to work with. This might not be the sort of film he might want to do, but he does it extremely well. There's something endearing about him in the zombie film, everybody wants him to be okay and survive."

The King's Speech (2010) involved a completely different set of creative muscles because it is an his-

THE KING'S SPEECH (1980)
JEFFREY RUSH, COLIN FIRTH, HELENA BONHAM CARTER
Licensed from Photo 12 / Alamy Stock Photo

torical drama set in 1939 England with the main characters being King George VI (Colin Firth) and Queen Elizabeth (Helena Bonham Carter). There are portraits and pictures and history books that chronicle these people's lives; the clothes they wore and the hair styles they sported are on public display. "The period is absolutely locked."

"I never try to make my actor fit the period. You have to be open and bring your research of the period to the actor and find something that might just put them in that space. I never say, 'This is the mustache you have to wear,' or, 'This wig is the right style for the period' because that doesn't necessarily make the actor look or feel right. For example, I didn't copy a photo of the Queen for Helena Bonham Carter; her makeup had the feel of the look, but it had the Helena finish to it."

According to Frances, **The King's Speech** was a low budget film, so she used a lot of what she had in stock. Wigs and bald caps were creatively used to recreate the feel of the period. "Nobody, nobody walked out of that trailer without wigs and facial hair. There was so much work done, but because it's not visible nobody has any idea. Colin Firth was going back and forth to America because he was nominated for an Oscar. He got a false tan, not makeup, the dye version, to look great for the Oscars. He did look great, but he'd come back to me with a nice tan he didn't have when he left. Now if you look again you might see various shades of skin tone."

Now You See It...

"I think, for a lot of contemporary stuff, if you're good at your job, you mustn't be able to see the work in general, whatever we do is not meant to be a distraction from what the story is about. I think sometimes in our industry the makeup can be a distraction."

In **Captain Phillips** (2013), the Somali pirates were actually mid-American guys who wore velour sweat pants with shapes shaved into their heads. "There was a huge amount of work to get them to look like they were Somalian. We broke their skin down, they wore prosthetics every day, and they had hair fill-ins. Then they had the process of the film story journey, blood and the glass and all the things that happened to them on the way. There was a lot of work that one never saw."

In **Now You See Me 2** (2016), Woody Harrelson plays two characters: a normal character, himself, and his not-so-normal brother. As the makeup and hair designer, Frances made up four different Woodys for the film. There were three look-a-likes: a body double, an acting partner, and a stunt man, each with two different looks. Each of these four actors had to be made up as both the normal character and the brother and back again because the two brothers talked to each other (in actuality, Woody was talking to himself). "We used full prosthetics, noses, chins, teeth, eyes, wigs, and everything. We needed to make a big difference in small ways that we could do in five minutes because Woody does not like the makeup chair. He had to swing from one brother to another and back again because they were doing motion lock. We'd go away, get him ready, back in, take him away again, get him ready with the brother character, back in. Somewhere along the line you can't lose the actor's performance. You have to let him, somehow, stay in that state he's in when he's responding to himself all the time." The logistics of making up the actors, preparing them for the shoot while allowing them to stay in character, and fulfilling the director's vision with an eye to expediency, is part of the job the general public never sees.

The stakes were high in **Victor Frankenstein** (2015) because the studios wanted to be sure Daniel Radcliffe's makeup wasn't straight out of **Harry Potter,** and "while they wanted him to look right, they wanted him to look like Dan because that's what sells." As the makeup and hair designer for the film, Frances wanted to show the degeneration of Daniel's Igor character through a subtle, old, cracked clown makeup. "I wanted it to look like it was real, that it had been layered over the years and had never been washed. They didn't use many close ups so the makeup and Neill Gorton's marvelous prosthetic designs for the monster didn't necessarily show."

"I think people think, 'She's done **Bourne** and there's no work on that.' It's so not true. Contemporary work is equally as involved and certainly equally as researched to get to the end result. It's just that if it's done well you don't see it."

The Hotel

"Wes Anderson asked me well in advance to do **Grand Budapest.** I went to meet him, read the script, did a huge amount of research, then met with Wes again. He said, 'That's just how I saw Bill Murray or Owen Wilson or....'" The periods of the film are 1930s and 1960s, "but they weren't locked; it was very fluid, moving from one period to another to get the stylized look Wes wanted." For Frances, it is more important to fit the mustache to the actor than the actor to the mustache, hence the fluidity.

Originally, Angela Lansbury was going to play the part of Madame D., but the shoot was delayed slightly and the dates didn't work with her schedule. "Wes called and asked, 'Do you think we could use Tilda [Swinton]? I don't want to change the whole age concept; can we make her the older woman?' I responded, 'Without a doubt we can make her sit well within it, but are you sure?'" At this juncture, Frances brought Mark Coulier into the project "because I love his work." Frances designed the hair and makeup and prosthetics, and Mark sculpted the pieces, made the molds and prosthetics for both Tilda Swinton and Harvey Keitel, and applied them, then together they did the hair, makeup, and tattoos.

THE GRAND BUDAPEST HOTEL (2014) © Fox Searchlight film
RALPH FIENNES AND TILDA SWINTON
Licensed from AF archive / Alamy Stock Photo

Budget was a major concern in transforming Tilda Swinton into a believable octogenarian. The wig was five pieces, the prosthetic was 11 pieces, which included back of hands, neck, chin, two nose-pieces, ear lobes, watery contacts to simulate cataracts, and yellow false teeth. "It's very expensive to do prosthetics, but Tilda's part was very small so we only did it for a few days. It's a very long process. By the time we got her ready, it was five hours into the day and we could only have her for a limited length of time. Time and available hours are an important consideration in anything you do."

Frances works with all her directors to determine budget and hour restrictions while factoring in the availability of actors. "In **Grand Budapest**, there were no makeup tests, no fittings, nothing because the most wonderful cast in the world didn't come on location until the day before they were on-set, with the exception of Ralph Fiennes. I did the work when they arrived. Hoped everything worked out as I planned. Cut their hair if I could; often they're locked into continuity on another film. Do the best you can within the limits you have and hope it works. It usually does. Your team of artists is most important. Without them, nothing would work. On *The Grand Budapest Hotel* my main team members were Julie Dartnell, Emma Mash, Norma Webb and Heike Merker."

The inspiration for Madame D. was Frances' mother. "My mother still now will pick up a lipstick and run it over her lips without looking in the mirror, leaving it slightly cockeyed. She still will put lipstick on her cheeks and rub it in for color. It reflects a certain time and a certain lady. The elegance of Tilda's character is absolutely a different thing from my mother. My mother is elegant, but she doesn't have the big 'dos."

While Tilda Swinton's Madame D. garnered much of the attention in *The Grand Budapest Hotel*, Frances's impeccable work and attention to detail is evident throughout the film in myriad mustaches and

wigs, cuts, bruises and blood, the birthmark in the shape of Mexico, and in crowd scenes of over 100 with each actor sporting appropriate facial hair and wigs. Her design captured Wes Anderson's vision, unifying the look of the film and supporting the actors. "It's so stylized, but most of the work you don't see. It doesn't mean it wasn't there."

Frances won the Academy Award for *Best Achievement in Makeup and Hairstyling* for *The Grand Budapest Hotel,* which she shares with Mark Coulier. She also won her third British Academy of Film and Television Arts award for *Best Makeup, Hair and Prosthetics,* also shared with Mark Coulier, as well as two Hollywood Makeup Artist and Hairstyling Guild Awards, one for *Best Period and/or Character Makeup* and the other for *Best Period and/or Character Hair Styling*, both shared with Julie Dartnell.

THE GRAND BUDAPEST HOTEL (2014)
RALPH FIENNES WES ANDERSON (DIR) MOVIESTORE COLLECTION LTD
Licensed from Moviestore collection Ltd / Alamy Stock Photo

In her Oscar acceptance speech, Frances thanked Bill Murray for introducing her to Wes Anderson, "Who made all this possible."

Frances Hannon likes challenges, always asking herself: how do I achieve this effect while satisfying my director, keeping my actor comfortable, engaged and on task, and fulfilling my vision? And, equally important, how does this translate to my life? "Be very open-minded, have guidelines, which of course we do with our job. If you're lucky, success will come by the way you approach your job or your life."

OUTTAKES:

On Working with the Costumer:

"I interact very much with the costume design. It's really important. There's no point at all doing what you do, and doing it well, if it doesn't match what's on the rest of the body."

On Making Do:

"You can usually find something, even in the kitchen, if you don't have your kit that will give you the effect you want. I use a lot of animal meat. I'd use a pig skin; you can make a great wound if you stick it on and slice it open. If you're making a wound by applying a prosthetic, use some animal flesh, a piece of steak in the wound, it's far better than building it into the prosthetic or making your whole prosthetic out of silicone. It works well to layer and add different textures - makes it far more believable."

On I'd Like to…:

"I'd love to do a film in Australia. I've never been there or Hawaii. Small pleasures in life, really, but I think, if I could, I would choose my projects by countries. I would love to film in Italy again."

On Light, Beautiful Light:

"People don't tend to light for the artist any more, as in the '40s, to make the women look beautiful. I haven't seen that in years. We did it on *Entrapment* for Catherine Zeta. I was making her up and I think it took them six hours to light the scene where she comes down the stairs in the red dress he bought her. She was breathtaking. That may have been the last time I've seen somebody who waited for the lights to make the actress or actor look gorgeous."

On Nurturing Your Actors:

"It's important that you create that space your actor needs, whatever that space may be."

"I wouldn't want somebody to turn up at five in the morning to make me up who is constantly talking, or doesn't pay attention to their job during the day."

"There are a million different people you have to be to make the right environment for the actor and I think that's very important."

On the Makeup Community:

"If you're working with an actor for the first time and you know somebody who has worked with him, you'll ask, 'Is there anything in particular he likes to use?' And if the designer has the information, they share it. I do with everybody."

"I think it's very important to share if you discover something new. If somebody phones you up and says, 'How do you do that?' Tell them, because they might go on and evolve that into something else that's even more interesting and then you can benefit all around. That's how I feel about the job. Share what you can."

On Commercials:

"Commercials these days are really like a mini film. If they're done well, they're as equally demanding as a film, except you shoot it in three or six days instead of months."

On Professional Makeup Effects:

"David Stoneman, who owns the company called *Maekup,* can create anything in the world for you. From duplicating 1940s lipsticks, to a porcelain cracking makeup, to a makeup to look like dogs poo for the film *Death at a Funeral*. He's a wonderful genius when it comes to making products."

On Personals:

"I love working with personals as a head of department. I don't think I've ever met a personal that I haven't enjoyed the company of. Brad [Pitt] works with Jean Ann Black, it's because he trusts what's going to happen to him with her. Whatever they do is their choice. I do not interfere with the look of that actor. When I do Bill [Murray], I design the look."

"The director and the actor, of course, have the final say, whether you are a designer or a personal."

"I'd be happy to work for the rest of my years with Tom Hanks, Bill Murray, Owen Wilson, Paul Greengrass, Ron Howard, Wes Anderson...there's an endless list of wonderful people."

On Her Team:

"I would never have been as successful as I've been or as lucky as I've been without an amazing team. If your team is not excellent at their jobs, it doesn't matter what you design, it won't look good on the day."

Catching Up!

We interviewed Frances on June 4, 2016. Since then, she has worked on

Inferno
Makeup and Hair Designer

For more of Frances' Credits, visit: www.imdb.com

LEADING LADIES
OF MAKEUP EFFECTS

2016
ACADEMY AWARD
BEST ACHIEVEMENT IN
MAKEUP AND HAIRSTYING

Mad Max: Fury Road (2015) USA / Australia
Director : George Miller ; TomHardy, Charlize Theron ; Movie poster (USA)
Licensed from AF archive / Alamy Stock Photo

LESLEY VANDERWALT

I saw this sculpture in a London park once, and it was all these coils;
a big, round thing with glass tubes coming out of it, all twisted and intertwined.
I thought, that's what my brain does when I read a really good script.
It starts going all colors.

Oscar Week, 2016. A whirlwind of parties and people and interviews. Lesley was on Australian time, fighting jet lag and nerves, answering emails, deciding whether to attend the 9th Annual Women in Film Pre-Oscar Party, Diane von Furstenberg's luncheon honoring female Oscar nominees, or the *Vanity Fair*, Lancome, and Clarisonic Makeup Artist Spa Day. While in Los Angeles for the awards, Lesley invited us to her room at The Beverly Hilton for our interview. She answered the door in the hotel robe and slippers, invited us in, turned off her electronics, settled us on the end of the bed, curled up in the chair, took a deep breath, and began.

"All these people are here that I've never met before, but oh my God, I go, 'Ahh, it's Ve Neil! There's Rick Baker!' They are my mentors, as they are everybody else's. It is extraordinary as we don't get to meet them. For me, coming here this time around, I am seeing people I've only ever seen pictures of in books." Lesley is striking, confident, comfortable, forthright, intelligent, and enthusiastic with a delightfully sly sense of humor and an honest, deep commitment to her art, unjaded by her success.

"It's been an amazing experience to go through this. Before [the Oscar nomination], I'd never done an interview. I don't have a social media presence. I have one Facebook page for my close friends and family so they know where I am. I've always avoided all that because it's something that's just not part of my life. It's part of my work and maybe I should start up a work thing, but I find it hard enough just getting the wi-fi on. It was great getting all the messages and congratulations when we won the nomination. I have just started an Instagram page, but I'm still not sure how to use it!"

It's in the Genes

Born in Cape Town, South Africa, Lesley's family immigrated to Wellington, New Zealand, when she was four to escape the injustices of apartheid and segregation. She attended school there, began her career there, and in 1981, Director George Miller asked Lesley to design makeup and hair for *Mad Max 2: The Road Warrior*. She accepted the job, went to Australia for the shoot, and to this day calls Sydney home.

Lesley credits her father's creativity as a major influence in her life. Experimenting with many careers, he was a photographer, a salesman, a policeman, and a sketch artist/cartoonist in his spare time. "All around the house were Dad's drawings; anything you picked up, Dad would have drawn on it. After he passed away, I made a book of his caricatures and cartoons because they were really good. If he thought something was funny, he'd do a drawing. My cousin, Lainey, started art school after her children were grown up and he thought it was hysterical. She was the oldest student there among all those young ones. He would draw cartoons of her in class and send them to her."

Even as a young girl, Lesley was busy creating, painting, knitting, and embroidering. She always had a project going and enjoyed the challenge of figuring out how to "make it work," something that drives her even today. "When I wanted to knit a jumper [sweater] with a pattern on it, I thought, 'If I get some graph paper and each square is a stitch…' I'd make patterns, do the picture on graph paper, and then work out the stitch. I would work things like that out even when I was really young, seven or eight."

"I remember, to my mother's horror, painting a mural of Aquarius on my whole bedroom wall. She came home and I, once again, had graphed off the wall and painted this very Pop Art graphic; hair with swirls and different colors in it. Very '60s, '70s. I was always very creative."

The Right Place…

Anxious to leave school as soon as possible, Lesley began her hairdressing apprenticeship at age 15 at Sigrid of Germany Salon in Wellington. She liked coloring hair and, at that time, during the 1970s, there weren't many career choices available for a young woman in New Zealand outside of nursing, office work, or hairdressing. "I never even thought about film and television." Cynthia Goodwin, one of her clients and head of makeup at the new Avalon Film & Television Studios in Wellington, asked Lesley if she was interested in the makeup and hair training program. Ms. Goodwin knew Lesley had the people skills and the hairdressing skills, she just had to determine if Lesley had the makeup talent as well. "I went and did some tests with her. She gave me some people to make up and a few days later she rang me up and said, 'I'd love you to come out here and I'll train you in makeup. You can finish your hairdressing apprenticeship while you're training with us so you can get your license.'"

Lesley trained at Television One New Zealand (TVNZ 1) in Wellington, where she learned makeup and honed her hair skills. She did a "few programs with them and the next thing I knew, I was offered a free-lance job for my first film, *Skin Deep* (1978), doing makeup, hair, and costumes. I was always interested in other things and in my spare time had been doing a correspondence course in pattern-cutting and designing. It was a contemporary film, thank goodness." Lesley's pattern-cutting skills were invaluable because the leading lady had just had a baby and was breast feeding. To accommodate her, Lesley "made little outfits for her that did up at the front, so it was easy when we were on-set. It was New Zealand. We were very, very low budget and we basically had to do everything, you know? It's amazing I wasn't doing catering as well."

Signs and Signals

"Right place, right time…and the same with moving to Australia, you know. There have always been, I believe, signs and signals in my life." In 1981, Lesley was working on *Bad Blood*, a film that called for bullet wounds and scrapes and blood, on the west coast of New Zealand. Bob McCarron, an Australian paramedic and prosthetic makeup artist, was responsible for the prosthetics on the film. "I hadn't even heard of prosthetics, to be honest. Vaguely, I had read about them, but hadn't had any experience with them." There was bad weather which closed the airport, so Bob was unable to get to the west coast. His gear had been sent ahead, so he called Lesley. "He guided me over the telephone. I applied the prosthetics with Bob's direction from long distance…and they worked, to my astonishment. When he arrived, Bob couldn't believe it. He finished the applications and I watched and learned, just like a sponge."

Shortly thereafter, Bob was asked to design the makeup for **Mad Max 2: The Road Warrior**, but was committed to another film. He recommended Lesley to George Miller, the director. "I went over and did **Road Warrior** with little experience. I was learning as I went. That's what it was all about in those days, you had to be working in the film industry, you had to have hair skills, makeup skills, and later on, prosthetic skills because the budgets were so small they didn't employ three separate people for those jobs." McCarron (affectionately nicknamed Dr. Bob for his ability to use his medical training in creating special effects) was responsible for the special makeup effects on the film; Lesley was the designer. "Bob McCarron was the guy who started Elka Wardega and me in prosthetics. He started a lot of women and men in film in Australia."

NO ESCAPE (1994) RAY LIOTTA
Licensed from Entertainment Pictures / Alamy Stock Photo

Gritty Sci Fi, Noir, and Futuristic Fantasy

Lesley's body of work spans genres and decades, and is peppered with interesting projects and recognition along the way. On her list of favorite projects is **No Escape** (1994), also known as **Escape from Absolom** outside of the US. Based on the 1987 novel **The Penal Colony** by Richard Herley, **No Escape** is a futuristic look at incarceration and punishment where prisoners are isolated on an island and ulti-

mately create their own society. Lesley was challenged because there were lots of extras in the film that needed different looks; the characters are filthy, rugged, and scratched, reflecting their conflicts, isolation, and will to survive.

In 1996, Lesley designed **Dark City**, a shadowy, stark murder mystery in which Murdoch (Rufus Sewell) awakens alone in a strange hotel to find that he is wanted for a series of brutal murders that he cannot remember. The makeup, lighting, and costumes combine to create a world familiar and unknown, frightening and stylish, desperate and sane. Lesley was nominated for the Saturn Award for *Best Makeup* and won the Australian Society of Makeup Artists Award for *Best Makeup* that she shares with Bob McCarron and Lynn Wheeler.

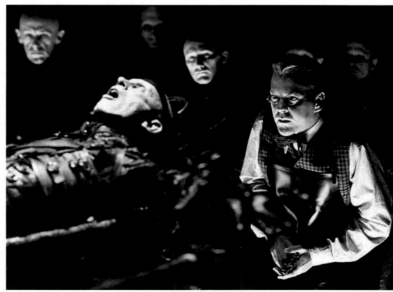

DARK CITY (1998) KEIFER SUTHERLAND
Licensed from United Archives GmbH / Alamy Stock Photo

In 1999, Lesley became the makeup supervisor (in the US this is the head of department) and designer for the television science fiction fantasy, **Farscape.** It was while on this series that Lesley worked, for the first time, with two prosthetic makeup artists, Damian Martin and Elka Wardega, who later played significant roles in **Fury Road.** Shot in Sydney and New South Wales and set in the future, **Farscape** revolves around astronaut John Crichton who finds himself thrown across the universe when an experimental mission goes badly. The series had alien makeups, prosthetics, and animatronics; Lesley conceived and designed the makeup for the humanoid aliens.

FARSCAPE (1999)
LANI JOHN TUPU, GIGI EDGELY, VIRGINIA HEY, CLAUDIA BLACK, BEN BROWDER, ANTHONY SIMCOE
Licensed from AF archive / Alamy Stock Photo

The look of Chiana, a new character to the series, actually evolved out of a frustrating meeting. Lesley still remembers the weekly creative team meeting discussing Chiana when the production secretary offered an idea. "'You could have her hair like this, get some mousse, do this, and add some lipstick.'" "Obviously, there's no point in me being in this meeting any longer," said Lesley as she left the room and went home, fuming. She couldn't let it go, "I thought, is this what it's come to? A can of mousse? And I looked down at my coffee table and there was a black and white brochure from **Belle Decoration Magazine** [a furniture homewares company] celebrating their 25th anniversary. I went, 'Oh, my God, that's what we could do! We can do a black and white person in this colored world.' I rang up my friend who is a DOP [director of photography] and asked, 'Could you send me over a grayscale now and put it in a taxi?'" She spent the night matching and mixing Dinair colors to match the grayscale, gray lipsticks, eye shadows, while rendering the lips, eyebrows, and facial shading. By the end of the night, she had created a palette, the right balance of grays that would make the makeup pop in a full-color world. In the morning she put the makeup on a crew-member and the makeup was met with enthusiasm all around.

"This all came from looking at a furniture magazine on my coffee table. You never know where inspiration comes from, and it can be all around you. It can be someone on the street. It can be in nature. You just suddenly go, 'Wow. Amazing.' I never know. It just comes. I never know where it comes from, when it's going to come. It's a funny thing…I don't know what made me decide to go to the catering table and get that date from the bowl of dried fruit and turn it into a wound. It's the sort of thing that just happens."

Lesley received the Australian Society of Makeup Artists Award for *Best Makeup* for her work on **Farscape** in 2000.

Everything's Connected

"I'm very much a collaborator that will spend a lot of time in other people's departments. I'll walk through it. I'll sit in it. I love touching and feeling the fabrics and looking at the texture. Quite often I'll introduce fabrics and their colors into my makeups. On **Gods of Egypt** (2016), I worked with milliners to create shapes, then made felt from hair and glued it on to create what we called W hats (Wig Hats). On **Gatsby**

(2013), I actually used some of the lace and material from the dresses to make masks and textures I glued on the face. I like to collaborate with the whole thing. It's all got to work, from the ground up to the sky, what they're driving, what they live in, it's all got to work."

When Lesley begins a project, she meets with and listens to the director's ideas, trying to get a feel for the concept. Then she puts together three different mood boards for each character that may have colors, shapes, pictures, or textures. "Then I see what the director's drawn towards and make a more defined board, one which is more about the character." She collects pictures from magazines, books, or the internet, often using a Pinterest board of the actors with long hair or short, blond hair or black, comparing different looks they've had over the years. "For instance, like Charlize, [Theron, **Mad Max: Fury Road**] she's a woman living in a man's world. You start looking at the whole character and then start defining the look.

GODS OF EGYPT (2016) GERARD BUTLER
Licensed from Atlaspix / Alamy Stock Photo

"I believe each character should have his or her own shape; like you did as kids behind the sheet with a backlight? It's a silhouette. You know who each character is by the lump on their head, or the big nose, or floppy ears. That's how I play with characters and their shapes."

The collaboration process involves scintillating creative exchanges among the director, producer, cinematographer, production designer, costume designer, makeup designer, and all other members of the design team. During one of those meetings, Lesley noticed the costumer was using an illustrator who sketched as they talked about a character's costume. As the ideas changed, the illustrator adjusted the drawing to the discussion. The team looked at the illustrations and evaluated the look: "'No, no, that should be higher.' 'I was actually thinking of putting him in a jacket.' 'Oh well, take that off the arms. You're not going to see them.' That is how we collaborate together."

And Lesley came up with an idea that would work similarly for makeup: using Photoshop. "With Geoffrey Rush in *Gods of Egypt*, he was going to be bald with a long, white beard. I worked with Matt Hatton, Photoshop expert, for about three days, just getting really good-looking stuff for Geoffrey. We sent it to the director and he'd say, 'Oh, can the hair start a bit lower? Or a bit higher?' We went up and down with the hairline until we got it absolutely perfect. I don't do Photoshop, but I use people who do. All these things that didn't exist when I started out, to go and learn them, taking time out of what I do to get really good at them, I might as well not be doing makeup. So I use their skills and sit alongside them and work with them."

"I remember years ago I did a film, *The Last Days of Chez Nous* (1992), where all these different actresses were a family. Janet Patterson, the production designer, called me up before we started work on the film and said, 'Listen, I'm thinking of doing all the walls this really deep aubergine [eggplant] color.' My first reaction? Half their heads are going to fade into the walls. Then I started thinking about it and called the director, 'What about if we made them all redheads so they stand out from these walls? They're all family and we can make them all different shades of red, which will look beautiful against the aubergine wall.'"

Lesley's creative process is collaborative, utilizing ambient stimulus, fellow artists, available technology, anything and everything that could possibly aid in the creation of a character's look.

"Doing the Big"

Mad Max 2: The Road Warrior (1981), ***No Escape*** (aka ***Escape from Absolom,*** 1994), ***Dark City*** (1998), ***Moulin Rouge!*** *(2001)*, ***Australia*** (2008), ***The Great Gatsby*** (2013), and ***Mad Max: Fury Road*** (2015) all have one thing in common (besides Lesley): they all have large numbers of extras. "I think I may have been one of the first people in Australia who started to do big crowd rooms. I mean, with ***Road Warrior***, it was two of us on it, you know? We were running like crazy nearly 24/7. We nearly lost our minds. I started building big things and I started looking at every project as a different thing. How do I make this work? How do I get these people out on time? How can I speed up the process? Is it better to have one person do individuals or is it better to break it up like a factory?"

No Escape was one of Lesley's first big shows where she organized the crowd rooms into an efficient unit. She figured out the needs of the film and how to maximize the time and energy spent making up the extras. "There were lots of different looks and lots of people in a rainforest location and we had to churn these people out every day." ***The Great Gatsby*** also had large crowd scenes, an average of 250 people, and Lesley divided the crowd room into makeup and hair to make it easier on her makeup artists and the actors.

Lesley ran ***Fury Road*** like a factory. "I had special areas for each stage of the makeups: airbrushing, clay, prosthetics. I really had to divide it up and work out a way of making it flow and having my head people there pushing them through. Everybody had to do ev-

THE GREAT GATSBY (2013) CAREY MULLIGAN & LEONARDO DICAPRIO
Licensed from AF archive / Alamy Stock Photo

erything. I had to have people who did straight makeup doing prothetics as well, otherwise I couldn't get all those people on. Eight people couldn't do it all; the makeups took two-and-a-half hours each."

"I always divide my work force into teams. The A Team handles lead actors or ones with featured bits. The makeup artists on A Team are the ones with the most experience and are the ones who I've worked with the most. The B Team takes care of the actors who are a bit further away from camera. For that team, I schedule a combination of experienced and newbie artists. The C Team works on the background actors who are furthest from camera; those artists are assisted by students."

Makeup artists often put in 12+ hours a day, starting early in the morning and, depending on the shooting schedule, can work six or seven days a week for months at a time. In addition to organizing the crowd rooms, Lesley puts together a schedule for her artists that is actually humane. "I try not to work everybody really long hours and wear them out. I stagger calls: the people who go in early one day, go in later the next. Then I have to organize the transport, who's going on what bus when. I really enjoy the logistics. Trying to get the look and the designs across in the most efficient manner without exhausting and drowning my people."

The "Event"

"In 2010, I had a left communicating artery blow out in my head. A massive aneurysm. I was at home on a Friday night, sending digital photos to my producers and I said, 'Whoa, I've got this massive thunderclap headache.' I can't exactly remember, but I know I was thinking there was something really wrong. For some reason I went into the next room and got my Medicare card, all my medical insurance cards, put a rubber band around it all, then got my phone and put it next to me at the computer. I actually thought something weird was happening. The next thing I knew, I came to on the floor on the other side of the room. I had been out cold. I couldn't move anything except one arm. I thought I'd had a stroke.

"I realized I needed to get help….I needed to get the phone. It's funny, you can only think one thought at a time; it's like having a whole lot of little cubes in your head and you have to check one off at a time."

Lesley is the only tenant on that floor of her building and access to her home is by swipe key alone. The fire escape is accessible, but only by key. "I dragged myself to the front door. Lying on my back, I was able to use my working arm to open the door and wedge a shoe, propping the door open. Then I dragged myself to the fire escape and propped that open with another shoe. Then I dragged myself back into the apartment and waited for someone to come.

"My next thought was, 'I have to get the phone.' I rang three people. My neighbor wasn't home, my friend down the road was out, but her kids answered the phone and I didn't want to worry them. Then my friend, Bec, who lives quite a distance away said, 'Just hang in there. I'm getting into the car and coming straight away. Just hang in there.'

"Everybody asks, 'Why didn't you ring an ambulance?' We watch so much American television I couldn't remember if it was 999 or 911. Of course, it's neither, it's 000. One box at a time.

"Bec got me to the hospital, it was a Friday night and it was busy. Where I live it's the middle of the night-life district and they assume you're taking drugs. When they finally did a head scan on me they rushed me straight to another hospital where the neurosurgeons were on duty. They coiled the aneurysm, which involves wrapping the aneurysm with wire, and I was in an induced coma for quite a while….

"After the operation, I got hydrocephalitis…fluid on the brain. They operated a second time, put drains into my head, and that's when they said they lost me. They called my family and told them it was over, but my sister said, 'You don't know my sister.' I survived. I was very lucky, many don't.

"My then-partner said it was like *Groundhog Day*. He said I'd wake up and say, 'What are all these?' and try to pull out all the tubes. And he said, 'Then they'd come along with another shot and put you back to sleep. Every time you woke up you said the same thing.' My surgeon said I was an absolute nightmare as a patient, grabbing the tubes and trying to pull them out because they were like foreign objects. There were times I thought I was in some sort of freaky film.

"I spent about eight months recovering. The first thing it does is knock all your confidence. You lose your confidence when you're trying to get back all your skills, walking, talking, all that, it was like one little box at a time and I thought, 'I can deal with this.' But I really didn't think I'd do another film.

I started looking at what else I could probably do.

"That's when Baz Luhrmann asked me to collaborate with Maurizio Silvi and Kerry Warn for additional designs and to be makeup and hair supervisor for *Gatsby* (2013)." Lesley had worked with Luhrmann on three previous films: as designer for *Strictly Ballroom* (1992), head of department for *Moulin Rouge!* (2001), and makeup supervisor and additional designer for *Australia* (2008). "First, they made sure I didn't have two heads and wasn't drooling. I talked to the doctors who said, 'Yeah, do it,' and so I did. That gave me my confidence back."

"I've decided now that I don't do films back-to-back. I've got to do one thing at a time. Don't go crazy. Don't get stressed out about it or try to do too many things all at once. I approach one thing at a time.

Then maybe delegate once I've gotten to a certain point. I hand it over to someone else to do on a daily basis, watching over it all the time. I think that's the way to approach a big film. I like to oversee the big picture, not concentrate on one character."

Mad Max: Fury Road

Fury Road is a post-apocalyptic film set in a desert wasteland populated by broken humans who are always searching for water, pure blood, and gasoline - the things necessary for survival. The film follows Imperator Furiosa (Charlize Theron), a woman committed to saving the innocent, and Max (Tom Hardy), who fights for justice in this unjust world.

George Miller is the creator, writer, and director of the Mad Max franchise, including the original **Mad Max** (1979), **Mad Max II: Road Warrior** (1981), **Mad Max Beyond Thunderdome** (1985), and **Mad Max: Fury Road** (2015). Lesley has worked on three films with Miller as makeup and hair designer: the second and fourth **Mad Max** films, and **Babe: Pig in the City** (1998).

MAD MAX: FURY ROAD (2015)
Licensed from Lifestyle pictures / Alamy Stock Photo

Mad Max: Fury Road is a high-concept film with diverse, unique communities. "We've got Gas Town where the residents are covered with burns because they live in a gaseous environment. The residents of Bullet Town are covered in chemical powders. Then there's The Citadel where the boys work on cars all the time, so they need to have black, greasy hands, covered in white clay, emulating their leader, Immortan Joe." There are also Immortan Joe's Five Wives, beautiful, sarong-wrapped young women, and other characters with names like Rictus Erectus (Nathan Jones), Organic Mechanic (Angus Sampson), and Nux (Nicholas Hoult), which means "hard nut to crack." Miller and Nick Lathouris wrote extensive biographies of each of the characters which, of course, informed design decisions. The challenge was to create unique characters that are true to Miller's vision while not succumbing to two-dimensional stereotypes.

Obviously successful, **Fury Road** won multiple critical and guild awards. The film also received ten Academy Award nominations including *Best Picture* and *Best Director* for George Miller. It won six: B*est Production Design, Best Achievement in Costume Design, Best Film Editing, Best Sound Editing, Best Sound Mixing*…and *Best Achievement in Makeup and Hairstyling*, which Lesley shares with Damian Martin and Elka Wardega.

The Team

Damian Martin and Elka Wardega, among others, worked closely with Lesley in the conception of the makeups, the applications, and problem-solving. "My right-hand woman for the War Boys was Elka, who did a brilliant job. She was with me initially when we started experimenting with clays, she helped figure out how to ensure the makeup lasted in the desert, and how to protect the prosthetics with sunblock. Elka was there from the beginning to the end." Damian, as the prosthetic supervisor on the film, was Lesley's "…right-hand man. He and his crew contributed a huge amount. I couldn't have done it without him."

Australia has a small, insulated film community where everyone knows everybody else. Lesley, Damian, and Elka have a work history that started in 1999 on the television series **Farscape.** Subsequently, Damian's company, Odd Studio, provided Lesley with appliances for **Australia** (2008) and **The Great Gatsby** (2013). Elka came on board for the films **Dark City** (1998) and **Moulin Rouge!** (2001).

The three of them were reunited, with Lesley as makeup and hair designer, for **Fury Road** in 2015, and **Gods of Egypt** in 2016.

A Leading Lady in her own right, Elka has a 20+ year career as a makeup artist, special effects artist, and prosthetic makeup artist working on such films as **The Matrix** (1999), **Chronicles of Narnia: The Lion, the Witch and the Wardrobe** (2005), and **The Hobbit: The Unexpected Journey** (2012).

With 20 years in the industry, Damian is a prosthetic makeup artist/creator who is co-owner of Odd Studio in New South Wales, Australia, which is at the forefront of prosthetic makeup, creature effects, animatronic characters, special effects, props, and models.

The rest of the international team included Anita Morgan, Brydie Stone, Tess Natoli, Troy Follington, Sean Genders, Rachelle O'Donnell, Jess Reedy, and Paul Pattison from Australia, Audrey Doyle and Catherine Biggs from Ireland, Ailie Smith, who led the crowd room and now owns Creative Media Skills at Pinewood, Kerstin Weller from the UK, and Nadine Prigge and her team from South Africa. Kylie Clarke from Kylie Clarke Wigmaking, Australia, made all the wigs. The crew totaled 35 strong.

Workshopping

In 2010 and 2012, Lesley workshopped the makeup, which entailed coming up with designs in a studio in Sydney, working with Elka, Damian, and other members of the team to create prototypes, photographing the pieces, and sending them to the producers. The detailed story boards, which evolved naturally over the years, the graphic novels, the extensive character backstories, and Lesley's research on the "oil fields of Angola, the workers of Salgado, the rubbish heaps in the Philippines, African tribal and Indian religious festivals, as well as Polynesian and Maori scarification" combined to create a peopled post-apocalyptic world which is foreign, frightening, and fascinating.

Sand, Sand, and More Sand

The production shot in Namibia, Africa, for seven months, May through December 2013. The natural elements were a force with which to be reckoned. "The early mornings in the desert had temperatures in the negatives, the afternoons could climb as high as 40 degrees Celsius [104 degrees Fahrenheit], and it would be freezing at night." The temperatures, the distances, the number of actors, and the elements influenced the day-to-day operation of the makeup crew.

A major obstacle for all the makeups was the Namibian Desert sand. "When that sand blows, it's like a fine powder, but it's red. It goes onto anything that's sticky and you can't clean it off. I needed scars that were fast to apply and non-sticky. Damian had done some Aboriginal scarring for me out of silicone encapsulated prosthetics for **Australia** in 2007. He made the same prosthetics for me in soft silicone molds so I could just apply them straight onto people really fast. Because a major character element for the War Boys is their scarification, these pieces were important. They were quick and practical and they looked good."

The sand wreaked havoc on the wigs; it would get into the netting and by the end of the day, the wigs would be orange and dirty. "I had Kerstin, our wig mistress, working at night. We would drop off dirty wigs after the shooting day and pick up clean ones on the way back to location in the morning." The sand also turned the white War Boys tan by the end of a day of shooting.

The Makeups

War Boys

The scarification of the War Boys came about in the workshopping process. The thinking was "because there are no books or art in this world, the boys carved the only things they know, their cars, on their bodies. It is their art form. Then the clay, which covered their heads and bodies, was war paint and protection, which mirrored their leader, Immortan Joe. The Imperator foreheads were inspired by a picture of African tribal women that wear clay across the top of their foreheads from the eyes up. One of them was a chalky brown color, which I ended up using on the War Boys."

MAD MAX : FURY ROAD (2015) *Warner Bros film*
NICHOLAS HOULT   RILEY KEOUGH
Licensed from Pictorial Press Ltd / Alamy Stock Photo

Nux's Chest

Nux's tattoo was a V8 engine block and it was "from a tattoo I saw on one of the Weta boys who did costume props, Matt. It was on his arm. I knew it would be perfect for Nux's chest. I photographed his arm, took it to George, and asked, 'What do you think about this?' He said, 'It's great,' and as we were talking, Peter Pound drew it bigger for the chest. It's amazing where you get your inspiration from."

Imperator Furiosa

Furiosa (Charlize Theron) is a woman living in a man's world, a violent man's world. "She would have to have been better than any of the men. She would have to be the best mechanic, the best driver, the best fighter. She would have come up the ranks and be accepted by the men. She would not have had hair that made her look feminine. Charlize is a statuesque, amazing woman and she decided on her own to shave her head. She was wonderful."

Originally, Lesley was going to use the same makeup for Furiosa that she used for the War Boys, but "we played with it and played with it and went into black. I knew that could be grease from the engines. I mixed a bit of bronze and a bit of silver together that could have come from metal shavings, rubbed it on her forehead to give a bit of illumination and light; and then we had it. The black forehead."

Miss Giddy

Miss Giddy (Jennifer Hagan) is the teacher and mentor to the Five Wives; therefore, as a teaching tool, she had the history of the

MAD MAX: FURY ROAD (2015) CHARLIZE THERON
Licensed from AF archive / Alamy Stock Photo

world tattooed on her body. "We made hair clips with nibs of fountain pens glued on them, that's what she tattooed herself with." Miss Giddy's makeup was the most difficult and time-consuming. "Basically, we did a scan of her body, made a model of it, covered it with acetate, and, with the help of a graphic artist, actually wrote the history of the world all over this dummy body. Then we sent the mannequin to the States to Tinsley Tattoos who made the tattoo sheets up. Mike Mekash came to Namibia to guide us through the intricate application. Then Anita took over; we'd spend nearly five hours applying those tattoos to her body: her chest, her back, her arms, her neck, her face, her ears, her legs. Then she'd go home with a pair of silk pajamas and a silk pillowslip and silk sheets, and she would sleep in those tattoos. Then she'd come back the next morning, we'd finish the makeup, and put the Belly Yak wig on, all of which took another two hours. She was literally a seven-hour makeup, the longest. But she could keep those tattoos on for three days of shooting."

Lesley would travel to location and use the hour of travel time to watch the dailies on her iPad. "Every day we would do 60-120 background War Boys, stunt doubles, and picture doubles. Two and a half hour makeups, a 12-hour shooting day, an hour in and out of town, and that makes for an 18-hour day. I would always try to stagger the calls." Once the makeups were finished, Lesley would travel back to the make-up base in town to prep and do fittings for the next day.

World-wide Acclaim

Mad Max: Fury Road received accolades around the world.

Lesley shares the Oscar for *Best Achievement in Makeup and Hairstyling* with Elka Wardega and Damian Martin

The British Academy of Film and Television Arts (BAFTA) awarded Lesley and Damian the award for *Best Makeup and Hair*

The Hollywood Makeup Artist and Hair Stylist Guild Awards recognized Lesley Vanderwalt, Nadine Prigge, and Ailie Smith for *Best Period and/or Character Makeup*

The Hollywood Makeup Artist and Hair Stylist Guild Awards recognized Elka Wardega, Damian Martin, and Jaco Synman for the *Best Special Makeup Effects Award*

The Australian Production Design Guild gave the *Makeup and Prosthetic Makeup Design Award* to Lesley, who shares it with Damian, Elka, Nadine Prigge, Paul Pattison, Audrey Doyle, Catherine Biggs, and Sean Genders

The Hollywood Film Awards bestowed the *Makeup of the Year Award* to the film

The Seattle Film Critics Awards gave Lesley Vanderwalt, Damian Martin, and Elka Wardega the *Award for Best Makeup and Hairstyling*

The Gold Derby Awards gave the *Makeup/Hair Award* to Lesley Vanderwalt, Elka Wardega, and Damian Martin

The Online Film & Television Association awarded *Best Makeup and Hairstyling* to Lesley Vanderwalt, Damian Martin, and Elka Wardega

The Academy of Science Fiction, Fantasy & Horror Films gave Lesley, Elka, and Damian the award for *Best Makeup.*

As we left the hotel room, Lesley was on the phone making arrangements to get supplies from Frends Beauty Supply; there was a party that evening and interviews and events filling the next few days. Even in her bathrobe and slippers, Lesley is inspiring. Her imagination soars. She is a woman who speaks her mind, is deeply committed to friends and work, and is open to a world full of creative impulses.

OUTTAKES:

On Being a Woman:

"I think women are naturally very caring, very nurturing. We're very gentle and patient with the actors. We use lots of initiative and intuition to put a project together. Sometimes when I'm sitting there trying to organize transportation and I'm going crazy, I think, 'Someone else wouldn't bother. They'd just bring them all in in a single van at the same time and let them all go at the end of day.' I'm, 'No, no, no. They all need as much rest as they can get.'"

"I think as women we have to prove ourselves over and over. Every time you start another project, you've got to do it again. I think as women, it's not in our nature to say 'No' or rock the boat. The hardest thing to learn is that it's okay to rock the boat, especially if it betters a situation, or if a task is impossible, or if there's a safety issue."

On Newbies:

"I try to see what people are really good at. Sometimes people are much better with SFX makeup, or beauty makeup, while others are better at styling hair and period work, and some are great with wigs and others with cutting. Their makeup may be very average, but wow, they may have done an amazing body painting. Once I see what they're good at, I try and guide them into it. I then put artists together who balance each other's strengths and weaknesses."

"I get lots of emails with questions and I feel they're really important. I never ignore them. I say if I'm in the middle of a shoot, 'I really haven't got the time now. Try me in June when I finish my next job. I'll try and give you some advice then.'"

"In Australia, Scott Lattimer runs ACMUSE, Australian College of Makeup and Special Effects, a school that I get students from. His final year students come on-set for work experience. I get people to guide them through the process. I bring them on in small groups so they can get some on-set experience while they're doing their course. I watch them and then the good ones, the ones I think have got the right qualities, I will bring in as assistants on the next job. If that works out, then next, they'll be on the main team. They learn on-the-job and we add to their knowledge, through experience, daily."

On the Aftershocks of the Aneurysm:

"I remember there were times people would say something to me and I might just start crying...I wasn't quite back to normal. About a year-and-a-half after shooting *Mad Max* I suddenly said, 'Wow, I'm back to normal. Now I'm back to normal.'"

"One of the guys who worked on *Gods of Egypt* came to me and asked, 'Do you mind if I talk to you? I know you don't know me, but my girlfriend was having a brain scan for something else and they scanned an aneurysm, which hasn't blown yet, but it's there and they're going to operate. I wanted to ask you about it, how you felt, what happened. Because one slip and...it could be all over, Rover.' They were both really nervous…I just talked to them about how I healed, what I felt. It's an experience I never want anyone to go through in their lives. It's a way I can help."

"I might only work six months a year and spend the other half travelling or doing whatever. I don't madly go after work. I see what comes up and then make a decision."

Once the Makeup Goes On:

"I think the best reaction is from the actor. As I'm doing the makeup, I start to feel them getting into the character. They start wearing the makeup like a glove, they're actually into the makeup, they're into the part. That's always my favorite reaction from an actor. And, I love it when the director walks in, and says, 'There's my Nux' or there's my whoever. And when you walk onto the set and crew says, 'Wow, that looks great.' Those are all positive reactions."

"I'm very, very self-critical. I think, like any artist, we all would like to go back and do it again. I can't even imagine how actors and directors feel. It's an incredible thing."

On Go-Tos:

"Just the word makeup itself, you know, make-it-up. Whether you get it out of the kitchen cupboard or the haberdashery or hardware shop, you find something and find a way of to make it work. That was always my thing. Cut up things, repurpose them, put them together, you know? Just make it work. It doesn't always have to come out of a box, bag, or makeup shop to be creative."

"I seem to have, on every film, a favorite thing that might not carry on to the next film. One of my favorite things we loved on **Fury Road** was Sunburn Pinky. I could put that in a spray bottle. If there were things that I wanted to look infected, I could just spritz it on and around it, and it would pop, look all sore and infected. We used it a lot for the burns. I used BECCA shimmers, Sunburn Pinky. I can't live without my Skin Illustrator or Bluebird palettes. I find something different on each job."

On Heat, Cold, and the Tropics:

"I remember saying to someone once, 'Sorry, I don't do cold, don't do extreme cold.' Someone asked me to do a film on, I think it was on a snow-capped mountain somewhere and I said, 'Oh, no.' I just couldn't. I don't mind the desert. I don't mind the heat, but the extreme cold I find really, really difficult. I remember working on **Beyond Borders** (2003) and we did all the extremes north of Quebec. Then we flew from there, where it was -44 Centigrade wind chill factor, to Namibia overnight where it was +44 Centigrade. Then we went on to Thailand where it was really sweaty and humid so I did all three conditions in one movie. The director, Martin Campbell, trying to convince me to take the job said, 'I know you don't do cold, but if I'm going to take you to the desert and Thailand afterwards, would you consider it?'"

On the Australia Film Industry:

"Makeup here is just completely forgotten. Even when we won the BAFTA, the local papers ran a story about the Australian nominations and that Cate Blanchett and so-and-so didn't win any awards. Right at the bottom of the article there was small paragraph, 'But we picked up these technical awards….'

"At the time of this interview, there was only one award that recognized makeup and hair in Australia, The Australian Production Design Guild Award. And starting in 2016, for the first time, the AACTA [the Australian Academy of Cinema and Television Arts] have introduced an Award for Excellence in Makeup and Hair. This first year, there will only be one award that covers both film and television; we hope to have one for each category in the future.

"There were 40 entries for the inaugural award, which was broken down to ten finalists and four jury nominees. The four nominees will be announced on October 27, 2016."

"The winner will be announced at a luncheon on December 5, 2016. The Award for Excellence in Makeup and Hair still will not be included in the main AACTA Awards ceremony, but at least we have got an award for our category. It has taken us 20 years or so for our contribution to the Australian film industry to be acknowledged, but we are very excited about it." [For further info visit: www.aacta.org]

Catching Up!

We interviewed Lesley on February 25, 2016. Here's the note she wrote us:

"Since I saw you last, I came back on the same plane as Ridley[Scott] from the Oscars and went directly onto *Alien Covenant* for 5 months.

I then took 4 months off and did *Peter Rabbit* from Dec 16 - Mar 17.

I then came directly on to *Aquaman* up here on the Gold Coast for 7 months with only a weekend off in between."

For more of Lesley's Credits, visit: www.imdb.com

LEADING LADIES OF MAKEUP EFFECTS

HOW A MAKEUP ARTIST IS NOMINATED FOR A

PRIMETIME EMMY AWARD FOR OUTSTANDING MAKEUP

The Academy of Television Arts and Sciences (ATAS) has 22,000 members who each belong to the Peer Group which reflects their special area of expertise. There are 29 separate Peer Groups, some of which are actors, directors, video editors, casting directors, costumers, and makeup artists.

To be nominated, a program, performer, or individual achievement must be submitted by a member of the Academy and a fee is paid. It is possible, even encouraged, for members to nominate themselves. In 2016, the Television Academy received 9060 nominations in 119 categories.

Ballots are then mailed to academy members. Each peer group member votes in his or her own category — costumers for costumers, makeup artists for makeup artists -- and everyone votes in the program categories, such as best drama series or best miniseries.

The votes are tallied by Enest & Young Accountants and the top five vote-getters become the nominees.

Thank you to the Academy of Television Arts and Sciences and the websites below for information on the Emmy Awards.

www.emmys.com/news/awards-news/infographic-how-emmy-won
and
http://www.emmys.com/academy/about/faq
and
www.http://entertainment.howstuffworks.com/emmy2.htm
and
http://www.goldderby.com/article/2017/emmy-nominations-process-explained-news/

Emmy Winners

Emmy Winners

In 1971, the Academy of Television Arts & Sciences presented the first Emmy Award for *Outstanding Achievement in Makeup* to Robert Dawn for the series ***Mission Impossible***, episode "Catafalque."

This first makeup Emmy was unique for a couple of reasons. First, the award was presented to the one person responsible for the makeups, the makeup department head. Secondly, the award was given for the makeup in a specific episode of a series.

Since 1971, the television industry has changed greatly, as have the Emmys. The number of awardees has grown beyond the department head to also honor other members of the makeup department. Additionally, the makeup award category expanded beyond makeup in a series to encompass mini-series, movies, specials, single-camera series, and multi-camera series.

Between 1971 and 2016, over 750 women have been nominated for an Emmy award in one of 12 makeup categories. Awards for makeup have become part of the *Creative Arts Emmy Awards* which acknowledge outstanding artistic and technical achievement.

Currently, there are four Makeup Award categories:

- *Outstanding Makeup for a Limited Series or Movie (Non-Prosthetic)*
- *Outstanding Makeup for a Multi-Camera Series or Special (Non-Prosthetic)*
- *Outstanding Makeup for a Single-Camera Series (Non-Prosthetic)*
- *Outstanding Prosthetic Makeup for a Series, Limited Series, Movie, or Special*

In 2002, a specific award for outstanding prosthetic makeup was added. Since then, 83 women have been nominated for the *Outstanding Prosthetic Make-up* category and nine have won. But what about the women who won Emmy awards working on shows that obviously included special effects and pros-thetic makeups before the category existed? If we focused only on the Emmy for prosthetics, women who worked on shows such as *Star Trek: The Next Generation*, *Star Trek: Deep Space Nine*, *Star Trek: Voyager*, *The X-Files*, *MADtv*, and *Saturday Night Live,* would be unrepresented. We decided to in-clude those Leading Ladies for their outstanding makeup effects contributions across the spectrum of television history.

The Emmy-winning Leading Ladies included on the following pages are: Bari Dreiband-Burman, Eryn Krueger Mekash, Jane Walker, Vivian Baker, Cheri Mon-tesanto, Karen J. Westerfield, Camille Della Santina, Jennifer Aspinall, and Tina Kalliongis-Hoffman.

We also congratulate the over 750 Ladies who have been nominated and/or won Emmys for Makeup since 1971.

And now…back to our regularly scheduled programming….

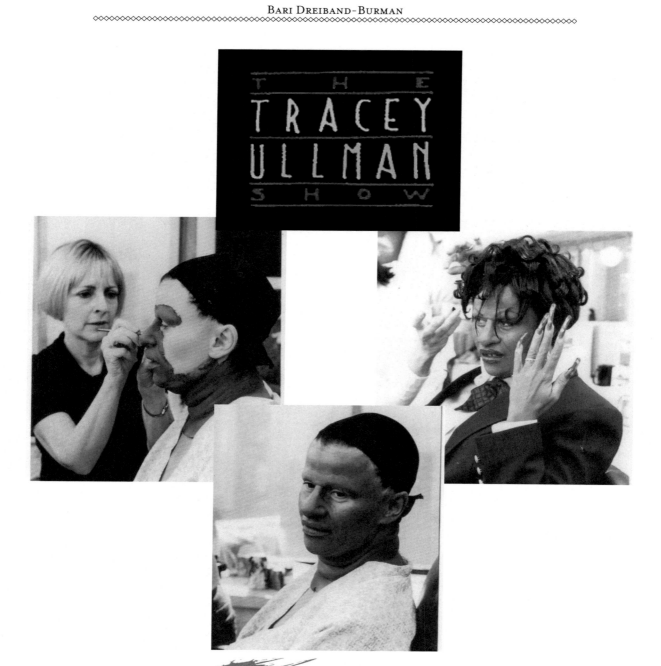

THE TRACEY ULLMAN SHOW

1990
EMMY AWARD
OUTSTANDING ACHIEVEMENT IN MAKEUP
FOR A SERIES

Tracey Ullman Show (1990) Bari and Tracey Ullman
Used with Permission of Bari Dreiband Burman

BARI DREIBAND - BURMAN

Keep learning, never let yourself be comfortable.
When someone says it's good enough, that is the kiss of death.
Once you accept 'good enough,' you enter the world of mediocre work.

"The members of my family were big movie fans. It was a fun thing for me when the Academy Awards were aired because we'd set up snacks and everyone would get their place on the couch. I couldn't touch the floor, my feet dangled over the edge, and my mother and I would analyze this and that, everything. The Oscars were a big to-do in my house when I was growing up."

"Just a little side bar, when we were nominated for *Scrooged*, I got the call at 6 AM. I was on-set for a commercial and the first person I called was my mother, then I called my husband. Mom was thrilled, beside herself. We took her to the luncheon and the Oscars. I think it's wonderful when we get to share this with our parents because they are our benchmark. Nobody, nobody adores you more than your family."

The Little Shop of Hollywood

Bari Dreiband-Burman is a petit woman with delicate features, a lilting laugh that punctuates her speech, wispy blonde hair, focused energy, intensity, and a clear sense of priorities. In her sleek, modern home with a view of the ocean, she is surrounded by fine art, her own sculptures and paintings, husband Tom's sculptures, oils by her brother and father, and two loyal dogs. The movie business is a family business: Tom Burman, Bari's husband and business partner, is a pioneer and innovator who coined the term "special makeup effects" and is attributed with the first independent makeup effects studio with credits like the original *Planet of the Apes* (1968), *Close Encounters of the Third Kind* (1977), and *Invasion of the Body Snatchers* (1978). Their son, Maxx, is a matte painter and art director with film credits including *Godzilla* (2014), *Her* (2013), *Iron Man* (2008) and television credits including *The Walking Dead* (2010-2011), and *Once Upon a Time* (2011-2012). Bari comes from a European family of artists. Her father and brother were painters and her mother was a fashion designer. They ran a combination art school, art supply store, and art gallery in North Hollywood in the 1960s. "We lived behind the store and were open seven days a week, so it was all I knew. At the art school my father taught the adults, my brother the teenagers, and I taught the children. I didn't know other families ate dinner at 6:00 and had days off...it was not part of my life. But I loved it. My work ethic and sense of excellence in fine art was forged there. It wasn't until Tom and I married and we had our son, Maxx, that I learned to play. I have since learned to play in my own way."

Anatomy

A fascination for the body, how it works, how muscles influence movement, how skin reflects the nerves, how blood determines color, inspired Bari's studies. "I have always loved anatomy...how we move, how we function, so at sixteen I went to Chouinard Art Institute and studied sculpting." Upon graduating from high school, Bari wanted to continue her studies in art, but she wanted to learn techniques and approaches from a variety of teachers; she felt students who studied with just one teacher and learned just one style were creatively stifled, straightjacketed. Instead, she wanted the breadth and depth of many influences and experiences which she gained through her studies at UCLA, Otis Art Institute, and Rhode Island School of Design (RISD).

At RISD, Bari's love of anatomy came to the fore when she was granted special permission to study anatomy with the pre-med students at Brown University. It was a pivotal point in her education for it reignited her fascination and passion for anatomy. She used those studies when she moved back to California and became a medical illustrator for the plastic surgery department at UCLA. "I was working with Dr. Ashley who did *pro bono* work for children with heartbreaking situations. I would draw the before and the after pictures, but I would leave work a basket case. I realized, 'I can't keep doing this. This is going to wipe me out if I do it forever.'"

Young Indiana Jones Chronicles (1992)
George Lucas, George Hall, Tom Burman, and Bari
Used with Permission of Bari Dreiband-Burman

Back to Fine Art

Because her professional focus had shifted, Bari was at a personal and professional juncture: what did she want to do and how she was going to get there? Fine art had been her inspiration and foundation growing up; therefore, she decided to refocus her energies and go back to school. CalArts provided the environment, stimulation, and fodder that fed Bari's creative drive and ignited her development as an artist.

She graduated with a BFA from CalArts, became part of the Feminist Studio Workshop (founded by CalArts instructors Judy Chicago and Miriam Schapiro), and was one of the founders of the Women's Building, the affiliated gallery. The Feminist Studio Workshop (FWS), which opened in 1973, was an innovative, first-of-its kind, women's-only collective, showcasing women's art within a collaborative workshop situation.

During this time, Bari started to find her own voice as an artist doing several series of paintings and gallery shows where she explored the human form. "It was a rich time. Most of the women in the Feminist Studio Workshop were edgy and a bit intense. They saw a woman's position in the art world as something to be angry about. I saw it as an obstacle to be overcome. I just wanted to be the best I could be. If there was a door I wanted to go through, I would find a way to go through it."

"The fine art world I came from was not very supportive of women. My parents were supportive, but they were from a time when men were the ones to be taken seriously, and while my brother and I were both talented artists, my brother was the star and I was going to make someone happy." The FSW provided Bari a platform and an outlet for her work which helped her clarify her goal: "Be the best artist I can be."

Freelance

Ironically, after her CalArts experience with the FSW, Bari became a freelance cartoonist for **Penthouse Magazine**. "I've always been a little bit of a rebellious person in a very private way. Everything I did is an ingredient of who I am today. My **Penthouse** work was appalling to the members of the FSW, but I thought, what better way to change the perception of women artists than to do great work in such a male-dominated industry?"

Concurrently, she was taking Michael Westmore's makeup class at Valley College where she learned the fundamentals of makeup which, of course, are the same fundamentals found in painting. Her class with Westmore led Bari to doing makeup on the **Penthouse** models, which in turn challenged her to creatively "cover up bruises and other unattractive things. It was a seamless transition, even though I didn't know the technical part, it was my critical eye, the use of highlight and shadow, attention to every detail, minimizing and maximizing, that informed my work."

Turning Point

On her 25th birthday, Bari took stock of her life: "Okay, I live in LA, I'm 25. What is it that I can do in LA? It's either the music business or the film business. My world had been fine art, so I thought I would go into film." So, Bari took her fine art portfolio to NBC where the scenic department was being pressured to hire women. With her training, she was more than qualified and became one of the first female scenic artists. However, she was not allowed to paint scenery. "I remember they used to make me carry five gallon drums of paint up 10 foot ladders to [the scenic artists], but they wouldn't let me do any art. They were trying to break me."

This, of course, was, and still is, the spur that motivated Bari to work harder to find her niche. During her coffee breaks, she would walk around NBC visiting all the departments, looking for what she could do alone. "I remember I popped my head into **The Tonight Show** and I thought, 'Look, that person is painting someone's face...I can do that.'" With her art training and knowledge of anatomy, doing makeup was a perfect combination of Bari's talents. Thus began Bari's career in makeup.

Union Work

In 1976, Bari learned the union had a window of opportunity for women to become unionized makeup artists; heretofore, women were allowed to be hair stylists and body makeup artists, but not makeup artists. Howard Smit, business representative for Local 706, called Nick Marcellino at Universal for Bari and she was hired in 1977 and became a union member.

Robin Hood: Men in Tights (1993) Bari with Amy Yasbeck
Used with Permission of Bari Dreiband-Burman

Capitalizing on her art training, Bari worked on multiple projects at Universal, moving from show to show wherever a makeup artist was needed who could paint and draw. "When I first started, there were some male makeup artists who said, 'Forget about it, it's never going to happen,' which, for me, was the perfect trigger. I just stayed focused on my work and passion. I was not in a hurry. I was never looking for someone else's job. I just could not believe that I got to be doing this work. I was tireless. I was excited to get up every day. It was a thrilling time. I didn't pay attention to the drama of 'No.'"

"Never get comfortable, it's a dangerous position. When I was at Universal, the makeup department was on top of a hill and I put my kit on a luggage roller to get it up the hill. I never asked for help; I had to hold my own because they were looking for any way to say I couldn't do the job. I think women have to always do more because even though we've come a long way, and we've come an incredibly long way, I really believe you can never get comfortable, that's dangerous."

On the other side of the spectrum, Bari received a lot of advice and guidance. "Jack Stone was wonderful to me. One day we were on location and he said, 'You know, Bari, if you're stuck on location and you're doing a western, and you have to lay a beard but you don't have any hair, you know what you do? If you see a dog, you shave its tail.' It was a different time. It wasn't fancy-dancy stuff."

"During my time at Universal, I met makeup artist Tom Hoerber who suggested I should meet Tom Burman of Burman Studio. He felt Tom would appreciate my fine arts background and critical eye. I had heard Burman Studio was a place where artists were encouraged to grow, learn new things, and expand their artistic skills. Very few makeup effects studios allowed that freedom, so I was enticed." However, that meeting wouldn't happen for a few years.

Bread and Butter

After working at Universal on various television shows such as **Buck Roger in the 25th Century** and **Women in White** (1979), Bari went to Warner Brothers and worked on the television series **Vegas** and **Bringing Em' Back Alive** (1982-1983). Both shows involved lots of beauty/glamour makeup. "That's your bread and butter. You do that probably 70% of the time, and then if there is a wound or a bullet hole, that's exciting."

"Makeup effects is a different animal. You have to be willing to be dirty and tired and relentless. It's not very glamorous. You have to be at the studio at two or three in the morning, get the molds out, and if the casting of the prosthetics are not good, you have to run the molds again until you get a good run of the prosthetics. It's not glitzy. You might get the win when you're applying it on-set and when you see it on film, but the actual work of sculpting and molding and casting is not necessarily a glamorous thing."

The Partnership

In 1982, upon her return from shooting **The Border** with Jack Nicholson and directed by Tony Richardson, Tom Burman asked Bari to bring a creative, female perspective to the transformation of Nastassja Kinski into a panther for the film **Cat People.** That was the beginning of a long professional and personal relationship that has spanned 34 years and promises to continue. Bari and Tom have strengths and weaknesses that complement each other: "We work entirely differently and we always work together. We know each other so well that we never even have to talk. I'm

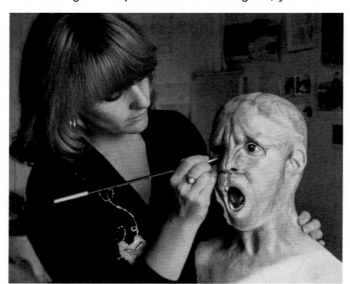

Cat People (1982) Bari sculpting the cat transformation
Used with Permission of Bari Dreiband-Burman

a detail fanatic and he's a ball-parker. It was a brave thing for Tom to ask me to design Nastassja Kinski's transformation because the field was male-dominated at that time. He doesn't categorize male/female roles. Whoever can do the best job is his only guide. Tom gave me complete freedom to design the transformation [for **Cat Woman**] and it was such a joyful experience that we've worked together ever since. It's an amazing partnership." Tom added, "There are some really great women makeup artists today. Really, really fine makeup artists. But the majority of them still don't go into effects. It's still kind of a man's sport in general."

Bari and Tom have worked together on film and television projects that span the fanciful, **The Goonies** (1985), the historical, **War and Remembrance** (1988), the contemporary, **The Bonfire of the Vanities** (1990), the classic, **The Godfather: Part III** (1990), **Wayne's World** (1992), the comedic spoof, **Robin Hood: Men In Tights** (1993), the adventurous, **The Mask of Zorro** (1998), and the medical, **Private Practice** (2008-2012). When Bari and Tom come onto a project it is usually for prosthetics and makeup special effects.

Goonies (1985) Steven Speilberg, John Matuszak, Bari, Tom, and Ellis Burman
Used with Permission of Bari Dreiband-Burman

Their Studio

The Burman Studio, Inc. was founded in 1973 to provide special effects for television and film projects. Tom Burman coined the phrase "special makeup effects" and the studio is credited with the first cable-operated, pneumatic, and remote-controlled animatronics, full body applications in foam latex and gelatin, and radio-controlled multiple bullet hits.

As co-owners, Bari and Tom turned the Burman Studio into the multi-award-winning premier makeup effects studio it is today. How to run a successful makeup effects studio and business presented Bari with another obstacle, one she faced like all that came before it, with uncompromising determination. The challenges were different, requiring her to learn the business of film while still maintaining her artistic integrity which, of course, results in great work. Bari jumps back and forth between producing and creative directing, two very different mindsets, but each requires attention to detail if the makeup effects studio is going to be successful. Her head for business drives decision-making while her artistic eye for detail elevates the work; she incorporates her artistic background and extensive knowledge of anatomy to create creatures and characters that feel real.

"The Burman Studio, Inc. is very much a reflection of who Tom and I are. We treat people like we want to be treated. We're not real complicated. I give everyone who works for me the same freedom as I need. By giving them the freedom to be their best, they give more than just an employee, they are a nurtured artist. We create an environment of elevation. We give people the opportunity to explore their talents. It's a wonderful studio to work at."

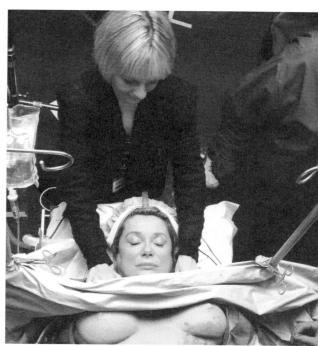

Nip/Tuck (1988) Bari with Catherine Deneuve
Used with Permission of Bari Dreiband-Burman

Bari Winning an Emmy in 1990 for *The Tracey Ullman Show*
Used with Permission of Craig T. Mathew/Mathew Imaging

"We currently have five employees who have been with us for years. It's like a family; we honed it to a tight knit group. We used to have a lot of people, which made Tom and me more administrative, but we were not doing art any more. We were organizing and orchestrating; it was just business. We realized that's not what we wanted, we wanted to do the work. So, luckily, we found and work with extraordinarily gifted people and are able to be as hands-on as we want."

The Burman Studio, Inc. has excelled in a difficult industry through exceptional work, innovation, and integrity. Additionally, their work has been recognized by their peers. As the consummate team, Bari and Tom garnered an Oscar nomination for *Scrooged* (1988), and together have collected 54 Emmy nominations. They have won 11 Emmy Awards for: *Outstanding Makeup for a Series*, *The Tracey Ullman Show* (1990, "High School Sweethearts"); *Outstanding Individual Achievement in Makeup for a Miniseries or a Special*, *The Young Indiana Jones Chronicles* (1992, Pilot Episode); *Outstanding Makeup for a Series*, *Tracey Takes on...*(1997, "Vegas"); *Outstanding Makeup for a Series, Miniseries, Movie or a Special (Prosthetic)* *Nip/Tuck* (2005, Pilot Episode); and *Outstanding Prosthetic Makeup for a Series, Miniseries, Movie or a Special*, *Grey's Anatomy* (2010, "How Insensitive") which they share with Norman T. Leavett, Thomas Floutz, Bart Mixon, and Vincent Van Dyke. Additionally, Bari and Tom have won two CableACE Awards (the precursor to the Emmy awards for cable television) as well as two Hollywood Makeup Artists and Hair Stylist Guild Awards for *Special Makeup Effects* for the pilot of *Nip/Tuck*.

Stand Outs

Over the years, there have been stand out projects that were creatively challenging, satisfying, or just great fun. For Bari, the top projects are *Scrooged*, for all the special effects; *Nip/Tuck* because Ryan Murphy is a dedicated supporter of the work; *Captain Eo*, which provided her the opportunity to design Anjelica Huston's makeup and work with Francis Ford Coppola; and *Grey's Anatomy* for the long relationship with the creative team.

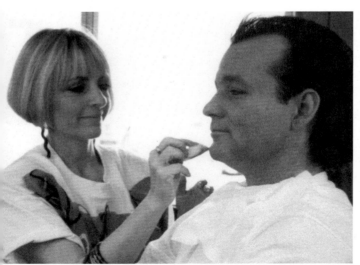

Scrooged (1988) Bari with Bill Murray
Used with Permission of Bari Dreiband-Burman

"When Richard Donner called about *Scrooged*, he laughingly said, 'Bari, there's not a lot of makeup. Do you want to do the show?' Adapted from Charles Dickens's *A Christmas Carol*, with the Ghosts of Christmas Past, Present, and Future, as well as a lot of other special effects, I deadpanned, 'Noooo, Richard, there're not many special effects. Not much work for me. Oh, alright, I'll do it.'" *Scrooged*, the madcap Bill Murray comedy, earned Bari and Tom an Oscar nomination.

"*Nip/Tuck* changed television because we brought feature quality to television. Ryan [Murphy, creator and director] shot our work inches away from the camera and it had to hold up. Basically, *Nip/Tuck* was sex and surgery. Our work was showcased in a way that had never been seen on television before. I loved it." Additionally, Ryan Murphy unequivocally supported the makeup team, fought for their vision, and trusted them to produce quality work. "When we did Vanessa Redgrave as a botched facelift victim, she came in a little freaked out. We did a full head cast, then a photo realistic duplication, and then production said, 'We don't want to pay for it.' Ryan called up and said, 'I'll pay for it.' His respect and the freedom he gave us was extraordinary. He's an incredible supporter of the arts. He's amazing."

"Another example of Ryan's support happened in the production meeting where Ryan introduced the Carver mask. 'We're going to have this mask; Props, you'll do it.' I'm listening to this and knew what the mask needed to be. 'Ryan, I really want to do the Carver mask. I've got this. The mask has to be disturbing perfection.' He agreed to let me design and create it. We got to do things out of the norm. It was exciting and it was appreciated, it was valued and respected, which is all we want." *Nip/Tuck* received six Emmy nominations for special effects makeup and one win in 2005.

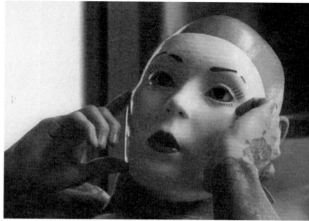

Nip/Tuck (2005) The Carver Mask
Used with Permission of Bari Dreiband-Burman

Captain EO, a 1986 3D science fiction film starring Michael Jackson, directed by Francis Ford Coppola, and produced by George Lucas, was shown at Disney theme parks from 1986 through 1996. In this short film, Michael Jackson, as a space captain, battles an evil queen, Anjelica Huston. The original design for Anjelica Huston's makeup, as conceived by George Lucas, completely covered the actress's face. Ms. Huston said she wouldn't do the part if her face was going to be completely covered, so Bari redesigned the makeup. To provide contrast to the colorful and human Captain Eo character, The Supreme Leader (Huston) is in silver, black, and grey tones. The makeup combined the mechanical with the organic, incorporating tubes and bolts which encircled the neck and head, extending down the arms and culminating in crab-like claw fingers that clacked when she moved her hands. The headpiece is a lobster tail-like spine topping highly chiseled cheeks with horn-like pieces coming out of her forehead. "I wanted it to be elegant and evil. I really loved working on that. It was really wonderful."

Captain Eo (1986)
© Disney

In 2005, *Grey's Anatomy* exploded onto the television scene to much critical acclaim and huge audiences. As of this writing, the show is currently in its 13th season and follows a group of doctors in a Seattle hospital, melding personal stories with the drama of illnesses and hospital life. Bari and the Burman Studio, Inc. have produced special effects for over 200 episodes from 2005-2017 with Bari in the roles of special effects makeup artist and prosthetic makeup designer. The special effects ranged from a pencil in the eye, to morbid obesity, to bark-like growths on a body, to leeches on wounds, to a man with a hole instead of a nose. "They've known me for years and know I'm not going

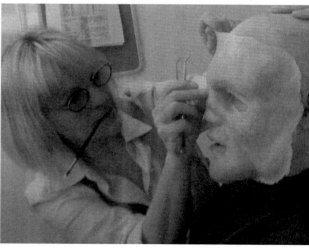

Grey's Anatomy (2005)
Used with Permission of Bari Dreiband-Burman

to compromise myself. They may say, 'We don't need that body,' because it's all about numbers, but I'm going to do it this way because I don't want to tie the director's hands. That's stepping over dollars and picking up pennies. You service the script, but the script is the broad stroke, it's really the director's vision. It's always our goal to make the director happy...without compromise." *Grey's Anatomy* received seven Emmy nominations for prosthetic and non-prosthetic makeup with one win in 2010.

Bari Dreiband-Burman is a tenacious and focused woman. Throughout her career she defined what she wanted and defied convention to achieve it. When obstacles presented themselves, she mostly ignored them. Want me to climb a 10-foot ladder with a five-gallon paint can? Done. You think I can't learn how to do prosthetics? Watch me. The union doesn't want women? Not true anymore.

OUTTAKES:

On Magic:

"That's part of the crazy fun of it, inventing out of your head. The rule in the industry is whatever looks good on camera. They don't care how you get there, as long as it looks good on camera."

"Collaboration starts with the script, then the director, the costumer, art director, cinematographer. When those ingredients are meshed, it's bliss. Think about it. If everybody gives 110%, what can be done? How amazing is that? It's exciting. That's what I love. I love being a part of that magic because it is magic. It's movie magic."

On Being a Woman:

"Did it get in the way? Of course it got in the way because they were not letting women be makeup artists. I didn't look at it that way, I just looked at it as a-door-that-needs-to-be-opened. I never looked at it as a problem. I looked at it as a challenge that needed to be corrected. I looked at it as something to solve."

"I think, as an artist, what you bring to the table is not gender-specific. I think when I started, other people made it an issue. It wasn't an issue to me. Physical strength was sometimes an issue, but I found a way to solve it; I used a luggage rack because I wanted to be an independent, highly functional person that didn't need help."

On Growth, Compassion, Ego:

"I've always believed you cannot skip a step of growth. You may think you can fast forward, but you're going to have to pick up that growth down the line. I think that when people are ego-based or not a generous spirit, it's difficult to work with them. I only find that to be the case if they're insecure. In actors, if they're really good at what they do, they're very nice. The same thing with my profession. If you're insecure, you're unkind. I think we're all in it together, that's how I approach it....everybody has to find their way. You can't skip experience, but I think the egos need to be dialed down."

"I've always believed there is enough light for everyone. When people are hungry and desperate, that's a bad place to be."

On Excellence:

"I continue to be an avid student of art as it is my passion and gift to keep my critical eye always intentionally sharp. I pay attention to everything. That's really my thing. People say to me, 'Will you stop looking? Because you will see the one crack, you always see the crack.'"

"Every time I do makeup it's like I've never done it before. I get giddy and excited and nervous. I want to do work better than I did yesterday. That's always the goal: better. When you live like that, you put your head down and think, 'I gave 100 percent today. What can I do better tomorrow?'"

"When someone tells me 'It's good enough, Bari, let it go,' I say, 'No, thank you.' Because no one is going to remember the relationship, but they will remember what's on film forever."

On the Future:

"If someone came to me with an amazing script, fascinating characters, a great director who is inclusive and appreciative, and I have the time to do it right, I would do it. I don't do things that don't take me to a higher place. It's a delicious place to be."

Catching Up!

We interviewed Bari on January 12, 2016.
Since then, she has worked on

Executive Producing the
upcoming documentary feature
Making Apes: The Artists Who Changed Film

Planning a one woman art exhibition

Painting and sculpting in her studio

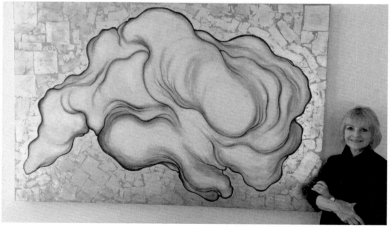

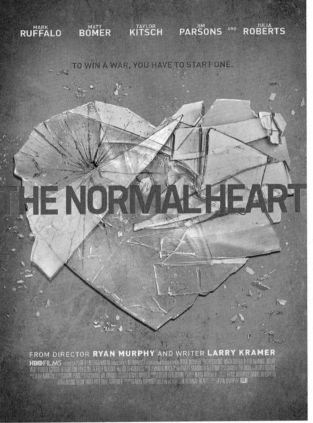

2014
EMMY AWARD
OUTSTANDING MAKEUP
FOR A MINI-SERIES OR MOVIE (NON-PROSTHETIC)

NORMAL HEART (2014) MATT BOMER & POSTER
Licensed from AF archive / Alamy Stock Photo

ERYN KRUEGER MEKASH

Makeup challenges and their solutions occur on a daily basis and are ongoing...from a crew member who missed an alarm and couldn't be contacted who throws off an entire schedule, to an actor with skin sensitivity to isopropyl alcohol but has to wear prosthetics. Situations, questions, answers, problems, mysteries, anomalies, happen all day long to a makeup artist. You have to be interested in being a detective/mother/teacher/therapist/MacGyver/producer, and pleasant to boot!

"'Don't watch HBO,' my parents would say to us as they went out for the evening. As soon as they walked out the door, my brother and I would switch on HBO and find something really scary like **The Shining**. We'd watch it from behind the couch, fingers curled, eyes glued, ready to duck down when we were scared. I wanted to be scared."

Yes, Yes, Yes

Eryn, with her stylish blonde hair, flashing green eyes, and quick smile, seems anything but scared. On the surface, Eryn appears to be a typical Southern California gal, but she is a woman of contrasts, complexities, and contradictions. She creates horrifying and beautiful makeups, loves skulls and the *macabre* while living a fun-loving, friend-filled, jam-packed life of work and play. Her decisions are guided by three questions: Does it scare me? Is it fun? Can I do it? And all three questions need the same answer...YES!

Between the ages of four and 14, Eryn underwent 14 surgeries to correct a congenital urinary tract anomaly that eventually influenced the way she lives her life. Eryn's father, a professor of business ethics, and her mother, an artist working in pastels and watercolors, devoted much of Eryn's childhood to guiding their daughter through treacherous waters. "My Mom and Dad would say to me when I was in the hospital, 'Suck it up kid, pull yourself together, let's keep going forward.'" From spending so much time in the hospital, Eryn still recalls seeing "a lot of unusual, difficult things for someone so young. I kept thinking, 'Now that I got through this, what now?' I needed to challenge myself to see how scared I could get."

At home, between all the surgeries, she and her younger brother, Brady, "loved watching **Creature Features** on Saturdays. My father would come in from mowing the lawn and ask, 'What are you guys watching?' 'We just watched a guy get decapitated!' Unfazed, he'd say, 'Okay'… and go back to mowing." And then there was Halloween. "[It was] a big deal in my house. Sometimes for my brother's or my birthday, we'd go to Universal Studios and see Frankenstein's Monster and Dracula. I would start planning my Halloween costume in June." Her parents also loved monsters, so, naturally, they bought her the Dick Smith book, **How to Make a Monster**, "the one where you could make a spaceman, or you could have the oatmeal face with ping-pong ball eyes. I just loved it. I'd do those makeups, ring the neighbors' doorbells, and lie on their porches. I was an oddball."

Teaching or Makeup?

Hospitals, horror movies, Halloween, and yet, "Nothing really scares me." Her parents, on the other hand, were "terrified what I'd do once I became healthy. I was a holy terror. I was a wild teenager and now there was driving and boys and…my poor parents."

As a high school freshman, Eryn and her cousin saw the double-feature **An American Werewolf in London** and **The Thing**. "I was pulling my face off thinking, 'Oh, this is it, this is IT! People, they DO this!' I loved makeup; it was a complete awakening at 14. I knew it was what I wanted to do."

With those movies as inspiration, Eryn and Brady started making 8mm films, figuring out the makeup effects along the way. "We wrecked the kitchen and bathroom." When Michael Jackson's **Thriller** came along, she recorded it, watched it, and watched it, and watched it again. When her high school did a Michael Jackson tribute, Eryn, as a dancer and makeup artist, chose **Thriller**. "We had zombie makeups and the choreography." Throughout school, despite distractions like parties, boys, and cheerleading, her path always returned to her love of creating scary makeup effects.

As she entered college, "My mom suggested I should be an art teacher since I'd always taken classes and was a good artist. The problem was I didn't want to be an art teacher. I loved makeup. I'd been doing it since I was seven or eight and I was passionate about it. But I didn't know how to do it as a job."

Fantasy becomes Reality

Then Fate dropped a flyer right into her lap. "It was one of those moments right out of a movie. 'Mom, I need to call about this. This is it! This is IT!'" A local makeup effects school, run by Sandra Burman, who, it turned out, was a friend of a friend, was offering classes. Phone calls were made and Eryn was enrolled in the eight-week class. "One weekend we got to see how to do face casting, and then we would do a little face cast. Then the next weekend we would learn about sculpting, and then we would get to do sculpting. Then we would do mold-making and run foam. It was taught by all these amazing people: Richard Ruiz, Ken Hall, Gil Mosko, and John Logan."

At the end of the course, Sandra Burman gave Eryn the names of people at several studios. "I just cold-called them and made appointments. I put together a crummy little book with photos of makeups that I had done straight out of the Richard Corson book with highlight and shadow, old age lines on my face, grey hair, and took it around to the studios." On the day of her appointments, Eryn and her mom headed out. "Mom said she didn't want me driving in those sketchy areas by myself, especially since I'd never driven more than two miles from home. Mom pulled up, I got out of the car with my little book clasped tightly in my hands and disappeared through the door. My mother sat outside gripping the steering wheel [thinking], 'I just sent my 18-year-old daughter into this building. I hope I see her again.' My mom drove me around all day sharing the excitement. My parents never discouraged me. They never said, 'You shouldn't be doing that.' They always said, "You can do anything."' Eryn's family has been an unwavering support system for her from her childhood surgeries to her current professional successes.

A few weeks after visiting the shops, John Buechler from Mechanical & Makeup Imageries, Inc. called and asked if Eryn wanted "an entry level job doing stuff to help keep the shop running. 'Oh, yeah, I totally wanted to do that.'" She talked with her parents, promised to return to college for 2nd semester of her sophomore year, and they agreed. "For a hundred dollars a week, I worked 10 hours a day, sweeping up and running errands at MMI in North Hollywood."

Eryn was 18 when she started working with Buechler. She was inexperienced, had never had a checking account, or a full-time job, or worked with people who were older. And yet, "As soon as I got there, I knew this was it! I'd run errands, handle petty cash, sweep up. But, John would also give me little things to sculpt and mold, run foam on, and take to set."

"John eventually gave me creatures and sent me over to Roger Corman's studio to do on-set stuff. He said, 'Just go make it work.' So, armed with superglue, fishing line, and duct tape, off we went. Scott Wheeler and I would drive to Venice with the monster in the back of my Honda Civic. We'd get there, walk on-set, and get to work. I still remember the smell of low-budget movies. It was an incredible experience!" Working in this commando style serves Eryn to this day. "Nowadays, if something goes wrong or falls apart on-set I can fix it. I can make it work. Back then, we didn't have time to go back to the trailer to fix something. Instead it was, 'No, no, no, we'll get through this shot and we'll fix it later.'" This was invaluable on-the-job-training. "I learned that from John: how to make something work on the fly. I never would have had that experience if I'd gone straight into a bigger shop that didn't have a hands-on approach to everything."

Eryn working in the shop
Used with Permission of Eryn Krueger Mekash

Eventually, Eryn left MMI and worked for both Stan Winston and Rick Baker at their effects shops. She quickly discovered at these larger shops everyone did specialized tasks. Eryn was especially skilled at mold-making and finishing work such as seaming and hair, but she felt she wasn't a great sculptor. "I was very slow. I could do little sculpting projects, but it didn't compare with anybody who was killing it out there like Steve Wang, Norman Cabrera, Matt Rose, and Tom Hester. All those guys, they're phenomenal. All the guys over at Stan Winston's, I couldn't get near that level. It just wasn't my forte; but, as a result, I have a huge appreciation for sculpting."

New Challenges

Eryn began to feel restless working in the shops. "There I was, actually working in a makeup effects shop, but I wasn't enjoying it anymore. I never wanted someone to come to me and say, 'You're not doing a great job here' and realize it was because I wasn't happy. I learned so much, and really appreciated getting the chance to work at Stan and Rick's shops, but I knew, for me, I had to make a change."

Trying to find her way, Eryn decided she would try different types of work. She worked for Rick Stratton on **Alien Nation** doing a little bit of painting and stenciling. Then she worked for Rick Lazzarini on **Radio Flyer** doing a bit of hair finishing and even some puppeteering. "I liked doing the puppet stuff and thought maybe I could do that. I even wrote to Jim Henson at one point." She also applied and got into Dick Smith's Advanced Prosthetics Course and started working through the curriculum.

After several false starts, she remembered a conversation she'd had with family friend and music editor,

Ken Hall, who had helped her get into Sandra Burman's school. "Ken's like my uncle, he's an incredibly lovely guy. He said to me, 'I don't want to discourage you from doing this work, but shop work can be incredibly hard, heavy lifting. Women don't do it very often; it's mainly a male-driven job. I know that you love it so much and I don't want to put you off, but you should keep an option open to doing on-set work. You may be more rewarded by and happier with a career as a makeup artist doing prosthetics.' He was right."

Smile and Wave

After deciding she wanted to try working on-set, Eryn started cold-calling ABC, NBC, and CBS because, at that time, television studios were allowed to hire non-union makeup artists. "Sandra Dunphy at ABC, the new department head for all the shows, wanted to get some fresh faces into the studio. So, at 22, she hired me for the Oscar show that year [1988] recreating *Baron von Munchausen* makeups for the costume category presentation. I was brought in to do one of the makeups which needed prosthetic ears and a bald cap. Little did I know I was entering a minefield. I walked around introducing myself to all these people, makeup artists who had worked at ABC for 20 years, people who were incredibly qualified to do the prosthetics that she had hired me to do.

"I learned to have a thick skin. I've had those skills since I was four. I knew I had to keep that kind of attitude at the Oscar show where I used my 'Smile and Wave.' Even though people didn't want to deal with me, I would just 'Smile and Wave.' This was a good way for me to approach the situation and try not to let anything bother me."

Can-Do Attitude

After her work on the Oscars, Eryn continued cold-calling the networks, which finally landed her on-set at CBS working with Barry Koper on *The Young and the Restless*. She also did some makeup effects work for Bart Mixon and Matthew Mungle making molds at home to bring in some cash, and even took a temp job for Warner Brothers. "I was the worst temp person. I'd disconnect executive producers all the time. I couldn't work the system. Everyone thought I could because my attitude was always, 'Yeah, I can do it,' then I'd try to figure it out."

Her, "Yeah, I can do it, then figure it out later" attitude served her well when she was hired at ABC for *General Hospital.* "They said, 'You have some experience with special makeup effects, do you want to do the prosthetics applications?' I said, 'Okay!' Then I dove into the books. I had my handful of books, my Richard Corson *Stage Makeup* and my Dick Smith Advanced Prosthetics Course materials. I thumbed through them thinking, 'Okay, this is how you do this.' I would practice, and say, 'Yeah, I can do it. I can do it!' It only took once for me to figure things out, and luckily those makeups turned out fine and they were happy with them."

Working on *General Hospital,* Eryn got to perfect her straight and beauty makeup skills as well. "Everything I knew at that point was self-taught. Makeup Department Head Donna Messina took me under her wing, and I basically was paid to learn how to do beauty makeup. I learned how to do contouring, and those big, beautiful makeups that they do on soap operas." Eryn also got the opportunity to work on *Good Morning America*, which had a 4 AM call time. She would get up at 3:30, go to work, do the makeup, and they would air it. "It was crazy, but it was fun."

Life Lessons and Union Work

Aside from her burning ambition, another driving force in Eryn's life is having fun! She relishes the enjoyment gained from positive, productive work that's driven by passion, coupled with interesting, energetic interactions on and off the set. "I didn't consciously know this when I was little, but my parents told me I wanted to have as much fun as possible. That has carried over into my adult life. If you're not having fun, make a change. If you're not happy doing a job, then you need to find what makes you happy. Learn to reevaluate. I learned that early on. Every step needs to be evaluated to make sure you're making the best choice for yourself, which all comes back to: are you having fun? Are you enjoying your job? Do you love what you're doing? If you're not, make a decision to change. This is what took me into doing on-set work."

Always looking to advance her education and skills, Eryn attended a seminar taught by Michael Westmore offered through UCLA extension. "We'd sit and watch Michael do every imaginable, out-of-kit make-up technique. This was the first time I watched somebody else actually do some of these techniques. Then we'd practice on a partner. I brought my book into class and said to him, 'I'm a mold maker too if you ever need a mold maker.' He said, 'As soon as you get in the union, you call me.'"

While working on *General Hospital,* Eryn qualified for union membership. At that time, a makeup artist had to work 50 days a year for three years within a five-year period in order to qualify. Every year she would apply, and every year she'd be told she didn't have enough hours because they wouldn't count her time working in special effects shops. In 1993, she finally had enough hours.

Feeling at Home

"When I got in the union, I called Michael Westmore and he said, 'Come over and start tomorrow. I'll get you all of your insurance hours if you can give me three months.' I said, 'Oh, yeah, absolutely.'"

The next day, Eryn started working with Westmore and she immediately felt at home. She did make-ups in the morning and mold making and foam running with Gil Mosko in the afternoon. Westmore's department was unique. "Everybody seemed happy. Everybody got to do makeups. Anybody that needed hours could call and he would have them come in." It was a model Eryn appreciated and re-members to this day. "Being a very talented makeup artist, Michael also has a lovely way of being a boss. The way he talks to people, supports people, is positive and inclusive. He was my model and my mentor. I knew if I ever ran a department, I wanted to run it like Michael Westmore runs his."

Once in the union, Eryn received a letter asking her to take the journeyman's test. "I was terrified. Really scared. It was a massive, full day test covering everything a makeup artist should know. My girlfriend said, 'Take it, because even if you fail, you'll know what's expected.'" The day before the test, Eryn received some hands-on advice from Dave Quashnick, one of the main artists in Westmore's department, who showed her how to lay a moustache. The last-minute tutoring paid off; Eryn took the test and passed it on her first try.

For the next three years, Eryn was the department head for low-budget films or a day player on big films; she took whatever union job came along. "At the time, we were using pagers and I'd get a call, 'They need somebody at such-and-such studio in an hour-and-a-half. Can you be there?' I would drop everything and just go. I got to meet a lot of people that way. Sometimes that one day would turn into two weeks or a month of work."

Success Breeds Success

In 1996, Eryn was recommended for *Sabrina the Teenage Witch;* she interviewed and got the job, one that lasted seven years. The show had lots of prosthetics. "When I first started doing *Sabrina*, I would do all the little gags myself. I would make stuff from off-the-shelf Woochie appliances and adapt them. I would do all these little funny makeups, like Unicorn Girl, as gags in the 'other realm' on *Sabrina*." Eryn had great success with her "make it work" methods. Working in a small department with only Key Artist Christine Steele-Smith by her side, Eryn became successful at improvising the various makeup gags. But success can grow out of hand. "The more we did, the more the producers knew they could incorporate. Finally, they were asking me for things that were beyond us."

As department head, she had to come up with solutions to the bigger demands which meant jobbing out some of the work. She called upon some of her former mentors who had shops, Westmore, Bart Mixon, or

James MacKinnon, to make gags for her. "I would job out these little things that I designed, they would make them for me, and then I would do the applications. I was doing what I had always wanted to do, applications on-set. That was 20 years ago, but I've always liked that way of working. I'm still part of the collaboration, it's my concepts, and it's their design. It kept rolling into bigger and bigger projects, which was great. I just kept taking it on. 'Yes, I can do it. Yes, I can.'"

Glee (2011) Kiss segment
Used with Permission of Eryn Krueger Mekash

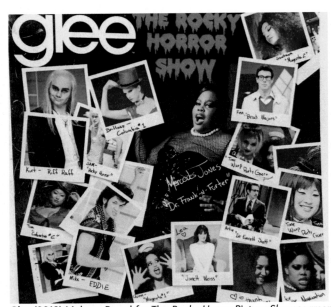

Glee (2012) Makeup Board for The *Rocky Horror Picture Show* segment
Used with Permission of Eryn Krueger Mekash

Continuing, Changing Challenges

In 2003, *Sabrina* came to an end, and a month later Eryn was hired for the show *Nip/Tuck* as key makeup artist for her friend, James MacKinnon. MacKinnon was department head on the show and Tom Burman and Bari Dreiband-Burman were responsible for all the prosthetics and surgery simulations. The 2003/04 season *Nip/Tuck* was nominated for two Emmy awards, and MacKinnon and the Burmans won for the prosthetic work they did for the pilot episode. When MacKinnon left *Nip/Tuck*, Eryn became department head and started working directly with producer/writer/director Ryan Murphy for the first time, a professional relationship that, as of this writing, has spanned 14 years.

The Ryan Murphy television projects Eryn has worked on include: *American Horror Story*, (2011-2016, 62 episodes as Makeup Department Head and/or Designer), *American Crime Story*, (2016, 10 episodes as Makeup Designer and/or Department Head), *Scream Queens*, (2015, 13 episodes as Makeup Designer and/or Department Head), *Glee*, (2009-2011, 43 episodes as Makeup Department Head), and *Nip/Tuck*, (2003-2009, 76 episodes as Makeup Artist or Makeup Department Head).

As a producer and director, Murphy likes to create a team on his shows using an impressive stable of actors such as Jessica Lange, Sarah Paulsen, Kathy Bates, and Angela Basset, as well as a crew he knows he can trust. Eryn is his "go-to" for makeup. As of this writing, she has worked on all seven seasons of *American Horror Story*, including *Murder House*, *Asylum*, *Coven*, *Freak Show*, *Hotel*, and *Roanoke* as makeup department head, overseeing both the makeup and prosthetics departments with Key Makeup Artists Kim Ayers (Makeup) and Mike Mekash (Prosthetics). Eryn is continually challenged by Murphy because he wants something new and exciting for each show. Murphy believes the hair, makeup, and wardrobe are where the character begins before they've even spoken a word. "I love doing character work like that, and Ryan is really amazing because he believes the first moment you see someone on camera, you can tell things about them, you begin to know them by what they look like. *American Horror Story* is completely geared to my sensibility because it changes every year. It's not like a cop show where every year it's the same over and over again."

One of her favorite makeups from *AHS: Asylum* was a makeup for Sarah Paulsen who played a successful Barbara-Walters-type journalist: a mature, beautiful woman. "It needed to be an age makeup with a beauty makeup effect, with a current hairstyle and clothing. It was hard to figure it out because we didn't want her to look too pulled or too much like a caricature. Sarah didn't want something that was going to be too extreme or heavy, so finding the balance was crucial.

American Horror Story: Asylum (2012)
Sarah Paulsen in Age makeup
Used with Permission of Eryn Krueger Mekash

"It was an eight-piece makeup. Chris Nelson and Mike Mekash did the application and I did the makeup and we tweaked everything as a team. When you're in the middle of something like that, all you want is to make sure that this beautiful makeup that Tinsley Studio designed for Sarah is represented correctly, is applied the right way, meets Ryan Murphy's vision, and Sarah Paulson can act through it. It's intense. You're just hoping that it all comes off the right way. Then, you see it come together and finally see it on camera and you think, 'Oh, look what we did. Yeah. That looks good.' In those moments, it's incredibly rewarding."

Season five of *AHS: Hotel* had several challenging makeups. One of the biggest makeups was the Addiction Demon, a four-hour makeup requiring three makeup artists. "He looks like a white dim sum dumpling. It had to be fabricated every day using full prosthetics underneath, with silicone pieces over the top, and Baldiez covering a lot of it. It was a huge, huge makeup." Also during season five, Lady Gaga starred as a vampiress who wore a deadly sharp-clawed glove. "We had tons of neck slashes; sometimes we did five slashes a day. We had it down to a science, all the rigs for the slashing and gushing blood. One episode I needed eight makeup artists to paint a group of dead parents who had been drained of their blood by their vampire kids. Everybody had a parent to do, so we were all on the set together, each of us making up a dead parent."

Creating a Cohesive Team

It's obvious that *AHS*, in its many variations, puts heavy demands on the crews, which vary in size depending on the needs of the show. On *AHS: Freakshow*, the crew was large due to all the unusual carnival cast, which included the bearded lady, the two-headed lady, and the three-breasted lady. Eryn can always rely on her core crew, Kim Ayers and Mike Mekash, but when the schedule gets heavy, "I call my 'guys,' Chris Nelson, Kevin Kirkpatrick, Mike Smithson, Richard Redlefsen, and James MacKinnon. These guys do effects, but they all do beauty as well. There're a lot of makeup effects guys that don't do beauty, and I don't have as much room for them. On a show like *AHS*, we do a lot of beauty. We have different units, sometimes I need someone I can send to one unit to cover a beauty makeup, and then come back to the other unit to cover an effect. Everybody that I hire, man or woman, can do prosthetic and beauty work. It is really fun, especially when I get to hire and work with my friends."

Eryn likes to hire women to cover both areas too, but women who do both beauty and effects are usually working. "I rarely can get someone like Christina Waltz or Carleigh Herbert, who both do beautiful effects and beauty work. Mara Rouse does beautiful work, and she's been coming in to help me out." In 2015, as makeup designer for *Scream Queens* and *American Crime Story*, Eryn was able

AHS crew: (L-R) Mike Mekash, Mike Smithson, Eryn, Ian Van Cromer , Kim Ayers, Cary Ayers, Silvi Knight, James McKinnon, and Careigh Herbert
Used with Permission of Eryn Krueger Mekash

Alpha Dog (2004) Eryn with Justin Timberlake (Tattoos by Tinsley Transfers)
Used with Permission of Eryn Krueger Mekash

to hire some talented women makeup artists. "On **Scream Queens,** I brought in Kelley Mitchell as department head and Melissa Buell as the key makeup artist; they both can do beauty and prosthetics. Then I came back to Los Angeles and did **American Crime Story**, which didn't have a lot of prosthetics in it, but I hired Zoe Hay and Heather Plott who both do prosthetics as well as beauty. Zoe took over as department head when I left after two episodes to return to **AHS.** For Ryan, I stayed on both of those shows as designer, so I read all the scripts and made sure that everybody was good-to-go with all the makeups on the shows."

Besides being able to hire friends to work with her, she's especially pleased to work with her husband, Mike Mekash, on **AHS**. They met in 2004 while working on Nick Cassavetes' film, **Alpha Dog**, "a fun project shot right before Christmas; it was really a good time." Mike started off as a graphic artist designing skateboards, waveboards, and snowboards. He then worked for Tinsley Studio drawing tattoos for their shows, which rolled over into doing prosthetics transfers. "He would say to me, 'Show me how to do a black eye.' I'd show him and he could do it right out of the gate. Mike is a natural artist who has worked very hard at his craft. His precision on his prosthetics and beauty makeups is stunning. He has an artist's mind and I'm always learning from him. He also has the kind of brain that loves putting things together, so he figures out our blood rigs, always making them simpler and more concise. He always wants to learn more. We work together well that way. It's all about learning from other people. 'How'd you do that? What is that?'"

Eryn has earned a reputation for juggling projects and maintaining high standards. At the 2016 Emmys, Eryn and her team received an award for *Outstanding Makeup for a Limited Series or Movie (Non-Prosthetic)* for **AHS: Hotel**. At the 2015 Emmys, she and her crew won two awards for **AHS: Freakshow**, *Outstanding Prosthetic Makeup for a Series, Limited Series, Movie or Special* and *Outstanding Makeup for a Limited Series or a Movie (Non-Prosthetic).*

In February 2016, she and her crews won three awards from the Makeup Artists and Hairstylists Guild, Local 706, for *Best Period Makeup and/or Character Makeup (TV Mini-Series or Movie of the Week), Best Special Makeup Effects (TV Mini-Series or MOW)* for **AHS: Hotel,** and *Best Contemporary Makeup (TV Mini-series or MOW)* for **Scream Queens.**

When asked about her recent awards she beams, "It's just incredible to get an award from your peers for something that you love doing."

The Creative Challenges Continue

On her hiatuses from working episodic TV, Eryn has also worked on several feature films: **Whip It** (2009), Nick Cassavetes' **My Sister's Keeper** (2009), **Prom Night** (2008), Clint Eastwood's **Letters from Iwo**

Jima and *Flags of Our Fathers* (2006), Nick Cassavetes' *Alpha Dog* (2006), and three of Ryan Murphy's films, *The Normal Heart* (2014), *Eat Pray Love* (2010), and *Running With Scissors* (2006).

"One of the reasons why I've stayed with Ryan so long is not only do I think he's a genius that loves make-up, but the projects that he picks are incredible and challenging for me." Eryn's first film with Murphy was the comedy *Running with Scissors*. Murphy wrote and directed the film, which included "lots of different character makeups, all out-of-kit character work."

In 2014, she worked on the TV movie, *The Normal Heart,* produced and directed by Murphy, for which she and her crew won the Emmy for *Outstanding Makeup for a Miniseries or a Movie (Non-Pros-thetic)*. "It is one of my favorite projects. I was on that film for two months in New York right before we started filming *AHS: Coven*. It was a difficult film to work on because of the subject matter; it was such a heart-breaking job. I did three weeks of research watching every documentary about AIDs that was out there and I would sit at my little desk wearing the headphones and cry and cry and cry."

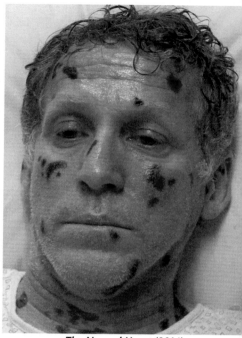

The Normal Heart (2014)
Stephen Spinella in AIDS makeup
Used with Permission of Eryn Krueger Mekash

In the course of her research, she met Dr. Alvin E. Friedman-Kien, who wrote *Color Atlas of AIDS,* the preeminent book on AIDS. Fried-man-Kien discovered this mysterious disease wasn't cancer, but a fail-ing of the immune system. "He was the loveliest man. After meeting him, I knew I had to do everything I could to accurately represent this illness." Many of the characters in the film were actual AIDS patients. "We used a lot of people that were sick. Sometimes we added sores and things to heighten the effects of their condition. We were trying to honor the people, the millions of people that have passed away."

Most of the sores and spots were done with either prosthetic transfers or tattoos, but Eryn found she couldn't use them on Matt Bomer, the lead in the film. "He had lost so much weight, I couldn't use the trans-fers on him because the nature of the transfers is to stay on. I couldn't take them off easily because his skin was so thin and dry, it was very fragile. I ended up painting all of them on so then he was able to go home and get in the tub to wash them off. On-set he was covered with blankets, so I would have to uncover an area, paint, and get him covered up again."

The Vanities? Nope!

Nick Cassavetes and Ryan Murphy believe makeup is as much a major component in character development as costumes or lighting. Unfortunately, this philosophy isn't always present on-set. "Not everyone agrees. Often the attitude is, 'Oh, right, we have to have makeup and hair?' When you're working for people with that mindset, you feel you're not an important part of the process. They call us 'the vanities' which makes it sound like we're an option, an unimportant part of the crew. When I hear that I always correct them, 'I'm not a vanity, I'm the makeup artist.' I make sure they know we're as important as everybody else. It's an old prejudice. Sometimes you have to remind people that everybody's part of the team to get a project done."

"There was a quote I read recently, from a major makeup artist that said, 'What you see in a close-up is acting and makeup.' That's stuck with me. Our work is front and center in the shot. They don't ever want to wait for what's actually being put on camera. We try to be proactive and do our touchups be-fore the actors go on camera so nobody has to wait, but they'll spend countless minutes, sometimes hours, lighting and setting up the shot. But they don't want to wait for actors to use the restroom, or wait for a final tweak of a costume, or the makeup and hair, all of which is the focus of what'll be seen on camera. They never want to wait anymore for a blood effect, which we are always fighting for."

Eryn appreciates Murphy as a producer who "likes blood gags and special effects to be practical. It's a fight all the time, getting to do real, practical effects. Nowadays, they'll say to you, 'Okay, we're going to put blood in this shot, but we'll do it in post.' Except, you never get the reactions from a digital blood effect that you do from a real blood effect. You don't get that excited visceral feeling. It still is a priority in the Ryan Murphy world, which is one of the things that I love about working for him."

Eryn had always wanted to do a war film, so another one of her favorite projects was getting to work as key makeup artist with her friend Tania McComas (department head) on Clint Eastwood's films *Letters from Iwo Jima* and *Flags of Our Fathers*. As in any good war film, there are lots of blood effects, sometimes one as simple as blood splashing onto an actor's face. As Eryn was preparing for this practical blood effect, "with my fingers dipped into a little bowl of blood, I hear Clint Eastwood's voice. There he is, 85-years-old, all 6'3" of him, an imposing presence, saying in my ear, 'In the shot, I just want it flicked on the actor. And, no pressure, but we're doing this in one.' I'm thinking, 'Oh my God, please, let me get this right.' In one way, it's an amazing thing, and in another way, terrifying."

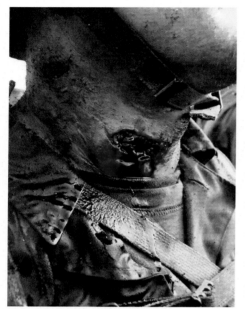

FLAGS FOR OUR FATHERS (2006)
Neck Wound
Used with Permission of Eryn Krueger Mekash

Eryn worked on the film *Wakefield* (2016) which stars Bryan Cranston as Howard Wakefield who lives in his own house, spies on his wife, and deteriorates as the film progresses. "Normally, Bill Corso does Bryan's makeup, but he was off on another film so he asked me if I could do it. It's an all-woman production: producers, director, and writer, and they're all wonderful. I've had a good experience with them. Bryan is a lovely person, fun to work with. For one look, he has dental plumpers and prosthetics around the eyes. In another of his looks he has this incredibly scraggly beard. Zoe Hay was my key on it and she designed all the beards for me. Robert Wilson was the hair department head, and he did all the wigs. Figuring out how to do this makeup on a dollar budget was creative and challenging. I love doing character work like that."

Changing It Up

"One of the good things about this business is you have the opportunity to do different things all the time. What else is out there for me to do? I'd like to do a really big prosthetics show. I already do that with the *AHS*, but I mean a film. My career has always presented itself to me as I've gone along. There have been times I don't know it's what I want to do until it comes up. Wow, it's so amazing I'm still doing what I've always want to do."

WAKEFIELD (2016)
Bryan Cranston in bearded makeup
Used with Permission of Eryn Krueger Mekash

Contradictions and complications define Eryn Krueger Mekash. It all boils down to three questons: "Does it scare me? I hope so! Is it Fun? Absolutely! Can I do it? Yes, I can!"

OUTTAKES:

On Me:

"I am lucky. I'm incredibly lucky. I'm incredibly lucky to be doing and loving everything that I still loved when I was 14. I'm the quintessential nerd boy. When people talk about that they loved monsters and they were in their basement sculpting monsters, I loved monsters like that, too. I get excited about horror."

"I have always been a very upfront and honest person as far as I can tell, as far as I know. I have a friend, Stacey K. Black, an amazing hairdresser who is now directing television. She's also a writer and a musician. She always says, 'As far as I know, I'm delightful,' which always makes me laugh. I love that. 'As far as I can tell, I'm delightful.'"

"I've also been accused of being Pollyanna-ish where everything is rose colored; I'm always trying to find the best in people. People don't like that. They say, 'Oh, you're just way too optimistic.' I try to just keep it to myself sometimes."

On Iconic Work:

"I got a few pieces from the Rick Baker auction this year. One of the pieces that I got was a set of *Thriller* prosthetics that were still in fairly good shape. I couldn't believe it. I get so excited about that stuff still. It's so amazing to get to be part of that community."

"I'm still a fan. I still love these books [Corson, Smith]. I still love talking about makeup. I still get excited about the process of researching and creating things, and thinking, 'I really want it to look like that; show how my design is influenced by my research.'"

On Working in Television:

"In television, you work very hard on a makeup, several makeups, the whole season, and you don't get to see that much of it on camera. It's very disheartening. The editing is so fast and you have to get all this information into an hour so you've spent all this time. You want to see more of it. It's a selfish thing. With the Addiction Demon, it's a four-and-a-half-hour makeup, they shot him for 10 minutes and then we took him out of the makeup. It's what we're all about, but you want, you know, you want a whole show about it."

On Artists:

"Everyone is an artist and everyone is passionate. We all put so much into it. We're not factory worker making the same piece over and over again. We're artistic people, with eccentricities, and ego, and passion that bring everything to the table. That's how you end up getting incredible things. But on the other hand, you also have people that are sensitive and protective and love what they're doing and want the most for it."

On Communicating:

"Instead of coming from an emotional state, I've always spoken very simply and clearly, and conveyed how I felt about things and asked for what I wanted, which tends to be an easier way to communicate with producers and directors who tend to be men."

"I know quite a few people who are incredibly dramatic, who cause trauma to the people that they work with, who place blame, and who are not good people, who are constantly let go from jobs. Everybody knows that they're a nightmare to work with because just don't know how to communicate with people. They especially shouldn't be in a position where they have people under them, or in a position where they hire people. The people that are successful communicate well. I have always found that being straight-forward and being simple with my requests is appreciated."

"I'm passionate and artistic, but so is my boss, so we both can't be that way. Do you know what I mean? Somebody has to be the one that's like, 'Okay, so you want this?' 'Yes, I want that.' 'Okay.' Then you give it to them. I love it. You have to be a good listener. You try to be a good communicator."

"I rarely get riled up about anything. I have a good perspective, I think, on what's important, what are priorities. Your health is important. Your family is important. These are the important things. If somebody gets sick at work, you're like, 'You need to go home now.' If something's happened, that's the priority. We can figure things out at work. I think I have a good perspective on those things. It makes for a calmer, better work environment when you actually keep the human element as a priority."

"You might occasionally get somebody in there that you realize doesn't handle stress well or doesn't handle their jobs well. You maybe don't bring them back on. It just doesn't fit in with your group. I always have people that I work with that are wonderful to be around and have the same work ethic that I do."

On Goals:

"Award winning is not the ultimate goal. I think keeping your passion is the way to be steadfast and to have staying power. Are you loving what you're doing? Do you need to do something different? Is it time to consider interior decorating or something else?"

On Growth:

"You have to constantly re-evaluate. There's a lot to be said for your off time where you really appreciate having time to just relax. This business just takes the toll on you. You have to have that time to reboot, to have your passion rekindle. I've found that that's really important as I'm getting older to have enough down time to still keep my passions alive."

Catching Up!

Eryn was our first interview on December 28, 2015. Since then, she has worked on

To the Bone
Makeup Design and Department Head

Anything
Makeup Design

Feud
Makeup Design and Department Head

American Crime Story: Versace and Cunanan
Makeup Design and Department Head

Star Trek: Discovery
working prosthetics for James MacKinnon

American Horror Story: Cult
Makeup Design and Department Head

American Horror Story: Cult
with a Producer credit

Game Face
Judge for the SyFy reality show

For more of Eryn's Credits, visit: www.imdb.com

Authors' Note:

On Sunday, September 10, 2017, at the Creative Emmy Awards ceremony, Eryn won two awards; the 1st for *Outstanding Makeup for a Limited Series or Movie (Non-Prosthetic) for* **FEUD: Bette and Joan** and the 2nd for *Outstanding Prosthetic Makeup for a Series, Limited Series, Movie or Special for* **American Horror Story: Roanoke.**

With these two new honors, Eryn has 30 Emmy Nominations and six Wins becoming the most awarded woman makeup artist in television.

We congratulate Eryn and all of her crews for this milestone acheivement.   Pat & Gary

2017 Emmy Awards: (LtoR)
Tym Buacharern, David Williams, Becky Cotton, Silvina Knight, Mike Mekash, Eryn, Robin Beauchesne, Luis Garcia, Kim Ayers, Carleigh Herbert, James Mackinnon and Jason Hamer.
Used with Permission of Eryn Krueger Mekash

2014
EMMY AWARD
OUTSTANDING PROSTHETIC MAKEUP
FOR A SERIES, MINISERIES, MOVIE OR A SPECIAL

GAME OF THRONE (2014) MAISIE WILLIAMS, RORY MCCANN
Licensed from Photo 12 / Alamy Stock Photo

Jane Walker

I was always a curious child, and as an adult I quite like to see what lies around the next bend and over the next hill. I want to know how that works and how this is put together. I think you must have a good wedge of that in your soul to do well in this job because your life will be full of adventure. They'll fry you to death in the middle of the desert and freeze you to death in Iceland and make you hike up the mountain. You've got to have that adventurous spirit.

"When I was young, there were only three TV channels, but I was obsessed with television. My brother and I would do film scenarios around the house. There were always Indians in the kitchen, cowboys ambushing them. I used to make little arrows and things to stab them with and I used to make blood out of beet root juice and ketchup. It's amazing actually. A couple of years ago we had just finished a huge battle scene on *Game of Thrones* and there were hundreds of people lying around in water and mud with arrows sticking out of them here and there and I was laughing my head off. I thought, 'This is the same game I played with my brother, but my toys have gotten a lot more expensive.'"

Jane's road from beet root juice to battlefields is a combination of talent, luck, drive, and an unquenchable desire to break with tradition. She was born and brought up in a small town, south of Edinburgh, Scotland, where her parents' life was dictated by 1940s societal norms and expectations. Jane's father went to work in the coal mines at age 13; her mother worked in the mill from age 14 until she married, at which time she stopped working to have and raise a family.

Jane is the youngest of four children: Mary is 16 years older, Kate is 15 years older, and her brother, James, is 11 years older. "It was like having three mothers and two fathers, not like having siblings at all. The other three created all the trouble and by the time I came along, it was like, 'Oh look, she's climbing a wall and juggling with knives and eating dirt, well, just leave it, it'll be okay.' So, it worked out quite well."

Mary and Kate married, had kids, and divorced. "My father could never understand. When he was sick and dying he said, 'I'm leaving you all on your own and none of you have any men to look after you. I have failed you.' We told him, 'No, Dad, it's quite the opposite. What you did is bring up really strong, independent women who can look after themselves. We are going to be absolutely fine.'"

"When I was growing up, there were no aspirations for me other than to grow up, be safe, and meet someone who would look after me. Those were my parents' best wishes for me. Even as a young child, I found that just completely unacceptable. I didn't want to have anything to do with it." With her wild mane of red hair, sharp and subtle sense of humor, quiet confidence, and unflappability, it is easy to see how and why Jane moved away from traditional Scottish expectations. She immersed herself in art and television, drawing what she saw, her imagination fueled by *Bonanza, Columbo, The Mary Tyler Moore Show*, and *Marcus Welby, M.D.* "Television was an educator and I had what my siblings did not, a window on the world through TV and film."

Breaking with Tradition

Science fiction, in the form of *Star Trek*, fantasy movies, monsters, and crazy costumes, captivated Jane's imagination. As she was basically an only child, she was often left to her own devices, and that's when "all the crazy imaginings took place. My mum would never have any trouble with me because I would just sit in a corner and draw." Drawing and painting were her constant companions; she was good at it, she enjoyed it, she wanted to incorporate it into her life, so she decided to pursue a degree at an art college. "My parents didn't have any problem with that because it kept me in education. My father did aspire for us to do better than they did."

Art college took Jane out of her small Scottish town. She enrolled in Duncan of Jordanstone College of Art and Design, affiliated with the University of Dundee, and she spent five glorious years immersed in art. She was introduced to sculpture in her foundation (first) year. "It was the first time I had ever sculpted anything or used three dimensions. It was much more satisfying. I have that kind of mind where I see things in the round. It doesn't have to be on a flat piece of paper. That was very exciting, so I ended up getting my degree in sculpture."

Jane's sculptures were huge, abstract, expressionist pieces using clay and metal and then later, glass. "I always felt a little dissatisfied because I was leaning toward figurative things, but they were not fashionable, so I was steered away from all that." Her sculptures were made from as many metal girders as she could find and weld together. Of course, at the end of a year, all projects had to be dismantled because there was no place to keep or store them. And from this experience, Jane learned a valuable lesson that applies to her work as a makeup artist to this day. "The work is transient. Don't get too precious about the things you make. It's important to be able to let go and reassess and rebuild."

Surprisingly though, at the end of her time at Duncan, Jane knew she wasn't going to be an artist. "Modern art had moved so much into conceptual art by that time…you put a brick on the table and you wrote an essay about why the brick is a work of art. That just wasn't for me. I can see the value in it, but it's not me. It's not my personality and I couldn't really see myself having a career that way."

Talent and Luck

College was over and it was time to get a job. Fortuitously, a friend of Jane's saw an advertisement for makeup trainees with the BBC, so both girls applied. It was 1981 and competition was fierce, with 800 applicants for the 12 available positions. "It was karma. The interview was on my birthday. I had to do an old age makeup on somebody. I had to put a long hair-piece on someone with short hair, then I had to make someone look pretty. I was used to building and constructing things so it was like do-do-do, done. I thought, 'This is the best fun ever.' It's drawing and painting on people. If I could have written a perfect job out of my wildest dreams, this would be it. I got the job."

The BBC training included three years in school learning everything: hair, makeup, and prosthetics. Following that was a two-year on-the-job traineeship, followed by either termination or a permanent contract. Jane got the permanent contract and stayed with the BBC for 10 years. During her tenure there, Jane worked on everything from period dramas to sketch comedies to the news and weather. She established working relationships with producers and directors that continue to this day. She also met her husband and had her daughter while working with the BBC.

Jane tells of a 12-episode children's program, **Think of a Number,** with a budget of 115 pounds for the entire series! The scripts had the five presenters dressed as different animals every week and they needed prosthetic faces of cats, pigs, dogs, and bears to go with the costumes. "Because the budget was so small, the pieces were homemade and slush rubber. I cast their faces and molded a little animal mask. Then I would literally slush the latex around and pour it out and keep doing that until there was enough layered latex to become a mask. It was the most economical but most time-consuming way to do the design. Because I was a permanent employee, my labor was free."

A few weeks before our interview with Jane, she taught a master class on casualty effects at the Christine Blundell Makeup Academy where she demonstrated the simple, unsophisticated yet effective makeup techniques she used while at the BBC. Frequently, when a makeup artist is beginning his/her career, these types of creative, inexpensive solutions are a necessity. Jane taught these "back-to-basics" skills to the young artists, highlighting survival skills and creative thinking in makeup effects. "Making wings by hand out of bits of tissue and latex, freehand sculpting, using collodion for scarring, and creating slush latex masks. I think I got so much more out of it than the students. It was a lot of fun."

Jane designed the makeup for **The Fast Show** (10 episodes, 1994-1996), a BBC sketch comedy show known for its blackout style and the brevity of its sketches. It was shot in front of a live audience and within 30 minutes there could be as many as 27 sketches, running from 10 seconds to three minutes in length. "It was the hardest work I've ever done. We were busy all day, putting the makeup on, taking it off again, and putting more back on as fast as we could. And the pressure of a live audience made the makeup fly on and off even faster. It was some of the best fun I've ever had."

Another BBC show for which Jane designed makeup was **The Smell of Reeves and Mortimer** (1993-1995), a sketch comedy show that featured Vic Reeves and Bob Mortimer. The show was produced by the BBC for one season then left the BBC umbrella for its second season.

"The makeup was extraordinary because it was the first time I'd done slapstick makeup. [Writer] Charlie Higson said, 'We want this chap to have a cardboard chin.' 'Really?' 'Just make us a chin. Just make us a chin out of cardboard.' As I was sticking it on, I was thinking, 'Good God, I can't do this. This is all wrong, innit?' I was trying to fill the edges and Charlie said, 'What are you doing? It's a cardboard chin. Leave it alone.' That was an education curve for me."

"We also had an art director on the show who used to do cartoon drawings of what he wanted us to make for him. I'd turn to my colleague at the time, Mark Phillips, and say, 'But Mark, it's got six chins and they come down to the middle of his chest.' And he'd say, 'Yes, Jane, and that's what you shall make. A face with six chins going down the chest.' It was quite challenging some of that, but it was really, really brilliant fun."

The Drive to Create

"The BBC in the latter years wasn't so much fun because they got a little tied up in bureaucracy and money saving and political things. I

THE SMELL OF REEVES AND MORTIMER
(1993) VIC REEVES AND BOB MORTIMER
Licensed from Fred MacGregor / Alamy Stock Photo

mean, the makeup bit is always the fun bit, but the rest of it..." So, Jane began a life of freelancing, working independently from project to project, searching for satisfaction in the artistic process. *The Smell of Reeves and Mortimer* (1993-1995) was Jane's first freelance design, a rollover assignment that originated at the BBC.

The more freelance work Jane did, the more connections were made: Producer Nira Park, having seen Jane's work, asked her to design the makeup for *Spaced* (six episodes, 1999). Edgar Wright was the

director and Simon Pegg was both a writer and actor on the series. Two other projects followed that involved Nira, Edgar, and Simon: *Shaun of the Dead* (2004) and *Hot Fuzz* (2007). In 2011, Jane worked on two additional films produced by Nira Park, *Paul*, where she worked as Simon Pegg's personal makeup artist, and *Attack of the Block* as hair and makeup designer. "This work is due to all the very generous people giving me jobs over all the years."

Personal vs. Head of Department

"Simon wanted me to design a film called *How to Lose Friends and Alienate People* (2008) but the producers had Peter King who has done *King Kong* and *The Lord of the Rings*, so there was no argument. Simon was disappointed so he asked me if I'd be his personal makeup artist. 'Well, I'll give it a go. I've never

SHAUN OF THE DEAD (2004) NICK FROST & SIMON PEGG
Licensed from AF archive / Alamy Stock Photo

done it before, but I'm sure it'll be fine.' He's in every scene in the film so it's not like I was going to be sitting around doing nothing. I wasn't sure how I was going to be received, so I was very apprehensive. Also, Simon was very much of the opinion that if I was his personal makeup artist, I would be the one who was designing his makeup. It worked out okay in the end, but that could have been really tricky because as head of the department, I know there's an overall feel to the film that's been discussed with the producers and directors. To suddenly have a spanner coming in and going, 'No, that's not going to happen' is not going to go down well. Luckily, we all concurred on everything."

Jane was also Simon's personal for the film *Paul* (2011) which provided her with the opportunity to work in the US and build connections there. There weren't any prosthetics for the film and "Simon said to me, 'Gosh, this must be the only time you're ever going to make me up when you don't have to stick any bits on me.' When we got out there, they wanted a big shotgun blast in his chest. Luckily, a lovely makeup artist came to the rescue and we got a nice shotgun blast made by Greg Nicotero."

Jane enjoys being Simon Pegg's personal because it provides her an opportunity to step away from the chaos and observe other processes and methods of working. When she worked in the US, she acquainted herself with a different system and diverse union regulations. "It was a fantastic opportunity for me. I experienced it instead of being in the middle of it. They have a military clock way of working; they only get paid by the hour. It's different working practices than we have, so it was nice not having the responsibility of department heading while learning the system."

"I've only ever done personal with Simon, and he's such a good friend and a lovely, lovely guy that I would never have any problems with it. But, ultimately, I do prefer the bigger responsibility [of department heading] because I enjoy the interaction. I enjoy talking about the makeups before we do them. I enjoy the whole design process and bringing it to completion. Having the concept drawings done as we do now because I'm so posh, I have to do them myself. I'm such a posh makeup artist. You know, going through all the concept meetings and tests, I enjoy that process whereas being a personal…I haven't become part of the creative process. I miss that."

Process

"I'm a very visual person, obviously being an art college chick. When I read a script, I always get a very strong end visual of the characters." To clarify her ideas for herself, the director, producers, and actors, Jane puts a mood board together. "No disrespect, sometimes the producers are not very visual, so sometimes it's best to just show them pictures of either other makeups that have been done in the same genre, or reference pictures or drawings. My poor daughter over the years has been covered in various bits and pieces of sticky stuff and photographed."

HOT FUZZ (2007) SIMON PEGG & NICK FROST
Licensed from AF archive / Alamy Stock Photo

The actor also has some input into the overall look of the character, and after all the discussions, conceptual drawings, and test makeups, a final design emerges that hopefully pleases everyone. Concern for the actor's well-being and comfort, whether they can walk and talk and see, are crucial considerations for the final design. "In **Shaun of the Dead** I couldn't make Edgar [Wright, director] understand why we needed to have pupil holes in the contact lenses. I said, 'Because people will be actually blind, Edgar.' 'Yes, and...?' '75 people, blind, in a pub on fire. Am I the only one who understands? Oh, yes I am. I am the only one. They have to see.' 'Okay, one pupil hole. One pupil hole.'"

Prosthetics are both time consuming and expensive, so it's important that everyone concerned signs off on a design. Another significant element to consider, especially for a show like **Game of Thrones**, which shoots in Ireland, is the availability of supplies. "I have things shipped from Tinsley Transfers, which is just outside of Los Angeles, to us. We can quite often get things sent over from America a lot quicker than we can source them from anywhere in England. The film industry in Britain is still relatively small compared to America. It's a proper industry in America. If I need contact lenses, there's only two people here who do them. Teeth or anything like that, false teeth, there's just one go-to person who does them really well. You have to be organized as well because these people are always very busy."

Game of Thrones

In 2014, Jane was asked to come on board as makeup designer for **Game of Thrones**, which was starting its fourth season. **Game of Thrones** is based on George R.R. Martin's best-selling book series, **A Song of Ice and Fire**, a medieval fantasy epic. It's the depiction of two powerful families, kings and queens, knights and renegades, liars and honest men, all playing a deadly game for control of the Seven Kingdoms of Westeros and the rule of the Iron Throne. Though she is still in the middle of her work with **Game of Thrones**, it is Jane's favorite project to date.

The makeups for the human characters need to be historically accurate, incorporating beards, hair styles, and beauty makeups that reflect the Middle Ages. When there are fights, injuries ranging from scratches to mortal wounds need to be meticulously planned and executed. The battle scenes, of course, demand lots of blood; there are wounds from arrows, axes, knives, ropes, spears, crossbows and myriad other

GAME OF THRONES (2014) Licensed from Photo 12 / Alamy Stock Photo

medieval weaponry, as well as animal gouging, trampling, and biting. Each and every wound has a different look and trajectory. "From a makeup point of view, it's got everything. It's got the monsters, it's got murder by makeup, it's got all the blood and guts and fantasy bits, and it's got pretty ladies as well. From a makeup artist's point of view, it ticks all the boxes."

The human characters and the supernatural characters provide different challenges, but Jane approaches her designs with a single guiding philosophy. "I try to make everything as real as possible, even if I'm doing a monster makeup, it has to work. Muscles have to be attached to bones somehow. I like things to be believable. I spend hours looking at dead bodies and gunshot wounds or deliberating crime scene photos. What makes that one look like a real crime scene? What makes that look like a real beating up rather than a makeup one? How can you tell?"

The Runaway Train

As makeup designer for **Game of Thrones**, the challenges for Jane are complex: there are two consecutive film units running all the time in separate countries. In 2015, there were sometimes as many as five film units running, and of course schedules can change daily. It's essential that Jane is able to understand what the needs are for each day on every set and prepare her team accordingly. "I have a big overview of it before we start. This season we're already on schedule number seven and we've only been shooting a month."

Any large prosthetics or fight scenes do tend to stay on schedule because the preparation is complicated and they're expensive to produce, much less reschedule or relocate. "[The producers] try and push any big prosthetic-y things a little bit into the filming schedule so that people have as much time to prep as possible. We have the big overview with the big, meaty, chunky things hopefully staying more or less where they are. After that, I try and keep it in two-week chunks that we tape around, and hope that they don't push things around too much. But they do. It's good, it's just like having a big jigsaw puzzle or being on a train…just get on top of the big old runaway train and don't fall off."

Teamwork

Jane was told when she was hired that the makeup and prosthetic departments needed to work more collaboratively, thereby creating a more unified look for the fictional worlds of Westeros and Essos. Additionally, because the story lines include a large contingency of supernatural beings, the demands of a full-time prosthetic team are great. A well-oiled working relationship between Jane and the prosthetic department is crucial for the smooth running of the series.

"They asked me who I wanted, and I've known Barrie [Gower] since **Shaun of the Dead.** He was my choice. Fortuitously for me, they settled on Barrie. It's been a wonderful, reciprocal arrangement. He helps me and I help him. We discuss design options together. He runs everything by me. As soon as the scripts come out, we have a shot at it and he goes, 'Yeah, you're much better at doing this bit and I'll do that one.' His work is meticulous; I don't have to worry about the stuff that's his. I don't have to have anything to do with the physical manufacture or the application of it. From a technical point of view, his pieces go on like a dream. They always fit beautifully, the edges are always immaculate. It's also in HD, so there's nowhere to hide with HD."

Jane has won four Emmys for her work on *Game of Thrones:* 2016 – *Outstanding Makeup for a Single-Camera Series (Non-Prosthetic)*, which she shares with Kate Thompson, Nicola Matthews, Kay Bilk, Marianna Kyriacou, and Pamela Smyth; 2016 – *Outstanding Prosthetic Makeup for a Series, Limited Series, Movie or a Special*, which she shares with Barrie Gower, Sarah Gower, Emma Sheffield, and Tristan Versluis. 2015 – *Outstanding Makeup for a Single-Camera Series (Non-Prosthetic)*, which she shares with Nicola Matthews; 2014 – *Outstanding Prosthetic Makeup for a Series, Miniseries, Movie or a Special*, which she shares with Barrie Gower.

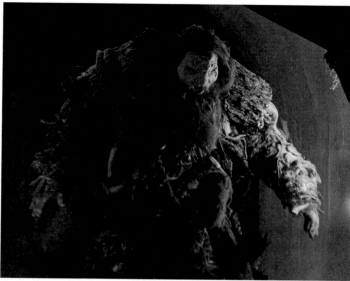

GAME OF THRONES (2014) Licensed from Photo 12 / Alamy Stock Photo

The Flip Side

The other side to success is often loss, and sometimes Jane feels a void. She is involved in such a large production she is unable to do the work she loves. She doesn't have the time to get her hands dirty and apply a makeup. She has to be on-set to ensure things are on target and well-done, and once underway, off she goes to the next location. She frequently does not even stay long enough to see one phase come to completion. "I'm quite greedy. I will take all the interesting makeups for myself, then my assistants will ask, 'What are you doing?'"

"I've got too much makeup going on, I can't be organized in what's happening next week or going to fittings or talking to the actors or doing the test makeups every few weeks if I'm also doing makeups. I have to start giving them all away because I physically can't do them all and do all the work that I'm supposed to do. It's a strange thing this process of doing bigger and more expensive projects; suddenly I get pushed away from actually doing the physical job, which is the part that is still very much enjoyable. But it is also fun to combine both parts of my brain. I enjoy that crazy momentum."

It takes four to six months to shoot one season of *Game of Thrones*, at the end of which Jane is both exhilarated and exhausted. Between her first and second season, she worked on two films, *Absolutely Anything* (2015) and *Man Up* (2015), and one film between the second and third season, *Patient Zero* (2017). In this manner, she is able to do some hands-on makeup, filling that void. "But at the end of this year, I've taken a big chunk of time out, not just because I've had my granddaughter and I want to enjoy her, but I needed a really good break."

It's a Hard Life

To the general public, being a makeup artist is a glamorous job that entails working on successful television shows with famous actors and directors and travelling the world creating iconic makeups. But, "TV-making is not a vocation. It's a business. The business is to make money. You're part of that business." And as a business, there are pitfalls and obstacles to overcome. "There will be lots of sacrifices along the way. There is no doubt about it. If you want to have a family…it's hard on your friends, just keeping your friends, not just your family. Any kind of personal relationship, you have to work hard to keep. You're away from home so often. I spend six months away from home at the moment. I probably have done all my life. I'm sure that's why I saved money toward buying a house, because I never saw my husband.

"A lot of the choices I made, especially in the middle of my career, were to ensure my family was cared for, looked after, and had a roof over its head. They weren't choices made with a career in mind, they were purely financially driven. It's harsh, not just on your children, but on yourself. Sometimes when my daughter was very young, I'd have to go abroad to film in somewhere like Morocco for four months. That's hard.

"You spend a long time away from your loved ones and your children and the people who you work with become your family. Then that evaporates after a few months. Sometimes you don't see people again for years. Sometimes never. I've had a great career and I'm hoping to continue to have a great career. It's been worth the sacrifices. It's also, getting back to money again, it's afforded my family to have a very comfortable life."

Sexism

Women are commonly asked if they are willing to leave their family and children to come and work on a film. But "it must be hard for fathers too, to leave their children. No one asks them, they just expect them to be able to do it. No one questions whether they're sitting in their hotel room crying at night because they miss their kids, and that's not fair. That's a form a sexism."

"As a woman, it can be quite frustrating when people will not listen to you and not take you seriously and direct all their conversation to your male colleague who's sitting on your right. It's easy to feel patronized. It's easy to get angry. You can't, because that's not what you're there for. You have to develop a thick skin and not get mad. It doesn't achieve anything and you've still got to do the best job you can possibly do. Even if it's a lousy film, you want the critics to say the only thing that rescued it was the high standard of the makeup. You can get frustrated, but there's no point in getting angry."

"I can see sexism works both ways sometimes. I sometimes wonder if the directors have a problem believing a woman could enjoy being blood-thirsty. It goes back to expected roles again. They don't take seriously that a woman could enjoy murdering someone. Gratuitous sex and violence are a trademark of *Game of Thrones* but in a non-sexist way because the women are as bad as the men."

It's Not Just Work

Jane not only takes her work home with her, she involves the entire family. One night a week is movie night, popcorn and all. "I still love it. Films and TV, it's my idea of heaven. I don't think about the makeup at all when I watch film or television. It's just entertainment. And we still go to the cinema regularly." She also records all the *Game of Thrones* episodes to watch at home since she rarely sees the finished cut when she's on-set.

"I'll tell you something about how geeky I am. I started watching *Firefly* and thought, 'How have I missed this?' It came on TV and I thought, 'Right, here we are, I've got it on series record. La la la la.' It gets to episode 14, and it's brewing up and coming along nicely, lots of stories and sub-stories, and it just disappeared. I was going bananas. A whole week's search on every single channel and I didn't understand why it was gone. I tell you, I am an addict, I do a series record and it says, 'Look for the next series.' There was nothing there, 'How could they do this to me?' I Googled it and it turns out years ago Joss Whedon had done the series and they pulled it after episode 11 because it wasn't getting any viewing figures. There were only 14 episodes, but Universal Pictures, God bless them, made a film of the whole concept. So, I was straight on Amazon. It was delivered the next day and that was it."

The Oyster

Jane brings life experience, a plethora of work experiences, and great joy with her to work every day. She has an unerring eye for reality, and an unlimited imagination that sparks her creations and those with whom she works. She understands that luck, drive, talent, and tradition have touched and directed her life.

"When you start out with no expectations of you, not really knowing which direction to take your life, your life can go either way. Either it's your oyster, or you follow a very narrow trail. Luckily, I was an oyster type."

OUTTAKES:

On Men and Women:

"Men are always taken a little more seriously, I think it's just the way it is. You find your behavior changing in order for you to be taken seriously. You know, talk a little tougher in some instances."

"The relationships I was expected to have when I was a child, the kind of male-female relationships I was expected to have…I look at my daughter's relationship. She's married. She and her husband are partners. They're proper partners, and they share everything. Chores, and the baby, and the financial responsibilities. A proper partnership. When I was young, the woman was very much dependent. Hopefully, all of that has moved along."

"Being taken seriously is sometimes an obstacle. Especially for prosthetics or special effects. If you've got a violent movie, they find it difficult to talk to you, I think."

"I see a lot of really talented young women coming through in prosthetics. I'm not seeing any as head of project yet, but second and third in command, certainly. Sarah Gower is project manager for Barrie and I don't think they could do without each other to be honest. She might not put the make up on, but she supports him completely. Barrie, himself, has a very high portion of women in his workshop."

"If you want children, you should not decide not to have children for this career. If you feel strongly about having a family and you want children, then you need to be there for them. There will be a point where you will have to put your career in second place and not be selfish, especially when they start going to school. You've got to fall in with their needs and your needs will be second, and they should be second. That doesn't last forever; children grow up and leave home. Hopefully, if you've got a good foundation on your career, then you can pick up and go forward again."

On Advances:

"Crikey, when I think back, I've got some pictures of work I did at training school which remind me how far we've come. I think the bar's been raised for makeup this past ten years. I think you can't compare the standard of makeup now to how it was when I first started. The bar has been raised so far."

"I think the advent of HD has impacted the field. There's no hiding place anywhere for any of it. Also, there's just been some fantastic work, particularly television projects like *The Walking Dead* and *Amer-*

ican Horror Story. I think the standards have been pushed so high. It's remarkable what people can now do."

On Zombies:

"I'd love to do a zombie western. Somebody's grabbed that one, but they could always do a sequel. I've enjoyed westerns ever since I was a kid."

"I do love a zombie movie, although I have to be careful when I watch them because they give me nightmares. I have an unreasonable fear of zombies. It's ridiculous really, considering I have done two zombie films. Yeah, they give me nightmares."

On Her Secret Weapon:

"I would not be without a pot of Pros-aide mixed with cabosil. I have made a horror shot gun wound out of it when I've been stuck and had absolutely nothing else. It's great stuff. It sticks. Especially if you've got someone fighting and they're having a good old tussle."

On Heroes:

"Ray Harryhausen, *The Valley of Gwangi* and *Jason and the Argonauts*, I thought his work was amazing. Boris Karloff, I loved Boris Karloff, especially the thought of him covering himself with tissue in the effects. Dick Smith is more contemporary."

On The Industry:

"When I was doing *Hot Fuzz* years ago, there was an old fella who used to wander about following the film crew all the time watching what we were doing. One of us had the courage to go up to him and ask, 'Well, you're watching us make the film. What are you thinking of it so far?' He said, 'Well, you hangs around a lot. You eats a lot. And then you panic.' I thought, yep, that sums up the film industry. Hang around, eat, and then panic."

Catching Up!

We interviewed Jane on June 2, 2016. Since then, she has worked on

Game of Thrones
Makeup Designer & Department Head

Slaughterhousz Rules
Makeup Designer

Patient Zero
Key makeup artist

For more of Jane's Credits, visit: www.imdb.com

LEADING LADIES OF MAKEUP EFFECTS

ON-THE-JOB

LOIS

"No one gets it right all the time. If you end up with things not working, puzzle out why, and figure out how and what turns that round. The more you do, the more you can. So, persevere. So you can make it work on the day, on the film set, because that's where it counts the most."

"As a new makeup artist, you should always be adjacent, but never obtrusive. Learn when to speak and when to be silent, even when you're itching. Don't chime in. At work, I don't necessarily give an opinion. Unless it's about the job at hand, I won't give an opinion until asked to."

JULIE

"You've got to have an understanding of people really, because you slot into them. You slot into your new surroundings, your new actors, your new production team. Particularly actors. You have to slot into them. Whatever personalities they are. Somebody might want to talk all the time. Somebody might want to have a bit of a laugh and a joke. You've got to be able to adapt. Be adaptable."

VALLI

"Listen to the director. Listen to what he wants when you have your meeting. Listen to the actors. Be kind to people that are working with you. Try to teach people to have respect for each other."

CHERI

"Being on time, being attentive. You're dealing with a lot of personalities so you just have to not put yourself first. It's not about you. This is about being part of a big picture. When you collaborate, the picture's going to be better. You're going to keep working if you're a collaborator."

MICHÈLE

"I don't come in and try to appeal using my sexuality. I become pretty much asexual, and I try to have that sort of androgynous thing about me, you don't look at me as male, or female, or otherwise. The actress or actor has to feel comfortable, they don't need to feel, 'Oh my goodness, this is a very sexy woman or really handsome hunk doing me.' We're not meant to be there to charm them and entertain them. They should just feel that whoever's come in to do their makeup is going to be competent and give them a great look."

"You've got to have people skills. You've got to be able to get along with people. You have to have the skills to deal with other people, because you work as a team."

"You have to be able to get along with your actor. We're never greater than the actor, or lesser than, and we have to always know to be the shadow in the background, that's there, always just there, doing the job."

BARI

"Hygiene is important. If you're Judi Dench, do you want to see a 23-year-old, full of tattoos, and things hanging from them, not properly clothed? You're the first person they see, you're touching their face Are your hands clean? For me, from THE 1st day and every day I would get up a few hours before and I would dress as a professional person, every day. I didn't come in in flip flops and shorts. You present yourself like you want to be paid."

TAMI

"A good bedside manner is very important. They [actors] have to trust you. They have to like you. You don't want somebody touching you if you don't trust or like them. You know? Because of that rapport, they'll respect what you do. They'll be on time, they'll be courteous. They might not be on their cell phone all the time. They're more apt to let you do your job."

"If you want to be treated seriously in this industry, respect yourself. Sometimes that starts with your appearance."

"You keep it light. You know you're there to have a good time because what we do is fun. You keep it clean. Cleanliness is a huge issue because we're in a clinical scenario. Nobody wants to walk into your trailer and see food from breakfast that was left there 5 hours ago. You play good music. Always have music, good music, nothing that's going to create angst or anxiety."

FRANCES

"Be open-minded. Do your research. It's really important. Do your research."

"Try to read what the director or actor is imagining. It's very important because everyone thinks differently. Put it in print. Do it. Show it. Then you're going to eventually find out what they're thinking."

LESLEY

"I look for someone who has great people skills and stamina. It's important to have stamina. The hours are long, the conditions can be brutal; you've got to be healthy."

CHRISTINE

"Plot it out, work out where you want to be and try really hard and be the nicest, smiliest person who knows when to talk and when to shut up."

"The most valuable skills are obviously your hands and your eyes."

KAREN

"For me, it's to try to be above all the craziness, and to learn when to speak, when not to speak, how to be kind and generous, but still be able to hold your place. To be able to put personal feelings aside and deal with what's going on in the shoot, or the dynamics of what's going on in your department. It's very hard to do, because when you work with somebody for 1 day, it's not a big deal, but if you work with them for 10 months, 5 days a week, 70 hours a week, personalities can clash. If you don't really care for somebody, being professional is that you don't allow those feelings to interfere with your work."

2009
EMMY AWARD
OUTSTANDING PROSTHETIC MAKEUP
FOR A SERIES, MINISERIES, MOVIE OR A SPECIAL

GREY GARDENS (2009)
DREW BARRYMORE
Licensed from Photo 12 / Alamy Stock Photo

Vivian Baker

I think the ease with which women jump into intimate relationships is a blessing and a curse. I feel as much as I think. A woman brings her intuitive, nurturing nature to work. What I give to my actors or actresses is my intuitive nature. I have to keep it on because that is how I know if she needs me there, or he needs me away, or he needs to be alone, or she needs me to protect her.

"'You realize I'm a zombie virgin,' I said to Joel Harlow and the [rest of the] makeup trailer as I came in to work on *Pirates of the Caribbean: On Stranger Tides*. All these really great artists looked at me like, 'Oh my God, where did you come from?' I don't do zombies. I think it's unusual for a prosthetic makeup artist not to want to build a monster. I would be that one…it was fun. I loved it. It was a great thing to do…but it's not in my head naturally."

Makeup effects transform and enhance characters, from out-of-the-kit bruises or false noses to full-face prosthetics. The ultimate goal of a professional makeup artist is to serve the script and the director's vision with the character being the guiding force behind the design. Vivian Baker, a veteran makeup artist of film, television, commercials, and print, found her passion when asked to do her first TV show, *I'll Fly Away* (1991), and "that was character creation. Then I got called to do some small movies and it was fantastic. I was hooked. I was hooked because I realized I wanted to create the character. The character is everything."

The Light Bulb Goes Off

For Vivian, the 1980 film *The Elephant Man*, the story of John Merrick (John Hurt), a uniquely and severely deformed circus performer, is a shining example of exceptional makeup that highlighted character and, through character, elucidated theme. "Seeing the film…makeup told that story. I mean were there great performances? Absolutely. Was it great directing? Without a doubt. Nothing was less than the makeup, but the makeup told the story. It impacted me and all that is important to me. The film validated makeup as more than a 'vanity.'"

"Throughout [*The Elephant Man*] we saw he had the most beautiful character. Every day we need to realize that no matter what the color of your skin, no matter what deformities you have, you can still be the most beautiful person because of who you are. These are messages the whole world needs to hear every day. But man, the makeup really told that story."

It's in The Blood

Growing up in Atlanta, Vivian's home was lively. The Baker Girls, or "The Four V's," Victoria, Vanessa, Valerie, and Vivian, filled the house with sports and cheerleading and Girl Scouts and boys and makeup. As a pre-teen, Vivian experimented on her sisters and friends creating makeup looks. Once the makeup was finished, she made them wash it off. It wasn't about showing off the work, it was about creating something new.

When it was time to go to college, Vivian told her father she was going to be a makeup artist. "My father was horrified. 'You don't even know if the job exists.' 'You're right,' I said, 'but I've seen credits, so there must be something.' Being from the South, I honestly believe, and this isn't tongue-in-cheek either, I honestly believe my mother, in her horror at what I was saying, must have got on her knees and prayed. And then, the next thing I knew, I was being paid to do models. It really must have come from heaven itself." Vivian's father regularly did her taxes for her, and "I remember the day my salary was greater than his and I think, at that point, he finally thought, 'I'm going to quit telling her she needs a real job.' I was the product of a mother who believed I could do whatever I wanted to do in a time when women were not taught that."

Vivian's father was an auditor, her mother a loan officer, one sister, Victoria, is a medical professional (a great resource for Vivian's medical dramas), another sister, Vanessa, is a computer programmer who first introduced Vivian to the concept of color theory, and her third sister, Valerie, is an educator who taught Vivian "what a real lady looks like." A strong artistic side also features prominently in Vivian's family, for the limbs on the family tree include writers Margaret Mitchell of *Gone with the Wind* fame, and Joel Chandler Harris of *Uncle Remus* fame. Margaret Mitchell, a great aunt on her mother's side, and Harris, a great uncle on her father's side, were philosophically and politically at odds, which spawned familial conflict and drama. "They were the only artists in my lineage. It's a very cool heritage. I think there are a lot of people in my family who have had some artistic bent, but I'm not sure they felt they could explore it."

Figuring It Out

Living in Atlanta and working in print and commercials, Vivian did not have easy access to products or other artists, so she did what she always does: figured it out. She would come up with an idea, reference the Richard Corson book, *Stage Makeup*, order the materials from LA, and play with them until the idea was realized. "I remember the first time I ordered latex. When it arrived, I thought, 'What is this? It doesn't make sense.' I still do the same thing, I come up with an idea, roll my sleeves up, and build what I want. Fortunately, now I have amazing colleagues who contribute to my thought process."

Vivian worked alone for years before collaborating or teaming with any other makeup artists. Her first jobs were model testing, making up models for their headshots, which is a job for a solo makeup artist. She spent a lot of time with the photographers learning about the cameras, the darkroom, the lighting; as a result, she developed solid, professional relations with the photographers who, in turn, asked her to work with them again and again. "I think a lot had to do with the fact I understood what they were doing. The first thing I'd ask is to see their camera test. It wasn't about me doing the makeup, it was about what character we were creating. How the photographer was filming and what size film he was using. What kind of light he was using. All of those things had to do with my decision about what I was going to do. It just worked out to be a nice symbiotic relationship with a lot of really talented people."

Fashion shoots and commercial print work followed the model testing, and Vivian continued to work and learn on her own. She did over 750 commercials in the Atlanta area, which "was a really good foundation for me. I worked with some really great crews and met a lot of people. Atlanta has a good base for film, and a lot of that comes from a big commercial market that has been in the South for years and years." Then she was asked to do a TV show and, for the first time, she worked with other makeup artists. "I never followed anyone because there wasn't anyone to follow. I'm self-motivated and self-taught. When I've been in large groups of makeup artists I find myself completely intimidated. There was a knot in my throat the whole time, because no one ever taught me what to do. I just did what worked for me. You get in a room with really talented people who know what to do and you kind of want to crawl under the table for fear they're going to say, 'Oh my God, where did they drag you up from?'"

"I wondered if it looked like it was supposed to look like. The next thing I knew, they asked me to be key, second in command at that time." She had obviously figured it out!

There Were Three, Four, Then More

As a personal, interdepartment head, or department head, Vivian still works alone. She calls the shots, hires the artists, and organizes the trailer as she sees fit. But when she works closely with others, she's open to new techniques, different points of view, and innovative approaches. Vivian cites three artists who have served as models and inspiration to her: Bill Corso, Kenny Myers, and Ann Brodie.

Vivian first worked with Bill Corso, personal makeup artist for Jim Carrey, on *Lemony Snicket's A Series of Unfortunate Events* (2004). "Yes, I did help him out there. Honestly, it was all Bill. I think what I really did was applaud him daily for his great work and make him a sandwich, which he needed." A future collaboration with Corso for *Grey Gardens* and a subsequent Emmy award followed five years later.

Kenny Myers has worked on such films as: *Bridge of Spies* (2015), *Lincoln* (2012), *Pirates of the Caribbean: On Stranger Tides* (2011). "Kenny and I…spent a decent amount of time together. He's such a talented makeup artist with an eye for color which is just incredible."

"I was never taught 'this is how you do stuff.' It wasn't until I saw work from Bill, Kenny, and other great artists, that I saw how they did things. That became a shot in the arm. 'Oh! I understand.' Bill and Kenny were a real impact on me and my work when I moved to Los Angeles and began to work there."

Ann Brodie is known for *X-Men* (2000), *Cinderella Man* (2005), and *My Big Fat Greek Wedding* (2002), as well as being Donald Sutherland's personal, when he took personals with him. Vivian worked with Ms. Brodie on *The Oldest Living Confederate Widow Tells All* (1994) and *A Woman of Independent Means* (1995). "She just has an eye. She taught me how to SEE."

"Every time you work with someone they bring things, a different way of thinking, to your world. It may be small, but that small thing may be the very turning point which opens up a much broader door. Anyone that I've had an opportunity to work with has always been an asset to my work, influencing where it goes and where I hope it will go; hopefully into some pretty groovy places."

And Then There is One

One of the jobs Vivian Baker does regularly is act as a personal, the makeup artist for just one actor, usually the lead, for a film. During this interview, Vivian was on set for *Guardians of the Galaxy Vol. 2* (2017) as the personal for Chris Pratt. "I am living the life. I'm finally sitting here, after all these years, with the most beautiful man in Hollywood as his personal."

When first asked to be a personal by Gwyneth Paltrow for *Great Expectations,* Vivian was conflicted. "I am very much a purist. I believe the department head should be the one who directs the makeup vision. Therefore, I was concerned about the unity of the vision. As a personal, my responsibility is to the actor,

GREAT EXPECTATIONS (1997) GWYNETH PALTROW
Licensed from Moviestore collection Ltd / Alamy Stock Photo

GUARDIANS OF THE GALAXY VOL 2 (2017) CHRIS PRATT
MARVEL STUDIOS/DISNEY/MOVIESTORE COLLECTION LTD
Licensed from Moviestore collection Ltd / Alamy Stock Photo

and I still very much believe in a unified vision." She was also concerned she would be bored making up only one actor. However, as her actor is usually the lead and has plenty of shooting days, she doesn't have time to be bored. And underlying this conflict was her personal mantra: "I don't want to spend time with people unless, at the end of the day, I'm a better person by picking up some of their traits. It is an honor to work for the clients who ask for me, and, at the end of the day, I am a better person for it. I have been blessed to have fantastic clients."

On the flip side of the coin, when Vivian is head of department, she often works with personals. She seeks them out to be sure the director's vision is clear and includes them in conceptual discussions. "Some artists are very receptive, some are not. These guys here (**Guardians of the Galaxy**), John Blake as head of department and I, we're working well together."

Where's the Light?

"My husband is the love of my life. The reason that I breathe. The air around me. The oxygen in my everything."

When Vivian and her husband, Michael Astalos, were newlyweds living in Atlanta, Vivian was doing a lot of commercial work. "They would me put me in the motor home in the morning, before God was up, with inadequate light. The guys would try to bring lights in but it burned the motor home up. I would come home frustrated. I needed light. My husband built the first makeup station and put Kino Flo bulbs in it. He gave it to me and said, 'You know, you're just not home enough to be that upset when you are home.'"

Before he was a lighting specialist, Michael Astalos was a professional photographer. After marrying Vivian in 1990, he built the first makeup station incorporating both daylight and tungsten lamps in a portable system that would become the industry standard for film, TV, and commercials. In 2014, he introduced a new line of LED lights, and his latest company, The Makeup Light, was born. TML offers a portable system that shows truer color than other lights, makes color matching easier, and highlights imperfections, thereby making it easier to correct them.

"All makeup artists have needed this. It's one of those things that respects and honors what we do. Makeup is a visual art. We need to see. I'm really proud of him for creating things that work and caring for makeup artists. I think it definitely comes from the love he has for me, and the love I have for what I do."

We're Not in Kansas Any More

"Vivian is the sweetest Georgia peach of a person. Her Southern demeanor makes you want to give her a hug every time you hear her slight Southern drawl welcome you into the main makeup room, 'Mornin', darlin'.'" says Howard Berger, special makeup effects supervisor of *Oz the Great and Powerful* (2013) in the book, *The Art of Oz the Great and Powerful*.

Vivian was head of department for *Oz* and remembers: "I had the great pleasure of designing every single person myself." It was a huge project with over two hundred cast members, thirty make-up artists, thirty hair stylists under Hair Designer Yolanda Toussieng, and thirty prosthetic artists under Berger, which, of course, was a logistical challenge for Vivian. "I've always been afraid that

Vivian working using The Makeup Light
Used with permission of Vivian Baker

getting a big group of makeup artists together would end up being utter chaos. It wasn't! It was really a great experience. We had a fantastic team of people. I had the right people in the right positions. As the film grew, everyone grew their role."

One of the biggest challenges of the film was facial hair. Every male character had a colorful, fanciful mustache or beard, everything from curled handlebar 'staches to circle beards to ringlet sideburns. Vivian also changed how the facial hair was glued on. "I brought in thirty artists two days before the shoot began and said, 'You're not going to use any of the glues you are familiar with. You're going to use this one.' 'What??' I watched all these really fantastic artists begin to do what artists do. Find a way to make it better."

Berger continues, "Vivian and her team…could do anything from specifically designed beauty makeups for the Quadlings, to hand-tying three hundred Emerald City residence mustaches with a multitude of colors subtly woven into the design. Vivian had a hand in every single makeup her department produced….I would come in at 3 AM and there was Vivian sitting cross-legged on the floor, hot cup of tea in her hands, as she reviewed every single facial hairpiece to make sure it was the way she wanted it."

"Here's the sad thing about *Oz*, so much of our work never made it to the screen. But it was a really incredible experience, and still, to this day, hundreds of background actors have friended me on Facebook."

The Eyebrows Have It

OZ THE GREAT AND POWERFUL (2013)
VIVIAN with SAM RAIMI (DIRECTOR) Used with permission of Chris R. Williams

Bill Corso was asked to do the makeup for *Grey Gardens* (2009) and he wasn't able to take the job, so he asked Vivian to step in. Vivian accepted and came on the film as prosthetics makeup supervisor and Drew Barrymore's personal artist. "I was completely terrified. It's interesting how each project in the beginning seems overwhelming, and then you just break it down, get in there and work it through." Corso designed and made the prosthetic pieces then sent the pieces to Vivian to apply. "Bill couldn't have been more wonderful. We were doing some tests and one piece wasn't working correctly. The problem was the shape, essentially the sculpt of the piece. I literally called him and, on the phone, he was able to determine the problem and how to solve it. He changed the sculpt, sent the pieces up, and they were perfect. Frickin' amazing, you know what I mean?"

GREY GARDENS (2009) JESSICA LANGE DREW BARRYMORE,
Licensed from Moviestore collection Ltd / Alamy Stock Photo

Grey Gardens was a challenge because the cast was two well-known actors, Drew Barrymore and Jessica Lange, who had to look like two well-know people, Edith Bouvier Beale and her daughter, Edith, aunt and cousin of Jacqueline Kennedy Onassis. The prosthetics took the actresses through four distinct stages of aging, from young to old. "We were, at the time, doing early Bondo appliances and testing their limits. There were lots of challenges. I swear I didn't breathe most of the time I was putting on Drew's makeup. I just couldn't. If I made a mistake, I'd lose everything. You can't fix it. You can't take the piece off and fix it. It doesn't work like that."

Vivian captured the iconic 1950s look for Little Edie (Barrymore) in the eyebrow: the arch, the strength, the subtleness; soft, yet defined, sexy, yet strong. "I had to move Drew through the ages of the character, none of which she actually was, and I did it through the brow. Like any woman, Little Edie found her place and her look at an early age and she held onto it. I wanted those brows to be charcoal grey and I knew it would be a thread for her character through her later years. I looked at her character through her face - the arc of the character was important to the look. I was responsible for using new techniques and technology. Prosthetics are a whole different ball game now, they're not all monster-oriented. Even though they were meant to age the characters, I wanted to see a level of beauty come from those women, and I think we achieved that."

GREY GARDENS (2009) DREW BARRYMORE, JESSICA LANGE
Licensed from Photo 12 / Alamy Stock Photo

"My experience has been that every job needs a different set of skills, all the way from management of cast, crew, and production to the actual art itself. **Grey Gardens** really hit high on all those points. Bill Corso carrying the project until close to shooting really set a great stage for the cooperation of the cast, producers, and Michael Sucsy, the director, who could not have been more fabulous."

Vivian won the Emmy for *Outstanding Prosthetic Makeup for a Series, Miniseries, Movie, or a Special* in 2009 for **Grey Gardens** which she shares with Prosthetic Designer Bill Corso, Head of Department Linda Dowds, and Prosthetic Makeup Artist Sean Sansom.

What's Right?

For Vivian, making design decisions centers around the arc of the character; where does the character begin and where does the character's journey take him/her? These questions guide her initial thoughts, and then consultations with the director inform and polish the design. However, filmmaking is a fluid, ever-changing art form. Things evolve and change daily, and it is incumbent upon the makeup artist to adjust her vision to the needs of the film, the director, and the actor. "I have to be flexible with the life form that the project has taken on."

"There is what is right for the film. There might be a hundred different ways to achieve a makeup, but ultimately each film will have what is right for it. The actors, what they will like, how it's being shot, what the conditions are, the heat, the sweat, what they're allergic to, what they're not, all contribute to what is right for each film. It will be different for everyone. To me, that's fun. There may be a thousand different ways to do a cut, but we need to find out what works best for this film. It just makes it interesting to me."

Vivian tells of a time when she was working with "one of the greatest actors of all time" to whom she described her vision: "Okay, I think we should blah, blah, blah and we should do this. He said, 'I don't care, whatever you think.' I've never had an actor give me so much freedom. He trusted me completely. Okay. Then there are some jobs where it's all about what the director wants. Sometimes it's a completely collaborative process. So, each situation is different. Flexibility is a crucial element to my process."

"There are no rules. There's not an absolute about anything. You have to be flexible and know your boundaries. Nothing is set in stone."

This Peach of a Woman

Vivian Baker hails from the South. She was raised there, has roots and a large family there, and began her career there. She has all the markings of a Southern woman, she is humble, gracious, grateful, passionate, and strong. She recognizes her incredible luck in love and work, and she is thankful. She feels as much as she thinks, and she gifts us her talent.

OUTTAKES:

On Succeeding:

"Don't be intimidated; follow your vision and manage yourself with dignity."

On Other Artists:

"Prosthetic artists are the most amazing artists around. They are the most sharing, unafraid, supportive group of people ever...because they're used to working with more than one person on a job, they are used to working in tandem. They work within a strong, united team."

On Surviving Set Life:

"I have a set kit. It is physically on my body and has a lot of different things in it. If I am on-set and the director wants something, I don't have to go back to the trailer, everything is right on my body and I can get it done. I can be in the jungle or I can be climbing a mountain and I have everything I need right there."

On Being a Woman in the Field:

"I have come to realize most men who have difficulty with working with a woman in authority have no idea they possess any misogynistic tendencies. I can say being good at what you do is the best leveling of the playing field. As a woman, you have to be good all the time."

"I love men. I've never been a male basher. I mean, my dad was amazing and my husband is ten times more amazing. I walk into every relationship believing that everyone likes me. My husband laughs at me for that. He says, 'This is where you get kicked because you actually think everyone is going to like you.'"

"What I have to do is to be good and worthy. If people, men, respect and honor what I do it is because it is honorable. That is all I can do. I think I am well-regarded as a woman artist, an artist."

On Longevity:

"I think work begets work. You have to stay in motion. If you're not in motion, there's a lot of people out there to take over."

Catching Up!

We interviewed Vivian on January 16, 2016. Since then, she has worked on

Guardians of the Galaxy 2
Chris Pratt's personal artist

Avengers Infinity War
Chris Pratt's personal artist

Passengers
Makeup Department Head and Chris Pratt's personal artist

Jurassic World 2
Chris Pratt's and Bryce Dallas Howard's personal makeup artist.

For more of Vivian's Credits and work, visit:
www.vivianbaker.com
www.imdb.com

LEADING LADIES OF MAKEUP EFFECTS

2014
EMMY AWARD
OUTSTANDING MAKEUP
FOR A SERIES

THE X FILES (1993)
DAVID DUCHOVNY & GILLIAN ANDERSON
Licensed from AF archive / Alamy Stock Photo

Cheri Montesanto

I like the "beauty and the beast" aspect of makeup. I like being able to do a beautiful sunset or a stormy ocean. I like to make a woman or a guy look incredibly beautiful and I also like to make them look dead. You know what I mean?

As a little girl, Cheri Montesanto remembers reading movie magazines and being drawn to special effects, film, and makeup. "I remember reading about movie people getting up at five in the morning and I used to think, 'Wow, it's dark out then.' I literally remember thinking, 'They go to work in the dark?' I must have been very small, because I was excited when my parents would wake me and my brother up early to go camping. We'd be excited because it was dark. I would think, 'This is what they do in the movies, they get up when it's dark.'"

No Fear

Born and raised in Rochester, New York, to a family that ran hair salons, Cheri always knew she wanted to work with hair. When she was 14, a freshman in high school, she applied for a waiver to attend vocational school. Normally, a student isn't able to attend vocational school until junior year, but because her parents owned a salon and she would be working with them, she received special dispensation. Cheri spent two to three hours every morning in hairdressing school and the afternoons working in the salon. By the time she was 15, she had her New York State Cosmetology license.

In 1979, Cheri's parents opened New York State's first unisex hair salon called Monty's Unisex. "When they went to get their license, the state didn't know how to license it. 'Are you a barber shop or a beauty shop?' 'We're going to do both.'" Monty's Unisex eventually grew into a six-shop franchise. Cheri's parents, with their creative thinking, fearless sense of adventure, and open minds, have inspired and supported Cheri throughout her life, allowing her to pursue her dreams. "My parents always were, and still are until this day, so supportive of me. They gave me lots of confidence and they instilled in me that belief that if you are a good person, that's the basis of everything."

"Working at the salon was a little bit funny, but I never felt I was missing out. I connected with everyone in the salon, my friends there were all older, in their 20s, and even on Saturday nights we would all go next door to the restaurant for a drink. Sometimes my teachers would come in and be my clients. Thinking back now, I wonder, 'What? How did this happen?'"

When she was 16, Cheri entered a New York State haircutting competition. Her parents used to compete nationally in hairstyling, so she decided to give it a try. There was no special category for youth competitors and Cheri won the New York competition, then moved on to a national competition, and also won it. "It's interesting because being young, I had no sense that I could do this or couldn't do that. I just decided I was going to do it and I won and it was really fun."

FEAR NO EVIL (1981)
Licensed from Photo 12 / Alamy Stock Photo

When Cheri was going into her senior year of high school, Avco Embassy Pictures advertised for locals to play extras in their film, *Fear No Evil* (1981). "I said to my mom and dad, 'I want to do makeup on that.' I explained I'd go down to the open call and talk to someone. My dad went with me and we told them, 'We don't want to be extras, we want to do the makeup and hair on the show.' My dad was a national haircutting champion many times over, so that got us the interview. I was hired as the department head and my mom and dad were my crew. The fourth crew member was Richard Jay Silverthorn who did the special effects."

"The director, Frank LaLoggia, was shocked when he found out I was 17. He thought I was 25. I guess I just looked and acted older. We had a little two banger trailer, not even a real makeup trailer, and it was a lot of fun. Looking back on it, I wonder, how did I know how to break down a script? How did I know how to do anything? I don't know."

Cheri couldn't go to school and work on the film, so she asked the school for three months off. They, of course, said it was impossible. Cheri told them she'd quit school because this was what she wanted to do with her life. The school found a way to grant her another special dispensation; she got the three months off, then came back and graduated with her class.

California, It's Not *WHAT* You Know...

Cheri decided after high school graduation to move to California to work in the film and television industry. "My parents tried to bribe me to stay in New York. My dad said, 'Look, I'll buy you a Corvette and fly you to California once every month for a week.' I told him, 'I have to do it because if I don't go, I probably won't go. I'll stay here because I'm close to you and I'll start building a life here, but I'll always think, what would've happened if I had gone?'"

Cheri met and impressed enough people on *Fear No Evil* that when she got to LA she found work immediately. Frank Birney, an actor in the film, was married to a production supervisor for the Disney Cable Channel, who hired Cheri to work on *Welcome to Pooh Corner* (1983-1986).

"It was a non-union gig, of which there were plenty in the '80s. All I had to do was make up Laurie Main, an English actor who sat in a chair the entire time. He was in his chair doing his thing and I was watching him in case he got sweaty. Then I decided to stretch, like this, right off-camera. He stopped and said, 'What are you doing?' Let me tell you, it stuck with me forever because I didn't know I was distracting him. I learned and I've never forgotten. That was my first lesson on set etiquette."

"When I go to Cinema Makeup School and talk to the students, I want to educate them on how to behave on-set. It's important because that can make or break your career. No matter how good you are, if you don't have the right etiquette on-set and good people skills, it could ruin you."

When Cheri is shooting, she follows her actors on-set and watches the scene from the monitor or behind the camera. In this way, if the talent needs a touch-up, or tears, or is sweating, she can fix the problem. She often sees the members of a makeup crew on their phones, reading books, playing games. "First of all, if I was a producer paying all these people, I'd be furious. I'd not be paying people to play games and not pay attention. The makeup artists who work for me, I make it clear in the beginning, should be watching their actors. We're not taking up valuable spots by the monitor to be looking at our phones."

Another important contact Cheri made while working on *Fear No Evil* was Production Coordinator Bernie Caulfield. Bernie is also from Rochester, which was the initial connection between the two women, but they have now worked on and off together on TV movies and series for years. Bernie came to LA and "hooked up with a new company called HBO. She started at the bottom level and obviously, it worked out really well for her. She is now the producer for *Game of Thrones*." Bernie also worked on *Welcome to Pooh Corner* and was responsible for bringing Cheri on to *The X-Files* (1998-2002).

Decisions

After ten years in the business, Cheri got her union membership on a film that flipped. "It didn't matter that it took ten years because I was always working. I never had any other job; I was always working in the industry. Those ten years was a non-union period which gave me time to establish my reputation and learn the business." *Robo-Cop 2* (1990) "was a huge non-union movie with a 40-million-dollar budget. I was department head for makeup and hair when it was non-union and my parents worked with me. We started shooting in Houston, Texas, and when we moved to LA, the film went union. That's how I got my union membership."

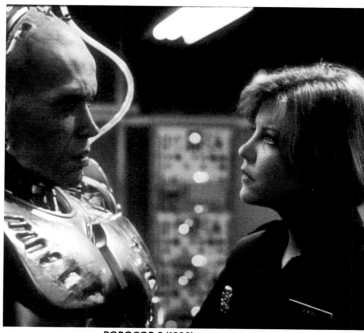

ROBOCOP 2 (1990) PETER WELLER NANCY ALLEN
Licensed from Photo 12 / Alamy Stock Photo

Once she was eligible to join the union, Cheri had to make some choices. Because she did both hair and makeup, she had to choose what she wanted to be, a makeup artist or a hairdresser. "I chose makeup because I like makeup better. When I am hired, I'm hired as department head for makeup and makeup effects. On all my shows I run both. In my personal life, I still do hair, and union makeup artists can groom men, so if I have time, I can do a man's hair."

For Cheri, hair remains a key element in creating the look for a character. "I was doing a project, a star request in Canada, someone I've done a million times. I would do her makeup and think, 'She looks great.' Then the hair person came in, a nice Canadian lady, and she did the hair, not good at all. After her hair was done, I thought, 'She doesn't look good. Oh, it's the frame. It's that ugly frame on a pretty picture. It just ruined the whole picture.'" If her favorite hairdressers are available, Cheri recommends them for the job to ensure she gets the hair looks she wants. "If they're not available, I leave it up to fate. I need my hairdressers to be good at hairdressing, be a good person, not cause trouble, get along with everybody."

On-the-Job-Training

Cheri has had no formal makeup training. She uses primary sources such as reference and forensic books to see what real wounds, gashes, broken bones, and death look like, then figures out how to create the makeup to simulate reality. "I'm artistic and I'm really good with colors and I have a really vivid imagination. I don't know, I just thought I could do it. It sounds ridiculous. I don't know how I did it. I honestly don't. It's like weird. Maybe sometimes inside I'm *American Psycho*. I dream a lot about my makeups, especially before a big or tricky makeup. I have little dreams and brainstorms that'll come to me in the middle of the night. I problem-solve in my dreams."

Using food is a favorite technique Cheri uses to create texture and body parts. For example, she needed to create a flap of skin to house a bleeding artery for the pilot of *The Night Shift* (2014). It was a hospital show, so she got a thin piece of tubing and painted it to look like a vein, made a prosthetic skin flap, and put dates in the wound to make it look "mushy and yucky. I use dates, I've used dog bones. I use a lot of that rawhide dog bone stuff. I love yogurt, cheese. Whatever gives it texture. It just pops into my head."

Ironically, Cheri has trouble with vomit. She can create arterial spray, but vomit makes her squeamish. And eyeballs. "Real eyeballs with veins, they gross me out. I was doing this one actor, he had all these veins in his eyes and I couldn't look in his eyes." And horror films. If there is something horrific, she can barely look at it. "If somebody else has done it, it freaks me out. My imagination's so crazy, I don't like to be scared. My husband makes me go."

One of Cheri's specialties is burn makeups. The verisimilitude is so detailed that some of her burn makeups are in classrooms or plastic surgery offices to show doctors and victims what a real third degree burn looks like. "I actually make myself crazy trying to make it look real. I'm such a stickler with an edge, I'm like insane. I hate to see edges. And coloring. I don't want any straight lines and I need color to look like it's coming from the skin, not just lying on top."

Variety, Longevity, and Respect

Since 1980 when Cheri was 18 and moved to California, she has worked non-stop on films, TV movies, and television series usually as head of department. 1998 marked the beginning of long-term work on series television. She worked on *The X-Files* (1998-2002, 105 episodes) which earned her three Emmys, *CSI: Miami* (2003-2011, 106 episodes), *Agents of S.H.I.E.L.D.* (2013-2014, 22 episodes), *The Night Shift* (2014-2016, 28 episodes), and she started on *Better Call Saul* in 2016. Her relationships, work ethic, creativity, and flexibility obviously make her an invaluable member of the production team.

"I like TV. It's come a long way. I like that every week there's something new and challenging instead of being on something for four months. I know what all the characters are like. I like when I get the scripts and I get to say, 'Oh, we get to do this or that.' I like the continuity of getting to know the cast and developing characters for long story arcs. That's fun."

Flexibility, creative thinking, and problem-solving are, for Cheri, necessary and crucial talents to being a successful makeup artist. She tells of an incident on *The Night Shift* when a character was to come into the hospital with a rake stuck in his head. She had had the special effects department make a balsa wood piece and she rigged it with monofilament which was to be hidden in his hair. "The actor came in and he's completely bald, which is problematic for the gag to work. I went to Tim Busfield, who was directing, and told him, 'The guy you cast has no hair.' He goes, 'I heard he has a receding hairline.' 'No, bald. He has no hair. We need the hair to hide the rig. Let me think about it.'" She ended up taking pieces of wig caps, cut them up, smoothed them over with third degree, took the monofilament off, and placed the rake on the actor's head. "It really worked. I'm really proud of that. My crew said to me, 'Most people would have such a meltdown.' But I don't do that. I will try to make it work. I'm production friendly, and I find you get more respect that way. People think if you're kind of a bitch you're going to get more respect, but I don't think you do. People don't want to deal with you. It gets wearing."

Working with actors is, of course, integral to any makeup artist's job. Before she meets actors, Cheri emails them, introduces herself, asks if they'd like her to know anything about their skin or favorite products so she can accommodate them. "I don't want to go in blind or unprepared. It makes the start of a project smoother. It's like the first day of school."

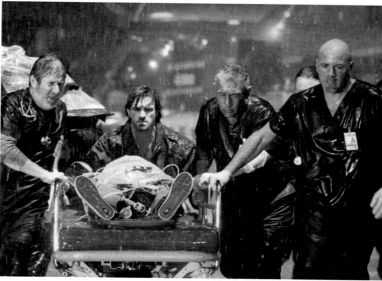

THE NIGHT SHIFT (2014) EOIN MACKEN
Licensed from AF archive / Alamy Stock Photo

"When I deal with my actors I have to find their personalities, how they are, what they like, how they like to be touched up, do they like a lot of attention, no attention, do they like to clean up after? The personalities are the most complex part of the job.

"I had an actress ask me for a lot of stuff I'd never heard of. She was very particular about what she wanted and then explained, 'I've hated my last five makeup people.' I got everything she wanted and we did a test. I did her makeup my way and then did it again with her makeup choices, then asked her which one she liked better. I remember as I was doing her eye makeup she was staring in the mirror. I kept thinking, 'Is it too much? Too little? Should I take it off? Add more? Different color?' And she's just staring. Then she looked at me and said, 'I love it!' I was dealing with her personality and her history. Happily, it worked out."

Eyebrows. Cheri knows that people are very particular about their eyebrows, and "not always in a good way." She will occasionally try to fix an actress's eyebrows, make them as flattering to the actress and appropriate to the character as possible, "but when you see yourself a certain way every day, it's hard to break out of that. It's a battle I don't fight. I will try, and if it doesn't work I have to make peace with it. It's not a battle worth fighting. And I'm not that makeup artist. Makeup FX is easier than beauty makeup because throw a little blood on somebody and they're thrilled, but try to make a nice arch on an eyebrow and it can be a battle."

There are also situations where an actor wants to look a particular way, oftentimes pretty, but it isn't appropriate to the character or situation. The director will have spoken to the makeup artist and given him/her specific direction, but some actors still don't want to look bad. Cheri just came off a film where one of the characters was dehydrated, dirty, and dying, but the actress said, "Just because I'm a refugee doesn't mean I'm ugly." So, on the second day of shooting, this actress came in with eyelashes, heavy foundation, and red lipstick. When she was asked to remove the makeup, she resisted. The director was brought in to tell the actress exactly what he wanted, which meant she had to remove her makeup. She spent the entire day having people block her while she reapplied the red lipstick. "I'm there to facilitate. The people that are in charge, they can argue. Some makeup people will argue. Why? I'm not gonna argue with people. I was nice and I was firm and I tried to explain it to her, but she wasn't having it."

The other side of the coin was a young, cute actress playing a dying cancer patient. Cheri put a bald cap on her and made her look ill. She was nervous because she doesn't usually play this kind of role, "but she got into it. I told her, 'It's fun being sick because there's no pressure to look good. Embrace it. You can just act and not worry about whether you need more lipstick.'"

It takes skill and sensitivity to work successfully with actors. A talented makeup artist takes the time and makes the effort to understand his or her actor to provide a positive, productive experience. Cheri prioritizes her actors and ensures they leave the chair in character and pleased with the results.

The X-Files

Cheri's friend from Rochester, Bernadette Caulfield, was a producer on **The X-Files** (1993-2002, 2016) once the production moved to California (1998-2000), and she was instrumental in hiring Cheri as the head of department. Cheri was working on a film in Georgia and was asked to fly to Utah to do a makeup audition on an actor. One of the producers said, "I like makeup FX to be done by guys, but I love your makeup FX," and offered her the job. But Cheri was reticent, never having done a television series before and she was committed to a film. "All my friends in LA told me I had to take the job; it was huge." She still couldn't commit, but fate stepped in when Cheri got heat exhaustion in Georgia and had to leave the film. She was now free to take **The X-Files** gig.

The same producer, Michael Watkins, asked Cheri to give him a black eye before every meeting he had with the studio. "I'd be on-set and I'd whip it out in a minute or two. Every time he'd go to the studio he'd have a black eye and nobody ever asked him why. This went on for years."

"**X-Files** was the pinnacle for me. There were very high levels of talent in the cast, crew, producers, writing teams, and makeup teams. Every aspect of it was a wonderful experience. It was also fun." Cheri was head of department for the four years **The X-Files** shot in California from 1998-2002. During her tenure there, Cheri was nominated three times for an Emmy for *Outstanding Makeup for a Series* and won all three times. "When Emmy time comes around, as department head, I'm the one that gets to choose the episode. We do 22 a year, so there are always a lot of choices. Nowadays there is a specific prosthetic category separate from the makeup category, but back then it was all one."

"The first Emmy we won was for an episode entitled "*Two Fathers/One Son, Parts I and II*" (1999). I was sure that episode would ruin my career. In that episode, we had to make these men, 50-80 years-old, look 25 years younger. It was hard work. So, I walked out on the set and I saw an extreme close-up of one of my actors and I immediately called Michael Watkins, the director, and asked him to come down and see if he liked it. When the episode came out with the special filters and everything on it, it looked spectacular. We ended up putting that up for an Emmy and we won." Cheri shares this Emmy with 16 other talented makeup artists.

The second Emmy Cheri won was for the episode entitled "*Theef*" (2000) starring Billy Drago as a "really creepy guy. It was difficult because he was cast the night before, so the only things we had to work with were generic prosthetic pieces. I wanted him to be a guy who would terrify you if you saw him looking in your window. It was a huge character makeup; he was a monster, but it wasn't a monster makeup. Fox said maybe we shouldn't put this one up for an Emmy because we were going up against shows like **Buffy** and **Star Trek**. In my heart, I knew it was the best choice. We were blessed; we won." Cheri shares this Emmy with Kevin Westmore, Laverne Munroe, Greg Funk, and Cindy J. Williams.

Cheri's third Emmy was awarded for her makeup work on the episode entitled "*Deadalive*" (2001) in which Mulder is buried alive and literally comes back to life, exploring the themes of salvation and resurrection. The makeup challenges were to create a realistic yet disconcerting death look for Mulder (David Duchovny). Matthew Mungle's lab, W.M. Creations, Inc., was given only six days to complete the special effects. "I love working with Matt. He's creative. There are no boundaries with him. I came up with a way the skin would fall off the leg and Matthew manufactured the piece. That's something you don't see even in features. It was a pleasure." Cheri shares her Emmy with Matthew W. Mungle, Laverne Munroe, Clinton Wayne, and Robin L. Neal.

"*X-Files* was always a challenge. They would change things last minute and they knew we could do it. I remember one night on Stage 5 they were filming an episode where a lot of women were killed. We were on Stage 6 doing another episode. We had eight makeup artists that night because we had a lot of dead women. It's 2 AM and we're in the 16th hour and they decided to come to me and say, 'Cheri, I would like this girl on the autopsy table to have an open chest cavity. How long?' 'When's the next shot?' '20 minutes.' 'Ok, 20 minutes.' You get your adrenaline going. Not to mention I had great people working with me. Every single makeup artist worked their butts off on that show."

X-FILES (2014) DAVID DUCHOVNEY
Licensed from AF archive / Alamy Stock Photo

You *CAN* Have It All

"I really try to impress on my family to remember it's life, not a dress rehearsal. You have to really enjoy your life when you can."

When Cheri was pregnant with her first son, Renton, she was worried no one would hire her again because they would think she wanted to be with her baby and not work. "That is so not true, they don't care if you have a baby. What was I thinking? It never affected me. No one ever said, 'Oh, you have a child? Maybe you can't do this.'"

When Cheri's second son, Logan, was six months old, she got a job in Utah. "I told them I couldn't stay in a hotel, I needed a place for a nanny to come with me. They were very accommodating and made the arrangements, found a place where my nanny could be." Additionally, when Cheri shoots out-of-state, she tries to get back to California and her family on the weekends. If there aren't any big makeup effects needed for Monday's shoot, she will leave Friday night and return Sunday night. The benefits to working in series television is the days and hours are almost regular; a makeup artist can plan a life outside of work. "It's a balance. You know what? My family keeps me centered, my family's what's important. I think my family makes me better at my job. I have a life outside of work."

Cheri's house is full. Her eldest, Renton Pexa, is a 23-year-old actor; her middle child, Logan Pexa, 21, is into music and art; her youngest, Dominique Pexa, eight, thinks she's the new Michael Jackson because he passed away in the year she was born; Cheri's "younger, improved" husband, Matt Pexa, is a writer and director; and her parents, both in their 80s, live with them. "There are seven people living in one house and they're all human. There's a lot of personalities. Sometimes I think this is the truth: my family is easier than my job. My family is way less demanding."

Cheri Montesanto decided when she was very young what she wanted to do as her life's work and she just did it. She was focused and determined and talented and ultimately, successful. She juggles a full work life with a full personal life, making time to meditate and connect with her kids and husband and parents, and if she runs out of time during the day, she'll problem-solve at night as she dreams.

OUTTAKES:

On Success:

"Some people get in and forget where they started. You can't forget where you start."

"Faced with a problem, I take a deep breath. People that work with me tell me I have a great sense of humor, so I think in times of stress, I become funny."

"I was doing a stuntman for **X-Files**, a last-minute change. He came in and he had a robe on and he took the robe off and he had little Speedos on and we had to do his whole body. He's like, 'This is not what they said. They said I was just gonna run around and scare people. I didn't know I was gonna be in seven hours of makeup or in a Speedo.' He had his arms up, and as we were doing under his arms I'd ask him, 'Who's happy to be here? Raise your hand.' Stupid stuff like that makes the time go faster when you have a laugh."

"I don't want to seem like an egomaniac, as far as mentors and the books, I don't oppose those. I think they're wonderful and schooling is great, it just so happens it didn't happen for me that way. I am always learning and experimenting and figuring things out."

"I know when we've done something cool when the crew starts taking photos on the set. That's a huge compliment."

"You have to remember there isn't one person on the film set that is there for charity. You're not here because we like to have an extra makeup person, you're needed here. By the same token, if you're not doing it, they're going to get someone else that will."

"Keep grateful, because at any moment it can change. You can't take anything for granted."

"People don't think of themselves as awful. So you have to search really deep and find the one thing that is redeeming. I always remember, that's somebody's dad or brother or son or friend. Somebody loves this person somewhere. That's what I have to do to get on with difficult people."

On Being a Woman in the Industry:

"In meetings sometimes, when I have my lab people there who are men, they'll defer to them over me."

"Sometimes we'll be doing a makeup effect and I'll have a guy working with me and the ADs or actors will gravitate toward the guy. By the same token, I've been on shows where the guys have done the beauty makeup and the ADs gravitate to me."

"I like red lipstick, bright lipstick. I always wear it. I remember all the men walked into the room where I was making up Ricky Shroder for a series audition and I got *the look*. The *she's-not-going-to-be-able-to-do-this-look*. That was before I even started. I'm just meeting them. Then I did the makeup and they loved it. They told me afterwards, when they first saw me, they didn't think I could do it, just based on how I look, red lipstick and all."

On Go-Tos:

"You can do pretty much anything with an Illustrator palette and a toothpick. By scraping it really hard you can make it look like coagulated blood. Hairspray and Illustrator palette. Seal it."

"I don't have any problems with personals. It's the actor's comfort, and usually if they're asking for a personal, 90% of the time it's somebody who they're comfortable with and does a good job on them."

On the Future:

"I'd love to do a musical. I think that would be fun because I like music. I love period pieces…one that has some makeup effects in it. Something fun and different, even character-driven. I love doing westerns, too."

"Based on my years of experience and knowledge of makeup, I'm developing a skin care and makeup line."

Catching Up!

We interviewed Cheri on September 15, 2016. Since then, she has worked on

The Night Shift
Makeup and Makeup FX Department Head

Better Call Saul
Makeup and Makeup FX Department Head

In 2018 she will launch her makeup cosmetic line including a new product for FX makeup

For more info about Cheri, visit: www.makeupbodyandsoul.com
For more of Cheri's credits, visit: www.imdb.com

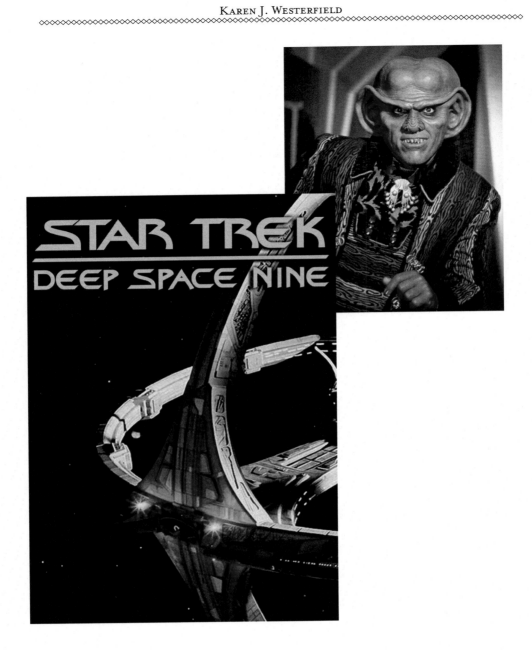

2014
EMMY AWARD
OUTSTANDING INDIVIDUAL ACHIEVEMENT
IN MAKEUP FOR A SERIES

STAR TREK: DEEP SPACE NINE (1993) ARMIN SHIMERMAN
Licensed from AF archive / Alamy Stock Photo

Karen J. Westerfield

Approaches evolve. There are ways to do it the long way, there's ways to do it the short way, but is there a right way? No, because everyone takes a different path to get to the end result. OK, so this is how you learned it in school, but it doesn't mean you can't do it a different way to end up with the same makeup. And everyone does it differently. We develop our own style of doing makeups and how we do things. But at the end, if they all look like they're supposed to look, does it matter how we got there? No, it doesn't.

The sign in the window read: "Hey GI, get your picture taken and send it home to your loved ones, family, and friends." The Merchant Marine entered the photography studio in Yokohama, Japan, and met the girl behind the counter. After a long courtship, they married and he brought her back to Long Beach, California, to begin their life together where they later had two daughters, Karen and her older sister, Roberta. "The second my mom stepped off the boat in San Francisco, she signed up for courses to become an American citizen. WWII had just ended and my mother, a Japanese woman, was hated by the neighborhood. My father's family disowned her. I was called names when I was in elementary school. I didn't get it. My dad talked to me about names like 'Jap' and 'Nip' explaining they were just abbreviations. It made me cry a lot and he didn't want me to continue to be hurt."

"My mother was totally accepted later. It's the same with every prejudice. Prejudice is an uneducated way of looking at a group of people and until you get to know a person on a one-on-one basis, on a personal level, the prejudice will not go away. But once you see the person, not the race or the gender, prejudice disappears."

Tomboy

While she was in elementary school and studying the pioneers, Karen and her classmates were all assigned pioneer-related projects. The girls made bonnets and the boys made Conestoga wagons. Karen wanted to make the wagon, not the bonnet, so her mother went in to talk to the principal to get special permission for her daughter to make the wagon like the boys. "We used wire hangers to make the frame of the canopy of the wagon, then took a white handkerchief and sewed it on. Of course, mine turned out the best because I could already sew. My wagon could stand up against any of the wagons the boys made."

Karen was told from the time she was young that "girls could never do this, could never do that. That was something I came up against my entire life. I wanted to do stuff that is traditionally men's work like working with tools, fixing things, being good with my hands, being able to replace a broken window. It was just fun. It was cool stuff to do. I think that's why I was a tomboy, because boys got to do the cooler stuff."

As a makeup professional, it is ironic that Karen never wore makeup as a young woman and her mother rarely did. However, she was fascinated by the process of "making up" and remembers "sitting, watching my mom do her makeup and watching my dad shave his face. That stuff is handed down from mother to daughter, father to son." The rituals of making up come into play every day as a makeup artist, whether through makeup, grooming, or making masks and monsters.

The Lure of Film & SFX

As a child, Karen's mother often took her to the movies, which provided her with context and an understanding of the American culture. "My mother was my major influence because she loved American cinema. Growing up, all those old movies that were on television, or the classic black and white films playing in the theater, we watched with my mother." And, as she got older, Karen went to the movies with her friends every Saturday during the summer. "That's when I fell in love with film. I love the Universal monsters; Frankenstein is my favorite." Her interest in film and curiosity about the makeups motivated her to "physically go to the library and learn to research to find out more. It's not like today where you can just Google something." She took out what few makeup books were available, including Richard Corson's *Stage Makeup*, to learn about the craft and art of makeup.

As a teen, Karen's interest in film led her to the local theater where she worked backstage helping however she could with props or lights or sound. Sometimes that meant making masks. Karen then started working with some friends who made Super 8 films, one of their specialties being special makeup effects. There was no budget and there were no rules, so they "MacGyvered" solutions, figured out how to make what they needed with what they had. Their original, creative approach, which included how to make a life cast, further sparked Karen's desire to be involved in filmmaking.

When the time came to choose a college and field of study, Karen went to UC San Diego as a chemistry major with plans to become a doctor. "I wanted to help make a difference in the world. But after three years doing summer work in hospitals, I realized I was a bleeding heart. I could not work with people who were injured or hurt. I wanted to take them home with me and take care of them. I didn't think being a doctor was for me, so I quit. Then I worked as a quality control lab tech at a chemical plant. After a year and a half of that, I realized I was going nowhere and went back to school." Her love for film reasserted itself and she "acquired a 35mm camera and went back to visual arts and specialized in still photography and film." During that time, Karen took a theatrical makeup course thinking it would be useful in filmmaking, but dropped the class because, ironically, she felt "totally out of her element."

Crafts, Not Craft

Once she graduated from college, Karen didn't immediately find a job, so she moved home with her mom and took some theater classes at Long Beach City College. One of her professors announced a job opportunity as a volunteer production assistant on a film. Karen had nothing else going on that week, so she took the job. "Basically, I was a runner. You answer to this guy or that woman or that department.

You do whatever they need you to do." On the same film, a young film school graduate was working crafts service and was more focused on the cinematography, filming, and writing than her job, so Karen was asked to step in and help her out. "It didn't take Einsteinian intellect. Empty out the ice water when there's no ice, take a wash cloth and clean the table, throw away the trash."

When the film finished shooting, the producers wanted to make a music video advertising the movie, and Karen was asked to come in and work crafts service because she had done such a good job as a production assistant. A year later, those same producers asked Karen to come work crafts service for *Masters of the Universe* (1987), a non-union film. *Masters of the Universe* flipped and became a union production, and as Karen was working crafts service, she was eligible to join the crafts service union, Local 727 (now Local 80) of I.A.T.S.E., International Association of Theatrical Stage Employees. This was her professional entry into filmmaking.

Crafts Service has evolved into the mini-catering group, providing coffee and snacks on-set, but according to mediamatch.com, "The Crafts Service person is available to assist the other crafts which include camera, sound, electricians, grips, props, art director, set decorator, hair and makeup, during the actual shooting of a motion picture, with tasks including providing snacks and cleaning the set."

For Karen, working crafts service was not just about the food. "One day I would be wrangling cable for the sound department, the next day I'd be buying props. Our basic equipment was a broom, a mop, a pickup, and a hammer because we were expected to help move sets or props and keep things clean. The main function is to help if a department is short on workers and they can't get someone to come out right away. CS is asked to help out, which is part of the mission of the union."

While on-set for *Masters of the Universe,* one of Karen's responsibilities was to help out the makeup department head by running errands. She spent a lot of time in the makeup trailer, enjoyed the people, and rediscovered her love for makeup. "I had done theater stuff, mask-making, sculpting, so after being on the movie for a while, I asked Michael Westmore [makeup designer for the film] if I could show him my work. He evaluated my work and said, 'If you ever get in the makeup union and want to work, just call me.'"

When Opportunity Knocks

In 1986, a pivotal job changed the direction of Karen's work life. She was working crafts service on *Throw Momma from the Train,* a dark comedy starring Billy Crystal, Rob Reiner, and Anne Ramsey in Danny DeVito's directorial debut. Tom and Bari Burman did the makeup special effects for the film and Anne Ramsey introduced them to Karen. A six-month internship in the Burman Studio followed where Karen worked in the shop, helped set up face casts and life casts, and learned basic skills. While there, she met makeup masters such as Matthew Mungle, who was a mold maker there at the time, Rob and Barney Burman, and Sonny Burman, with whom she later worked on *Star Trek.*

She then spent some time working in Matthew Mungle's shop, and then a year at Rick Baker's where she worked in the mechanical department. "I was the only girl in the mechanical department and we were working on *Gremlins 2: The New Batch* (1990), and my boss, Phil Notaro, showed me how to make gang molds and the digits that went into the articulated hands of the gremlins. I got to make the pneumatic chest pieces for the breathing gremlins and the electrical stuff that made the embryos glow. I'd started learning makeup effects through these apprenticeships and jobs in the labs, but I had no idea how to do beauty makeup. Beauty makeup is the bread and butter of makeup artists, so I knew I needed to learn how to do it. I went to the Westmore Academy to learn beauty makeup."

Still an active member of I.A.T.S.E Local 727 (now Local 80), Karen discovered an incentive program available to all crafts service workers. If the member wanted, he or she could take any class related to the film industry, anything from acting to video feedback. All she had to do was to sign up, pay for it, take the class, and apply for reimbursement by the union. Once the paperwork was completed, the member was eligible to join that union. "I took the exam and that's how I got into the makeup union. I'm the only one that ever got in that way." And Karen's work life changed.

Open the Door and Walk Through

Karen got into the union in 1990. To prep for the journeyman's exam, she called Michael Westmore to ask if he would help her with her hair work. He told her to come down to the Paramount lot and he'd give her some time showing her techniques for laying hair and floating off hairpieces. She went to the lot and worked in the prep trailer. "I got to practice under his tutelage," which honed her skills and prepared her for the practical exam.

"Then when I was finally able to work on the show, Michael brought me onto *Star Trek*. My first makeup was a Klingon." Karen had watched the original *Star Trek* series, but hadn't really been following the new series, *Star Trek: The Next Generation*. She showed up with her kits ready to work, but didn't really have any idea what she was supposed to do. "I went to June Westmore, whom I'd met and was friends with from *Masters of the Universe*, and she said, 'I'll let you know exactly what you need to do.'"

Karen worked *Next Generation* and then was asked to go over to *Star Trek: Deep Space Nine*. On *Next Generation*, Karen occasionally created aliens but mostly worked on Starfleet officers with their special sideburns. On *Deep Space Nine*, "We had lots of interplanetary aliens working as well as visiting on the space station, so there was a lot more effects work on that show."

"Usually as a background makeup artist you're not privy to the script. They'll tell you, 'Bring your beauty kit, you'll be doing beauty makeups tomorrow.' When you're working on *Star Trek*, you're expected to be ready to make up aliens. Mike Westmore came to me and said, 'Hey, I want you to come in and do this Ferengi makeup tomorrow.' I had no idea what a Ferengi looked like because I hadn't been watching *Next Generation*. So, the next day, I did the makeup." When Karen did her first Ferengi, the components of the headpiece (which included a large cranium, a heavily creased forehead, and gigantic ears) came pre-painted so she could match the colors on the face and facial prosthetics to the headpiece coloring.

STAR TREK: DEEP SPACE NINE (1993) ARMIN SHIMERMAN
Licensed from AF archive / Alamy Stock Photo

"Since I hadn't been working with principal actors I assumed this character was background. But then I found out he was one of the main characters on the show. I was making up Armin Shimerman as Quark, the owner of the space station bar. Mike came to me and told me I'd be doing this character and all the prep on the appliances from then on."

Even though the Ferengi coloration was established, Karen added some of her own touches. She remembered that on *Batman Returns* (1992), where she ran the foam latex Penguin noses, Department Head Ve Neill used a special color around Danny DeVito's eyes to create a sunken look. "Ve told me she was using a Kryolan maroon color. Armin has big beautiful eyes and I wanted to see the whites of his eyes pop out of the darkness from the deep set of the eye ridges. That maroon color worked perfectly."

Prepping the makeup included the headpiece and the facial appliances which took most of a day. Luckily, she could use one headpiece several days in a row before she needed a new one. In the beginning, it took about three hours to apply the Quark makeup, but by the end of the show's run, Karen had it down to about 90 minutes. A day on-set with Armin Shimerman began for Karen at 4:30 AM. She got a

30-minute set-up before Armin came in at 5 AM with two hours allocated for Karen to apply his makeup. She first applied the prosthetic head and face pieces, blended the edges, and patched the air bubbles. She then used Pax paint (a mixture of acrylic paint and Pros-aide), painted everything, and powdered it. Armin then went to rehearsal, changed into his costume, then returned to makeup where Karen removed the powder and applied KY Jelly to give the face a sheen. She then did his hand makeup and fingernails. Karen would go on-set with Armin to maintain the makeup and at the end of the day, she stayed and removed everything. "I stayed because that's the deal I made with production. At the end of the day it takes about 45 minutes to remove the makeup. I took my time because I didn't want to hurt his skin. In seven years, he never had a problem, so I apparently did a good job."

Karen worked on all seven seasons of *Star Trek: Deep Space Nine*, principally making up Quark, but also other alien guest stars. Under the leadership of Michael Westmore as makeup supervisor and designer, she won three Emmy Awards for *Outstanding Individual Achievement in Makeup for a Series* for *Star Trek: Deep Space Nine* for the episodes "*Distant Voices*" (1995), "*Captive Pursuit*" (1993) and *Star Trek: Next Generation* for the episode "*Cost of Living*" (1992). She shares these three awards with designer Michael Wetsmore and an extensive cadre of fellow makeup artists. In addition, she has been nominated for nine other Emmy awards: *Lackawanna Blues* (2005), *Star Trek: Enterprise* (2002), *Star Trek: Voyager*, (2001*), Star Trek: Deep Space Nine* (1999, 1998, 1997, 1994), *Alien Nation* (1997), and *Star Trek: The Next Generation* (1993).

LACKAWANA BLUES (2005) Alamy Stock Photo

Since leaving the *Star Trek* universe, Karen has worked as a makeup artist on: *Spider-Man* (2002), *The Polar Express* (2004), *Mr. & Mrs. Smith* (2005), *The Dead Girl* (2006), *Pirates of the Caribbean: At World's End* (2007), *Beowulf* (2007), *13th Annual Prism Awards* (2009), *14th Annual Prism Awards* (2010), and *Listen to Grandpa, Andy Ling* (2012).

A Few of Her Favorite Things

"Who doesn't like Dr. Seuss? To see it live action, in Whoville on the back lot of Universal, with the Who cars? It was really fun." *How the Grinch Stole Christmas* (2000) ranks as one of Karen's most memorable jobs, partly because the project was so delightful, partly because her daughter was able to come to work with her and stay at the Universal Studio Lot nursery, and partly because she was in charge of the Who children.

"I didn't want to work full time after my daughter was born, so one of the things I did was a lot of background, making up the crowds. That gave me the flexibility to spend more time with her. When I was hired to work on *Grinch*, my daughter was four. I was good with kids, and they asked me if I'd be in charge of the children." That meant the children came in at 9:00 AM instead of 5 AM and they had a shorter work day, no longer than nine and a half hours (unlike adults who can work 24 hours a day as long as they get a turnaround). "The makeup was far less extensive than the adult Who makeups. Mostly ears, or a nose tip, or just painting. I got to drop my daughter off at nursery school, come over and go to work. I took care of the children, then would start prepping stuff for the next day. I'd pick my daughter up from nursery school and they would let her hang out with me on-set. She loved it. The hairstylists would

HOW THE GRINCH STOLE CHRISTMAS (2000)   Alamy Stock Photo

give her Who hairdos and she would sing and dance." The makeup artists who came in early had to get off the clock, so Karen cleaned the makeup off the actors. "That was really my favorite film."

One of the most fulfilling makeups Karen did was for a play called *900 Oneonta*, named after an address in Louisiana, written by David Beaird. The play was rejected by most American theaters, but played in London at the Lyric Hammersmith Theatre, The Old Vic, and the West End Theatre to excellent reviews. The play revolves around the 76-year-old family patriarch, Dandy (played by Leland Crooke), who spends his last day on earth skewering his family members before telling them who will receive the sizeable inheritance.

Karen's challenge was to make Leland Crooke, who was 40-years-old at the time, look a convincing 76. "I was able to design the makeup, sculpt it, and fabricate the prosthetics. Basically, he was in a bald cap with a wrap-around neck piece and eye bags and a nose tip to make his nose look bigger. I had a comb-over hairpiece done for him." The play was first performed in a small theater in Los Angeles before moving to London. "Nobody wanted to wear makeup. I told them, 'In order to sell this guy being 76, you guys have to wear makeup. It's too far a stretch from him being in full prosthetic makeup to you being in no makeup up at all.' I was finally able to convince them to wear makeup. Leland was only in the first act, so we took off his makeup during the second act and he took his bow as himself."

While creatively fulfilling, the experience went south when the producer did not pay Karen for her work or her products. "The actor paid for everything out of his pocket. I made all the bald caps and the prosthetic pieces for him to take to London, then sent the bill to the producer who stiffed me. I did the project for me because I got to do the sculpting and construction of the pieces."

Loss

Karen J. Westerfield has severe arthritis and is no longer able to do makeup. The arthritis is centered in her lower extremeties. It started in her hips, moved to her knee, foot, then ankle. This impacted her ability to do her job because she couldn't move quickly or get up from a chair in a timely manner; she couldn't "hustle." Karen has had both hips and a knee replaced, but she can't stand for the long hours necessary to be at a makeup chair. "I really loved being a makeup artist, and I really, really love makeup effects."

"I needed some type of artistic outlet, which is what makeup was. When I didn't have that any more I needed to fill that void. A friend stepped in and asked me, 'What have you always wanted to do that you never did?' After I thought about it, I answered, 'I always wanted to learn silversmithing and jewelry fabrication." Ever mindful of her illness, Karen took a course at the local community college to see how much she liked it and if she could do it. "I've been doing jewelry-making for two and a half years and at times I get very frustrated because I would like to be selling more stuff. There's a bajillion jewelry makers out there and I'm not a big fan of trend jewelry. I like artisan jewelry. So, do I want to do this to make a living? Not really. It'd be great, but that's not my ultimate goal. It's the art, the creation that I love."

OUTTAKES:

On Career Choices:

"Well, first of all, I ask makeup students, do you want to work in the motion picture industry, or television industry? Ask them could they be a makeup artist at a makeup counter or doing runway work or whatever. Because people think working in films is very glamorous. If you want to do fashion forward stuff, filmmaking is not the place to go. You need to go to the fashion industry and do runway stuff, or glamour stuff. It's very different than filmmaking or television. So, they have to decide if that's where they want to go. But mostly, what drives them to want to do the makeup, and knowing if that's enough to be happy, because it's not an easy role to get into the union."

"I would never discourage anyone from pursuing any kind of dream that they have. Most people get into the profession in their 20s, early to mid-20s. I started in my 30s, which was considered late. But you have to decide how long are you going to pursue this. Until you give up? Or pursue it 'til you make it?'"

"Everyone has a different story. But the biggest thing is, you can't give up. If you really want it and that's your dream, then you keep going and you try to learn everything that's out there. There are new glues out there. There are new ways of doing things. You have to stay up with the new products, you have to stay up with trends, you have to stay up with what's going on, and you have to watch a lot of films. That's how you continue your education. There's a lot to be good at your craft."

"I learned how to 'see' shooting photographs. I learned about tonal range shooting black and white and about color shooting and printing color. It helped me to be a better makeup artist because I think the artistic skills you have to have is understanding about color, what compliments, what contrasts. You need to know about tonal range and you need to know about film. And you really need to know about lighting, especially when it comes to makeup effects."

On the Working Environment:

"There are two kinds of bosses out there in the makeup world. There's the kind that hire people that are just as good as they are, if not better, and their department shines. They know they can trust and rely on their team to step it up. And then there are bosses out there that hire people that are not as good as they are so they always look really good."

"I did some commercials in Brazil and hired a better makeup artist than me, hands down. And that's why I hired him. I knew if I dropped the ball, this guy would know what to do, and it worked out great. And I got him the same pay as I, because we were doing the same job."

"I've worked on shows where the department head pulls big money and you get little money but you're doing the lion's share of the work. It's kind of crappy."

On HD and Continuity:

"There was a time when we'd say, 'Don't worry about it, it's just TV.' But now it's high definition TV. It's 'Oh-my-god-you-can-see-everything' TV!"

"Doing a makeup on a TV show requires continuity; they have to have the same look they had yesterday. The same lipstick, mascara, eye shadow. But part of what we do is that illusion of the same day, but it took you three months to get it."

On Working with Foam Prosthetics:

"Prosthetics are interesting because, especially when it comes to foam latex, they fit about 90-95 percent of the population.   Unless the actor has a very odd shaped face or a very pointy nose, or a huge nose, or eyes widely spaced apart, you can pretty much retrofit a foam latex piece to fit anybody."

"There's lots of little tricks that you learn along the way, like how to cut away foam on the inside to make more space to fit the person without affecting the outside sculpt. Or, if they have a smaller nose you can lay in some foam and glue it in place to fill up the extra space and to make the piece fit better. I mean, there's all kinds of different things you can do."

On Women:

"Ve Neill has been and still is the matriarch of makeup effects.   As far as women are con-cerned, Ve Neill will always be the forerunner. Lois Burwell is another makeup artist that I've real-ly admired and have worked with. Those women are very inspiring. Just working with all kinds of different women that are good at their job, that are good at being a leader, that are very ar-tistic, that are kind and nurturing, you know, that kind of thing. There's a handful of wom-en out there that are really good that way and I know there's more and more coming up the ranks."

"When I first started 25 years ago, it was 95% men, 5% women, and you were always battling for a place. You always have to prove yourself. Like a guy can come in and just work. A woman comes in, you still have to prove yourself, that you're good at what you do. I don't care what any-one says, I feel it still, other women still feel it. It's not really talked about very much, but there is a difference. A lot of guys don't treat women differently, but a lot of guys still do."

"Well, I think they've shown that women are better multi-taskers. We have a higher pain tolerance for sure. A lot of women can work long hours alongside any male coworker. I notice that women don't have a tendency to sit around and talk about what movies they did or what makeups they did, just work. Women talk about other things than work. If you're lucky enough to have a career and a family and children and stuff, it's a very different thing. So there's other stuff that's talked about on-set. Not just makeup. But I notice guys, they talk about makeup. Is that a good thing or a bad thing? I don't know. But there's more to life than makeup, that's how I look at it."

Catching Up!

We interviewed Karen on March 2, 2016. Since then, she has worked on

creating her jewerly for sale online

For more of Karen's Credits, visit: www. imdb.com

LEADING LADIES OF MAKEUP EFFECTS

STAYING POWER

FRANCES

"In our industry, you have to work hard and be smart to survive. Now, I also think it can be excruciating, but even more so than it used to be. We can do 16-18-hour days. That's very hard, but you must be willing to do that when you're young, because at the end of the day, that is going to get you your future."

MONTSE

"If you lose your passion, you lose everything. It is sad because what you feel first is passion; when you are doing something that makes you happy, even with headaches and stress, you want to keep going. If you don't have that, then finish. I think that, yeah. Passion."

LESLEY

"My thing is always, like anything, 'Do you really want to do it? Do you understand the hours? Do you understand what you'll give up? Do you understand you'll be away a lot? It might not work in your relationship. It might not work for having children. It might not work.' I go through it in great depth with aspiring makeup artists and say, 'It's not all bells and bows. It's really hard work. It's early, early mornings. It means not going out to dinner with your friends and not going to this party or that party because you've got to be up at 3 AM. Are you ready for that?'"

"Also, I encourage them to save their money and have enough money in the bank to have at least six months out of work so they can pick and choose their projects. I say, 'Get a profile. Learn how to pick and choose your projects so you work on the good ones.' Please, whatever way you can, save every cent you've got, put it away so you have choice. You don't just go from one job to another."

LYNN

"You have to be ready for everything. We were in the sun last week, with not a shred of shade in sight for hours on rocky terrain. You can't sit anywhere. You're fighting off bugs. You've got to be passionate about it, otherwise, you're going to be miserable."

VALLI

"Go to a lot of movies, go to art galleries, look at magazines. Keep things fresh and keep up with the times."

TAMI

"It is about attitude. A lot of people in this industry, get so jaded so quickly. The hardest thing in this industry is not to become jaded. You always kind of change up what you do and how you do it. This year is my 20th year in this industry, and I still want to do all. I'm still learning to do different things. With the innovations within the makeup industry, you need to keep learning new techniques and new product and new people. It's an incredible time for makeup effects right now."

KAREN

"You need to know how to do make-up, but I think doing make-up is not enough. You've got to have people skills too. The film industry and the television industry are very ego driven, and so ego is a dangerous thing. I learned over the years you have to be able to be a good leader, but you also have to be a really good follower. It's hard when your boss asks you to do something their way, when you've been taught a different way. You need to put your ego aside and do the job or task that you're asked to do."

JULIE

"You've got to have a lot of patience. Never think you know, because you don't. Always look. Never stop learning and listen."

JANE

"It's not enough to just be good, you've got to be exceptional."

CAMILLE

"You've got to love it, of course. Absolutely love what you're doing. That's the only way you'll be able to get through those hours."

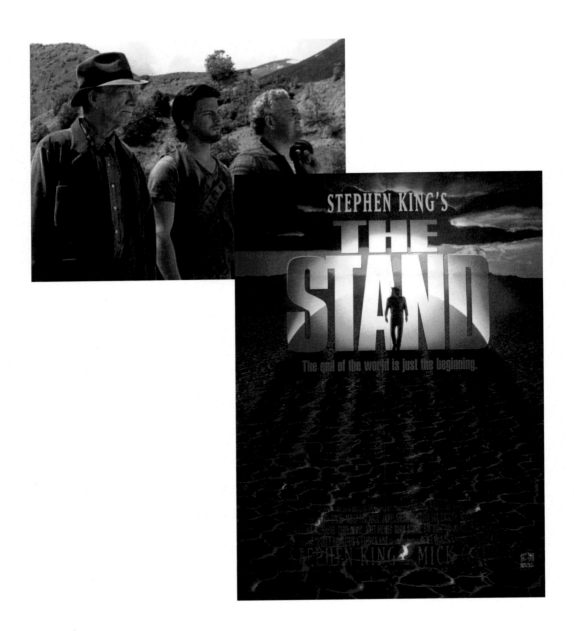

1994
EMMY AWARD
OUTSTANDING INDIVIDUAL ACHIEVEMENT IN MAKEUP
FOR MINISERIES, MOVIE OR A SPECIAL

THE STAND, (1994) ©ABC/courtesy Everett Collection
Licensed from Everett Collection, Inc. / Alamy Stock Photo

CAMILLE DELLA SANTINA

I always had a thing about wanting to do something that's considered a man's job.
I've always wanted that for some odd reason.

"Know your craft! That's my mantra. You need to know everything; beauty makeup, straight makeup, makeup effects, hair work, wig-making, sculpting, mold-making, running foam…everything! Get a good background, go to makeup school, then just get out and keep pushing. Never say no, just keep pushing, don't stop."

Camille Della Santina's career has veered from screenwriting, to makeup effects artist, to beauty product innovator. Well-known in the film and television industry as Camille Calvet, she has won two Emmy awards, one each for *The Stand* (1994) and *Star Trek: Deep Space Nine* (1995). Her most recent television work was as makeup department head for *The Cape* (2011). At the warehouse for her specialty beauty product line, Calvet Cosmetics, LLC, Camille tells us about the swerving arc of her career.

The Initial Celluloid Flicker

The women in Camille's family were artistic even though Camille's father was a New Jersey bank vice president and her mother an accountant. Her great-grandmother, grandmother, and mother were all artists, but "No one was really an 'Artist.' Except my great-grandmother who was a painter. Her work was shown at MOMA in the 1930s, and I've collected all her paintings I can find." Even though Camille grew up among artistic women, "I didn't really do a lot of art work when I was a child, that came later." Her artistic genes kicked into gear when she discovered her love of film.

At the age of 13, Camille knew she was going to be in filmmaking. She took a class on television production and she was smitten, specifically with screenwriting. She credits her English teacher, Therese Matill, as the major influence that sparked her interest. "She always backed me, always pushed me, and always said nice things about my writing. She told me I was going places." As a result, Camille collected every book on filmmaking she could get her hands on and cajoled her parents to take her to the movies as often as possible. "I was a little obsessed." Little did she know just how far her obsession would lead.

"I loved Woody Allen films. I didn't see a lot of horror films and I wasn't into monsters. Yet I was obsessed with *Planet of the Apes*. I wouldn't ever miss a *Planet of the Apes* film." She was also an avid reader of fantasy fiction, "things like *The Dragonriders of Pern, The Lord of the Rings, Watership Down*. I guess I was always involved in the fantasy aspect of it, but it never dawned on me at that age that that's where I was heading."

Film School...Course Corrections

After high school, Camille enrolled in film school at Stockton State University, one of the only schools in New Jersey that offered a degree in film. While her initial intention was to become a screenwriter, her innate desire to do a man's job led her to change her emphasis to directing and producing. "They had a really good film program. They had a lot of money, there were only 35 of us students, and we were using 16mm cameras. An unbelievably good program." Unfortunately, a new dean came in and eliminated the film program in favor of a business school. "I probably would have stayed back east except they told us, 'You can graduate with a photography degree,' and I said, 'That's not what I want to do.' So I didn't. But I also couldn't afford NYU, which was where I would have loved to go. I decided, 'I'm going to California, the heart of the film industry. I'm just going to move out there.'"

Camille made plans to move across the country with three classmates who were also looking for a good film school. Her parents were concerned about their 20-year-old daughter driving a car and camping across the country, so "they sat me down, asked what I was going to do, what was the plan, and made sure my head was squarely on my shoulders. My dad, being Italian, sat down with the two boys and had quite a talk with them. Once things were clear, my parents were 100% behind me."

California Here She Comes

When Camille arrived in California, she had very little money. She heard that if a person lived in California for six months he or she could apply for residency and attend school as a resident. She applied and got accepted into UCLA film school and attended for one semester, but once again, the money situation raised its nasty head.

Camille knew she wanted to work in the film industry. She also knew she wanted to do something that was a traditional "man's job." But she didn't know exactly where she'd fit in, what she'd enjoy doing, or how to get there. "I transferred to Cal State Northridge, majored in film and minored in screenwriting, which led me to my first job in the industry as a production assistant on a movie. I knew I had to find my niche." She thought she'd like to direct, so she "started training as an assistant director at the Directors Guild of America and worked as an assistant to Chico Day, a famous production manager who worked on *The Ten Commandments.* I liked production managing and was good at it. I helped Chico with a series of workshops at the DGA for production managers. I was working that directorial angle, pushing towards that. Then, I was placed on a film, *X-Ray,* as a PA and working crafts service."

Camille was sent to work in the makeup department headed by Allan Apone, and her life changed. "They were doing a cut-throat gag and my job was to clean up the blood at the end of each take. I was fascinated with what they were doing, so I started hanging out in that makeup room. When that film was over, I kept going to [Apone's] shop until he told me to get out. I'd finished film school at that point and Allan said, 'You have to go to makeup school.' I knew now what I was going to do." Camille had found her niche.

Following the Lure of Makeup

Acting on Apone's suggestion, Camille starting researching makeup schools. At the time, there weren't many in Los Angeles to choose from and she was looking for one with effects training. "There was Blasco's school and Elegance International. I chose E.I. because they had a small effects component in their training."

"I took the full program and I was there almost a year. I learned all the aspects, everything about TV and film makeup. Because the focus was regular makeup, there were a lot of women in class and few men. Most of the women weren't interested in effects, but I was, me and the guys." When she finished at Elegance International, she went back to Apone: "'Okay, I'm out. I'm back.' And he hired me. He gave me my very first job in the lab."

Her first task in Apone's shop, MEL, Inc., was cleaning up, so Camille jumped in, eager to get started. The crew had just pulled an all-nighter after working six days straight, so when she walked in that first morning "the shop looked like a disaster area. I thought, 'Oh no' and I started cleaning up. Boy, did I clean up. I cleaned up too much." Unbeknownst to her, the mold that the crew had been working with the previous night had broken into pieces. "I cleaned it all up, and put it in the garbage. They came in and they looked around, 'Where is the mold?' I said, 'What? There was a bunch of plaster on the table.' As I dug the pieces out of the trash, I was thinking, 'Oh oh, I've gone too far.' After gathering the chunks, they showed me how to piece it all back together. Yeah, that was my first day."

"Gung Ho!" - Working in the Shops

Camille threw herself into the work at Apone's shop, always ready to tackle whatever job she was asked to do; it wasn't always easy, and sometimes it was at her own peril. "One of my next jobs was pouring polyfoam, or polyurethane foam. We were making some big heads. I stood over the molds thinking this was the best thing ever. 'Look at the foam, oh my God, that's great.' I didn't know it gives off a gas and you're not supposed to be standing over it and breathing it; it turned out I was highly allergic to it. In 1983 we didn't have OSHA. We had nothing governing us in these shops. I broke out and had horrible bumps, hives, all over me, none of us knew what it was all about." Undaunted, Camille worked in Apone's shop for the next four months.

When Camille left MEL, Inc., she made the rounds of the makeup shops looking for work. "All I had was my resume with only one credit on it and pictures of the sad little molds that I had made. I went to all the labs looking for work. At the time, there weren't a lot of women working, but there was word on the street that this one guy, R. Christopher Biggs, hired women." So she headed over to Biggs' shop, Art & Magic.

"These boys in the shop were all nerds. They'd been making monsters in their basements forever and [Biggs] was the smart one. He hired women, so I went over there. He was working out of his garage, and sure enough, he had already hired Jill Rockow, then he hired me, and next he hired Eryn Kreuger. We joke with each other because Eryn always thought of me as 'The Pioneer' and I'd say, 'I only got here three weeks prior to you!'"

In 1985, Camille started working at Art & Magic and her first film was **Teen Wolf**. Over the next five years, she would work with Biggs on films such as: **Silent Night, Deadly Night 2** (1987), **Programmed to Kill** (1987), **Le Avventure di Tennessee Buck** (1988), **A Nightmare on Elm Street 4: The Dream Master** (1988), **The Unnameable** (1988), and **A Nightmare on Elm Street 5: The Dream Child** (1989).

In 1987, Camille became the first female shop foreman at A&M. One of her first tasks was working on **Unnameable**

A Nightmare On Elm Street 5: The Dream Child
(1989) Used with Permission of Camille Della Santina

The Unnameable (1998)
Used with Permission of Camille Della Santina

(1988). "I got to do the body cast of the actress and sculpt the body, because I am female. I also did all the ventilated hairpieces for the body. Then when it came time to do the applications, I applied all the sensitive parts and then helped the actress when she needed to go to the restroom. This was an eye opener for me; a woman was needed to work with other women."

At the time, the women would move from shop to shop, working a while, building resumes, learning skills, then moving on to the next shop. "Yeah, we were all over there [at Art & Magic], we worked, and then we'd move on. Eryn went over to Rick Baker's shop and was there forever. We all made the rounds. Each shop had their token female. That's just how it was. It's funny now. It's not really funny, but it's tongue-in-cheek funny. We laugh about it now because it's changed, thankfully."

While Camille was at A&M, she also got jobs working at other shops. She went over to Kenny Myers' shop to work on *Return of the Living Dead, 2* (1988). Myers kept the men and the women segregated. "He didn't want any fraternizing." Working at Myers', Camille already knew how to make molds and run foam, so she and another woman, Lisa Doering, ran foam in the mornings and in the afternoons "we'd go upstairs and make wigs. We were not allowed downstairs. If Kenny caught us we got in trouble. When Kenny wasn't around, I used to sneak down to the sculpture room where Mike Smithson was working because he had these great tapes, that's how long ago this was, I'd grab a tape, and run back upstairs before we got caught."

Learning To Work Around Problems and Finding New Skills

Return Of The Living Dead, 2 (1988)
Camille working upstairs in the hair room
Used with Permission of Camille Della Santina

"One of the ways I used to pour foam latex was the 'Burman' method. As you mixed the foam latex you would sniff the ammonia, when it started going off, you'd pour the foam into the mold. I learned this method from one of the Burman boys, Rob. I would sniff, sniff, sniff. Then I woke up one day and I couldn't move my joints; it was ammonia poisoning." After her experience with polyfoam, and then ammonia, Camille realized she had sensitivity to many of the chemicals used in the shops. "I used to get sick a lot from chemicals in the lab. It wasn't just me, a lot of the women were affected by the chemicals." She remembers working at Myers' shop the day OSHA showed up for an inspection and almost closed down the shop "because we didn't have masks that fit the women. They were all made for men and were too big for us." OSHA's presence and oversight provided the necessary safety net for women working in the industry.

So, working upstairs making wigs was actually a blessing for Camille. She developed her wigmaking and hair skills in makeup school, now she was able to hone those ventilating and punching skills making hairpieces and wigs. "When I was at Kenny's, I did hair and wigs. It expanded my resume. It was something else that I could do, another skill I could get hired for at other shops. Steve Johnson hired me over at his shop to do wigs."

Then, back at A&M, Chris Biggs, acknowledging Camille's management abilities, wanted her to learn to do budgets on the computer, which was, at that time, a new element in the business world. "I would do all the budgets for him. Chris was a computer whiz, he always has been. I, on the other hand, was not. He wanted me to learn, and I did learn, which added yet another facet to my skill sets. I started getting calls, 'Could you come over and do this budget?'" Camille's talents now ran the gamut from running molds, making hairpieces and wigs, to doing budgets. Ultimately, however, Camille wanted to get out of the shops and get on-set doing makeup.

Getting On-Set, the Girls, and the Union

"I wanted to get on-set. Even my first day at Allan's shop I knew that. I didn't want to be stuck in the labs all the time, especially once I found out I was having problems with the chemicals. I had to get out there. A lot of us girls were just 'lab rats.' The only one that had gotten out of the lab at that point was Ve [Neill]. She's always been a mentor to me. I could call her up and she'd say, 'Just keep trying.' She was out there." Margaret Prentice at Rob Bottin's shop and Michèle Burke were other women who had broken out of the lab and onto the set. Burke, a makeup artist from Canada, had burst onto the scene as the first female Academy Award winner for her work on *Quest for Fire* (1983). "We always kept up with the women. We always knew where they were, what they were doing. We were very supportive of each other, too. We had each other's backs."

Camille was trying to get into the union, which would guarantee her set work; she needed to accumulate enough hours working on-set to qualify for membership. The hours spent working in a shop have never counted towards that total, which was another reason to get out of the shops. Camille had some set experience and some hours from working on the films at Art & Magic with Biggs and over at Kenny Myers'. She also worked non-union films hoping they would "flip," which would help secure union entry. "I happened to live on the same street the union office was on, they were in this little house. I would go down there and walk in, just annoy them, like I did with Allan. They'd say, 'You have to get your 30 days' and 'We never go off [the union] roster, ever.' I wasn't stopped by that, I would periodically just go in and check, 'Hi…roster?'"

"Sure enough, one day I got the call to go down to *My Two Dads*. They needed an old age makeup and there was nobody to send that could do it. I went in off roster. I went down there and they needed extra hands, I called the shop, told Chris Biggs and Michael Key, 'Come on down. We're going to get in the union.' We all got our first day, the first set of hours that counted toward membership. Once I got that, there was no stopping me."

It was 1989, and Camille started picking up days at CBS on *The Young and the Restless* doing straight and beauty makeup, every day accruing hours towards her 30 days. In 1990, Camille got into the union.

From "Lab Rat" to "…But Can You Do Beauty?"

Being able to do both makeup effects and beauty makeup created a dilemma for Camille when she went out on interviews. "[Producers] were used to the men not knowing how to do beauty and women not knowing effects. So, I had two books, one for effects and one for beauty. I had to separate them because the minute they would see the monsters, they'd say, 'Can you do beauty makeup?' and vice versa. In interviews, I found I had to show them what they wanted to see."

Working with the right people and being in the right place at the right time plays a role in every successful makeup artist's life. "I did *The Runestone* in 1991 and I was head of makeup. I knew straight, beauty, and character makeup, so I could do it all. *The Runestone* was a horror film, but I was doing the beauty makeups. Lance Anderson was doing the makeup effects. He found out that I knew effects and that I came from the shops. So, when we had to shoot in New York and Lance couldn't go, I got to take the monster to New York for him."

Camille got a surprise when she interviewed with Joe Dante for the short-lived TV series, *Eerie Indiana*

Eerie Indiana (1991) Bigfoot
Used with Permission of Camille Della Santina

ARMY OF DARKNESS: EVIL DEAD 3 (1992)
BRUCE CAMPBELL
Licensed from AF archive / Alamy Stock Photo

(1991-92). She came armed with both her books and when the producers asked to see her work, "…because it was Joe Dante and there were a lot of makeup effects on the show, I passed around my effects book. It went around the table and sure enough the question came up from one of the producers, 'But can you do beauty makeup?' I went to hand them my beauty book and Joe Dante said, 'If she can do this. She can do anything.' Bam. Hired on the spot. Best interview ever!" *Eerie Indiana* was a kid's show that featured lots of interesting characters every week, including Big Foot and a fully articulated werewolf. "I had to get all those characters designed and dealt with while I was also doing the makeup on the show. I was able to use my strengths."

In 1992, Camille worked with Director Sam Raimi on *Army of Darkness*. For this film, a sequel to *Evil Dead*, she was selected as makeup supervisor specifically because of her expertise with both effects and beauty makeup, and got to work in conjunction with KNB EFX. "It was a big show. We had all the prosthetics to do on Bruce Campbell and his stunt doubles. It kept me really busy taking care of the makeup and makeup effects."

Her next big project was *The Edge* (1992-93), a variety TV show starring Jennifer Aniston, Tom Kenny, and Wayne Knight. Every week, the show featured the actors playing different characters. "We had tons of prosthetics to create, so I opened my own little lab in my garage. We had forty pieces a week working. We were constantly pulling them out of the oven and taking them directly to set. I had people working at the house, sculpting in my back yard. Then we would go in for two days a week and shoot all the sketches. Jennifer Aniston was great, I loved working with her. We'd do the most horrible prosthetics on her and she'd be absolutely fine with it all."

Going Where She'd Never Gone Before, But First...

Once she finished *The Edge,* Camille got a call to start day checking for *Star Trek: The Next Generation*…but just as she was settling in, she got a frantic phone call from Steve Johnson. He needed a head makeup artist to jump in on *The Stand* (1994), which started shooting five days later. It was a five-month gig, so she said goodbye to *Star Trek* and flew to Utah. This was another time when her well-rounded background played in her favor. "I had worked for [Johnson] in his shop on various shows, and he wanted a HOD that could help out with prosthetics. It was a huge undertaking. I had to do a complete continuity breakdown in two days." The film, a road movie, was shot out of sequence "and all the actors did several scenes a day with varying beard lengths. This was something else I brought to the table; I was really good at hair work. We needed to hand lay beards, but beard lengths changed within the shooting day. Beard lengths were a problem." Then she remembered a trick she'd learned working with Richard Schell on *The Edge*.

"We were doing a Three Stooges sketch and we had to do fast changes, so we needed bald caps with hair already applied. Richard came in, flopped a bald cap on a form, and used a flocking gun to "flock" short hair onto the cap. We'd done this technique for animal fur in the shop and now on bald caps. Richard was always finding solutions. He was the makeup MacGyver. Now on *The Stand* we had a similar problem. I wondered if you could flock straight onto the actor's face? So, we gave it a try and it worked beautifully." Since the hair for flocking is short, Camille found a trick. "Since I couldn't change the length, I used lighter hair for less density, which looked shorter. Then I'd go darker and denser to have a longer, heavier look. After all this flocking, I got the nickname The Flocker." In 1994, Camille won her first Emmy Award for *The Stand* in the category of *Outstanding Individual Achievement in Makeup for a Miniseries or a Special* along with Johnson.

And Now...Back to *Star Trek*

When she got back from *The Stand,* Camille was hired on *Star Trek: Deep Space Nine* working for Michael Westmore,

THE STAND (1994)
Licensed from AF archive / Alamy Stock Photo

like the famous voice-over states, "to discover strange new worlds." "When I went over to *Star Trek*, I had to relearn the whole world. I had been heading shows myself by that point, but I had to learn everything new."

Working on *Star Trek*, Camille refined the mantra she'd already developed from her past experiences: *Know your Craft*! "On a show like *Star Trek,* you had to really know your craft, every ounce of it because you did it every day. I had to do beauty and straight makeup. I had to do hair. I had to sculpt. I had to make molds. Michael would just throw you in there."

Camille considers Westmore her beloved mentor and role model; he taught her everything from understanding what a makeup needs, to the treatment of makeup artists, to running a department.

"[Westmore] would come in the room and he could see immediately what needed to be done with a makeup or a color, but he wasn't one of those people that would tell you, 'Okay, you have to do it this way, dah dah dah.' He would say it in such a way that it was your idea. He treated each artist as an artist. The minute he would walk in the door we would want his input, 'What do I need?' He'd catch it. Just like that. He wasn't judgmental if you were doing it differently than he would do it. I learned from him how to tell somebody how you want it done without sounding like you're demanding it. So it looks like the idea is theirs."

Bajorans, Klingons, Ferengis...Oh My!

After two months, Westmore made Camille key makeup artist on *DS9*. For the next six years she was responsible for actress Nana Visitor's Bajoran character, Major Kira Nerys, and when Michael Dorn moved from *Next Generation* to *DS9*, his Klingon character, Commander Worf. Also, as key, her duties included the makeup for whatever actor was guest starring each week.

DS9, a space station where alien ships stop to do their interstellar business, always had a menagerie of alien makeups. On the days they shot scenes on the promenade there could be as many as thirty makeup artists working. "I really learned how to coordinate. Michael's schedules were beautiful. He taught me that. He does battle plans. Everyone used to make fun of me because I

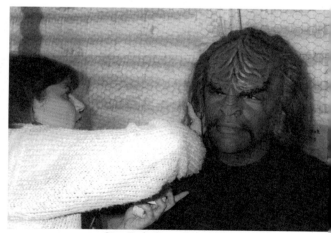
Star Trek: Deep Space Nine (1995)
Camille with Michael Dorn as Worf
Used with Permission of Camille Della Santina

Star Trek: Deep Space Nine (1995)
Camille with Nana Visitor as Kira
Used with Permission of Camille Della Santina

walked around with a clipboard all day long."

Camille's organizational skills and sense of expediency served her well on the set of *DS9.* "I remember we had a huge Klingon day. I had some new artists I told to touch-up the Klingon extras off-set. Michael Dorn had wandered over from the ***Next Generation*** set to visit in his Worf makeup. We were chatting at the AD's booth and one of my eager, new makeup artists ran up to him, touched him up, glued his beard on, and ran off. I started to say something but Michael said, 'just let him do it.' I laughed and told him, 'I did tell them to do touch-ups off-set.' This artist had no idea it was Michael Dorn." The assignment was accomplished, the artist fulfilled his obligation, and things moved smoothly due in no small part to Camille's grasp of the job and how to handle the large number of actors and crewmembers.

She'd finally gotten her wish to be on-set, but with the massive workload on *DS9,* Camille found she and her crew were perpetually exhausted and constantly working overtime. Then she had an idea.

Teaching Old Dogs New Tricks

"The hours were killer for us, but at least we had a clean-up crew who came in to do removals. They waited upstairs until we hit our nine-hour turnaround time, then we'd be out the door. I thought, 'This isn't working for me.' As key makeup artist, I was doing the artists' schedules. When I looked at the budgets, my inner production manager realized production was spending a lot of money keeping us on golden time (overtime) when we had people like Kevin Haney, an Oscar winner, upstairs just waiting around to do removals and cleanup. I thought, 'They are very capable of coming down and taking over for us on-set.' I brought it to Michael and he said, 'Hmmm, Okay.' He told me to go sell the idea to Bobby Della Santina, who's now my father-in-law. I presented my case to Bobby in my production manager mode, looking at the finances. I said, 'This is how much money you're going to save if you bring those makeup artists on-set and take us off golden time.' We worked it all out and I finally got to implement the new schedule. It was now possible to get us off the clock sooner so we could have a life and maybe get some sleep."

From 1993 to 1999 Camille worked on *DS9,* and in 1995, Camille won her 2nd Emmy for *Outstanding Individual Achievement in Makeup for a Series.* "It was great working on ***Star Trek****.* It was wonderful. It was the hardest work I think I've ever done." But as *DS9* was wrapping up, Westmore wanted her to come over onto the new franchise, ***Voyager****.* "By this time, I had done all the movies and Michael would keep me working. On hiatus, we had to make plans to go on vacation or else he'd have us in. He wanted to keep us working. It was his love for us." But after six years, she was having an itch. "I wanted to go out. I want to go over the wall."

Going Over the Wall

Camille went over the wall and met Michèle Burke. Between 2000 and 2002, Camille assisted Burke on four films; ***The Cell*** (2000), ***Vanilla Sky*** (2001), ***Minority Report*** (2002), and ***Austin Powers in Goldmember*** (2002). Burke is another woman who had to work her way into makeup effects when women weren't common in the field. "She understands women effects artists and she hires a lot of them. She's wonderful."

On ***The Cell****,* " I was her third. That was a lot of work and [Burke] did a lot of designs. I learned a lot from her, seeing how closely she worked with the director, the production designer, and costume designers on that level of film."

On **Vanilla Sky**, "Michèle did several designs for Tom [Cruise]. The film was hinging on our makeup, it had to be flawless. He expects 110% of you because he gives that himself. You give it to him. You become a better person because he will throw things at you. On **Vanilla Sky**, we finally got it down to a look that he liked."

On **Austin Powers**, "I always put moles on all my characters. We had a character on **Austin Powers** that had a big mole, and I swore he was looking at my mole when I did that. Yeah, all my aliens, they all get a mole, that was my signature."

Back to TV: *Firefly* and *The Cape*

In 2002, Camille was lured back to episodic TV with the Sci-Fi series **Firefly** (2002-2003). The show was created by Joss Whedon and starred Nathan Fillion as captain of a renegade spacecraft running from the authorities while evading warring factions in a far-flung corner of the galaxy. Camille was the key makeup artist on the series, and she brought in her **Star Trek** colleagues Tina Kalliongis-Hoffman and Mary Kay Morse. The series ran 14 episodes and gathered a large cult following.

FIREFLY (2002) ADAM BALDWIN SUMMER GLAU SEAN MAHER NATHAN FILLION MORENA BACCARIN GINA TORRES ALAN TUDYK JEWEL STAITE & RON GLASS
Licensed from AF archive / Alamy Stock Photo

In 2005, **Firefly** was resurrected as a cult film, **Serenity**. This time Camille came on as makeup department head. "I knew all the characters and I was really into Photoshop, so I got to design all the makeup looks. I loved working with Joss Whedon again and Nathan Fillion. It comes from the top and he's just a charmer. I also got to work with my beloved KNB to do all the Reavers and other alien makeups. I've worked with them since we were together in the '80s. It's like I've always been with those guys. It was a great experience."

Her last foray into TV was in 2011 on **The Cape** as makeup department head. The show was about a divorced cop who wanted to reconnect with his estranged son, so he adopts the identity of his son's favorite comic book character, The Cape. "It was a huge prosthetics series. I had gone in deciding to only do the pilot, but was won over by the cast. One of the best since **Firefly**! Even though my business was doing well, I decided to take on HOD [head of department]."

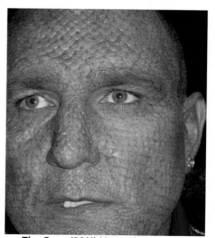

Camille knew one of the producers of **The Cape** from **Star Trek**. He knew her capabilities and experience, but the other producers didn't, "which created a big challenge in trying to get the work produced." The show was challenging, calling for up to 10 new prosthetics a week and the workload was so heavy Camille used two different FX shops, Matthew Mungle and KNB, to produce the required prosthetics.

Vinnie Jones played one of the most difficult prosthetic characters on the show, Scales. "He had a full face of scales sculpted to where his face met his hairline, but he always varied his hairline. So we had to hand sculpt in a new hairline every three

The Cape (2011) Vinnie Jones as Scales
Used with Permission of Camille Della Santina

days. Vinnie is known for being difficult, but was one of the best actors I have ever worked with! I think our success was because of my assistant, Christopher Nelson; I couldn't have done it without him, his wit, talent, and height, he stood eye-to-eye with Vinnie!" In 2011, Camille was nominated for *Outstanding Prosthetic Makeup for a Series, Miniseries, Movie or a Special* for her work on **The Cape.**

Camille, CEO of *SilcSkin* specialty anti-aging products
Used with Permission of Camille Della Santina

The Present

In 2005 Camille had twins and realized that while she was fortunate to be working at what she loved, her life would have to change. Calvet Cosmetics, LLC, a beauty product line which specializes in silicone anti-aging pads for the face and *décolletage*, was born.

"Working with silicone prosthetics, I noticed when I did the removal, the actor's skin looked smoother and reju-venated. I did some research and found out silicone gels were being used to help treat scar tissue. I wondered how this would work with wrinkles. I started experimenting and developed my silicone anti-aging pads, *Silcskin*."

"I'm so very blessed because this all came about around the time I had my twins. Working on films, I was gone most of the year and I couldn't really do that anymore. I didn't want to miss out on their lives. My business affords me the chance to go pick them up from school and help them do their homework. So, I basically turned my prosthetic life and knowledge of silicone into an anti-wrinkle business. Now I'm in the beauty biz and *Silcskin* has products in 28 countries around the world."

The Future

Camille (Calvet) Della Santina has truly embraced her mantra of *Know your Craft*! Zigging and zagging her way through life and work, not unlike her race-car-driving husband, she's evolved from film student, to makeup artist, to beauty product entrepreneur. What maneuver lies ahead for her? "It's funny, I always wanted to do a western and I still haven't done a western, even though I think of some of my Sci-Fi work as 'space westerns.'"

"Every once in a while, I want to call Eryn [Kreuger Mekash] and say 'Hey, I want to come in and make a monster, okay? Or maybe, just throw some blood around? It's been a hard day.'"

OUTTAKES:

On Getting in Sync with My Alien:

"On **Star Trek**, I used to dress in the color of the alien I was doing that week because I'm a mess. I'm not someone who can actually wear a suit and not get a thing on it. I usually have a full apron on when I'm working and I still get stuff all over me. I used to dress in browns and blacks and oranges if we were doing Ferengis. I started dressing in dark colors because I would get the paint on me all day long. I'm going to believe it's a symbiotic connection with the actor and the character. That's what I want to believe."

On Going Back On-Set:

"I'll go back if I get a personal call. On **Ted 2**, Howard [Berger at KNB EFX] called me up and said, 'We have one of your actors here from **Star Trek**, Michael Dorn.' I was the last person to take his Klingon head off and [Dorn] said, 'I'm never ever wearing this head again.' On **Ted 2**, they convinced him to put on a Klingon headpiece for a Comic Con scene. He said to Howard, 'I'm not putting it back on unless Camille comes and does it.' I went to Germany with KNB to make up Mike Myers on **Inglourious Basterds** because we'd worked together on **Austin Powers.** Stuff like that, I'll definitely go back. I haven't hung up my brushes yet!"

On The Differences Between Working as HOD on TV and Film:

"With television, you're meeting with all the writers and producers and they're telling you what they want, except they don't all know what they want. You hope there's one that has a vision, but they all have different visions. So you submit your designs, many designs, but if they don't trip something in their brains, that's it. It's difficult. Then there's the tight time frame because you've got to get it done."

"With film, it's a much different process. You have much more time in the beginning to go through the script, breakdown what you're going to be doing with the characters, and, hopefully, you have a director that has a vision, that can see it right away. You're primarily working with the director and the other designers."

On The Differences Between Being a Makeup Artist and HOD:

As a makeup artist: "Working as a day check makeup artist allows you to create art while in a controlled environment. You are given parameters and directions, which can be quite fulfilling with the right HOD."

As an HOD: "It is all about who you hire, who is controlling your talent, so your 2nd is of utmost importance. You are dealing much more with production, especially on episodic TV. On films, it's much different because everything is set in production prior to actual shooting."

On Working with Actors:

"When you're doing effects, you're taking away some or all of their senses. A lot of times they can't hear, can't see, and they still have to act. They're not just a piece of meat you're going to glue stuff onto. It's all about their persona; they have to feel that character. It's got to be about the actor and them feeling at ease and helping you with the design. They know themselves and they know the character so they can help."

"When I've finished a makeup, the first reaction I want to see is from the actor. Did we nail it? Did they become that character? That's what we're working for; do they feel the character? When we were working with Mike Myers playing Austin Powers, it was brilliant because he would start getting into character as the makeup was progressing. If he did that, you knew if you were getting it right."

Catching Up!

We interveiwed Camille on February 24, 2016. She sent us this letter about her latest work.

"I'm continuing to grow my brand *SilcSkin.* We are now carried in over 1000 retail outlets throughout the US. We distribute to over 30 countries. We have a *SilcSkin* European Office in Rotterdam, Netherlands, that distributes in Europe.

SilcSkin is getting a lot of attention and I'm doing a lot of press and Podcasts. There is extreme interest in how I went from being a Special Effects Makeup Artis to a Beauty Entrepreneur using my knowledge of silicone prosthetics.

I have spent the last year working with chemists creating two new products. A Hand Treatment, that debuted with great results in New York at the International Esthetics Conference and a Gel Cleanser."

For more of Camille's Credits, visit: www.imdb.com

2009
EMMY AWARD
OUTSTANDING MAKEUP
FOR A MULTI-CAMERA SERIES OR SPECIAL (NON-PROSTHETIC)

MADtv, Alex Borstein, Stephnie Weir, Jordan Peele
Used with Permission of Jennifer Aspinall

JENNIFER ASPINALL

I believe that if you're doing something through joy, then the universe will provide and you will be supported and blessed. It won't matter who is competing with you or who thinks you shouldn't be doing it. If you're coming from that place of joy, then the universe is going to give you what you need.
That is the way I conduct my life; that is the reality in which I live.

"I got into this because I was painfully, painfully shy. I really didn't have friendships or relationships with anybody outside of my immediate family. Then, when I was eight or nine, I found Richard Corson's book, **Stage Makeup**, and as both my parents were artists, I related to the highlights and shadows of the makeup and started practicing on myself and my family. That led me to disguising myself, and disguising my brother, and disguising my father. That was the joy for me, finding the ability to create illusion. That started to bring me to life as a human being."

It's in the Genes

Everything from the art on the walls, to the research books, to projects in-process and completed, to mood lighting, and the five vociferous parrots informs the visitor that Jennifer's home is the home of an artist. It's an homage to the creative process.

Born and raised in Pennsylvania to an artistic family, Jennifer was encouraged to explore her passions. Her father was a painter and started teaching Jennifer, from the age of four, the basics of painting and drawing. Her grandfather was a stonecutter, a carver, and a sculptor. His work in the form of "gargoyley-things" can be found on buildings and in the cemetery in Bolton, England, where the Aspinall's originated. Her grandmother loved to draw and her brother, Brian Aspinall, also draws and sketches, but excels in creative food preparation.

So, as a child Jennifer lost and found herself in Richard Corson, literally. "When I started doing disguises on myself I found I could be a different person. There was no pain other than my own insecurities, but I think anytime you're in another person's face or being, you're not you. That helped me fight my shyness."

Mrs. Reilly

Jennifer's father was her first influence, Richard Corson her second, and Mrs. Reilly, the next-door neighbor, her third. Mrs. Reilly produced dinner theater and summer stock and once she knew Jennifer was interested in makeup, she made sure Jennifer had professional products. Then, when Jennifer was eleven, after she completed her five-mile paper route after school, she would go to the theater. "I started doing basic makeup, or painting sets, or acting. I literally was building beards and bald caps and everything for various shows and doing good, old-fashioned techniques that no one would ever even know about at this point in history. Mrs. Reilly was the first one to provide me makeup and get me to the theater. Once I was bitten by the theater bug, that was it. I was in love. Being around people that were in that space was very joyful."

Theater is the business of creating illusions through scenery and lighting and sound and makeup and costumes and acting and producing. Jennifer's attraction to illusions, in all forms, was satisfied in the theater.

In 1979, at 17-years-old, this passion for theater inspired Jennifer to produce *The Rocky Horror Picture Show* in Philadelphia in which she played Dr. Frank-N-Furter. "I saw the movie and the fans dressing up in makeup and costume, and the visual appealed to me, very glitter-rock/punk-rock. Playing the role of a man challenged my ability to create illusion. Frank was a strong, self-confident character, something I was not at the time. Somehow *Rocky Horror* gave me permission to become someone else, to come out of my shell. Frank-N-Furter was also one of my first "look alike" character makeups where I tried to create that face on mine, creating more illusion. *Rocky Horror* was also the beginning of my character makeup career." *The Rocky Horror Picture Show* taught Jennifer about department heading and creating and producing a show. It also acted as a conduit to getting her work in New York.

Another Mrs. Reilly

Jennifer had a fan club, The Jennifer Aspinall Fan Club, which began in honor of her portrayal of Dr. Frank-N-Furter. The mother of the president of her fan club had a friend, Peggy Owens, who was a hairdresser in New York working with actors like Al Pacino and Woody Allen. When Jennifer moved to New York after her stint in *Rocky Horror*, she worked with Peggy, who helped her land her first television commercial jobs.

Jennifer has no formal training. "I did take some sculpting classes at the Art Students League of New York, but other than that, I taught myself. This is a very collaborative art form, so I learn from almost everybody. And I was lucky enough to have parents who were artists and I had an inherent understanding of highlight and shadow. I started teaching when I was 17 and I've been teaching ever since." The Richard Corson book is a requirement for all her students.

The Rise of the Low-Budget Horror Films

Once Jennifer got to New York, she started taking any project that she could. Her first major project was *The Toxic Avenger* (1984), a low-budget horror film by Troma Entertainment, Inc., a company known for making, "Not exactly romantic comedies…low-budget sex comedies, that's what they were."

"Troma wanted to get into producing more, to their minds, serious films, so they had written this story about a superhero from New Jersey, a shy janitor kid who fell into a toxic waste kettle and became a superhero."

"There's a scene where this guy turns into the monster. *The Howling* had just been out and Rick Baker had done *An American Werewolf in London*, so I talked them into letting me do a transformation scene that wasn't originally in the script. That was the first time I ever had to do special effects makeup. That was the first creature I ever sculpted. That was the first sculpture I ever sculpted. That was my first-time department heading. I also got to create, storyboard and direct the transformation scene. It was very exciting. They gave me the crew for a day and said, 'If you can shoot it in a day, have at it!' So I did!"

The Toxic Avenger got Jennifer's career in makeup effects started. Because the film was set in New York, had a superhero creature, and was designed by a woman, it got the attention of *Fangoria Magazine*, a horror film magazine. "*Fangoria* did two big articles on me, and that sort of started me in that world doing low-budget horror films. That was my world for a while."

The Toxic Avenger (1984)   Used with Permission of Jennifer Aspinall

Other horror films followed: *Spookies* (1986) features a sorcerer who kills his victims to steal their vitality to keep his wife alive, *The Ambulance* (1990) focuses on an ambulance that picks up female patients who then never arrive at any hospital, and *Street Trash* (1987), which revolves around a liquor store owner selling alcoholic drinks to homeless people who are unaware the bottles actually contain a toxic brew. This last movie became a cult-classic and a making-of documentary was shot, *The Meltdown Memoirs* (2006), in which Jennifer appears and talks about the makeup effects for the film.

During this period, Jennifer jumped between working in New York and London. "I did a few horror films under the table over there [London] while I was in that low-budget-horror-film-period of my life, pre-*Saturday Night Live*."

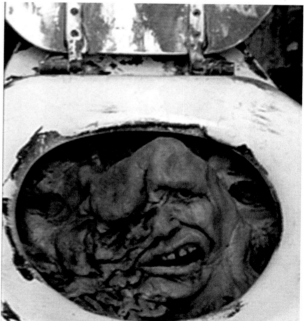

Street Trash (1987)   Used with Permission of Jennifer Aspinall

"*Live from New York ...*" Working Live Comedy

In 1987, in the midst of working horror films and working at New York City Opera, Jennifer started working on *Saturday Night Live* doing a lot of the off-site commercial parodies. Then in 1989, she became head of department for three seasons until she left the show in 1993.

Jennifer was nominated for an Emmy for *Outstanding Individual Achievement in Makeup for a Series* on *Saturday Night Live* (1993) for the episode with host Harvey Keitel. "I just found out a couple of days ago that I was the first person in the makeup department of *SNL* to ever be nominated. I was shocked

Keegan-Michael Key in makeup for
Various characters from *MADtv*
Used with Permission of Jennifer Aspinall

to find that out. I guess the guys before me, Peter Montagna and Kevin Haney, never submitted. I was surprised."

Creating the Character

Jennifer is in a unique position because she works not only on television, but sketch comedy on television. Because of the demands of sketch comedy, everything has to be done quickly and sometimes at the last minute. To facilitate that process, Jennifer works closely with the actors. "A lot of the stuff I do is character-driven, so I get from the actors what they're thinking. I've been lucky enough to be in situations where I can help them more with, say, a gold tooth or a missing ear. My job is to get them what they need and be there as their support team."

Additionally, Jennifer has a team of people she trusts and with whom she enjoys working. As department head, she goes to the meetings with the directors and producers, designs and builds pieces, then communicates the makeup needs to her team members. "The benefit of working with people I trust is I can say, 'Okay, I need this, go knock that out for me.' I can hand things over to people like Scott Wheeler, who's become a friend, or Ed French who helped me for years on *MADtv*, and trust the work will be done and done well. Various people that are ego-less enough to let me do that with them."

"I'm all about collaboration. For me, that's the big thing. We're creating so many characters in sketch comedy, clarity and respect is necessary. There's always going to have to be dialogue and communication. Since I know how to do hair and costumes, I can communicate in their world also, so I can accommodate what they need."

And for Jennifer, everything relates to the actor and his or her needs. What can she do to make the actor comfortable? To assist her in creating the character and the performance? "It all goes back to my passion for illusion and acting. I know what an actor needs to help build layers into the character."

The Mad *MAD* World of LA

In 1995, Fox Television brought Jennifer out to Los Angeles to do *MADtv*. She wasn't planning on staying. "I was just here for three months while we did a pickup show for the summer. But they kept picking us up. We got picked up for fourteen years. That's how I landed here in LA."

MADtv was a late-night sketch comedy show based on the humor of the classic *MAD Magazine*, famous for its parodies of American culture. The show was a mixture of pre-recorded and live, real-time comedy sketches. During Jennifer's tenure as makeup department head (251 episodes 1995 – 2008), she supervised the creation of makeup for impersonations, fake advertisements, spoofs of movie trailers, and scenes from current and iconic films and television series. Some of Jennifer's favorites include spoofing *How The Grinch Stole Christmas*, *The Nutty Professor*, *The Lord of the Rings*, and *Star Trek*. "I was asked to replicate a lot of well-known movie and TV makeups, except I had only a week to build those makeups that the movies had months to perfect. But I found that challenging. Working quickly makes me work more efficiently and I like that."

"We shot the show in front of a live audience, which meant the makeups were done live, fast, and in the moment. Other segments were inserted, so we shot them ahead of time and it was more like working on a movie or regular TV. We had time to do the applications and get the makeups just right."

"I think that one of the best things that we ever did at *MADtv* was a sketch about *The Wizard of Oz*. It was about a slave that Dorothy and everyone runs into on the yellow brick road. It was supposedly footage that got cut out of the movie. It was one of those moments where everybody's performance, everybody's creative and artistic endeavors, came together, and really worked; we recreated this scene from *The Wizard of Oz* and everything just fell into place. Wardrobe, hair, makeup, everything. It was really beautiful."

MADtv spoof of *The Wizard Of Oz*
Used with Permission of Jennifer Aspinall

Jennifer won an Emmy for *Outstanding Makeup for a Multi-Camera Series or Special (Non-prosthetic)* for her work on *MADtv* (2009) for the episode #1405 *(Season 14, Episode 5)* which she shares with makeup artists Alexei Dmitiew, David Willams, and Heather Mages. #1405 featured pre-recorded spoofs of *I Love Lucy* with Lucy and Ethel raising money as hookers which required the classic looks and hairdos for the two ladies plus a bald cap, hair fringe, and fat chin for Fred; the gay wedding of George Takei with an impersonation of William Shatner as the clergyman, two Romulans as special wedding guests with bobbed wigs and pointed ears, and two Klingons in full regalia from *Star Trek*.

Live segments included Condoleezza Rice at her last press conference after eight years in the Bush administration going all "gansta" with wig-disguised-corn-rowed hair; a spoof of *The View* with impersonations of Whoopi Goldberg, Joy Behar, and Elisabeth Hasselbeck in which a stage hand gets his arm torn off and Whoopi get her head torn off by a female American Gladiator; an ongoing sketch involving a Muslim minimart owner with beard and mustache; a Barack Obama impersonation with short cropped wig, eyebrows, ear extensions, and a prosthetic nose.

Jennifer was nominated 12 other times for Emmy Awards for her work on *MADtv*. In 2008 she was up for *Outstanding Makeup for a Multi-Camera Series or a Special (Non-Prosthetic)*; in 2007, 2006, 2005, 2003, 2002, for *Outstanding Makeup for a Series (Non-Prosthetic)*; in 2007, 2006, 2005 for *Outstanding Prosthetic Makeup for a Series, Miniseries, Movie or a Special*; in 2003 for *Outstanding Makeup for a Series (Prosthetic)*; and in 2000 and 2001 for *Outstanding Makeup for a Series*. In addition, Jennifer was nominated nine times for a Hollywood Makeup Artists and Hair Stylist Award and won five times: once for *Best Character Makeup - Television Series* in 2003 with Scott Wheeler and Randy Westgate; twice for *Best Special Makeup Effects - Television (For a Single Episode of a Regular Series - Sitcom, Drama or Daytime)* in 2002 with Randy Westgate, James Rohland, and Stephanie L. Massie and in 2001 with Randy Westgate; and twice for *Best Character Makeup - Television (For a Single Episode of a Regular Series - Sitcom, Drama or Daytime)* in 2002 with Randy Westgate, Julie Purcell, and Deborah Rutherford, and in 2001 with Felicia Linsky and Ed French. In 2016, Jennifer had one last curtain call with *MADtv* for its short-lived reboot.

The Tonight Show with Jay Leno
Used with Permission of Jennifer Aspinall

The Craziness Continued

Jennifer's work on live TV comedy also led her to work as make-up designer on other comedy shows: *The Jamie Kennedy Experiment* (2002), using her disguise skills to help Kennedy with his "Candid-Camera-style" show pranking unsuspecting victims; makeup artist on 10 episodes of *NESN Comedy All-Stars* (2008) making up stand-up comics for the show; makeup artist on *Presidential Reunion* (2010 video short directed by Ron Howard) working with Will Farrell and Jim Carrey playing their famous *SNL* impersonations of George W. Bush and Ronald Regan; make-up effects artist and makeup artist for the guests on *The Tonight Show with Jay Leno* (2010-2013).

In 2016, Jennifer's most recent foray into live disguise was on Disney TV's *Walk the Prank*, a hybrid scripted hidden camera show where kids prank adults in real-time video. She had two especially difficult pranks for the show. For one she had to transform a boy, in stages, into a lizard "in front of a babysitter. Every time she left the room, or he went to the bathroom, he'd get more prosthetics put on his face. He'd go back to bed, and she'd come back and go, 'Oh, he looks a little sick.' He'd come back in the bathroom again, and we'd add something, like contact lenses, and he'd go back to bed. The poor woman thought he was the devil and she ran out of the house.

"I had a 12-year-old girl we wanted to put a mask on that made her look like she had no face, which means she couldn't really breathe through the mask. We had to create a rig for her to breathe through, then we had to put her in it and hide her in a room to play a joke on a real person. The gag was a hidden camera prank on a babysitter. The mark goes away, comes back to check on her, and the little girl with no face appears behind her (via a spinning bookcase). It all had to happen in live time in less than a couple of minutes. Getting a 12-year-old into a rig where she couldn't breathe, couldn't see, and couldn't get herself into place was a challenge."

BASQUIAT (1996)
Licensed from MIRAMAX / Ronald Grant Archive / Alamy Stock Photo

Creating Between Gigs

During her early comedy years, Jennifer was also involved in several film projects. One of her favorites was working with David Bowie on the film *Basquiat* (1996) as department head and makeup effects supervisor. The film is the story of Jean-Michel Basquiat, a young black artist from Brooklyn of Haitian and Puerto Rican descent. He came into notoriety in Manhattan during the 1970s doing graffiti, which eventually led to an international exhibition of his neo-expressionistic paintings. He died in 1988 at the age of 27 from a heroin overdose. In the film, David Bowie played Andy Warhol, the famous modern artist who was friend and mentor to Basquiat. Jennifer worked with Bowie transforming him into Warhol. At the time of this interview David Bowie had just passed away.

"Creating with him was definitely one of the highlights of my life. I could probably almost stretch it, and put him into a mentor place, because he...I will try not to cry. He's just very inspiring. We jived creatively. He was just one of those people for me. Watching him as a person who's gone through a lot in his life, and to see where he was creatively, how he never stopped creating, I related to that. Like Bowie I'm one of those people that if I don't create then I know I'll die, so I have to keep creating."

Other movie projects include: department head on *The Tic Code* (1999), makeup artist on *Gone in 60 Seconds* (2000) and *The Mexican* (2001), and special makeup effects artist on *Bad Boy* (2002), *Highway* (2002), *Indiana Jones and the Kingdom of the Crystal Skull* (2008), *Star Trek Into Darkness* (2013), and *Guardians of the Galaxy* (2013).

Picking and Choosing Work

Jennifer rarely says no to a job offer, which is why she is one of the few makeup artists who works almost 100% of the time. She takes jobs that are interesting and challenging because she wants to do them. "I don't really work. I get to do what I like to do and get paid for it. That's why I don't think I'm working. I think I've only worked, if I add it all up, probably a couple of years, because the rest of it has all been fun.

But, given an unlimited budget and time, Jennifer would like to produce a Broadway show, harking back to her *Rocky Horror* experience in front of a live audience. Or, "It would be incredibly satisfying to be partly responsible for creating some major illusions for a big film. Big enough meaning a decent time and budget so we could use cutting edge technology and have the time to perfect something."

On with the Show

In 2016, Jennifer worked on *Westworld*, a television series based on the 1973 science fiction Western film based on the book by Michael Crichton. The TV re-imagining takes full advantage of 2016 makeup technology to depict the violence of the Wild West with white-hatted good guys, black-hatted bad guys, and comely saloon girl hookers. The humans live out their fantasies interacting savagely with androids until the androids turn on the humans.

Human Vase
Used with Permission of Jennifer Aspinall

"It was very inspiring working on *Westworld*. There were a lot of amazing, creative people working on that show - makeup, hair, costumes, everything. That was really a lot of fun, to be in the mix with a lot of what I consider really incredibly talented people. I'm just really lucky, knock on wood, that I keep doing it."

And More Work...

As if she isn't busy enough, Jennifer also has two other businesses.

The fanciful side of Jennifer creates living art through a company founded with a friend, Alison Franchi, called *Human Vases*. They cover a model with elaborate body paint, prosthetics, or stones and incorporate flowers; the model is the vase.

Her other business is selling her specialty *Skin Saver Barrier Lotion*, that she created to protect her actors; it is also useful for gardeners, doctors, or anyone who can benefit from extra skin protection.

Jennifer is energetic and devoted to her art. She has committed her life to creating things without putting a plan together; she trusts the universe will provide what she needs to have a happy, fulfilled, creative life. "Art is the crux of all this."

OUTTAKES:

On The Evolution of the Industry:

"The whole industry, television, film is changing. We are in a time period right now where the paradigm is changing dramatically. And changing fast!

"I think there are a few main factors attributed to this shift. We are seeing the way we watch entertainment change. People don't watch TV anymore. They don't tune in on a weekly basis like they used to. I'm not even sure they go to the movies as much. They watch on their computers or their phones. Whenever and wherever they want. This can be very exciting but also a little scary as a working professional. This has opened up the field for a lot of content; however, many productions are being done on very low budgets and many are non-union.

"In an effort to unionize this new medium, the union has been forced to create extremely low budget contracts to accommodate these low budgets. I believe, as the Internet becomes a more established viewing base (and it probably will be by the time people are reading this book), the production budgets will increase as the desire for better production increases. Unfortunately, the union contracts will have already been in place and I'm not sure we will be able to get our hourly wages back up to what they have been in the past. This has been happening with TV and film contacts as well. Kind of sad.

"I've also seen the perceived value of makeup shift over my many years in the business. It feels like producers, or the corporations that produce, at this point in time don't see the value of what a makeup artist brings to a production and don't want to pay for it. I think there is a combination of factors that have lead to this. It could be young producers and business men have no attachment to a system that has been in place since the studios ruled Hollywood; it could be that the technology, ever-changing and developing, can tweak effects in post, so there is less need for a live makeup artist. Or it could be a trend towards grittier, more organic 'no makeup' looks, or it could be that the market is over-saturated with makeup artists, driving competition to lower the costs. Or it could be just good, old-fashioned greed! Whatever the reason, makeup artists have fallen down the food chain. Or maybe it's just the circle of life. It doesn't really matter, the good will survive and the mediocre and the bad won't. They'll find something else to do with their lives and hopefully, they'll be happy.

"I'm not sure if it's because budgets have gone down, but I've also felt the value of quality shift. I feel like the level of quality is suffering. It seems like people are willing to accept less quality as long as it is done in the time allotted (which is usually short) and done under budget. No time to make illusions from scratch or money for test make ups, that's for sure. As an artist this is incredibly frustrating. But sometimes it forces us to think outside the box, so maybe all is well. lol

"It's going to be interesting to see what will end up happening for us in the makeup industry in the next 20 years. Schools should have a disclaimer saying, 'The job you're training for might be dead in the next 20 years, so you might want to re-think it.' Just kidding, I don't actually believe the job category will disappear, but it is changing. Which just makes it more important that we all become adaptable, keep our skill sets current, and keep our attitudes positive."

Authors' Note: In the interest of full disclosure, Jennifer Aspinall is a Trustee of IATSE, The International Alliance of Theatrical Stage Employees, Local 706.

On Conflicts and Choices:

"Making a choice between home, motherhood, business, career, all of that, I don't feel like I had to. I didn't make it because I feel I was living my course. I was lucky enough to find someone who came in and went into the groove with me. It seemed like, that is what I am and this is what I do, and anybody who gets involved with me is going to have to understand what I am."

"I never sat down and made a conscious choice. I was lucky enough to start doing this when I was nine-years-old and I just haven't stopped. So here I am, 40 years later, and still doing it. I'm very blessed to keep doing it."

Catching Up!

We interviewed Jennifer on February 11, 2016. Here's her letter about her work since then:

"I, and my team, got nominated for an International Guild Award for *Walk The Prank*. We lost, but it was great to be included.

Westworld won an International Guild Award. Although, I was not on the ballot I was very proud to have been part of Christian Tinsley's team.

We shot the second season of the hit Disney show *Walk the Prank*, which wrapped in April. This season included many more makeup effect illusions; some of which I can't believe Disney approved! In August we will be going back to shoot the third season.

I worked as a Makeup and Special Effects Artist on *Skull Island* (2017)

When *Westworld* comes back in July (2017), I will be helping out as much as I can before returning to *Walk the Prank.*

Alison and I are continuing to create *Human Vases*. Most recently, we did *vases* for a party at MGM honoring Rob Lowe and a rose festival at Descanso Gardens in Pasadena. We are also working with a charity in downtown LA and the Descanso Gardens to bring our art and passion for creating to underprivileged kids.

Skin Saver Barrier Lotion is slowly but surely growing. We will be adding a sun block in the upcoming months, making it the ultimate skin protector!"

Human Vase
Used with Permission of Jennifer Aspinall

Promotional makeup for Jennifer's Skin Saver
Barrier Lotion
Used with Permission of Jennifer Aspinall

For more of Jennifer's Credits, visit:
www.jenniferaspinall.com
www.imdb.com

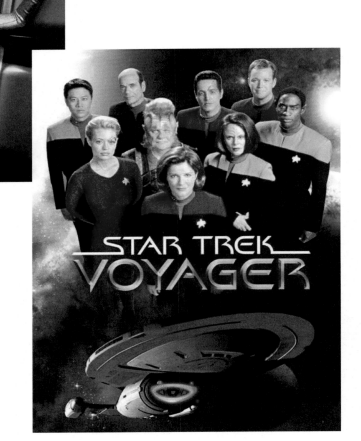

1996
EMMY AWARD
OUTSTANDING MAKEUP
FOR A SERIES

SEVEN OF NINE STAR TREK: VOYAGER (1995)   JERI RYAN
Licensed from AF archive / Alamy Stock Photo

Tina Kalliongis-Hoffman

I love the art of makeup so much. You have no idea.
When I met my husband, I told him, 'This is my first love. You know that, right?'
He said, 'I know.'

Tina Kalliongis-Hoffman is a daughter of Greece, the land of art and knowledge, beauty and passion, heroes and heroines. She is at once a passionate artist and a humble heroine, a woman of endless positive energy, a defender of children, a woman who forges her own path.

The Odyssey Begins

"I remember the exact moment I realized what makeup is. You know how little kids sit in front of the TV, two inches away? I was four or five years old, watching **The Munsters**, and I realized Grandpa's nostrils were not real. They must not have painted it perfectly because I could see they were painted to look bigger. I started noticing those little things and they started growing on me. I remember as a child, getting into trouble because I was always doodling on people's photos, changing how they looked and ruining the photos."

While her imagination was changing how people looked, Tina's family emphasized the academics. The family moved to New York from Athens to ensure all four children had every educational opportunity. While she was a good student and committed to her academics, when Tina got her first job at the age of 16 the first thing she bought with her money was a Bob Kelly Disguise Kit. "You know, those kits that came with some crepe wool and crème

THE MUNSTERS (1964) AL LEWIS
AF archive / Alamy Stock Photo

color sticks." But having the Disguise Kit wasn't enough for Tina. "I went up to Bob Kelly's Cosmetics and I met Bob Kelly. That opened a whole new world to me, meeting him."

"Art was never encouraged in my house. I was always pushed to be academic. My family expected me to go to college and become a chemist. So, I found my own way." Following her parent's wishes, Tina attended Adelphi University in Long Island, New York, and studied chemistry. But after classes every day she went into the City and worked at Bob Kelly's. "I don't have any formal training, but he taught me everything about makeup and how to ventilate hairpieces. He was very patient with me. He would introduce me to makeup artists who would come in to purchase and order supplies and he'd say, 'Teach her how to do this. Teach her how to do that.' I was very fortunate that I had some amazing makeup artists that taught me and believed in me."

When she was 17, Tina also started face painting for $25 a face to augment the pre-packaged costumes available at Halloween. "You know, those *Rubie's* costumes? I would do the face paint to spruce them up. That gave me the face-painting bug. **The Munsters** and face-painting opened the door to another new world for me."

"Still, at that point, makeup was just a hobby, because I was going to be a chemist. This was an after-school job." But Bob Kelly had a vision and understood Tina's talents. "He had a makeup lab and introduced me to his chemist. I started working with him [the chemist] actually making the makeup. One thing led to another. Artists would come in and ask, 'We need such-and-such to do so-and-so.' I would help them develop it and show them how to use it. They started saying, 'Oh, no. You just come in and do it.' That's how I started going on-set and working." Her work fulfilled the requirements for union membership and in 1986 Tina joined the New York makeup union. "My studies in chemistry help me even today with the new silicones and gelatins. It definitely comes into play. Bob Kelly was a major influence in my life."

The Siren's Call...Hollywood

Even though Tina was working as a union makeup artist in New York, the industry was going through a dry spell in the early 1990s. Kelly encouraged her to go west, to Los Angeles, to find work. So, Tina started calling around to makeup artists in LA and telling them, "I'm available. I'll do anything."

She got an interview with John Caglione and became a lab rat. "He taught me how to make molds in the shop. He let me hang out." Working in Caglione's shop, Tina learned the process of creating a character from the beginning and then was able to practice the whole craft: taking the life-cast, sculpting, molding, and finally, applying the piece. Caglione introduced Tina to his foam-runner, Donna Drexler, who taught her how to run foam; thereafter, "I made my living running foam."

"The makeup artists that I work with, the ones I admire the most, have one thing in common: they don't just apply makeup. They know the process. They know the whole process. I think those are the stronger makeup artists. They follow the whole makeup from the start. Not necessarily making it themselves, but being involved in that process somehow. I think that's pretty major."

Tina's favorite projects at Caglione's shop were assisting Drexler running foam appliances for *Chaplin* (1992) and assisting Caglione on a *Fanta* commercial where "we took someone who was alive and made them look like a statue. It was fun because I worked with a lot of different mediums, used different textures, and helped John apply the appliances."

"I've been very lucky with the people around me, people I really respect. I got to learn from the ground up and truly grow as an artist." Tina worked non-union gigs as well as doing lots of lab work, which kept her busy. She got into the LA union Local 706 working with Todd McIntosh on a show, *Great Scott!* (1992), with Tobey Maguire and Kevin Connolly, which flipped right before it wrapped. The Muse of Luck continued to smile on her with her next job.

Lured to the Heavens

After getting into Local 706, Tina got a call from her friend at the union, Jerry Quist, who sent her over to work for Michael Westmore on *Star Trek: The Next Generation.* "He needed a body to do clean up."

"Michael Westmore was my next mentor; he became like a daddy to me. When I started at *Star Trek*, I was 21, but I was 21 from a Greek household, which is like 15. I was very young and I knew makeup. But he was tough on me and he re-taught me how to do everything, refine everything." Tina committed to learning all she could from Westmore, which included watching him apply the makeups and then critique them the next day. Every day he would watch dailies. "It was the favorite part of my day. I'd go up and have lunch in his office while he'd watch the dailies and analyze my makeups. I learned a lot from those critiques.

"There is so much more to our job than just makeup. We deal with actors and other makeup artists and production. I didn't just watch Westmore doing makeup, I watched everything he did, including how he worked with production and how he dealt with actors. I learned a lot more than makeup from Michael Westmore. He's definitely someone I hold very, very close to my heart because of that."

Tina worked as a makeup artist with Westmore on most of the *Star Trek* films: *Star Trek V: The Final Frontier* (1989), *Star Trek VI: The Undiscovered Country* (1991), *Star Trek: Generations* (1994), *Star Trek: First Contact* (1996), *Star Trek: Insurrection* (1998), *Star Trek: Nemesis* (2002).

From 1995-2001, Tina worked on the television show *Star Trek: Voyager* as makeup artist for Jennifer Lien as Kes and Jeri Ryan as Seven of Nine. She found both the makeups for Lien and Ryan had similar challenges: Lien's character, Kes, had latex ears that blended along her jawline and ended mid-jaw; Seven of Nine, Ryan's Borg character, was originally introduced with some major Borg appliances that were eventually reduced to a brow-piece and hand appliances painted to look like metallic and electrical components. These makeups were complicated because the edges had to blend without a trace where the appliances overlapped smooth, beautiful skin. The work on *Star Trek: Voyager* was continually challenging, since once Tina finished working on her principals she would move on to the various guest aliens for the day. "The challenge of working on *Star Trek* is that you have people wearing prosthetics playing against people who're not in prosthetics and you still have to

STAR TREK: VOYAGER (1995) JERI RYAN (SEVEN OF NINE)
Licensed from AF archive / Alamy Stock Photo

STAR TREK: VOYAGER (1995) JENNIFER LIEN (KES)
Licensed from AF archive / Alamy Stock Photo

make the aliens look as realistic and organic as the humans!"

In 1996, Tina won an Emmy award for *Outstanding Makeup on a Series* for *Star Trek: Voyager*, Episode "*Threshold,*" which she shares with department head and designer, Michael Westmore, as well as the other talented makeup artists on the team. Tina has been nominated six other times for *Star Trek*, once in 1994 for *Star Trek: The Next Generation*, twice for *Star Trek: Deep Space Nine* in 1994 and 1999, and three more times for *Star Trek: Voyager* in 1995, 2000, and 2001.

Westmore and *Star Trek* played other significant roles in Tina's life as well. Tina met her husband, Key Costumer Matthew A. Hoffman, working on *Star Trek*; when they got engaged, the first person she told was Westmore. "He was also the first person I went to when I got pregnant because I had my kids during *Star Trek*. I was going to quit the business when I had kids, but they gave me an office, actually Michael's old office, which they turned into a nursery for me. That was pretty major and forward-thinking. I brought my baby every single day, did makeup, and never had to stop working."

Having her baby along with her at work had some interesting ramifications later for her daughter. "Marissa was graduating from high school and needed to bring in baby pictures for her yearbook. We looked and looked and couldn't find any baby pictures where she wasn't being held by aliens. I remember her saying, 'Why can't I have normal parents like all the other kids?' Every picture we had she was in the arms of one alien or another."

Baby Marissa with Neelix (Ethan Phillips)
Used with permission of Tina Kalliongis-Hoffman

"My first day, all Michael needed was a body, anyone would do. If someone could carry a Kleenex, that was good enough. He just needed someone for cleanup. I came into work one day and I never left. 10 years later, I was still there. He kept me busy every single day which was great. You know what? When he hires you on *Star Trek*, 'you move up from clean-up.' That's what he said, and that's where I grew. I grew as a makeup artist and as a person." Tina stayed with the *Star Trek: Voyager* until the series ended. By the time *Star Trek: Enterprise* began she had committed to other work.

FIREFLY (2002) Photo 12 / Alamy Stock Photo

Growing Beyond *Star Trek*

After *Star Trek: Voyager* wrapped in 2001, Tina worked as makeup artist on two films in 2002, *Minority Report* and *Star Trek: Nemesis*. She then did television's *Firefly* (2002-2003, 14 episodes), and the follow-up film, *Serenity* (2005), where she reunited with fellow *Star Trek* alumnus Camille (Calvet) Della Santina. *Star Trek* (2009), the film reboot of the original TV series, followed.

After working in sci-fi for so many years, Tina switched it up by working on the TV legal drama *The Lyon's Den* (2003, 13 episodes), the film comedy, *The Santa Clause 3: The Escape Clause* (2006), the TV mystery-thriller series

Vanished (2006, 13 episodes), and the crime drama *Bones* (2008-2009, six episodes).

In 2007, Tina started her tenure on *NCIS* as special effects makeup artist and has worked on the show for the past 10 seasons. "The jobs that I take, I need to be growing. I've done the alien thing, the monster thing, the fantasy thing, and character work. With *NCIS*, I'm in my medical phase. Every episode, I'm researching. I'm talking to medical people. I need that. I need that for my makeup."

NCIS is a crime drama involving autopsies and injuries that change weekly, which makes the job ever-challenging. Tina's process begins with reading the writer's draft then meeting with the writer. "We talk about the script, what they want, and how severe that week's injury will be." Meanwhile, when the actor is cast, she immediately sends them for life-casting of whatever body part is necessary. From there, she puts a budget together of everything the episode will need and then submits it to the unit production manager. A few days later, she'll attend a production meeting with the producer, writer, and director, and "we'll decide what we're actually going to do, talk about budget and what we need to do next. After a couple more days, production 'passes' on the show and then I can actually get started getting things ready." Once the show passes, prosthetics are created according to Tina's instructions. The day of the shoot, finished appliances are delivered onset. "We don't have the luxury of makeup tests on the show. We just have to go."

NCIS (2016) MARK HARMON, BRIAN DIETZEN, EMILY WICKERSHAM, DAVID MCCALLUM
Licensed from AF archive / Alamy Stock Photo

Tina has a library of medical reference materials, books, journals, encyclopedias, but what she enjoys most is working with medical professionals. "I love collaborating with the coroners and the medical teams to get things done and make them realistic. But, when it comes to realism, we must balance what CBS will allow. When something is too realistic, we have to adjust it to meet standards."

NCIS has many scenes in the morgue where victims of burns or drownings or stabbings or shootings are laid out on the slab. Tina works with Matthew Mungle's lab for creating prosthetics with life-like injuries. "We send our actors over to him and he creates the special prosthetics for us. He's also been doing *CSI* and other injuries shows, so he has a good stock of things that can fill in at the last minute. He's good about giving us what we need."

"I love getting letters from the medical world. *NCIS* is huge, especially in Europe, and I love getting letters from the people who watch it and see the realistic work we do."

A Good Crew Makes for Smooth Sailing

Sometimes the best laid plans go awry, which can happen for any number of reasons such as time limitations, budget, actor availability, or last-minute changes. To accommodate these unknown factors, Tina makes sure the people she hires on the show are well-rounded in all areas of makeup.

"I call in people that can pull something out of the hat if they need to. I have a handful of makeup artists I always use and they all have one thing in common: they started out in a shop. They have the knowledge to build stuff. Things happen. So many times makeup artists come on shows and something goes wrong, maybe an appliance doesn't fit. They need to know how to build and how to problem-solve."

Tina used an example of an episode with a Vietnam vet who, it was decided with two days' notice, was supposed to have a blown-off leg. With no time to have it cast and have an appliance made, "We, me and the makeup artists I'd called in, were able to build something out of our kits. I had skilled people with shop training who knew how to build stuff. We made something and built it rather than have an appliance handed over to us premade to glue on and just paint."

For Tina, her makeup artists also have to have talents beyond doing makeup, they need to know how to make someone feel comfortable in makeup. "I know some very talented makeup artists who come in and are Prima Donnas. I can't and won't call them in. When an actor comes in in the morning, we are the first face they see. We can make or ruin their day. It's very, very important. It's not just about putting the makeup on them. They need to feel comfortable. They need to feel welcome. They need to know it's a safe place being in the makeup trailer. They need to know that we are on their side to help them develop the character, especially if they are in prosthetics.

"I know if a problem arises, like an actor is allergic to a certain product, I need an artist that can build something right on him using a different product. I don't want my department to be known for holding up shooting. If we are not noticed, we are doing our jobs.

"I've seen makeup artists putting makeup on someone who's very uncomfortable in it. I've seen people in full-face masks that have a complete meltdown. Keeping the actors calm, working with them, helping them, that part of it is very, very, important. Don't just put the makeup on. Their facial expressions are very important to them. Involve them in the process. Ask them, 'What are you going to be doing today?' Involving the actor makes them more comfortable and they're going to be able to sell the makeup with confidence."

There is something more important to Tina than whether the makeup is good. She doesn't want the work or the techniques to stand out; for Tina, the focus needs to be on the overall effect. "If someone says to me, 'I like your beauty makeup,' I don't like that compliment. If someone says, 'That's a beautiful girl!' Now I know I did my job. The same thing goes when I do effects. If someone says, 'That's a really cool makeup!' That bugs me. If someone says, "Wow! That's a cool monster!" I am satisfied because people forget that it's a makeup. That's when I know I've done my job."

Fair Winds and Following Seas

Tina has been working primarily in television for the past 19 years to be able to be at home with her family. "I wanted to stay in town, but I wanted to work. Having the security of TV and something new each day is wonderful. I'm very fortunate to be in that position. I like the process. I like the 'get it done quick.' Rush, rush, rush, I like that."

By the end of 2017, Tina's daughter and son both will have graduated from high school, "I've been saying, 'Now is when I'm going to start working on my career.' I keep telling them, 'You just wait. It's my time next.' I was fortunate enough to have had hands-on training, maybe I'll go to makeup school."

Whatever is on the horizon for Tina, she knows one thing for sure, "I want to do makeup every single day of my life."

OUTTAKES:

On Working Together:

"You can't live on an island and do makeup on a show and that's it. You need to collaborate with your fellow artists. You need to have relationships with them. I think, honestly, that is major."

On Interns:

"I know there is incredible talent out there and a lot of them have gone to makeup school. But I don't use interns because I don't want to put my makeup artists in that position. It's not fair."

On Design:

"Sometimes if things are too realistic for CBS, I need to do some re-design work. Let's say I might have a big cut across someone's face that needs to work for five days. You need to look at the actor, see how their face moves. You can't just put it anywhere because the makeup needs to work 16 hours that day."

On Forging a Career:

"I made my own roadmap. I knew very early on that I needed to work harder so they would see past me being a woman. I never had any bad experiences, but I know I had to do that early on. I knew that's just how it had to be and that's what I was going to do."

"I think there are some people who still believe that a good FX artist is male and a good beauty makeup artist is female. I think that gap is closing. I think women are closing that gap."

Catching Up!

We interviewed Tina on February 20, 2016. Since then, she's been working on

NCIS
2016-17 & 2017-18 Seasons

1
a film directed by Andrzej Kozlowski
Makeup Department Head

For more of Tina's Credits visit: www.imdb.com

LEADING LADIES OF MAKEUP EFFECTS

Emerging Artists

Emerging Artists

The idea of a section focusing on Emerging Artists in the Makeup Effects Industry sounded like a fabulous addition for this book. But once we began considering how to make a selection, the task was more daunting than culling down the 750+ Emmy nominees and winners!

As mentioned at the start of this book, the number of young women graduating from makeup schools, globally, is astounding; they are one of the major impetuses for this book. But choosing Emerging Artists from the sheer number of women entering the Makeup Effects Industry was like grabbing a drop of water from a tidal wave headed for shore! How could we choose the few drops that exemplify the oncoming wave? We were drowning before we could swim.

Like any grand project, it's about setting parameters. We decided to cull out any award nominees, those Ladies had already climbed high enough to be acknowledged for their work. Next, we decided to narrow the field from global to local, meaning local to us in Southern California. Then, we chose to exempt students or graduates without some major experience beyond schooling. What about Local 706 Union membership? Or union members who were working and had never been nominated for an award? The waves were rising again.

Ideally, we wanted Emerging Artists who had some major experience working in non-union independent film, or TV, or internet media and had recently, or were on the brink of, entering the professional world with union membership.

Our five Ladies have met these criteria and are emerging into the professional makeup industry. Ordered alphabetically, our Emerging Artist Leading Ladies are Carleigh Herbert, Mo Meinhart, KC Mussman, Erica Preus, and Chloe Sens. We had been following the careers of these five young women long before the book was conceived; the depth and breadth of their work demonstrates talent, passion, and drive, the likes of which led us to believe they may be the award-winners of the future.

All of our Emerging Artists were interviewed in early 2016 and, since then, their careers have exploded. Therefore, their chapters begin with their "*Catching Up!*" information so our readers can see where they are now, then read about how they arrived.

Keeping up with these Ladies has been like wading into a rushing river headed to sea...but it was worth it!

And now...introducing our Emerging Artist Leading Ladies....

Catching Up!

We interviewed Carleigh on March 6, 2016; here's her *Catching Up!* letter:

"Dear Pat & Gary,

Since I was interviewed, I've been up to a few things including department heading several projects back-to-back.
- I've completed all 20 episodes of the final season of *Teen Wolf*
- I've had an amazing time doing Stan Lee's makeup for *The Extraordinary Stan Lee Tribute*
- I've finished filming on the MGM remake of the 1980s feature film, *Valley Girl: The Musical*

Carleigh's Lucifer Falling (2017)
at Monsterpalooza for PPI
Used with Permission of PPI

All of these projects were possible because of hard working teams and awesome creatives who allowed me to be a part of their vision.

A fun moment for me this year was a makeup I created, my version of *Lucifer Falling*, for the Premiere Products, Inc. (PPI) booth at Monsterpalooza. I designed, life-cast, and roughed up some sculptures to hand off to awesome FX artists to do the finishing touches, clean it all up, and do the lab work. Creature creation and designing is a world I would like to move into, and this makeup was extremely challenging and rewarding. Actress Amanda Hall portrayed Lucifer with full scale wings, silicone back piece, collar bone appliances, face appliances, and various wounds. Frederick Faith created the costume. Eryn Krueger Mekash saved the day and jumped in, op-site tape and all, and helped me glue down and get the makeup started. I'm really grateful to PPI for allowing me to be a part of their lineup, working alongside artists who continue to push me and support me. I'm already in the works for another stage of this makeup that I will hopefully get to apply at another makeup convention.

Carleigh's Lucifer Falling (2017)
at Monsterpalooza for PPI
Used with Permission of PPI

The past year and a half has been a complete whirlwind. I went from heading smaller feature films to heading television shows and larger features, which was an incredible growth period for me. I've gained more respect and understanding for all my relationships including those with actors, directors, and other makeup artists.

I have been enjoying the process of helping bring characters to life. This is something I have always dreamed of doing. The work is hard, the hours can be stressful, things and people are in constant demand and change. But it's all worth it. When you create something that fits right and it lands correctly on the screen, that's the moment I remember why we do what we do and why we push ourselves so hard to pursue this career.

Currently, I am lucky enough to be working for and with Eryn Krueger Mekash, Mike Mekash, Kim Ayers, Silvi Knight, Dave Anderson, and team on Season 7 of *American Horror Story*. I am also gearing up to start a Marvel pilot that will fall into a full season. This year I have also received my first Emmy nomination for *Outstanding Makeup For A Limited Series or Movie (Non Prosthetic)* for *American Horror Story: Roanoke.* I still can't believe I get to work with this group of artists, let alone be on the nomination roster with them. I'll be forever grateful for the opportunity to be a part of that show. Someone pinch me.

Now off to research some comics..."

- Carleigh Herbert

CARLEIGH HERBERT

It's weird how things always end up happening and unfolding upon you.
The thing is, when something life-changing happens, you've just got to keep going
because you never know what's going to be on the other side of that.

In 2016, Carleigh Herbert became head of department on **Teen Wolf** as it entered its sixth season on MTV. Carleigh, with a shock of pink hair and a devilish smile, has an energy which is barely contained in her lithe and wiry frame. Her apartment reflects her personality: comfortable and eclectic, full of projects-in-progress, a human anatomy textbook, a worktable stacked with pictures and drawings, two guitars, walls filled with artwork ranging from Mike Mekash personalized skate boards to monster silhouettes in color and black and white, all capturing both the beautiful and the horrific. Her current life is not one she ever imagined. "I threw myself into pursuing the makeup world, so I wasn't really sure what direction I was going or what I was getting myself into."

She's a Dance Machine

During her high school years, Carleigh discovered her passion for dance. It was the only thing she ever planned to do with her life. Specializing in postmodern jazz and lyrical, she attended Cal State Long Beach and majored in dance. And then her plans were interrupted.

Carleigh developed a schwannoma, a benign tumor made up of a bundle of nerve cells, which began growing and pushing against her esophagus causing breathing difficulties. "At 19, I had to have neuro-surgery."

"I couldn't breathe. I had to get it taken out immediately. It was also one of those things where they had to clip pre-existing nerves, which could have changed the way my body worked. I could have ended up with a droopy face or a seizure disorder. They did their best when I was under to pinpoint what every nerve connects to, but you just never know. Within a couple weeks' time, my body configuration changed.

My pupils don't dilate properly now and my sweating is off, so being overly physical creates difficulty. Basically, after six months of going back and trying the dance thing, I realized I couldn't move the way I wanted to anymore."

Carleigh was down, but she wasn't out. She needed a plan, a goal, so over the next semester break she went home to San Diego and began wracking her brain: what could she do instead of dance? Weighing the options, "the only thing that really clicked and stuck with me was doing makeup for dance productions. I could help create a character or mood for the audience before the performer even took the first step." That way she could still be in the dance world while learning and pursuing a new art form. Being a career-driven person, she immediately started researching makeup schools.

The Leap into MUD

Within a month, Carleigh completed her research, took out a loan, and enrolled in the beauty, hairstyling, and character training classes at Makeup Designory (MUD) in Burbank. The plan: to design makeup for dance productions. "When beginning school, I didn't understand the impact prosthetics and lab work had in the dance and makeup world, so I hadn't enrolled in those classes. Now that I've been working as a professional, I see how knowing every aspect of makeup can influence other makeup styles."

Carleigh was faced with some initial challenges, first of all, being up close and personal with strangers. "I'd never touched anybody else's face until I went to makeup school, so that was a huge test for me. Touching faces, moving into people's intimate spaces, and being comfortable." In the character course, she was introduced to out-of-kit effects, and "I started getting into the gore and the character effects like dirt and wounds. I wasn't one of those kids that watched movies and knew all of the monsters. Dance and performing had led me to makeup. I had always found beauty in the darker things, so changing someone's face dramatically and making the audience uncomfortable was something that clicked with me. The more I work, the more I fall in love with the movies and the filmmaking process, which still holds true today." By the time she was finished at MUD, Carleigh had a new path, film.

Student Films to Syfy Channel

After leaving MUD, Carleigh began working on student and independent films such as *Escaping Grey* (2008), *Theo* (2010), and *Peach Plum Pear* (2011) to gain experience. "It's a route that artists I respect have taken. Being brand new to an industry that requires years of learning, messing up, trying new techniques, and honing skills laid a firm foundation for me as an artist. I believe it's necessary to work for less, do the small jobs, and start gaining experience. To me, true artists aren't handed their careers. School is great and it gives you the basics, but I got the best experience doing student and low-budget films, making mistakes and learning how to do better." While working on the indie films, Carleigh also attended Santa Monica College where she got her cosmetology license which expanded her skillset and made her more versatile.

By working on those low-budget movies, Carleigh got involved with the company known for the *Sharknado* films and met Line Producer, Devin Ward. "He does a lot of cool indie movies and projects. He gave me my start as department head. When I started working with him on Syfy Channel movies, he told me, 'I want you to department head.' 'Okay. Yeah.' He just threw me into it."

"Those Syfy Channel days were so important because I had the power to play. I knew it wasn't always going to look great, but I learned so much from it. Like the first time I pumped blood or saw a throat cut, 'Oh my god, this is amazing!' Even though it was rigged incorrectly and looked like hell. Stuff like that was so exciting. It's how I started learning what I was doing wrong and what I needed to know more about."

She started department heading on films such as *Zombie Apocalypse* (2011) and *Nazis at the Center of the Earth* (2012) for Ward. These films were "much smaller than union stuff, but everything still applies to the biggest productions. Every day was a different challenge, and learning what is right and wrong is a very intense thing when, every day, whatever you create will be sent to camera. No pressure at all!"

Working on **Nazis at the Center of the Earth**, Carleigh learned more than she expected. "It was the hardest indie film I ever worked on. I had never created prosthetics or blood tubing gags. I just went for it, reading books and referencing professional makeups. That movie showed me I knew nothing about the prosthetic process, and that experience led me to seek work in a makeup FX shop to learn the ropes behind the scenes."

Getting into a Shop

Taking what she had learned in makeup school and her experiences in low-budget films,

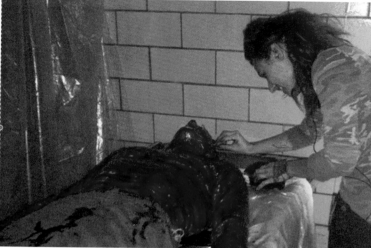

Nazi's at the Center of the Earth (2012)
Used with Permission of Carleigh Herbert

Carleigh set out to get shop experience, which she found when she met and started working with Kenny Myers.

"That was my introduction to the professional makeup world. It was really cool working in a makeup lab under artist Kenny because that was the first time I was around real prosthetics. I got to see someone create multi-piece prosthetics and layer them together. I wasn't sitting there with third degree [a two-part silicone product] or off-the-shelf foam prosthetics trying to make do. I saw how things were supposed to be done. I got to life cast, I got to see how things were sculpted, I got to see how things were molded, and see it done the right way. I think that was what pushed my training as an artist and got me looking at things differently."

Working at the shop, Carleigh had some unique opportunities. "It's funny, I met a lot of well-known effects people when they came into the shop and saw me scrubbing floors; nowadays I get to work on-set with them, which is totally crazy." Working with Myers, who created the highly popular makeup line Skin Illustrator, Carleigh got the chance to assist some of these big-name makeup artists at Monsterpalooza, a monster-themed convention.

"[PPI] started bringing me to all these conventions and had me help the artists. At Monsterpalooza the PPI station has some of the biggest effects people in the industry. They fly people out from London and all over the world, to do these demos and these artists are incredible. Being able to be that close and that involved with PPI over the years has deepened my skills."

One of Carleigh's favorite makeups she did for PPI in 2014. "I had just started doing FX lab work and they asked, 'Why don't you build your own makeup?' I'm like, 'Okay.' It was the first time I sculpted and did just basic plate molds and a little life cast thing for a makeup that I built for Monsterpalooza. It was a gear girl, the

Carleigh's Gear Girl for PPI at Monsterpalooza (2012)
Used with Permission of PPI

gears were coming out from her chest, which is a simple makeup, but at the time for me it was a huge deal because it was the first time I created it all myself. They gave me a chance. A lot of people have thrown me chances. I've been very lucky."

After two years working for Myers and continuing to freelance on indie films, Carleigh left the shop. She met Chris Gallaher, who was doing the special effects and teeth for *Teen Wolf*. He brought her on as a makeup assistant to help him with setting up and working on small projects for the third season. Her path was ready to turn.

Next Steps and a Bit of Kismet

Working on Syfy and indie films, Carleigh had been collecting hours towards the 60-60-60 requirement (60 days in each of three years within the last five years) to get into the union. By happy happenstance, two films she had worked on flipped (went from non-union to union status). The first was a film for Syfy called *Bigfoot* (2012), and the second was an indie film released as *Angels in Stardust* (2014). With the hours she had already accumulated over three years coupled with the two flips, she was eligible for union membership. Now she had to pay her dues and her mom, Connie Roberts, stepped up to lend her a hand.

"My mom was one of my biggest influences because she was always behind me in everything I did, full force. She supported me as a dancer, she supported me as a makeup artist. She was always there through all the ups and downs of becoming a professional artist. When I was accepted into the union, neither she nor I had the money for the union dues. So she took out loans to help me pay for the first half. She passed away two years ago, but she still remains my biggest hero and inspires me to push forward, to keep climbing."

Now in the union, Carleigh could officially work for Gallaher assisting on the effects side of *Teen Wolf*. In addition to working on *Teen Wolf*, she began keying other shows like *Children's Hospital* and *Gortimer Gibbon's Life on Normal Street*, and she was co-department heading the new *Insidious: Chapter 4* (2018) feature film.

Teen Wolf (2016) Final Season show poster
Used with Permission of Carleigh Herbert

"[Gallaher] was the first person to throw me out there and have me do prosthetics on a TV show. Even though I screwed it up and muddied it up, he gave me more shots and he let me keep going. Then, I started day playing in the makeup department doing beauty makeup. Eventually I moved up to being the full-time third and worked in that capacity for a couple years. At the beginning of this year [2016], the makeup department head position opened up and production decided to play a wild card and bring me up and give me my first union department head job. I started as a makeup assistant for [Gallaher] and now I get to department head next to him, which is pretty wild."

Teen Wolf is a show made up of a large main cast, with many day players, and Carleigh keeps track of several different units going all at the same time. "The makeup changes daily between bloody, sweaty looks and regular makeup looks. Some days we have 20 principal actors, 60 background, stunt doubles, and photo doubles. I've got to be on my game and always ready for what's thrown at me next; it keeps me on my toes." On top of maintaining and establishing new looks and keeping the actors and production happy, she deals with scheduling, hiring additional help, keeping the trailer stocked with products, and attending production meetings. "I can't take all the credit, I have an amazing team with me and great artists that come out and help."

Meeting Heroes

In 2014, Carleigh got a call to work on *AHS: Freakshow* and she got to meet one of her makeup heroes, Eryn Krueger Mekash. "That was probably, still is, one of the biggest moments in my career, meeting all those artists I've known about for years. Going on that show, being flown to New Orleans to be in the effects trailer, that was a huge moment for me. The makeups that I got to do were amazing and fun, and I got to be surrounded by all these artists that were doing all these incredible makeups next to me. Dave Anderson was to the right of me in the trailer, and I was like, 'Don't have a panic attack. You're standing next to Dave Anderson. He's right there.' It was intimidating in the best way. I was just geeking out."

American Horror Story: Roanoke (2017)
Carleigh & Mike Mekash
Used with Permission of Carleigh Herbert

Beside the opportunity to work with Eryn, Carleigh looks up to her as a role model. "She'll answer any question. She's a phone call away and she shares her knowledge. She's also somebody who really brings up her team. I have a lot of respect for that. Obviously, she's an amazing makeup artist, and incredible at what she does, but the way that she runs her team, and the way that she treats people, and the way that she is with her actors, she's who I want to model myself after as a department head."

The Realities of the Biz

Even though she discovered makeup when her dance ambitions were quashed, Carleigh never had any grand illusions. "I'm kind of a weirdo in the sense that I knew it was going to be hard. I had researched the field going into it and I'd read about the lifestyle. I was broke for five years, eating top ramen, wondering if it would ever work out, but I just keep pushing and pushing forward. I work probably 15-16 hour days on average. That kind of lifestyle is something you can't really prepare for. No personal lives. I've always been a lone rider. I have so much respect for people that have children and families and travel home to see their kids on the weekends.

"People see you with celebrities and on all these nice sets and making decent money, but there are only so many people who get to do that. It's really about honing your craft and working your butt off. I always knew it was going to be hard. We're all crazy people. No normal person does this."

Carleigh considers herself very lucky to have moved so quickly along her career path, but some credit should go to her strong, positive attitude, work ethic, and level-headedness. Her first year in the union, Carleigh remembers feeling intimidated. "I didn't walk into it all cocky. 'Oh yeah. I'm in the union, I'm amazing. I got in and I was like, 'Oh, shit. Look at all these people around me who've been doing this for 20 or 30 years, and I'm over here just figuring out who the hell I am.' But it was intimidating in the best way, because it was like, 'You got to get your shit together.'"

"Three years before, I was working on Syfy Channel movies. A year after that, I was scrubbing the effects lab floor, thinking, 'One day I hope I'm back on-set.' Then suddenly, I was in the union, day playing on shows like *AHS*, and now I'm department head on *Teen Wolf*. I still can't even believe it, really."

OUTTAKES:

On Professional Understanding:

"On a film set you're bringing so many different people together. You have grips, you have cameramen, you have art directors, you have people that do props, you're bringing in all these different genres of what we do and mashing them in a group together. It's what makes it so amazing, because you all get to feed off each other and work and learn from each other. But at the same time, sometimes with some people, they brush makeup and hair off, because it's something that they understand the least about."

"The term 'glam squad' makes me want to pull my teeth out. There's nothing wrong with doing beautiful, glamorous makeup. That's all good, but do not refer to me as a 'vanity' if you expect me to come in and sweat them up, make them bleed, do all those things. I'm not a vanity. I'm a makeup artist. I do it all."

On Straight Makeup & Effects:

"When I was in the lab, an artist told me, 'Don't ever let these boys get you down for doing straight make-up, because when you are good at both you will be so much more well-rounded.' They both play into each other. If you know all your techniques of straight makeup, they will help you with your effects makeup, and vice-versa, like the correct placement and the way you highlight and shadow. I think it's good just to be well-rounded in everything."

"I do straight makeup as well. I do both, but I do kind of pride myself on being able to do them both well. The thing that's so weird to me about straight and effects makeup is I find them both difficult in different ways. For effects makeup, it comes more naturally to me. The more comfortable and better I get at straight makeup, the more obsessed I get with it. It's a lot more than a foundation and a blush. Like making a natural look, that's my favorite thing to do, because it's so complicated, with the use of color choices and the way they're blended. On eyes you may use four colors, and on cheeks three colors, but it's all about the way they blend to look natural. It is a total art within itself."

"One thing I don't like is people who bash straight makeup, effects artists who are like, 'I don't need to.' It's like, come on, get your head out of your ass and respect your art. You don't have to go do straight makeup, but at least respect it and know the basics to understand what they're doing is just as important as what you're doing. It's just different, but it all plays together."

On Working in the Boys Club:

"They would joke around with me, giving me shit about being a girl and all that stuff, but it was always playful and it was always fun. I really didn't have it that bad, but I think being the personality type that I am, I don't mind being around all men. I just give them shit back. For me, it was always playful. Will I say that I had to work harder sometimes because I was a girl? Yeah, absolutely, but that's just the way it is."

"As a female artist in a male-dominated industry, I've had the pleasure of working with amazing artists that have never put me down for being a female and embraced women being more dominant in the film and TV world. That being said, I've also worked with artists that have sexualized me, made remarks about me being a girl in effects, or pushed me aside because I'm a girl. I had always ignored those situations, but looking back on parts of my career, especially the beginning, I have been ragged on for my sex and put in unfair positions. I never spoke up because I always wanted to be one of the boys. I love the makeup boys in my industry and am proud to work in a trailer full of men; I'm also proud to be in a trailer full of women."

"I've just always worked my ass off to try and lift as much and do as much and be right there with the guys. I feel like if you want to be respected as one of them, you need to treat yourself at the same level. Maybe that's just kind of the way I was raised into it and just kind of the way I worked through it. I guess, maybe that was my defense mechanism, to be one of the boys."

On More Heroes:

"Lois Burwell is a big role model for me. I haven't had the pleasure of working with her yet, but I've been around her, I watched her do some makeups, and she's just incredible. She has a light touch; she knows exactly what she wants from her subject and from the medium she is using with every brush stroke. She exudes confidence and class and I've never heard one bad thing said about her. Who doesn't love a strong woman who doesn't need to be in your face and ranting on and on about herself? She walks in a room and demands your attention without trying or saying a word."

"Kenny Myers was a huge influence because he introduced me to this whole professional world. Anybody who knows what Kenny knows…he's a crazy perfectionist. He is very detailed and very much 'do it this way,' 'do it that way.' I still get to work with him and it makes me a better artist."

"Mike Mekash is an artist I truly admire, because he's just the coolest guy ever and he's so down-to-earth. The first time I was in the trailer with him, I saw him paint. I was like, 'Oh, my god, I'm obsessed with this guy.' I got to work for him again on Season 6 & 7 of *AHS*, and my adoration grew for the way he is as an artist, the way he plays his makeups, and the way he helps run the show. He's right up there with the director and DP during gags and speciality shots and has a way of improving the way his makeups are shot through an artist's eyes."

On Full Circle:

"I will say what's so cool about having my dance background is that I have been able to work with dancers and do live events, so that's really cool. There's a saying, 'Once a dancer, always a dancer.' It's good to be around it, you feel the energy, it's still a rush. It all comes full circle a little bit."

On Future Goals:

"I am constantly working to become a stronger and more established artist. I would love to continue running shows, getting to work with the artists that inspire me, and putting myself and my art in different mediums to accomplish that."

For more of Carleigh;'s work, visit:
www.carleighherbert.com
www.imdb.com

RBFX Giger Girl Makeup
Used with Permission of Lara Solanski

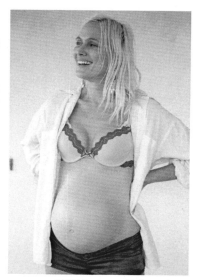

RBFX Pregnant Belly makeup
Used with Permission of Lara Solanski

Catching Up!

We interviewed Mo on February 26, 2017; here's her *Catching Up!* Letter:

"Dear Pat & Gary,

Since we last spoke I've honestly been busier than ever. As of January 2017, I moved into a house and set up a small shop. I don't think I've had a day off since.

My first big job of the year came from seasoned artist Kerrin Jackson. She brought me on as her key for an Indy, LLC production — a horror anthology, which included iconic horror directors such as Mick Garris, Joe Dante, Ryuhei Kitamura, Alejandro Bruges, and David Slade. To make things even better, KNB FX was the shop for the film. Smaller features such as these are tons of work, but also so much fun since we get to work in every department. I applied prosthetics, did beauty makeup, and styled hair. I believe working is always a good thing, but the relationships that develop from each job are of the greatest importance to me. Not only did I grow as an artist working under Kerrin and KNB, but I found an amazing and talented group of individuals who are now my dear friends.

In a Foreign Town (2017)
Two faces of the Showman Actor: Dave Snyder
Used with Permission of Mo Meinhart

From there, I department headed a small period film set in the 1920s freak show circus genre called **In a Foreign Town** with production company Butcher Bird Studios. I was referred to this job by Spectral Motion. For this film, I designed and created a freak show character called "The Showman" from start to finish with fellow artist Tanner White. I also designed the period hair and makeup for the other on-screen talent. I love period projects and the research that goes along with executing the perfect look.

In the last couple of months, I've worked on two back-to-back horror film features as head of special makeup effects for the production company Diablo. Diablo has had several films premiere and sell at Sundance in the last year.

As my new shop continues to grow, I partnered up with friend and fellow artist Tanner White to help me build everything from bodies, blood rigged prosthetics, and character makeups.

In June, I was called to day play for three weeks on **The Walking Dead**. Working with artists like Greg Nicotero, Jake Garber, Kerrin Jackson, Kevin Wasner, Gino Crognale, Lee Grimes, and Chris Nelson was an invaluable experience. I was a sponge soaking up all the years of experience and knowledge these artists have to offer!

Mo modeling Serpentes makeup by Kerrin Jackson
Used with Permission of Brad Stanley Photography

As this year continues to progress, I see nothing but opportunity and new relationships on the horizon. It's a relief to finally see substantial progress in my career as the scale of productions grow; but I never stop learning, no matter the size of the project. It's true what they say, follow your dream, never stop working hard, and anything is possible."

- Mo Meinhart

Mo Meinhart

When I moved to Los Angeles, I didn't know where to start. I didn't know how things worked. I knew I wanted to be part of the industry, so I started asking a lot of questions. My focus was to build quality relationships, learn from my successes and mistakes, and benefit from the experience of others.

Mo bounds over the back of her sofa into a cross-legged sitting position with a warm, bright smile on her face. Tall and athletic, she is enthusiastic, warm, and grounded. "I wish I had a really good story for how I got the name Mo. I was an athlete all my life and I think it came from my coach doing something silly, like calling me 'Mo-lissa' and then everyone started calling me Mo, Mo-girl, Mo-babe, Mo-money. Even my parents call me Mo."

In high school, Mo played volleyball, basketball, and softball. Both her parents and older brother are athletes, "so it just was a natural progression." Her father always told her, "Be proud to be tall." Growing up, going to the gym and getting involved in sports were valuable ways to spend her time. "Athletics promoted good team building, time management, and basically kept me busy." At home, Mo's family encouraged her to explore and find a passion "to do what you want to do." Her mother still rides horses at 65 and her grandmother used to ride motorcycles. "I come from a line of strong women, 'pull-up-your-big-girl-panties-and-straighten-your-crown' types."

Like most younger sisters, Mo often followed her big brother around. Before he found his career as a musician, Michael was an artist who was always drawing. "I thought it was cool. I might've been annoying to him, but he inspired me to get into art, which led to drawing, painting, sculpting, art classes, and eventually, to makeup."

"I have to thank all my friends who were my guinea pigs. They would let me cut their hair and do their makeup. Halloween was a big event for us when I'd create crazy costumes and face paintings. I didn't know that's what I wanted to do for a living, at that time it was just my creative outlet. It was fun." The sports and art classes paid off when Mo was accepted to the University of Toledo, Ohio, as a fine arts major on a volleyball scholarship.

University, Florida, Graphic Design...and Sales?

Being in college, studying fine arts, and playing volleyball worked well for Mo. She found the creativity of the artist and the discipline of the athlete satisfied both sides of her personality. "I was the jock and the artist. I loved it. Athletes have a reputation for being meatheads; I wanted to break that stereotype."

When she had school breaks, Mo enjoyed leaving behind the cold weather of Ohio to visit her grandparents at their condo in Naples, Florida. As graduation approached, Mo needed to find a job, and with a traditional college degree in fine arts it seemed the most practical place to use her skills was in graphic design. Inspired by the artists she studied in school, she considered two options: "I could be a painter, or I could go into an office and work on a computer. The latter seemed a more lucrative choice. Universities have this way of funneling you into a corporate environment. I didn't know there were other options." She moved to the warmer climes of Florida, interned for a short while, and found a graphic design job.

Mo found her interest in graphic design waning when she found she wasn't as creatively fulfilled as she thought she would be. As an entry level graphic designer, she didn't have any creative license. "I made document corrections and followed the designs of the senior artists. I remember thinking, 'I'm going to make how much money? In how many years? Oh, no. No, no.'"

As a young woman in her early twenties trying to make her way in the world, financial success was important to Mo. So, when her graphic design plan went awry, she spent the next two years as a sales representative for Budweiser. "I wasn't a 'Bud girl,' I was a sales rep." Traveling her territory for Budweiser, she built a network of relationships with bar managers and restaurants owners, and "I discovered one of my strengths was creating and maintaining relationships. This proved to be one of the most useful skills I've ever learned."

Selling beer provided a living for Mo until something more lucrative came up in the form of pharmaceutical sales. "I liked the science behind it, so for the next five years I was a pharmaceutical sales rep and I was pretty good at it. I was number one in the nation one year selling drugs." The success she achieved from selling was addicting, but in order to move up the ladder in the pharmaceutical industry, she went back to school and earned a master's degree in business.

During those years when Mo was earning her college degree, working as a graphic designer, selling beer and pharmaceuticals, she also continued to do makeup on the side for fun. Finally Mo realized, "I was financially successful, but unfulfilled. I had an itch that needed to be scratched. I needed to do something creative."

Mo continued to experiment with makeups when a friend, a successful model, introduced her to a photographer who gave her the opportunity to create any makeups she wanted. Through his photography, she saw her work come to life for the first time. "It was magic. I knew then that I wanted to pursue makeup."

"I started experimenting with not only makeup, but different materials. We did one photo shoot where I incorporated latex into the makeup. At that time I didn't know latex should be powdered. When the models posed close to one another they stuck together, when they pulled apart it created strings of latex between them. This was a happy accident, taking the makeup up a level and making the images more captivating. This was the first of many happy accidents I've discovered in makeup. The photographer submitted the photos to magazines and they were published. Together we got some great portfolio pieces."

From Drugs to Makeup

Eventually, Mo was laid off from her pharmaceutical job and started thinking about other career choices. It gave her a chance for a reality check. "Do I keep doing something I'm not passionate about, or dive headfirst into a career that I love?" She had tried graphic design and sales, but she loved doing make-up. "I thought a makeup career was selling makeup behind a counter. So, I started to Google all things makeup, came across *Make-Up Artist Magazine*, got a subscription, and realized, 'Oh my goodness, this is a thing? This is how they do it in film. This is fantastic.' I had this urge, 'I have to do this. If I don't try it, I'm going to regret it.'"

In the meantime, her brother, now a professional musician, had been living in Los Angeles and was pushing Mo to come to California. Having some money saved, coupled with her brother's coaxing, she made a decision: "Okay, screw it. I'm going to change my career. I'm moving to LA and I'm going to find success as a makeup artist."

CMS and Building Networks

Mo moved to LA and found the creative outlet she'd been searching for when she enrolled at Cinema Makeup School (CMS). She took their television and film program which included beauty makeup, hair-styling, and character makeup. She knew she'd made the right move when, at the finish of the program, she was driven to know more about makeup effects. So, she quickly signed up for the special effects program which "was awesome: science, baking, and blood. I loved it." She appreciated the programs at CMS because she received instruction on the most up-to-date techniques and materials from actual working professional artists such as Don Lanning, Mike Spatola, Nelly Recchia, Scott Ramp, and Joel Harlow.

"For character class, Craig Reardon taught us techniques used in earlier film-making. You never know what you're going to have to pull out of your Mary Poppins makeup bag. Scott Ramp and Mike Spatola have become amazing mentors. They've provided opportunities, shared their knowledge, and even opened up shop space, helping me evolve and grow as an artist."

Having had several careers before attending CMS, Mo found that, at 28, "I was that one in class that the younger kids are annoyed by because I was always asking, 'How do you do this?' Or 'How does this work?' And they were like, 'Old person, stop asking so many questions.'"

"I wanted to be immersed in makeup, so I got involved with as many things as I could: assisting teachers, attending seminars, going to makeup conventions, and taking advantage of the many opportunities CMS provides their students. There's nothing like actual experience. I learn by doing."

Mo also began collaborating with her fellow students Chloe Sens, KC Mussman, Melissa Jimenez, Jamie Leodones, and Erica Preus on projects and work. "I started my network at CMS. I work with Erica the most. We're like the dynamic duo. She's my better half. She's talented, composed, genuine, and practical; a real girl's girl. We have fun. I'm fortunate to be surrounded by so many strong and talented women. We look out for one another."

Getting Behind the Makeup...Literally

As Mo worked with her friends on more and more makeup projects, the group eventually talked about who could bring the makeup to life, who could model it correctly. Mo would jump into the fray saying, "'I know exactly how this creature should act, put it on me.' That's how I got started modeling these makeups." Working in collaboration, she found she not only liked being immersed in creating and applying the makeup, she wanted to move with it, play with it, and wear it.

From her modeling experiences, Mo gained interesting insights into performing. When she was younger, she dabbled in traditional modeling, yet always felt awkward and uncomfortable. But, "put a prosthetic

Mo modeling for **Monstrous Makeup Manual 2**
makeup by Eryn Krueger Mekash
Used with Permission of Michael Spatola

on me, or make me into a monster, I'm someone else complete-ly. It's like an alter-ego you can wear like armor, giving you permission to access different parts of yourself; you have a reason to act crazy. I love it."

Being in the makeup also helps Mo understand how the make-up affects the performer. Now, when she's crafting or apply-ing the prosthetic, she understands what the actor is going through. "If their mouth or eyes are covered, I try to make it as comfortable as possible. I understand what that means on a practical level as the actor and as the makeup artist. It's a unique perspective."

Mo has been fortunate to have had several truly unique ex-periences when modeling for seasoned industry professionals. "You can tactily feel how they're applying the makeup on you. I've learned a lot from just sitting and talking with them about how they're doing it and what products they're using. They share their tips and techniques. You had better believe, when Eryn Krueger Mekash or Kerrin Jackson is doing my makeup, I'm going to ask questions and absorb everything about being in that chair."

Mo has modeled for makeup demonstrations at IMATS LA, Monsterpolooza, Cinema Makeup School, and Comic Con for makeup artists including Eryn Krueger Mekash, Bruce Spauld-ing Fuller, Kerrin Jackson, Ana Gabriela Quinonez, Mireille Ber-trand, Nelly Recchia, Tanner White, as well as her former CMS colleagues, Melissa Jimenez, KC Mussman, Erica Preus, Devan Weitzman, Chloe Sens, Jamie Leodones, and Kaity Licina.

Mo has also appeared as a makeup model in **Monstrous Makeup Manual 2**, written by Michael Spatola, one of her teachers and the Chief Academic Officer at CMS. She modeled a large tattoo transfer applied by Kato DeStefan, realistic scrapes and wounds for Spatola, and a gothic Vampire named Loisine Zinkin for Eryn Krueger Mekash. "I'm happy to sit there for hours and be a part of the makeup process. I like helping them 'let their makeup flag fly.'"

It Takes an Army

"In film and television, it takes an army to create everything. There are many working parts and people that make it happen. I always try to surround myself with people who have more knowledge, so I am constantly learning." This attitude goes beyond just working with the makeup department. By under-standing the language and terms used by the director, the director of photography (DP), the grips and electrics (G&E), and other departments, Mo has found, "I can have discussions with them, and that helps me with the makeups I'm doing, and ultimately the final product."

In the Fall of 2015, Mo had the opportunity to travel down the California coast with **Food & Wine Maga-zine**. She was doing basic touch-up makeup on farmers and vintners, but "because it was a small crew of nine, I helped grip and electric and filled in as production assistant. It was hard labor, but it was enlight-ening. I had the chance to work with each of them as they taught me the intricacies of their departments and how they work. I have a huge appreciation for each department and their role in film-making. It was an invaluable experience."

On-the-Job

Since leaving CMS, Mo has been busy working as a freelance makeup artist, building her resume and reputation, establishing relationships, and working hard towards union membership. "I'm working on all types of projects: commercial, film, television and print, applying beauty makeup, special makeup effects, or both, sometimes I even make props."

"For me, on a professional level, everything is balanced. Sometimes I find that my time gets split between projects that I really feel passionate about and the ones that pay the most, like commercial jobs. They can be creative and exciting as well, but typically these are the ones that help me keep my finances healthy enough to support the work that is more in line with where I see my career ultimately heading."

While Mo sees her strength as on-set application, she also wants to keep learning about different materials, fabrication, sculpting, molding, and building. "I do have some skill in the shop, but there are so many products, applications, and ways of accomplishing things. There's almost an infinite number of ways to do something. I'll never stop learning, and that's exciting."

She's begun getting department head positions on independent films, which include design assignments and hiring responsibilities. This gives her the opportunity to assemble her dream team. While working on these films, step-by-step, she's collecting the hours that will count toward getting her into the union. "I feel union membership will open a lot of doors, so I'm working towards it."

Her most exciting project to date has been department-heading ***Nosferatu: The Vampire Lives*** (2017). "It's the highlight of my career so far." The film is a feature length remix of the classic vampire tale from the 1922 silent film. The current incarnation stars Doug Jones as Count Orlok and is directed by David Fisher. "It was an amazing opportunity and a dream project." Mike Elizalde of Spectral Motion (***Birdman, Hansel & Gretel: Witch Hunters***, and ***Hellboy I & II***) sculpted the Count Orlok pieces for Jones, a well-known and respected creature-actor (***Crimson Peak, Pan's Labyrinth***, and ***The Strain***).

Nosferatu: The Vampire Lives (2017)
Used with Permission of Mo Meinhart

"Mike and everyone at Spectral Motion were invaluable in helping me realize the vision for this next evolution of the classic character. Working with Mike's design for this project was an honor; the wealth of knowledge and the creativity within Spectral Motion is inspiring. Working with Doug Jones…what can I say? He exudes such positive energy, it's contagious! His prestige and professionalism are exceeded only by

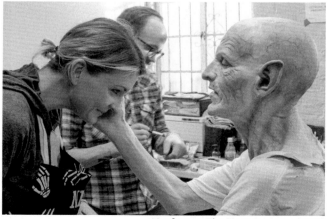

Nosferatu: The Vampire Lives (2017)
Used with Permission of Denéa Buckingham

Ascension (2017) Alien fetus puppet Asst: Tanner White
Used with Permission of Mo Meinhart

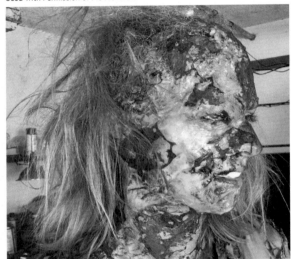

Ascension (2017) Face burn makeup   Asst: Tanner White
Used with Permission of Mo Meinhart

Dark Legacy : An Unofficial Star Wars Story Concept artwork with makeup FX
Used with Permission of Anthony Pietromonaco

his sense of humor and warm heart. Working with these prominent artists is a makeup artist's dream."

"This film has all my favorite things; period hair and makeup, blood gags, bites, injuries, and monsters. The film is edited with de-saturated colors, almost black and white. We had to figure out the perfect combination of colors so the makeup looked just right. I loved designing the looks for the characters with Erica Preus, my makeup key on the film and having Ben Ploughman working with me on prosthetic effects. Researching the period styles and testing the makeup colors in desaturated light was a fun process that taught us a lot. In this case everything looked completely different in person than on film. I learn something new every time I'm on a job, whether it's a brush stroke or a color palette. Every experience is valuable."

For another recent project, *Ascension*, directed by Ross Wachsman, Mo headed up the effects department for the film. In this sci-fi thriller, she hired fellow makeup effects artist, Tanner White. "We made a skin suit that the actress had to hide in, a distended pregnancy belly, a mangled cat, a drill-in-head gag, a full face burn makeup, and a womb complete with a puppeteered alien fetus. We cut a couple throats and got messy with a few blood gags. I loved it, we experimented with different materials, painting techniques, blood rigs, and bladders. I learned so much from working on this project."

Mo is fortunate to live in a very creative environment, sharing a house with her boyfriend and director, Anthony Pietromonaco, and her older brother. Each has their our own creative talents in different fields and inspire one another. "It's especially fun when we work on a project together, whether it's a commercial, music video, or feature film. I'm really proud of *Dark Legacy: An Unofficial Star Wars Story*, a short film we did that's close to being released. It represents our collective efforts as a small team. Anthony wrote and directed it, Michael composed and arranged the score, and I did the practical and makeup effects. I know they always bring their best, so I have to do the same; their art inspires me to push mine to the next level."

Onto the Future

Collecting her hours to get into the union is the next goal for Mo, so she's always working on something, whether it's a film production or a personal project. "I'll collect the hours I need to get in. But until then, I'm going to enjoy the journey."

"I would love to be department head or key on a big feature film or a television show. I love to do everything. I want to design the look, I want to apply the makeup, I want to style the hair, I want to fire off that blood effect. I want to create the monster, I want to apply the monster, sometimes I even want to *be* the monster. There are so many cool aspects and every day is different."

Mo is certain about one thing, she'll keep working with her female colleagues. "We support one another and our individual goals. If one of us is unable to do a job, she'll pass it to me, and vice versa. There is a lot of trust when passing a job to someone, they represent you and you represent them. The ladies I work with all believe we will have a lifetime of working together, and it's not worth losing that friendship by taking someone's client. You better believe, if I'm teaming up, I like to pull in the people I can trust."

OUTTAKES:

On Professionalism:

"I think that as a makeup artist, you're in everyone's personal space. I think there's a level of trust that you need to earn with an actor and the people on-set. You have to have good bedside manner, be ahead of the game, notice things before other people notice them, and bring value to every opportunity."

"Clean. I think Mike Spatola told me, 'You can never be sick, and you always have to have clean hands.' That's very good advice. Being a special effects makeup artist it is sometimes hard to keep clean 'looking' hands, so I always paint my nails black, which a lot of us do."

On Heroes:

"My role models are the women who forged the way before us, the women in this book. They broke down barriers and opened up the industry for us. Now there are more women in makeup and effects."

"I would say my hero is Eryn Krueger Mekash. She's obviously very talented, but she is also compassionate and supportive. She's willing to take the time to help the next generation of women trying to make it in this crazy industry. Her passion is contagious, and she not only inspires me but also many others. She once told me, 'You're so lucky to have all these strong ladies around you, working with you; working together.' She's right."

On Being a Woman in the Biz:

"As females in the indusrty, most of us do beauty makeup, but we also style hair and create and apply effects as well. So on smaller sets, independent films, a lot of times I'll get hired to do all three. That's been extremely helpful."

"I think women who work in special effects shops are just badass."

"I always say, 'I make blood, guts, monsters, and beauty queens.' The tomboy side of me loves getting messy while building and creating. The nerdy side of me loves the science and engineering behind it all. The feminine side of me loves the glamour and luxury of beauty makeups. It's incredible when you apply makeup to someone and you see them come to life, whether it's making someone feel and look their best with beauty makeup, or an actor getting into character after applying prosthetics."

"The process of building something from start to finish is hard work accompanied by sleepless nights, but it's so satisfying to see the final result."

"The makeup community is very supportive. The artists that I absolutely admire and look up to are open to sharing their processes and techniques. That's so cool."

On Being Resourceful:

"The question of special techniques is a hard one because we're not inventing anything new. Everyone that forged the way before us has done these things, and they're passing their information and their knowledge on to us. We're trying these techniques for ourselves. Those techniques are new to us, but we're not re-inventing the wheel."

"As a makeup artist you have to be resourceful, I think that's the fun part. Sometimes you have to think outside the box to figure out ways to create the effects and what materials to use. In **Monstrous Make-up Manual 2**, Steve LaPorte uses gelatin in a unique and practical way for a burnt face, and I think it's brilliant. On a piece of paper he will draw out the shape and size of what he wants the prosthetics to be, then he will cut and split open a zip-lock bag and place it over the paper. Applying gelatin with a chip brush, he'll stipple and brush the gelatin just inside the pattern, making textures as it cools and thickens. After it hardens he powders it and rolls it up, making them easy to store and carry in your kit. Some of my most successful makeups I've done have been using that technique. I'll even keep a few in my kit, just in case. It's cost effective and the result is amazing."

For more of Mo's work, visit:
www.imdb.com
Instagram: @momeinhart

LEADING LADIES
OF MAKEUP EFFECTS

Catching Up!

We interviewed KC on February 23, 2016; here's her *Catching Up!* letter:

"Dear Pat & Gary,

Since our interview, my company and shop, *Nocturnal Designz,* designed and created all the make-up effects for the Primetime Emmy Nominated Webseries **Making a Scene with James Franco**, with Department Head Nana Fischer.

Nocturnal Designz is the only shop in LA offering a work study program. We work with makeup school graduates and give them a platform to acquire more hands-on experience and skills to enter the makeup effects industry while learning high work standards, community values, and ethics.

I also was department head of hair and makeup on the pop drama **Daddy Issues**, a highly anticipated film in the LGBTQ community which is coming out in 2018.

In the Summer of 2017, I was one of the three Finalists for Season 12 of **FaceOff** the reality TV Show about makeup effects and design. Unfotunately, I didn't win, but the experience was fantastic!

- KC Mussman

KC's Asmodeous and Hesperian the Imp makeups for the Finale and KC with her interpretation of *Vivaldi's "Summer"* all for **FaceOff Season 12**

All images used with Permission of KC Mussman

KC Mussman

If you're striving to work on a big movie set and you're just starting out, you might not be qualified enough to be on it yet. Keep it where you're supposed to be. Grow from there. Push the envelope a little bit further every time you go out, and grow and develop yourself. In that aspect I'm really enjoying myself. I think it's good.

"Every day I'm here in my shop. It provides more opportunity for me because I have a place to go. On days that I'm not doing a project for someone else, I'll usually try stuff for myself. I learn a lot here. This shop is my training ground for new things."

KC Mussman is the owner of Nocturnal Designz, one of the only female-owned and operated makeup effects shops in Los Angeles. Sitting surrounded by shelves of molds, chemicals, half-finished sculptures, and other tricks of the trade, with her crimson tinged braids and her broad smile, she is at home.

"I feel that having my own space to use, and using it, develops my skills further. I always come in here to test, try, practice, have fun. Other artists join me and we have fun together. It also opens the door, quite literally, for a lot of collaboration with other artists, which I love."

KC has a colorful past that ultimately led her to Los Angeles. As the middle child of five siblings, she was born in Long Island, New York, and spent her childhood in Alabama before moving to Israel at age ten. "My mother is Israeli, her entire family is over

KC working in her shop   Used with Permission of KC Mussman

there, and she wanted to bring us closer to her homeland." So, her family relocated to Tel Aviv, where KC lived until she was 26. She grew up, went to school, served in the Israeli military, and LARP-ed, which is where her interest in costuming and makeup began.

KC's specialty makeup characters
Used with Permission of KC Mussman

Necessity, the Mother of Invention

"I had this hobby, LARP-ing (Live Action Role Play-ing). Basically, what we would do is dress up as characters from **Lord of the Rings**, or **Dungeons and Dragons,** or from some other fantasy story, go to the forest, reenact battles, and play out the characters." KC enjoyed creating her charac-ters by detailing the makeup, hair, and costumes. Her fellow LARP-ers began to notice her charac-ter work and asked her to help them with theirs. "They'd come over to my place before the LARP-ing began, and I'd do them up."

KC's friends wanted to play more fantastic char-acters, such as Orcs and Elves, and wanted KC to help with the transformations. It became more and more challenging for her to create them. "I really wanted to create unique looks so my friends could look like the fantasy characters. For exam-ple, I would take a band-aid, fold it up on the ear, take my mom's hair removal wax, put it over the band-aid, cover that in foundation, and there you go, elf ears." She started making ears, horns, noses, and cheek pieces. At that time, she had no idea what a prosthetic was, much less how to make a mold for one.

"Back then, it was in the late '90s, early 2000s, there was no YouTube, no Facebook. It was hard to find information. I got **Fangoria** magazine from the magazine shop; they only had one and it was really old. I read that magazine every day, over and over, to try and learn how to do these characters. The maga-zine literally fell apart from all my reading. That's how my fascination started. Then, some of my friends started making films and they asked me to come on and do the makeups. As I was doing those makeups for the camera, I realized that I needed to learn how to do this professionally. It wasn't enough to do the wax and band-aids anymore."

Until then, she hadn't considered a career in special effects makeup, but she started researching and found a makeup school in Los Angeles that could give her the training she needed, Cinema Makeup School (CMS).

Stepping Beyond...CMS and Opportunities

KC chose to attend CMS because all the makeups she saw coming out of the school were creative and challenging, but, more importantly, all the faculty are working makeup artists. "I knew the education I would get was current and up-to-date, which was very important to me. Also, [the school] is here in Los Angeles, the heart of the film industry. If I was going to go somewhere, it would be here, to the center of the action."

She moved to LA in 2012 to attend CMS and start her training, but it wasn't easy because she had to leave Or, her husband of one year, behind in Israel. Originally, she moved to LA to study, planning to re-turn to Israel after completing school. But she decided to stay and work. She and Or started working on his paperwork immigrate to the US, and it was three years before they were finally reunited.

While she attended CMS, KC learned all the basics she wanted and needed to begin building a career as an artist. But even beyond those basic technical skills, she also had opportunities to meet and work with other professionals and forge long-term relationships with her classmates.

KC met one of her personal mentors, Wendy Ann Rosen, at school. Rosen taught her beauty makeup and recommended her for the Leonard Engelman Fellowship, an honorary program offering a select group of students the opportunity to study directly with Engelman. Engelman is the CMS Emeritus Director of Education and serves on the Board of Governors for Makeup Artists and Hairstylists for the Academy of Motion Pictures Art and Sciences (AMPAS).

"When I was in school, I also met Francesca Tolot, a very unique artist. She's a beauty makeup artist, well-seasoned, very well-known, except not to me at the time. The day I met her she was wandering around the back of the school, looking for help. She looked a little lost. I went up to her, and she said, 'I'm looking for a special effects artist to help me with prosthetics for my book.' I said, 'Sounds great. Let's do it.'" KC recruited a fellow classmate, Mo Meinhart, and together they helped Tolot with her project. "Mo and I worked for three days on it. We had our special effects makeup finals during the day, and then we stayed over nights to do Francesca's project for her. She did a beautiful makeup with the prosthetics we created for her and it ended up in her book."

KC's "Galilea, Queen of Europa." Model: Mo Meinhart
Used with Permission of KC Mussman

Engelman found out that KC had a background in graphic design and another opportunity presented itself. He had a friend whose agency represents makeup artists and she needed a graphic designer to help build artist webpages. KC went in for an interview for the short-term intern position, which turned into a long-term, part-time job at The Milton Agency. "It's a small agency, but they do big work. They are a team of incredible women who hold everything on their shoulders." The Milton Agency represents makeup artists such as Lois Burwell and Frances Hannon. In 2016, KC was added to their LA roster as an Emerging Artist.

Stepping Out...Opening a Shop...Finding a Community

After graduating and moving on from CMS, KC started making the rounds looking for work in film and/or in a shop. "I realized suddenly, there were many people working in this field, there's a lot of competition. Even people that are trained can't seem to get work. I went to a lot of shops trying to get an internship. Most of the opportunities presented to me were ones that were on a volunteer basis. I absolutely have no problem with that idea, but I didn't have the luxury of not receiving a paycheck for days on end."

"Eventually, I was meeting actors, producers, and directors and I started getting work. I wasn't hired into a shop, but I was working. This gave me a notion,

KC working in her shop Nocturnal Designz
Used with Permission of KC Mussman

'Ah-ha, you know what? I'll be my own shop.'" Her first year out of school, KC jumped into doing projects from her home. "I started taking on work, but I was doing everything in my kitchen. It wasn't working out. I found this place, a very small, hole-in-the-wall studio. But I knew when I saw it, 'This will be home base, no more kitchen projects." It's a little shop inside a big, open-space artist community. I can see everyone working on their art, which is fun and inspiring. Having a shop has allowed me to take on a lot more work."

Once KC opened Nocturnal Designz, she started collaborating with other small shop owner-operators. "I learned from these other artists with small garage shops, worked on projects, and made a paycheck. I started helping other artists who came to my studio, and I'd go to their studios and they'd help me. We founded this nice community system of helping each other out." By working alongside these other artists, KC learned new skills and improved upon the ones she had.

Running a "Girls' Shop"

As a successful woman running her own shop, KC has unfortunately, run into some sexism. "People have asked me, 'Who lifts your molds? Who makes your molds? Who uses your power tools for you? Who do you get to do this? Who do you get to do that?' I'm like, 'What do you mean? I do all that myself.'"

KC and "The Nocturnal Girls" Used with Permission of KC Mussman

"I've had a lot of good friends and mentors that brought me on projects and did not doubt me for one minute. They'd say, 'Here, use this,' and hand me a drill. I think I'm very fortunate that I've found positive people that were open to teaching me, helped me succeed, and lifted me up. I feel very blessed for that, and that's where I learned these skills."

KC tries to honor the help she received along the way by bringing other women on to get them started down their own career paths. "I have a lot of girls coming into the shop. Nocturnal Designz is often referred to as 'The Nocturnal Girls.' I love the fact that we have a big female force working here. One of the reasons is a lot of these girls either get rejected or mistreated at shops. I like to work in a team. Around here it's me and my girls."

"I believe that the future of the industry lies in working together and sharing the knowledge which helps us grow and strengthens ourselves and the community. When we take on projects, we also take on interns; we collaborate with schools in a work study program. Nocturnal Designz helps students gain some experience and increase their skill sets as they enter the industry by giving them jobs and opportunities along the way."

Bringing in the Work

Since she started her business and opened her shop, KC has been working with a lot of directors on indie films, music videos, and fashion projects; professionally they are all at the same level. "We're not exactly starting out, but we still have big stars in our eyes and we want to do big things. Getting a chance to work with other people who are also ramping up and experimenting is fantastic."

A memorable project KC worked on was a promotional video for ***Paranormal Activity: The Marked Ones*** with Paramount Studios. The video was shot in 360 degrees so it presented special problems. "To shoot 360, you're shooting in a room where all angles are shot at once; you cannot be in the room. I had to, for the first time in my life, do everything blind. I had a lot of blood gags to rig. I had to tube up my actor, feeding the tube every which way, behind a chair, under a lamp, underneath the rug, and finally out the garage and into my hands where I have my controllers and my blood cannon. At that point, I didn't know what was really going to happen. They closed the garage door, the director yelled, 'Action!' I pressed the controller. At the end of the shot, the garage door opened up and there was blood everywhere. All I could do was ask the actor, 'Did it work? What did it look like?' It was very challenging and fun. We got the shots, everything went great, and we did it all blind."

KC has also done some advertising work, including a particularly special Coors Lite promotion. "We did this *Walking Dead* kind of promotional poster where all these zombies are hiding behind a door, and they're all holding Coors beer cans. It was fun to see all these zombies running around inside the promotion office. It was also a bit of a promotion for Noctural Designz because we got to use the prosthetic transfers we make and sell."

Coors beer commercial a la the Walking Dead
Used with Permission of KC Mussman

The "Horn Lady"

KC has a personal fascination with horns. She met her husband while she was wearing horns and they have figured into many facets of her life. "I always loved making horns and wearing them. During my LARP-ing days, when I didn't know what I was doing, I would cut up my socks and wrap them with saran wrap and then put glue on them and shape them. Since then, I've been making hand-sculpted horns. I like to see them in fashion, on film, and on creatures."

Horns are a staple of Nocturnal Designz. "They're our bread and butter. We have over 40 different styles of horns that range in size from small to large, tall to short, wide to narrow." KC has a booth every year at the major makeup shows in LA, Monsterpalooza and IMATS. "Michael Key [publisher of *Make-up Artist Magazine* and producer of IMATS] gave me the nickname 'Horn Lady' when we started having our booth at IMATS Vancouver."

KC is "The Horn Lady"   Used with Permission of KC Mussman

The Israeli Film Industry and Workshops

KC's greatest goal is to bring special effects makeup to the Israeli film industry. "I'm out here [in LA] to actually help develop the industry over there [Israel]. I'm hoping that everything I learn here, and everything that I accomplish here, can inspire others to grow over there."

"Israel is a country that is very modern on one hand, but behind-the-times on the other. The film industry in Israel, while big, has many primitive departments, like the makeup department. There is limited access to materials, knowledge, and information. The entertainment industry itself is pretty old-school. Lots of drama and comedy, but not a lot of fantasy or horror. In fact, the first horror film produced in Israel has only come out in the past few years."

Many people she LARP-ed with, back in the day, are now in the Israeli film industry and, "we're talking. In fact, one of the directors, a female directors I work with, Rona, is very much into special effects makeup. She thought it would be impossible, but after I worked with her on her film, and we did all these really cool effects, it really pushed her to start putting more special effects makeup into her scripts. She gained the confidence that it's actually something that can be done."

KC originally intended to open a shop in Israel, but soon found the obstacles were too great. Obtaining materials and chemicals was impossible, so she's given up the idea for now. But she decided the next best thing would be to be based in LA and continue working with directors and makeup effects artists in Israel. "They can design a look, have it manufactured here in LA, and have it brought to them; it's not hopeless anymore. They stand a chance to get their special effects makeup on film."

To help rectify the situation further, KC has started teaching makeup effects workshops in Israel. She has hosted courses for local makeup artists before Purim, a Jewish costume-based holiday, and she has held classes for the Israeli Animation College (IAC), a school that focuses on visual effects. In 2016, KC held four sold-out workshops.

"Initially we were scheduled to do two workshops with ten students each, but the demand was so high, we ended up selling out four with 20 students each. Several makeup artists and teachers came to participate, including, Neta Szkelly, senior artist for MAC Israel, and Richard Takach, one of the leading practical effects artists in Israel. Most of these artists had never experienced foam latex appliances, alcohol paints, pros-aide or pros-aide transfers. Learning about these materials and the techniques gave them a whole new outlook on makeup effects."

"After the workshops, we hosted a pot luck and we talked about the responsibility of each artist to support the community, to teach and help and elevate each other so they can all rise and eventually thrive."

Looking to the Future

KC wants to eventually work on major films and she's not afraid to say she'd like to win awards. "We, all of us, I think, are going for the gold rings, which of course, are awards, Oscars or Guild Awards.

"This was what I was thinking before I came out to LA. 'Yeah, I'll go, and I'll learn this stuff. I'll come back, and I'll open a shop. I'll start doing these really big makeups for an Israeli film. It'll go to America, it'll go to Hollywood, it'll make it to the Oscars. I think a lot of people are kind of scared to say it, but yeah, you know what? I'd like to see that happen."

OUTTAKES:

On The Importance of Molds:

"I absolutely love mold-making. I like the mathematical aspect to it. Figuring out the different angles, figuring out how to really create a mold that can take that sculpt and turn it into the best possible prosthetic. I realized that I love this through making some really bad molds."

"At first, I addressed mold-making like a lot of young artists do, as a means to an end. Today, I realize that it's an art form in its own right."

"Basically, once you're done with your sculpture, if your sculpture is perfect, but your mold is terrible, that prosthetic's not coming out correctly."

On Beauty and SPFX:

"When I came out to L.A, the first jobs that I was able to get onto were fashion. I love doing beauty make-up. I'm very passionate about fashion, the *avant-garde*, and all these really cool *haute couture* looks. When I started doing beauty, I was one of those artists that would always try to push more ideas onto my clients. I'd say, 'You know, lipstick and stuff, that's really good, but what if we did some prosthetic work? Yeah, let's put some cheekbones there. Let's put some pieces on her.' A lot of times, I'd get raised eyebrows because most of the fashion designers don't know about special effects makeup. It's not a big thing in the fashion world, but I've started doing a lot of fashion effects. I like to create *avant-garde* prosthetics for the runway and a lot of my horns go to fashion designers to incorporate into their work."

On Crazy Expectations and Reality:

"We have a lot of people inquiring about work. Today, a lot of directors do not know or are not aware of what it takes to do special effects makeup. We'll get the craziest phone calls all the time. 'Can you make a creature suit in two days?' 'We need seventeen zombies tomorrow morning.' We even got a gig to make prop antlers for 20 reindeers from an animal wrangling company. Once castrated, male deer stop growing antlers. Projects like these require planning, budget, and a ton of work."

"We have to pick and choose projects. We have to talk with, and sometimes educate, our producers and directors so that they know exactly how much time it's going to take and what the budget needs to be, and then we see if we can actually schedule it."

On Heroes:

"I've always had a huge fascination with Dick Smith's work, and Rick Baker's, as well. That one magazine that I had, it had Rick Baker's work in it, and I had it on my walls and really studied it. I did get to meet him on several occasions, the first time as a student. It was during beard finals at Cinema Makeup School. We went to see Rick get his star on the Hollywood Walk of Fame. I ran out with my beard still on, and stood there in the crowd. I yelled at him, 'Hey, Rick Baker. We love you.' He came over, and he checked out my beard, and he said, 'Why, thank you, lady in a beard.'"

KC in beard with hero, Rick Baker
Used with Permission of KC Mussman

"Eryn Krueger Mekash is a great inspiration to me. One thing that really gave me a lot of motivation is seeing her work with her husband, Mike Mekash. They're such a good team. It's so important, especially in our industry, where we work such long hours, under high stress, to have someone on your side, to be there for you."

"If Dick Smith is the godfather of special effects makeup, then for me, Ve Neill is the godmother. She was one of the first ones out there, breaking the molds, pun intended. She really set a path. To this day, when I hear her talk, and she's says, 'Yeah, go ladies.' I'm like, 'Yeah, Ve, we're going!'"

For more of KC's work, visit:
www.nocturnaldesignz.com
www.imdb.com
Instagram: @kcmussman

LEADING LADIES
OF MAKEUP EFFECTS

FIGHTING THE STEREOTYPE

MICHÈLE

"I always had to fight my corner to make sure that it was understood that no one was coming in to do the special effects makeup work. That was me. I also do that. It was more often to production managers and people like that who would say, 'Who should we bring in to do that particular makeup?' I'd say, 'Nobody. I'm doing it.' They would look surprised, 'Shouldn't we bring somebody in?' I'd say ,'No.'"

FRANCES

"One producer said to me, 'I'm doing a project down the Amazon. We'll be camping and I'm going to look for a male makeup artist.' Why? Do you think we can't work? Can't camp? Can't carry our own equipment? We do it all. I've lived on ships. Lived in Greenland. Lived in Iceland. Walked the fjords, climbed the glaciers. There's no reason it should be male or female."

MONTSE

"You know, I think maybe I'm lucky because the people that surround me are not *machista*. As a woman, I am not conscious I am a woman; it's like I feel like I'm a person."

TAMI

"Sometimes ignoring the boys club means you hire the right person for the job. For instance, on a recent film I worked on our actress was in a bikini all the time. She gets messed up. It's a deterioration makeup, but she's in a bikini. To get her into makeup, she's nude. I was hiring an assistant. Somebody said, 'Oh, what about this guy? Blah blah blah.' I said, 'You know what? This isn't just the actress, it's both her doubles, all naked in the makeup trailer. I would prefer not to have a male in here. Not for me, not because it matters to me, I was just being sensitive to them. One of the doubles, this was her first job ever. I didn't want her to have a weird experience. That's the only time the sex of a makeup artist comes into play. It's about what exactly are we doing? It wasn't that this guy that production wanted me to hire wasn't capable. I was thinking of the girls."

Catching Up!

We interviewed Erica on March 1, 2016; here's her *Catching Up!* letter:

"Dear Pat and Gary,

Thanks so much for offering me the chance to expand my *Catching up!* information! Two years can bring so many changes to a career in this industry; it certainly has for me.

Dwayne Johnson with Erica & Crew
Used with Permission of Erica Preus

Jimmy Johnson with Erica
Used with Permission of Will Akana

At the time of our interview, I was still pretty green in the union (ok, I'm still relatively a bit green, but then I was reeeeeaallly green). Since then I've had the honor of working with several talented and generous artists whom I admire to no end and who have taught me so much.

Shortly after our interview, I was fortunate to have the opportunity to day play for *American Horror Story: Roanoke*. I can't even begin to describe my excitement being on that set working alongside two women I hold in high regard (Eryn Kruegar Mekash and Kim Ayers). From there I also went on to day play on *Feud*, *Bright*, *Teen Wolf*, and *Kings* (meeting Jacenda Burkett has been one of the highlights of the last year!). Another major highlight for me was working for Keith Hall on *Jean Claude Van Johnson*. I'm very grateful to Keith for his trust, and really look forward to working with him more in the future! And of course...the day I was on set with Dwayne Johnson was (if I may get a little colloquial) pretty damn awesome.

I also had the opportunity to run my own show as head of department for a Disney pilot called *Forever Boys*. We got to turn four kids into unlikely teenage vampires, and I was able to build a team of all my favorite rockstars to help (Mo Meinhart for lab FX work, Abby Lyle Clawson as my key artist, and Courtney Ullrich as hair department head).

One particular gig I'll never forget was right at the beginning of 2017 when I applied a bald cap to sportscaster and former NFL star Jimmy Johnson for a Geico commercial. I love bald caps, and he was so laid back even though he'd never sat for FX or character makeup before. Terry Bradshaw was there hanging out, too (I'm a football fan, so I was geeking out). But best of all was the standing ovation from the entire crew when we walked onto the set. It was one of those humbling moments that makes you realize you chose the right career! Everyone raved about that bald cap. Sometimes it's those simple things that really make it all worthwhile.

And of course, another major highlight of the last two years has been undertaking my latest editing project. I've been privileged to read, edit, learn, and stand in awe of each and every chapter in this very book. It's been like studying a textbook about the female pioneers in this industry, learning the unique career paths of every Leading Lady gracing these pages. So I also want to thank you, Pat and Gary, for including me in your journey to see this project to completion.

It's truly an honor to share space in this book with the other magnificent women featured here. I cannot wait to see what the next few years brings for us all. Cheers!"

- Erica Preus

ERICA PREUS

I liken my career to a snowball. You roll your snowball and it gets bigger and bigger.

Then, at a certain point, it starts rolling on its own.

I never know what job I'll be offered on any given day.

The snowball keeps rolling on and that's the fun and the mystery of it.

Erica Preus lives in Orange County, about 30 minutes from Los Angeles. She lives in a nice detached house on a quiet street, perfectly suited for a family in the OC. Erica is married to Kevin, her husband of over 10 years, and they have a darling little girl, Delilah, nicknamed "The Wild Moo" by Mo Meinhart, Erica's friend and colleague. "I really enjoy having my family to come home to every day. We were married before I got into makeup, so my family life is very important to me. Kevin is extremely supportive of my career and insane schedule, so I'm lucky that I get the best of both worlds."

From Dance to Literature, The Evolution of a Makeup Artist

Erica grew up in home full of academics. Her mother was an English major and still works as a librarian, her father is a computer programmer with a Ph.D. in Chemistry, and her brother, gifted in drawing and painting, is a successful accountant. As for Erica, she grew up focusing on her passion for literature and creative writing.

Erica credits her early interest in makeup first, to her fashionable grandmother who gave her Estee Lauder lipsticks when she was a child, and second, to her years and years of dance training. From the age of three until she was an English major at UCLA, Erica was a competitive dancer in ballet, jazz, lyrical, contemporary, and hip-hop. In her teens, she combined the two interests as captain of her dance squad and became the go-to performance makeup artist. "By the time I was sixteen, throwing on eyelashes and contouring other people's faces was really normal for me. A few times, I also went to my friends' houses to do their hair and makeup for prom. I remember packing up a bunch of random items in a Caboodle, which was kind of like my first version of a kit!"

While attending UCLA, Erica's interests in dance waned because she was pursuing her other passion, literature. Erica is the ultimate student, loving the classroom, books, and learning. She graduated *Summa Cum Laude* and *Phi Beta Kappa* from UCLA with a Bachelor's degree in English and a minor in Classical Civilizations. Erica's interests lie "in all things antiquated, old, and boring. I still read Shakespeare in my spare time. Give me **Paradise Lost**, and I'm going to read it again and again. I'm kind of a nerd that way. I always thought I would either be an English professor with a Ph.D. at some Ivy League school or a writer." But her plans went off course in her senior year.

Best Laid Plans Go Awry

At the end of her senior year at UCLA, Erica was newly married and decided to take a break from school to pursue an internship at a prestigious Beverly Hills literary firm. At the last minute, the internship fell through. "Now I had a major wake-up call and no plan. So, I did what I always did when I needed to shut my brain off and comfort myself…I went to the mall."

While she was at the mall, Erica saw a sign at the Macy's department store advertising a cosmetics career fair the following day. She decided with her interest in makeup and current lack of employment, she'd return and see what it was all about. It turned out not to be a career fair, but an actual interview to work at the Lancome counter at the store. She was hired on the spot. "I knew people would say 'You've spent all those hours studying in college and now you're just going to go do makeup?' But at the time I thought it would be temporary until I figured things out."

Erica began as a beauty advisor behind the counter at one of Macy's stores then, after six months, transferred to the freelance artistry division where she traveled all over the state representing Lancome. Trained by "my first real mentor, Darais, a national artist for Lancome on the West Coast, he showed me many artistic things I could do with makeup. He's brilliant. I still look up to him and credit him with my falling in love with makeup. He also showed me that makeup wasn't something I had accidentally picked up as a dancer. I was good at it, too."

"I'll always be grateful for those working experiences behind the counter. It was the ultimate training in customer service, which I think is essential for being a makeup artist. You have to be able to handle any color, age, gender, anyone who might walk in that day, and every type of personality." She worked at Lancome for the next six years and also picked up work with other brands including Make Up For Ever, Bobbi Brown, Smashbox, Armani, and Calvin Klein, making contacts and doing weddings and events. "Pretty much everything I learned about beauty makeup came from my time as a freelancer for beauty lines."

It was also around this time that she was asked by a social media management company, Two Stray Dogs, to do some editorial makeup for a photoshoot that would be featured in a local magazine. Pleased with her work, the owners asked her to also write online content for their clients' websites and blogs. She readily agreed. "It was the perfect blend of all my skills. I saw this as my segue back into using my English degree; I had such creative freedom in those photoshoots. Marco Ciappelli, one of the original owners, is still one of my best friends to this day."

More Life-Changing Moments

"After I'd been freelancing for a few years, I toured several makeup schools looking at SFX programs and considered just going for it, but I was always too scared of the financial commitment, not to mention the uncertainty of the profession, to truly pursue it as my full-time life. Plus, I was always a nerd at heart and felt like an artistic career just wasn't me in the long run. So, academics it was. I planned to continue doing weddings and some freelance here and there, but figured that would phase out once I was a professor." She made the decision to scale back on everything else to go back to school at UC Irvine and get her Master's Degree in English.

Around this time, Erica also noticed she was developing a small bump on her left middle finger. Eventually, it grew to the size of a kernel of corn, and she saw her makeup clients were noticing it while she worked. Erica consulted a doctor, thinking she might have it removed purely as a cosmetic procedure. She had the bump removed in June 2010, and was told at her post-op appointment that everything was normal. But later that same evening, she received a call from the surgeon himself who admitted he hadn't actually received her pathology back until hours after the appointment; the news was not good. "I was told the bump was a tumor called a malignant epithelioid sarcoma. Extremely rare and also very aggressive. One in ten million is what he said. He told me they would probably have to amputate my finger, if not my hand, and I would be scheduled for chemo treatments and radiation. So just like that, everything was turned on its head."

The type of cancer she had was so rare that her medical team at UCLA sent her pathology for review to Harvard Medical and the California Tumor Board to get more detailed information. Her hand surgeon and oncologist scheduled her surgery, for whatever procedure would be deemed necessary, during her midterm exams at school. Her surgery was scheduled and canceled four times over the next month as they waited to hear back from Harvard. "Essentially I had to be on-call for surgery within a day's notice. That wreaked havoc on my school schedule because I couldn't plan anything. If there was a big test the next week, I didn't know if I'd be able to attend or even have a working hand! I was so happy being back in the classroom, I felt like my life was back on track. I had no choice but to drop out, figuring I'd go back the next year if I came out of the whole ordeal alive."

Erica and her doctors eventually received a recommendation from Harvard that only the tip of her left middle finger be removed and several lymph nodes on the underside of her left arm to see if the cancer had spread. The surgery was finally completed and when the pathology came back the margins of the tumor and lymph nodes were clear. "I'm left-handed, so I had to retrain myself to write and use my left hand. I remember doing a wedding makeup and having a brush flip out of my hand and fly across the room." Erica still has regular CT scans to check the cancer hasn't returned, and she has residual pain from the surgery. But, as she was recovering, she made a resolution.

Makeup School...Monsters Raise Their Scary Heads

As often happens after a major life trauma, priorities become clearer. Previously daunted by the expense of makeup school and the vagaries of the profession, Erica determined she couldn't live afraid anymore; she wanted to go to makeup school and devote herself to becoming a makeup artist. But she wanted to learn more than just beauty, she wanted to make monsters.

Erica has always been enamored of monsters, zombies, and creatures. She credits this interest to her father who liked all things gory, gruesome, and weird. Her mother was always squeamish and could never go to haunted houses or watch horror films, but, "My dad is the exact opposite. If something weird and bizarre was on TV, he'd pause it and call me and my brother in to see it, and we both still love that stuff to this day."

"When *The Exorcist* was rereleased in theaters I was in high school and he took me to see it. I had seen it at home, but he wanted me to see it in the theater like he had. We went to a midnight showing. I had dance practice the next morning at 5 AM, but he let me do it anyway. I grew up loving horror. Stephen King was one of my favorite authors." She and her father would attend the haunt at Universal Studios and, not being a squeamish girl, she always wanted to grab a monster and "see what was really going on with their makeup. That was a huge part of my identity, loving things that were creeptastic."

"My dad tells a story that at one haunt, when we were waiting in line for a maze, I said to him, 'I'm coming back here one day to do this kind of work.' He called that my 'Blood Oath,' which has always made me laugh. When I started making monsters, he reminded me about the vow I swore that day. He was so proud and excited for me when I worked for two years at Six Flags Fright Fest for my dear friend Scott Ramp, which will always be one of my favorite career memories. My dad and I still go to a haunt every single year together and always will."

Erica's *Phantom* Final project at CMS
Used with Permission of Michael Spatola

So, after a traumatic bout with cancer that forced her to drop out of university, Erica, with the help of her parents, enrolled at Cinema Makeup School to begin her formal training as a makeup artist.

Making Monsters

Erica did the full course of training at Cinema Makeup School which includes beauty, character, prosthetics, and special effects, 40 hours a week for five months. While attending CMS, Erica met a number of makeup artists who were to become future colleagues and friends with whom she still collaborates on projects. Mo Meinhart topped that list.

In her character makeup course, Erica created an original **Phantom of the Opera** makeup. This makeup was one of the highlights of her work at CMS, so much so that her instructor, Michael Spatola, asked her to recreate it for the second volume of his series of books, **The Monstrous Makeup Manual 2**. "It was for sure the best makeup I did at CMS. It was my first ever foam latex prosthetic and the makeup turned out really well. For being a student at the time, I'm really proud of that makeup." When Spatola asked her to repeat the makeup for his book, Erica took the opportunity to make it even better.

"I got to do it again, but this time he taught me how to make a fiber-glass injection mold. My original prosthetic was foam latex, but I did the new version as an encapsulated silicone piece, so it was really done right. My model was one of my fellow students, Taylor Lawson Caldwell, who was just perfect. He's an actor, so he played the character as well as modelled for it. That was such a special day, just seeing my makeup come to life how I really wanted it; it was not simply as a student assignment. That was so much fun."

Erica's *Phantom* for **Monstrous Makeup Manual 2**
Used with Permission of Michael Spatola

Working with Spatola also afforded her an opportunity to meld her love of English with her passion for makeup when he asked her to be the editor on his second book. "I was so pleased when Mike asked me to assist him. Not only did I get to contribute a makeup to his book, but also to help with the editing. It was such a privilege. And now of course, I have the extreme honor of editing another book, one very near and dear to my heart...all about amazing women who work in special effects makeup!"

Working with Mo Meinhart is another one of Erica's greatest pleasures. One of her favorite memories of their partnership was when they teamed up to create a full-body gelatin boogeyman for creature actor Alex Ward. They sculpted a spinal prosthetic, a face prosthetic, and covered Ward in gelatin burn-type makeups from head to toe.

It took six hours to apply and several hours to remove. "Alex is everywhere now and he is such a treat to work with. I can picture something evil-looking and he just makes it happen. Mo's one of my very best friends in the world, so whenever we get to collaborate, it's a good time."

Getting Out Into the Biz

Attending CMS changed Erica's life because she'd found her true calling as a makeup artist. After completing the program, she immediately began working regularly, most memorably as a personal makeup artist for actress Jane Seymour. She credits it to being lucky, but also acknowledges, "It's about being at the right place, at the right time, with the right people. I've so many people to be grateful to for where I am today and being able to call this my career."

In late 2015, Erica got into the union, Local 706, after being key artist on *Joe Dirt 2* starring David Spade reprising his cult-favorite role as a down-on-his luck, mullet-haired, loveable loser, and personal artist for Charlotte McKinney. The film was a Sony Studio production for Crackle, a pay-per-view online streaming service. Erica got a call to work on the film, packed up, and flew to New Orleans five days later.

Boogeyman created with Mo Meinhart
Used with Permission of Anthony Pietromanaco

"It was such an experience. We were gone for almost two months and it was a fun, crazy, wild ride of a movie. My department head was a phenomenal woman who I really look up to, Abby Lyle Clawson. As a young mom in the industry, she is an incredible example. She's taught me pretty much everything I know about being on-set, running a department, and how to treat your people. I'm so lucky to know her and call her a friend."

Erica knew she would get qualifying union days working on the film and Clawson helped her get into the union. "When I got home I submitted all my paperwork, and I qualified for union trainee status on the roster. It was an example of being in the right time at the right place."

A New Life Brings a New Perspective

Union membership was a well-timed happenstance for Erica who found out she was pregnant shortly after *Joe Dirt 2* wrapped. During her pregnancy, Erica worried about having to step back in a very "out-of-sight, out-of-mind" industry. But getting into the union secured her a place. "Getting that pinky hold on something that's stable and solid, where it will still be there even if I have to take a step back, means I'm a part of something bigger. I've taken that next big step. That's an amazing feeling."

Jane Seymour with Erica
Used with Permission of Erica Preus

"When I found out I was pregnant, I was very, very happy and excited, but I was terrified, not at all of being pregnant, but of what it would do to my career. I didn't tell anybody in the working world until I was about six months along and I couldn't hide it anymore. That was absolutely on purpose. Anyone who could possibly hire me, I did not want them to know. And yes, it absolutely affected who called. I would love that to

Joe Dirt 2 (2015)
Charlotte KcKinney and David Spade

change someday."

For Erica, like many other young working mothers, having a small child to come home to is a great joy, but of course, it also presents some extra logistical work when it comes to managing her calendar. "I'm lucky that I have so much support around me at home. Having my parents and in-laws living nearby means I still have the freedom to take last minute jobs with crazy hours. As a woman with a family, it's even more important for me to constantly prove that I'm still in the game. I never want to be counted out because of my personal life.

"It often happens that I leave when Delilah is asleep and come home when she's asleep, so I do understand why other women in this industry choose not to have children, or choose to scale back when they do. For me personally, that raises my feminist hackles. Of course I'm going to rise to that challenge and make both worlds work together, because that's what men do! No one thinks that male artists can't handle both. So far, juggling the two has worked out great thanks to what I call my nanny-brigade-of-grandparents."

Some Interesting Work

Shortly after getting into 706, Erica got to fly to San Francisco for eight days to work on Nickelodeon's *The NFL Experience* (2015) making up Nickelodeon stars at a convention leading up to the Super Bowl. This was her first big union gig and she discovered the value of her union membership. "Working under the union contract we worked reasonable hours, were paid and treated well. I realized, 'This is why we have a union. It's really nice, I understand now what my union dues go for and do for me.' It was a very good experience."

In 2016, Erica had the opportunity to work as key makeup with her best buddy, Mo Meinhart, on *Nosferatu.* With Mo as department head, and fellow makeup artist Ben Ploughman on for effects, the team of three recreated the characters of the iconic vampire film. "It was a dream come true to be able to work on a film like that. Bringing to life not just the vampire, but all the other characters, too. It was a lot of fun and very satisfying."

Mo Meinhart as *The Bride of Frankenstein*
Used with Permission of Eric Anderson

The Future ...

Erica feels very lucky to have progressed quickly along her career path since leaving CMS. She has made good choices about projects and made connections within the makeup community. Erica's sense of the future right now isn't structured, "I feel my current career path and where I am today has mostly been left to chance and fortune. Since the cancer incident it's hard for me to put a goal and nail it down to step A, step B, step C, step D. I'm better at 'Let's see what happens next month.' To me that's part of what's so beautiful about this industry."

"I mean, I think most women in my age and career bracket would admit that they want to be just like Eryn Krueger Mekash someday. And it's not just her talent and accolades; it's her spirit and attitude towards others that are so beautiful."

"I definitely would love to make more monsters. I know colleagues who say, 'Oh, I really want to win an Academy Award' which is great, but I don't necessarily feel that way. I feel if I'm able to keep working exclusively as a makeup artist full time, then that to me feels like success. As long as I'm holding a brush, I'm really happy. I know that's not the sexiest answer, but that's how I feel."

OUTTAKES

On Expectation and the Industry:

"This may sound cheesy, but if you put in the time and have the dedication and are willing to do what it takes to meet the right people and get the right experience, I think you can do it. There's a misconception that you have to do ten years of free work before you're able to get good substantial jobs. I don't think that's the case.

"That being said, the schedule is intense, 12 to 14 hour days is the norm. I don't think people really understand what they're signing up for because it's a lifestyle, not just a job. Your whole life centers around it. Your days off and your time off are going to be different than everybody else's outside the industry.

"It's not even just the work. Being in the industry is a full-time job. There's so much planning and managing of your time, you must be a good organizer. There are invoices to manage and W-2s to track, 1099s, submitting hours at the union, calendars, maintaining your kit and supplies, building and keeping up with your contacts and resume, organizing pictures, keeping your skills up. It's not like working for one company where everything is linear."

On...Is There Enough Work for Everyone?

"No, absolutely not and there shouldn't be. I'll say this very frankly about my class. I think that there were probably a total of twenty to twenty-five people in my class at CMS, depending on where we were in the curriculum. There were probably three or four people who I thought could actually end up working. Of those three or four, I'm the only one who still calls makeup my fulltime job. I've been in classrooms my whole life. That's what I do, so for me it was sort of easy to see who's dedicated and who's not. Honestly, I think it's kind of good to weed out who actually wants it and who maybe isn't quite cut out for it, but thought they were. And I don't think there's any shame in bailing out once you realize the lifestyle isn't really for you. Everyone should go find and do what works for them."

On Working in the "Boys Club":

"I've considered myself a feminist since I was a child. Since I learned the term, it's my favorite 'F-word.' I don't mind throwing it around at all. Special makeup effects is considered more of a man's world, but that makes no sense to me whatsoever because the numbers show there is more female interest now, especially when you look at the classes coming out of the makeup schools."

"When I've been in concept discussions I once had someone say, 'Well, isn't that going to be messy for you?' Like I was too dainty. I wouldn't be able to handle something messy and I was like, 'Really?' Look how many females who are into this world who don't mind getting covered in blood and making a mess in a lab and rubbing their hands raw scrubbing Ultracal out of molds. We're fine with that."

On Pregnancy Prejudice:

"A word about being a young mother in this industry — it opens up an entirely new set of rules and politics you have to navigate, especially depending on who you're working with and for. At the stage I'm in, just getting started in this industry, I can never use my child as an excuse to say no to a gig, or miss out on work, it's seen as a weakness. When I was pregnant I had several physical complications that limited how I could move my body, but no one ever knew that, even though I was sometimes in excruciating pain. I pretty much pretended not to be pregnant because I never wanted to be counted out of the game. But it happened anyway. I know for a fact I lost work when I was pregnant and when Delilah was an infant because people either thought I was a liability or just plain figured I wasn't going to work anymore."

"I would say I had potentially more problems from women. There were several women who said, 'Oh, I just assumed you weren't going to work anymore.' Which was just baffling to me, especially because some of my clients are working mothers, one with four kids. It's just the assumption that you're not going to. That's certainly something that men don't have to deal with. No one asked my husband, when he told them I was having a baby, if he was going to come back to work. As a feminist that really gets under my skin."

On It Takes a Tribe:

"It makes me so sad when I hear the stories of people cutting each other down because, in this industry especially, if one of us succeeds, we all have a chance to succeed. If my good friend gets a job that I wanted, but she's a department head, she can hire me and we still both end up working. It irks me so much that we don't see it that way. We're artists; this is a collaborative process. If someone I know gets a good job, or a student who I've taught now gets a good job, maybe they'll hire me some day. Likewise, they shouldn't burn a bridge with me, because I'm always looking for people to bring along on jobs to things, and I've also been asked for recommendations and for opinions about other artists."

"You have to have a tribe. You have to have a group who you trust, who you can call, not even just to collaborate with but to pass things to. It's really so important. If I'm already booked for something and one of my steady clients calls me, I need to be able to pass that job to someone I trust who isn't going to take that client from me, but it keeps it in the family, and then ideally that person will do the same for me. I have my core group of like four ladies and we all do that for each other. I think 50% of my work comes from that, the little circle that you build. It's so important for women to do that."

For more of Erica's work, visit:
www.ericapreus.com
www.imdb.com
Instagram: @ericapreus

LEADING LADIES OF MAKEUP EFFECTS

Catching Up!

We interviewed Chloe on February 22, 2016; here's her *Catching Up!* letter:

"Dear Pat and Gary,

When I moved to LA it was days after my 21st birthday. I drove the 23 hours alone, nervous and excited as all hell, wide-eyed and passionate beyond belief about being a 'Hollywood Makeup Effects Artist' with my life in my car and not knowing a single soul.

Makeup for Season 2 *Miss 2059* (2017)
Used with Permission of Will Akana

Gucci advertising campaign (2017)
Used with Permission of Chloe Sens

What I didn't know was what it was going to take and how the journey would play out to get to where I saw myself in my dreams.

Over the past 5 years there've been a lot of hurdles, hard days, no money, lots of money, and then no money. On paper and in photos, it all looks so easy. It plays out like a well-written resume highlighting all the accomplishments; when you squeeze them next to each other, all the bumps in the road disappear.

To onlookers, it looks like every day is a good day, as if I haven't had to fight for the opportunities I've had, worked my butt off, haven't had to hold on tight to the relationships that are special to me, or prove myself to the ones I look up to the most.

But to me, that is one of the special parts of my career, the true journey. I remember sitting in my first LA studio apartment in Hollywood on a cold December night and there was no heat. The building was old and I could hear cockroaches scatter when the kitchen light came on, but I was so incredibly proud of that place because I had made it to LA. I also remember sitting in the apartment homesick and upset and scared that I had made the wrong choice to move. But I reminded myself why I was here. I was here because I had huge dreams of working on big productions, meeting my idols like Howard Berger, Rick Baker, Eryn Krueger Mekash, and Dick Smith. I dreamed of being in the union. But it still felt so daunting.

As the years went by, one situation led to another, and I met those people. As my relationships grew, my idols started to see the artist I was becoming and became people that I could talk to, ask advice of, and confide in. Pieces of my wildest dreams started to fall into place in those years.

As I started to get noticed more, I started to work more. I learned how to live on-set. I fell in love with that life so much that I had to force myself to learn how to create balance with the rest of my life. I still have to. How can I be there for my friends and family? If I have more than a few days off without the prospect of upcoming work, how do I not have a complete mental breakdown and become depressed? I had to learn to never take a paycheck for granted because sometimes you don't know where the next one will come from. I had to learn not to take things personally and that, unfortunately, this industry has an ugly side that will bury you if you let it."

(continued on Page 291)

CHLOE SENS

The day you stop being a good artist is the day that you decide that you know everything and stop learning. I think that everybody can always learn more, especially in our industry where new things are always coming out.

"My heroes are Jack Pierce and Rick Baker. And Rob Bottin; I did a Meg Mucklebones makeup that was really a tribute to him. Other heroes, artists who are currently working, I would definitely say are Eryn Krueger Mekash, Tami Lane, Howard Berger, and Kim Ayers." Sitting in the studio she shares with three other makeup artist friends, Chloe is surrounded by her creations: a sculpture of a steam-punk Tin Man, a Sasquatch she created for a commercial, gory monster heads, and other prosthetic body parts perched here and there among the shelves. Today, she has purple tinged hair and her makeup is immaculately applied. Pointing to her left leg she says with a bright smile, "I have a Jack Pierce portrait this big on my thigh." Chloe has a deep love for Pierce's makeups and has enjoyed reimagining them as passion projects over the years. She has reinterpreted Pierce's famous creations Frankenstein's Monster, The Bride of Frankenstein, and The Mummy. "Yeah, I have this little obsession with classic monsters."

An artistic inclination has always come naturally to Chloe as both her parents are artists; her father is a jewelry designer and photographer and her mother is an interior designer and decorator. As a young girl, she was always interested in makeup and constantly experimented on her friends. Eventually, this interest led her to investigate the Blanche Macdonald Centre in Vancouver, British Columbia, when she was 14 and living in Canada. Visiting this professional beauty makeup school planted a seed in her for the love of makeup artistry, but her life took a turn when she moved back to Austin, Texas, to live with her dad.

While attending high school in Texas, Chloe discovered a love for cooking; she was the president of the culinary club, and continued training in the culinary arts after graduating. She eventually landed a job as an executive pastry chef at a local bakery, but in time, "I kind of got burned out on it. It wasn't everything that I thought it was going to be. So, I started looking at makeup schools again, watching a lot of film, and researching the industry."

Chloe's Meg Mucklebones nakeup tribute to Rob Bottin at IMATS LA
Used with Permission of Eric Anderson

What a Difference a Film Makes

"I saw *An American Werewolf in London* for the first time when I was 18 and it changed my entire life. I had always loved film and horror and special effects, but I never really understood special effects was a real job until I saw *American Werewolf*. *The Thing*, *The Lost Boys*, and *Bram Stoker's Dracula* were hugely inspirational as well. At that point I realized, 'This is a thing.' I decided that that's what I wanted to do. I became obsessed with it; that's all I could think about."

Freshly motivated to explore the makeup field, Chloe researched makeup schools and was most impressed with Cinema Makeup School in Los Angeles, especially their special effects program. Never having visited LA, she and her best friend made the journey to explore the school. It was there she met Lee Joyner, CMS Director of Admissions, who gave her a tour and discussed the admission requirements. At the end of her stay, she decided CMS was the right place for her.

Returning to Austin, Chloe saved every penny to build a tuition fund to pay for CMS. At the end of a year, she had saved enough money, so she called Joyner and arranged for her admission. She was ready to head to LA to start her training, until…

The Accident

"I was walking down a bike path and I got hit from behind by a rollerblader. I did a flip in the air and ended up with a third-degree concussion and a broken collarbone. The rollerblader took off. I was in bed for two months, couldn't work, and spent all the money that I had saved up for school on medical bills."

Chloe might have been laid up and recovering, but she certainly wasn't idle. "While I was lying in bed I watched films nonstop and read everything I could about special effects. That's when I truly fell in love with the art form." Once she had recovered from her injuries, it was time to restart.

LA IMATS

On her 21st birthday, a year and a half after her accident, Chloe gave herself a birthday gift. She headed back to LA for the International Makeup Artists Trade Show (IMATS). "I came out by myself. It was my first time at IMATS and it was mind-blowing. It was the year that Rick Baker did the keynote and I cried. It was so incredible, seeing all these people I'd only read about." While she was attending the tradeshow, one of the people she ran into was Lee Joyner at the CMS booth.

"He asked me, 'What happened to you? I thought you were coming to school.' I told him about my accident, and that I'd spent all my money, and I didn't know how long it would be until I could save all the money again. He said, 'Okay. Why don't you come talk to me tomorrow morning before you fly out?'"

She met with Joyner and he offered her a work-study internship. In exchange for working at the school during the day, she could attend the makeup courses at night. "That would be my dream come true. I want to do it. But then he said, 'Great, but you have to be here in a week for the start of the session.'"

Running Fast and Furious to Keep Ahead

When she arrived back in Austin, Chloe's boyfriend picked her up from the airport, and she dropped the news on him without any warning, "I'm moving to LA in two days. I hope that you can come, but I've got to go."

Within two days, she had packed up her car and drove to LA to start working at CMS and attending evening classes. The internship covered the cost of her tuition, but Chloe had living expenses as well. She found herself spending every minute of her days at CMS working or studying. She managed as best she could by sleeping on friends' couches and borrowing kits, but after a month, "I couldn't afford to live. I didn't have any type of work to cover rent or food or incidentals. It just wasn't working out."

In LA, there's another yearly convention, Monsterpalooza, which caters to all things monster-related. That year there was a contest for the best monster costume and makeup; the prize was a scholarship to CMS. Chloe thought if she entered and won, her tuition would be paid, she could attend classes during the day, and work to make enough money to cover her living expenses.

"I dropped out of [CMS] to build this female version of the Creature from the Black Lagoon and put every penny of my money into it. At the time, I didn't really know anything because I hadn't been in school very long. I talked to everybody. I talked to people at Nigel's, at Frends, anybody that would listen and give me advice, and a lot of people were really helpful."

She entered the contest at Monsterpalooza and her female Creature from the Black Lagoon won the prize! Now she could restart her education at CMS on scholarship.

Rebooting at CMS

Chloe started back at CMS following the Master Program. To fully maximize the experience, she focused her training on makeup effects. She skipped over the beauty portion of the training, trading it for a class in creature maquette sculpting where she met Don Lanning. Shortly thereafter, Chloe met Norman Cabrera. "They are my biggest sculpting influences and inspirations. Each has a distinctive, individual style, and I think that my style pulls from both."

Sculpting project   Used with Permission of Chloe Sens

"The special effects industry was daunting to me because there are so many techniques, products, and chemicals. Having teachers available to help me learn how to use the products and answer questions was invaluable. Especially something like mold-making. When you're physically doing it for the first time, learning how chemicals react or how Ultracal needs to feel as you work it, a teacher is a great help."

At the end of her 18-week program, Chloe stepped out and started looking for work. "The first year is hard for everyone. Our industry is so word-of-mouth. There is no database to apply for jobs or anything like that. I did a lot...I bar-tended, did makeup on student films, and worked for free. It's all about getting through the first year or two." While she was finding her way into the industry, an opportunity presented itself.

FaceOff

Chloe received a call from the producers of *FaceOff*, a reality television show featuring special effects makeup artists in competition. The artists are challenged to create fantastical characters from a variety of genres. "*FaceOff* had been contacting me for a while and I kept saying no. I didn't feel like I was ready. And, I didn't know if I wanted to do it because of how a lot of the industry views it." Eventually, she decided to go out on a limb and audition for the show. She appeared in Season 6, which aired January 2014.

Chloe on FaceOff   Used with Permission of Chloe Sens

As with most reality television, the concept of reality is relative. On *FaceOff*, the extensive makeups are created over a period of three days and can involve prosthetics for the model's entire body as well as fabrication of costumes. Extensive makeups such as these would normally (in a film or television situation) be created over weeks, not days. So, on *FaceOff*, the pressure is immense. Chloe made it through to the 10th episode of Season 6 and was the last woman standing that season. "I'm happy I did it…because it gave me a lot of opportunities. It helped build my portfolio, and I met a lot of people. I met my roommates working on the show. It was a once-in-a-lifetime opportunity." This opportunity led Chloe down a new path.

Mummy makeup for Bdellium Tools at IMATS LA
Used with Permission of Eric Anderson

IMATS Tour

Being a contestant on *FaceOff* inevitably creates a certain level of celebrity, and Chloe found herself being asked to do demonstrations at IMATS LA for vendors such as Kryolan, Bdellium Tools, and Iwata. Chloe decided to do what she calls the IMATS Tour. "I love traveling. So, I went with Kryolan to almost every IMATS around the world and did demos." For the next year she traveled, following the IMATS conventions. She started in Los Angeles, went on to New York, London, then Vancouver, until she finally returned home to LA. "It was great getting to meet and know so many artists."

"I came home from the Vancouver show and I was like, 'You know what? It's been great, it's been fun, but I really want to focus on my career as a makeup artist. I started to feel a bit like a show pony. I don't want to do just demos. I reached out to established makeup artists I respected and explained what I wanted to do, showed them my work, and asked for a job. They all said, 'Well, I can't do anything with you until you're in the union.' So, I was like, 'Alright, well then, I'll get in the union!'"

The Pathway to the Union

Over the next year, Chloe worked on several projects that moved her toward her new goal. A breakout moment occurred when she was hired as department head on *Oscar's Hotel for Fantastical Creatures*, a web series. "*Oscar's Hotel* was a lightning in a bottle show for me to work on. The cast and crew were one of those rare combinations of artistic brilliance and personalities that made the entire experience incredible. It was my first big show to department head, so I was under a lot of pressure to not only run a department of five, but to design all the makeups as well. I flew out my best friend and partner in crime, Nix Herrera, to be my key. He has an eye for these kinds of fantastical, hyper-artistic looks and I couldn't have done it without him. In addition, I brought on my dream team of artists to fill out the rest of the department. I chose carefully to make sure the strengths of each artist contributed to a well-rounded department. We were running sometimes up to 35 talent through our six-station trailer in two hours each morning with a behind-the-scenes crew also jammed in the trailer doing interviews and videotaping. I was designing a lot of makeups on the fly, supervising, as well as doing makeup myself. I made sure to give the artists creative freedom and in the end, it created a really cool aesthetic that was a little bit of all of us."

Oscar's Hotel For Fantastical Creatures (2016)
Used with Permission of Chloe Sens

The next step along the path was going to New York with fellow artist Mo Meinhart. "I went to do a commercial for Optimum Online, and what an incredible adventure that was! We went on very short notice. I had a week to prep and in that time, I had my roommate, Niko Gonzalez, build a beautiful set of fairy wings, I pre-painted two reptilian aliens and a Sasquatch with prosthetics supplied by RBFX. It was a mad dash all week and then we packed everything into crates and suitcases and jumped on a plane. It was my first time taking such a big project across the country like that. Just getting through the airport with oversized crates as big as me and wings is a comedic and intense event in itself."

Getting into the Union

Sasquatch makeup for Optimum Online commercial
Used with Permission of Chloe Sens

In 2016, Chloe had two major projects that finally led to her goal of union membership, *Miss 2059* and *Mr. Student Body President.*

"*Miss 2059* [another web series] was an absolute blast to be on. I was key artist for that. Jim Ojala was the mastermind behind the special effects and the makeup designs. He was on-set as much as he could be, but things were still being built during production so he gave me the reins for the makeup effects. The biggest makeup I had on that show was one of the principles named Tri. This makeup seemed so simple in theory, but turned into one of the hardest I've ever done. She was covered head to toe in pearl white with blue and silver gill-like appliances on her forehead and cheeks. To top that off, she had a half bald cap and lace blonde wig. The makeup took about four hours each morning and she worked almost every day. The tricky part was she had very sensitive eczema-prone skin. I had to develop a paint mixture combining a couple of different brands to have the right ratio of alcohol to pigment to elasticity because if not, as soon as I airbrushed her, it would crack. I've never seen anything like it. I tried everything. Creme makeups, skin prep, barriers, combinations of everything but the kitchen sink. Nothing was working. I talked to a lot of my mentors (Tami Lane gave the best advice on this) and finally came up with the right

Chloe working on *Miss 2059*   Used with Permission of Chloe Sens

proportions of everything. But the trick was also making it bulletproof enough to be in 100 degrees at Vasquez Rocks for 12 hours and look right on a stage."

"For *Mr. Student Body President* I was department head. This is probably the most mentally and emotionally hard show I've done. For the most part it was all just straight makeup and hair, but we had many looks and a gigantic cast. Continuity was the name of the game on this show and with the way it was shot, it was always a challenge to keep up. I had an incredible key, Alex Perrone, who is amazing with continuity and I couldn't have done this without her.

We had days when we were cramming four to five artists into a three-station wardrobe/makeup combo trailer. So, the trailer would be shaking as we're trying to nail down a perfect cat eye, bumping butts with the artist next to us, controlling flying brushes while it's pouring rain outside. It was everything from hilarious to frustrating to an amazing bonding experience with both our department and the cast."

"Four days into shooting, IATSE [International Alliance of Theatrical Stage Employees] came out to set and began negotiations to turn the show union. We chose to picket and walk off property. It was a wild, eye-opening experience, but it's what got me into the union." Both *Miss 2059* and *Mr. Student Body President* flipped, going from being non-union to union productions, so all the hours Chloe had been working on these shows were now applicable toward union membership. In 2016, Chloe became a member of the New Media division of Local 706.

The Future

While Chloe likes working in the shop sculpting, painting, and mold-making, her true ambition is to continue being an on-set makeup effects artist and a department head for film and television. "[When I'm a department head] I'm in all the production meetings, we talk about the looks, we look at concept photos, work with the script break down, and figure out the budget. I like dealing directly with the director and first AD as well as running the team and saying, 'Here's the plan and the looks, how can we make this happen? How can everyone's strengths and weaknesses work together to meet our goals? Department heading is what I want to do. Even if I'm there at 4 AM, it doesn't matter. It never feels like work to me."

OUTTAKES

On Being a Woman in the Industry:

"It's definitely impacted and affected me. I don't know that it's affected my progress in a negative way...I think it's almost pushed me, because I feel like I'm constantly having to prove myself and to prove that I can be in a shop, I can fiberglass, I can also go on-set and do application and run a department, and I'm just as good as the males in the industry."

"I think the industry is shifting as well. I've talked a lot to Eryn [Krueger Mekash] about this and a little bit to Ve [Neill] as well as Lois [Burwell]. For them, it was different coming up as a female. I think they have paved the way for the younger generation of women to get in a little bit easier and have more support. But I still have encountered some prejudice towards being a female in the industry. It happens in the shops more than it does on-set. You've just got to go, 'It's fine that you feel that way, but I'm not going anywhere.' Fortunately, we have a very supportive community here for advice and support. "

On Work Ethic and Philosophy:

"Not everyone is going to like you, and I think that's the most important thing that I've realized in this industry. I do my best to do right by everybody and keep my word and be kind. I have to focus on my career."

"I'm always watching...I have my eyes all around me. I'm watching what other people are doing, both bad and good because you learn from both. You think, 'Well she did that and maybe it doesn't look good, and this is why it doesn't' look good.' Or, 'That person did this, and it looks amazing because they used A, B, and C.'"

"When you are on-set, you are not just a makeup artist, you're almost like a therapist and a caretaker. I'm always very aware of the actor and how they feel, and how they feel in the makeup, because it's not easy what we're doing to them. I try to make sure that they are taken care of."

"It goes beyond just putting on makeup. I think it's going that extra mile for the actor that shows a true professional and yeah, it's four o'clock in the morning and you're tired, you're cranky, you're stressed, whatever. But to not let any of that show or bleed onto the actor, I think is really important."

On Beyond Formal Education:

"To continue my education, I've watched a ton of Stan Winston School videos. I learned how to paint, I learned how to seam and patch, I learned how to do hair work, there's everything on there. I still watch those all the time."

For more of Chloe's work, visit:
www.imdb.com
Instagram: @beauty_efx

Catching Up!
(continued from Page 284)

"Getting into the union was bittersweet because of the contract I signed. But I've never lost faith that that is just another piece of the story and the journey. As are the jobs I've had and the ones that meant so much to me that I lost. Every step has been worth it and contributes to the next.

More and more over the past few years I've had younger artists contact me and ask, 'How did you do it? How did you get in the union? How do you go to set all the time? How do meet these people?' My answer is always the same. My story is only, and can only, be mine. There's no formula or checklist. Nothing is certain and things change daily. Today I might not have work and tomorrow I might get a call to leave next week for a month. It happens all the time. You have to be head-over-heels in love with the art to survive the ride. But I find that the artists that are, you can see it in their work.

In 2017, I was Department Head for Gucci International Fall campaign, makeup artist on *The Orville* and three music videos. One video was nominated for an APMA [Alternative Press Music Awards] 2017, for *Memphis May Fire*, on which I worked as personal to Matty Mullins. I did 6 months on the paint team at Legacy Effects working on *Avengers: Infinity War*.

I am so grateful that every year is bigger for me than the last. I have a few really incredible projects coming out that I can't reveal yet, and I find that each job leads to the next. After the dust settles from each project, I always have the same feeling, I couldn't imagine dedicating my life to anything else. It's my whole heart."

- *Chloe Sens*

LEADING LADIES
OF MAKEUP EFFECTS

LIFE LESSONS

MONTSE

"You have to do what your heart tells you to do, no matter If you want to clean houses or drive a bus. There's nothing better than another. You have to do what makes you happy. That's all. Not thinking about money. You have to follow your intuition. Then, if awards come or you get famous or not...you have to be happy day by day, doing the things that make you happy."

LOIS

"Never underestimate good fortune smiling upon you, whether at the beginning or middle of a career. The good fortune to work with stunningly talented people has been mine."

"Life has a way of going round in circles and you will be where you're meant to be, at whatever time it's meant to happen. No matter how much I've tried to force things over the years, no matter how much I think that's what I want, it's about luck to a certain degree."

JENNIFER

"Make sure you have passion. Then, technically, make sure you understand art; you can learn the craft, you have have to have the art to make it better. If you have the art background, you'll be able to take those skill sets in to lots of different areas, whether it's beauty makeup or wedding makeup or makeup effects. That will keep you working because the more varied you are, the more possibilities you have to work, the more you'll have in your toolbox to keep you employed if your goal is to be employed by this industry. First, have passion and then have art."

JANE

"I'd say for any young person to want to be a makeup artist, if I could do it, anyone can do it really. It was beyond my aspirations to even dream about it. I didn't even know it was a job. Here I am, and I've had the best time. I've had the time of my life. The whole of my working career is just a brilliant adventure."

ACKNOWLEDGEMENTS

Special Thanks go to our Beta Readers
who took valuable time to read, evaluate, and react to the raw manuscript:

Jenny Hussein

Michelle Paolilli

John Fisher

Kathy Calkins

Thank you to the following school representatives who gave us invaluable insight
into the training and students currently in makeup schools.
(Our next book will be devoted to you!)

Michael Spatola
Chief Academic Officer, Character and Prosthetics Instructor,
Cinema Makeup School (CMS)
Author: *Monsterous Makeup Manual, Vol 1 -3*

Jarrell Mosley
LA School Director
Make-up designory (MUD)

Elissa Frittaion
Curriculum Manager and Instructor,
Vancouver Film School

Special Thanks to
Beverly Norcross
who nudged us into this project!

Overwhelming Thank You to Family and Friends
who believed in our vision and our work and
supported us throughout the process!

EXECUTIVE PRODUCERS
GARY CHRISTENSEN
PATRICIA L. TERRY

PRODUCERS
SCOTT & PAM MORRIS
KAREN WELLER
JOHN FISHER & JAMIE MCALLISTER

ASSOCIATE PRODUCERS

ANNE COLTEN

BEVERLY KRIVOKAPIC

CHRISTINE CAMERON &
BILL BUTLER

DAHLIA & GLENN MALIN

GAIL POLACK

GARY & MARJIE TOOPS

MARIA GERMANA
DE CARLI

GLORIA HICKMAN

JUDY VRABEL &
MANUEL ADAME

JOHN AUGUSTINI

KARIN MAYER

KRISTAN CLARK

LESLI SPENCER

LYNNE CRYTSER

MAGGIE POMEROY

MARK NICHOLS

MARY IVES

MICHELLE PAOLILLI

P KATHLEEN CALKINS

RACHEL COENEN

SARAH BROWN

SIAN JEFFRIES-JONES

STUART BRAY

SUSANNE BUETTELL

TONY LAUGHLIN

BUSINESS SPONSOR
SILCSKIN
WWW.SILCSKIN.COM

LEADING LADIES
OF MAKEUP EFFECTS

Patricia L. Terry
Gary Christensen

THE AUTHORS

Patricia L. Terry is a Theater Director who has directed over 100 productions at theaters in Southern California. For 13 years she served as Artistic Director of the **Alternative Repertory Theatre** (a small non-profit theater in Orange County) for which she oversaw all the productions and directed 35. She won a Drama-Logue award for her direction of *The House of Blue Leaves*; other favorite projects at ART stylistically ranged from *Seascape,* to *No Exit,* to *Macbeth,* to *Long Day's Journey Into Night*. In addition, she was Producing Artistic Director of the **Pandemonium Word Ballet and Literary Circus**, a travelling educational company producing Theater for Children. She also directed and taught acting at several colleges in Orange County. For the past six years, she has written a blog, *Pat's Musings on Living La Dolce Vita*, about her experiences living in retirement in Italy where she spends six months of the year.

Gary Christensen is a Makeup Artist and Designer for Theater. In the area of Makeup Special Effects, he has won a Drama-Logue Award for his prosthetics make-up design for *Comedy of Errors* at the Grove Shakespeare Festival. 2013, 2014, and 2015, he designed silicone makeup effects as a demonstrator for Mouldlife and Neill Gorton Prosthetics Studios at the London International Makeup Artists Trade Show (IMATS) and United Makeup Artists Expo (UMA Expo). In his tenure as Founding Member and Producer of the **Alternative Repertory Theatre**, Gary designed make-up for over 30 productions. Also, as a Theater Makeup Instructor, he has taught and designed at several colleges and universities throughout Southern California including CalArts, California State University, Fullerton, Mesa College, San Diego, and Riverside City College. For two years, he served as *"Backstage"* columnist for *Make-Up Artist Magazine* for Issues #11 (Feb/Mar 1998) through #23 (Feb/Mar 2000).

For more information, visit: www.leadingladiesofmakeupeffects.com

MARTINI SHOT

Pat: "So ... is that it?"

Gary: "Yep! We're all through!"

Pat: "Completely?!"

Gary: "Finito!"

Pat: "Now what?"

Gary: "Volume 2?"

THE END

LEADING LADIES OF MAKEUP EFFECTS

Made in the USA
Lexington, KY
17 June 2018